To the memory of J. L. AUSTIN

The Philosophy
of Wittgenstein

George Pitcher

PRINCETON UNIVERSITY

PRENTICE-HALL, INC., *Englewood Cliffs, N. J.*

Current printing (last digit):
12 11 10 9 8 7 6 5

PRENTICE-HALL INTERNATIONAL, INC., LONDON
PRENTICE-HALL OF AUSTRALIA, PTY., LTD., SYDNEY
PRENTICE-HALL OF CANADA, LTD., TORONTO
PRENTICE-HALL OF INDIA (PRIVATE) LTD., NEW DELHI
PRENTICE-HALL OF JAPAN, INC., TOKYO

Library of Congress Catalog Card Number 64-12550

Printed in the United States of America
66445-C

Preface

Wittgenstein is one of the great philosophers of the twentieth century. He may be the greatest. This book is meant to be an introduction to his thought. Wittgenstein's writings are not easy to understand —there is no use denying it. Indeed, if they were, no such book as this would be needed. There are, however, many ways in which a philosopher can be difficult, and different kinds of difficulty call for different kinds of treatment. There are at least two Wittgensteins: the early one of the *Tractatus Logico-Philosophicus* and the later one of the *Philosophical Investigations,* and the difficulties presented in these two masterworks are not of the same kind.

The *Tractatus* is difficult sentence by sentence. On first reading it, one often simply fails to understand what is being said, what the individual sentences mean. There are several reasons for this, but two main ones are that Wittgenstein uses some ordinary terms in special technical senses without explicit warning, and, more importantly, that the considerations lying behind his cryptic remarks and the arguments in support of his conclusions are sometimes only darkly hinted at, sometimes not mentioned at all. Mainly, the *results* of a great deal of profound thinking are presented rather than the actual *process* of the thinking itself. And so the opening sentence of the Preface to the *Tractatus* is quite true:

> Perhaps this book will be understood only by someone who has himself already had the thoughts that are expressed in it—or at least similar thoughts. [*T*, p. 3.]

Accordingly in Part I of the present book, where the *Tractatus* is dealt with, I try to explain how Wittgenstein uses his key terms, and to supply the arguments and reasoning which I take to lie behind, and thus to constitute the necessary background for understanding, what he says there.

In the *Philosophical Investigations,* on the other hand, we find not so much the results of philosophical labor, as the labor itself. We see Wittgenstein thinking. Here the sentences are usually easy enough, considered one by one; their meaning is reasonably clear. But sometimes one does not see how they hang together, what they are leading up to, what the *point* or significance of the discussion as a whole is. Accordingly in Part II, I try to give an over-all picture of the sort of thing Wittgenstein is concerned with in the *Investigations,* the fundamental issues that worried him, the aims he was trying to achieve—in short, the motivating forces behind his thought. So I seek to provide a general framework within which the various sections of the *Investigations* can be understood. The strokes in Part II are thus broader than in Part I.

I repeat that this book is an introduction to Wittgenstein's thought. If this introduction be a happy one, the reader will go on to become better acquainted with Wittgenstein on his own. He will read the man's works, for that is the only way, in the end, that anything more than a superficial understanding can be gained. The book will have failed if it does not lead to the reading of Wittgenstein's works, for it is in no sense a substitute for that.

This book is necessarily selective, in ways that must be noted here. First, it deals primarily with the *Tractatus* and the *Investigations.* The *Notebooks 1914-1916* throw much light on the *Tractatus* and anyone seriously concerned with that work must read them. I refer to them quite often in Part I, but give them no special consideration in their own right. *The Blue and Brown Books* represent the first stages of Wittgenstein's later period, and contain some transitional ideas which he later abandoned. They are not separately treated in Part II, but are appealed to only as they illuminate aspects of the *Investigations.*

Second, I have largely ignored those parts of the *Tractatus* which deal with technical problems of logic and the foundations of mathematics. I have little competence in these matters. Hence I have made no effort either to discuss Wittgenstein's later views on these subjects, as contained in *Remarks on the Foundations of Mathematics.* Readers interested in this important part of his philosophy may wish to consult the relevant works cited in the bibliography.

For first suggesting the idea of writing this book, I am indebted to my colleague Walter Kaufmann. I owe an enormous debt of thanks to G. E. M. Anscombe, Alice Ambrose Lazerowitz, Paul Benacerraf, Brian McGuinness, David Pears, and Peter Strawson, who read all or large parts of the manuscript and gave me the benefit of their knowledge and considerable critical talents. They saved me from any number of blunders and mistakes, and helped me to clarify my thoughts about Wittgenstein. Those errors and infelicities that remain are no fault of theirs, but are attributable rather to my occasional stubbornness in persevering in my own way against their criticism. James Griffin, Walter Kaufmann, Gregory Vlastos, and Bernard Williams read parts of the manuscript, and were also most helpful: I am happy to record my debt to them. For liberally providing me with material and information in their possession, mainly concerning Wittgenstein's life and character, I thank Mrs. Dorothy Moore, Dr. Max Bieler, Roderick Chisholm, Herbert Feigl, Dr. W. W. Nowinski, David Yalden-Thomson, G. H. von Wright, and Dr. M. O'C. Drury.

To Princeton University and the Procter and Gamble Corporation I am grateful for a term's leave of absence, without which this book could not have been written. To Patrick and Elaine Brunner, my gracious hosts at Wotton House, Wotton Underwood, I owe a debt of thanks for providing me with a most beautiful and friendly setting for writing and thinking during my stay in England. For her impeccable typing of my manuscript, I thank Mrs. Helen Wright of Princeton, New Jersey; and I am grateful also to Robert Jaeger for so ably preparing the index.

Acknowledgments

For permission to quote from the following works, acknowledgment and thanks are due to their publishers:

L. Wittgenstein, *Philosophical Investigations* (Basil Blackwell, Oxford); L. Wittgenstein, *Notebooks 1914-1916* (Basil Blackwell, Oxford); L. Wittgenstein, *The Blue and Brown Books* (Basil Blackwell, Oxford); L. Wittgenstein, *Tractatus Logico-Philosophicus* (The Humanities Press, New York); G. E. Moore, *Philosophical Papers* (The Macmillan Company, New York); B. Russell, *Logic and Knowledge* (The Macmillan Company, New York); N. Malcolm, *Ludwig Wittgenstein: A Memoir* (Oxford University Press, London); J.-P. Sartre, *Being and Nothingness* (The Philosophical Library, New

York); Plato, *Protagoras and Meno* (Penguin Books, Baltimore); G. E. M. Anscombe, *An Introduction to Wittgenstein's Tractatus* (Hillary House Publishers, New York); St. Augustine, *Concerning the Teacher and On the Immortality of the Soul* (Appleton-Century-Crofts, New York); and P. A. Schilpp (ed.), *The Philosophy of G. E. Moore* (The Library of Living Philosophers, Inc., Evanston, Illinois).

For permission to quote from the texts of their talks on the BBC, my thanks are due to Lord Russell, Karl Britton, and Dr. M. O'C. Drury. I also thank the British Broadcasting Corporation, publishers of *The Listener,* in which the talks were printed, for permission to include these excerpts in the present book.

G. P.

Table of Contents

PART II: *Philosophical Investigations*

Abbreviations

BB   Ludwig Wittgenstein, *The Blue and Brown Books* (Oxford: Basil Blackwell, 1958).

NB   Ludwig Wittgenstein, *Notebooks 1914-1916,* edited by G. H. von Wright and G. E. M. Anscombe, with an English translation by G. E. M. Anscombe (Oxford: Basil Blackwell, 1961).

PI   Ludwig Wittgenstein, *Philosophical Investigations,* translated by G. E. M. Anscombe (Oxford: Basil Blackwell, 1953). *Note:* In all references to this book, section numbers refer to Part I.

RFM   Ludwig Wittgenstein, *Remarks on the Foundations of Mathematics,* edited by G. H. von Wright, R. Rhees, and G. E. M. Anscombe; translated by G. E. M. Anscombe (Oxford: Basil Blackwell, 1956).

T   Ludwig Wittgenstein, *Tractatus Logico-Philosophicus,* translated by D. F. Pears and B. F. McGuinness (London: Routledge & Kegan Paul; New York: The Humanities Press, 1961).

1   Life and Character

There have appeared in history certain extraordinary men who can justly be called passionate thinkers—men, that is, whose thinking was infused with passion. Plato was one of them, and so were Augustine, Kierkegaard, Nietzsche, and Wittgenstein. These men were completely absorbed in their philosophical work and deeply preoccupied with the problems that confronted them. They rightly considered the questions they raised to be of the highest importance and also of the greatest difficulty. Hence, being men of dedication and high purpose, they lived with their questions and wrestled with them. Those with little confidence that they were making progress were positively tormented by the questions that faced them. Wittgenstein was one of these. Driven on by the conviction that his journey had to be made, sustained by the firm belief that he was traveling in the right direction and even that he had achieved some real advance, he nevertheless kept finding the horizon of complete understanding as remote as ever, as new problems constantly appeared. And so he had to push on. "The real discovery," he said, "is the one that makes me capable of stopping doing philosophy when I want to." (*PI,* sect. 133.) He never made that peace-giving discovery; the demons pursued him to the end.

Any thinker of such dedication is bound to have followers and his ideas are bound to exert an important influence on the thought of his day. But Wittgenstein was endowed with additional qualities. He had a remarkably original mind. His ideas have freshness and vigor; they are new, they have just been born. This is not to say that none of his thoughts had ever been thought before; but even when they had, Wittgenstein rediscovered them for himself. His originality lies not only in the making of new points, but in the raising of new questions, the seeing of new difficulties. Wittgenstein was the first to detect certain monsters lurking in the apparently friendly countryside of familiar facts.

At the same time, his thought is profound, he takes things deep. Wittgenstein used to compare thinking with swimming: just as in swimming our bodies have a natural tendency to float on the surface so that it requires great physical exertion to plunge to the bottom, so in thinking it requires great mental exertion to force our minds away from the superficial, down into the depths of a philosophical problem. Wittgenstein continually made this superhuman effort, and it cost him dearly.[1] What is more, Wittgenstein was able to express his ideas in such a pungent and compelling way that he has been ranked among the modern masters of German prose. The brilliance of his style, the dramatic turns in the discourse which sometimes baffle the audience but always intrigue them, the stunning aphorisms, the witty questions (usually unanswered), the fantastic and amusing examples which he uses to illustrate his points—these and other features of his writing and speech gave the expression of his thought overwhelming power and fascination.

Given these endowments, it was inevitable that Wittgenstein should have exerted an enormous influence on contemporary philosophical thought. There is wide agreement that no other philosopher has contributed more to the present state of philosophy as practiced in English-speaking countries, and many would argue that none has contributed so much. What the decision of history will be concerning Wittgenstein's ultimate importance, or, granted his importance, concerning the value of his work—whether he will be judged an enlightened savior or a barbaric destroyer of philosophy—remains to be seen. But the spirit of Wittgenstein is present everywhere in current philosophy and is certain to remain so for years to come.

Life

Wittgenstein was born on April 26, 1889 in Vienna, and was given the name Ludwig Josef Johann. He was the youngest of five

[1] See Norman Malcolm, *Ludwig Wittgenstein: A Memoir* (London: Oxford University Press, 1958), p. 55. No one interested in Wittgenstein will want to miss reading this revealing and moving book.

brothers and three sisters. The family was of mostly Jewish descent, but not of the Jewish faith. Wittgenstein's mother was a Roman Catholic and he himself was baptized in the Catholic Church. The family was a wealthy and cultured one. Wittgenstein's father Karl was a man of intelligence and forceful character, who was both feared and respected. An engineer by profession, he became one of the founders of the steel and iron industry in Austria. Wittgenstein's childhood was spent in the family's country estates or at their palace in Vienna.

The Wittgenstein home was something of a cultural, and more particularly, a musical center of Viennese life. Clara Schumann gave informal recitals there, Gustav Mahler was a frequent visitor, and Johannes Brahms was a good friend. It was Ludwig's mother who was primarily responsible for this artistic interest of the family; his father was very musical, but, in his businessman's way, he did not consider the arts to be much more than pleasant diversions in a busy life. All the children had considerable musical talent, and one— Ludwig's elder brother Paul—became a famous concert pianist. Ludwig himself developed a passion and talent for music which lasted throughout his life. He played the clarinet and considered for a time the possibility of becoming a conductor. He had a quite extraordinary ability as a whistler, and in later years he would give his friends what must have been somewhat uneasy pleasure by whistling whole concertos and symphonies, punctuating the performance with occasional comments on features of the music. Malcolm reports that Wittgenstein frequently discussed aesthetics and that "the depth and richness of Wittgenstein's thinking about art were very exciting." [2]

Up to the age of fourteen, Wittgenstein was educated at home, and then for three years at Linz in Upper Austria. He had developed a childhood interest in machinery, and decided to study engineering at the Technische Hochschule in Berlin-Charlottenburg, where he remained until the spring of 1908. This interest in mechanisms and machines was another lifelong one. According to von Wright, "Even in his last years he could spend a whole day with his beloved steam-engines in the South Kensington Museum. There are several anecdotes of his serving as a mechanic when some machinery got out of order." [3]

---

[2] *Ibid.*, p. 53.

[3] G. H. von Wright, "Ludwig Wittgenstein, a Biographical Sketch," *The Philosophical Review*, LXIV, No. 4 (October 1955), 529. This excellent article is reprinted in Malcolm, *op. cit.*

His writings contain frequent allusions to mechanisms; they were one of his richest sources of analogies and examples.

Upon leaving the Hochschule, Wittgenstein went to England. In the autumn he was registered as a research student in the engineering department at the University of Manchester, and remained there until the fall of 1911, devoting himself to research in aeronautics. During this period, his interests gradually shifted to pure mathematics and then to the foundations of mathematics. This was to be the gateway through which he entered philosophy.

The first reading which Wittgenstein did in the literature on the foundations of mathematics was probably Bertrand Russell's *Principles of Mathematics,* which had been published in 1903. This doubtless led him to read the works of Gottlob Frege, whom most consider to be the father—or perhaps the grandfather—of modern mathematical logic. Wittgenstein visited him in Jena, Germany, to discuss his plans for further study, and Frege apparently advised him to go to Cambridge and study with Russell; this he did. He was admitted to Trinity College and registered in the University from the fall of 1912 through the second term of the following academic year, 1913-14. Then, he lived on a farm in Norway most of the time until the outbreak of war in 1914.

Wittgenstein listened eagerly to Russell's lectures and had long talks with him. "Getting to know Wittgenstein," Russell tells us, "was one of the most exciting intellectual adventures of my life." [4] Russell tells the following story. Wittgenstein had come to him at the end of his first term at Cambridge and asked,

> "Will you please tell me whether I am a complete idiot or not?" I replied, "My dear fellow, I don't know. Why are you asking me?" He said, "Because, if I am a complete idiot, I shall become an aeronaut; but, if not, I shall become a philosopher." I told him to write me something during the vacation on some philosophical subject and I would then tell him whether he was a complete idiot or not. At the beginning of the following term he brought me the fulfilment of this suggestion. After reading only one sentence, I said to him, "No, you must not become an aeronaut." [5]

We know from Wittgenstein's first published work, the famous *Tractatus Logico-Philosophicus,* that Russell's views strongly in-

[4] Bertrand Russell, "Ludwig Wittgenstein," *Mind,* LX, No. 239 (July 1951), 298.

[5] Bertrand Russell, "Philosophers and Idiots," *The Listener,* LIII, No. 1354 (February 10, 1955), 247; reprinted in Russell's *Portraits from Memory* (London: George Allen & Unwin Ltd., 1956), pp. 26-27.

fluenced him. But Russell soon ceased to consider Wittgenstein a mere student, and thought of him as a friend and colleague. His own thinking, furthermore, was profoundly influenced by that of his former pupil.

Russell was not the only philosopher at Cambridge who was impressed by this strange young Viennese genius. G. E. Moore, who must also be listed among the outstanding philosophers of this century, writes with characteristic generosity:

> In 1912 I became acquainted with Wittgenstein. During the first year in which he was at Cambridge he attended my lectures on Psychology; but it was only during the next two years that I got to know him at all well. When I did get to know him, I soon came to feel that he was much cleverer at philosophy than I was, and not only cleverer, but also much more profound, and with a much better insight into the sort of inquiry which was really important and best worth pursuing, and into the best method of pursuing such inquiries.[6]

This, coming from an acknowledged master, and spoken of a young man who had just begun his study of philosophy, is praise of the highest order.

Although he had been exempted from military service because of a rupture, Wittgenstein felt called upon to enlist in the Austrian army as a volunteer when war broke out in 1914. He was trained as an officer, fought on the eastern and then on the southern fronts, was captured by the Italians in November 1918, and spent about nine months as a prisoner of war in a camp near Monte Cassino in southern Italy.

Wittgenstein had been thinking about various fundamental logical notions since 1912, jotting down his thoughts in a notebook, a practice he kept up during the war [7] and indeed for the rest of his life. A little later, after the beginning of the war, he became engrossed in problems connected with the significance or sense of propositions. These preliminary studies received their final formulation in Wittgenstein's first work, completed while he was on military leave in Vienna in August of 1918. As *Logisch-philosophische Abhandlung,* it was published in the original German in 1921. The next year it appeared in a German-English parallel text, with the impressive Latin title reputedly suggested by G. E. Moore: *Tractatus Logico-*

[6] G. E. Moore, "An Autobiography," in P. A. Schilpp, ed., *The Philosophy of G. E. Moore* (New York: Tudor Publishing Company, 1942), p. 33.
[7] Wittgenstein's notebooks for the years 1914-1916 have been published.

Philosophicus. The impressiveness of the title is no more than the work deserves; it is already a classic of the philosophical literature and has exerted a profound influence on subsequent thought.

When the war was over, Wittgenstein did not return to Cambridge. One can scarcely imagine what effect fighting in a war must have had on a young man of Wittgenstein's sensitivity. During this period of crisis in his life, he came across a volume of Tolstoy on the Gospels (perhaps the one called in English *What I Believe*) in a village bookstore, and this book influenced his view of life very deeply. In addition, Wittgenstein believed that in the *Tractatus* the problems which had been exercising him had been basically solved, once and for all. He wrote in his preface to that work: "I . . . believe myself to have found, on all essential points, the final solution of the problems." (*T*, p. 5.) Given the passionate integrity which Wittgenstein possessed, these circumstances help explain his course of action after the war— a course of action that might otherwise seem incredible—he became a village schoolteacher in lower Austria. A man of acknowledged genius who, after knowing next to nothing about logic and philosophy, had made important contributions to both fields within a remarkably short period of time, a man who could not help having a brilliant future in one of the most sophisticated of all intellectual disciplines— this man turned his back on all that and devoted himself to the humble task of teaching young children in remote villages.

It was inevitable that the Austrian villagers should look upon Wittgenstein as an odd, indeed mysterious, character; he could not fail to be the subject of their feverish curiosity and gossip. Although he had inherited a considerable fortune on the death of his father in 1912, upon his return from the war he had immediately given it all away to two of his sisters and his only surviving brother, so that he was now a relatively poor man. Shy and withdrawn, somewhat shabbily dressed, he chose to live in the simplest of surroundings—a tiny whitewashed room that was like a monk's cell, or a small cubicle in someone's house. At one point, when dance music was introduced at the inn where he had a room, he slept for a while in the school kitchen; at another time he lived in a tiny disused washroom in a villager's house. He had a few carefully selected friends. In the evenings, he would read or play the clarinet, and sometimes he could be seen at his window, gazing for hours at the stars. But the townspeople must have suspected that an exceptionally gifted and fundamentally kind man was in their presence. Once, for example, he astounded the personnel of the local weaving mill by repairing in short order an elaborately broken steam engine. (He accepted in payment, reluctantly, a package of cloth, and only on the understanding that he would distribute it among his pupils.) Several old sewing machines in the village also received the benefit of his scrupulous mechanical attention.

What his young pupils thought of him is difficult to imagine. He was actually a skilful and extremely conscientious teacher. He carefully wrote out in a big book his preparations for each hour. There was never enough time for all he wanted to do. The next class would often be kept waiting outside his door, and he regularly kept his young charges one or two hours—sometimes longer—after the rest of the school had been dismissed. The accepted teaching procedures held no interest for him; he was always experimenting with new methods and devices of instruction. He dissected animal corpses and assembled their skeletons, explained models of steam engines, set up with his students a potter's wheel on which they fashioned clay pots, and compiled for them a book containing a long list of commonly used words. If he happened by chance to meet some of his youngsters in the evening, he might give them instruction in astronomy on the spot. In mathematics, he had great success; he took his students well beyond the ordinary requirements for their class, and introduced the older, more gifted ones to advanced problems in algebra.

But, although fond of children, Wittgenstein hardly had a suitable temperament to be a village schoolmaster. He demanded a great deal of his pupils; occasionally their childish behavior would enrage him, and he might physically discipline an erring boy too roughly. There were complaints from parents, and Wittgenstein voluntarily resigned his post in April 1926 and returned, a profoundly unhappy man, to Vienna.

At this point, the idea of entering a monastery, which had occurred to him before, occupied his thoughts; but nothing was to come of it. Instead, he worked for some months in the summer as a gardener in a monastery near Vienna, camping all the while in the garden toolshed. But this life of the soil was a short one. In the fall of 1926 he undertook to design and build, in collaboration with his friend, the architect Paul Engelmann, a mansion for one of his sisters in Vienna—a task to which he devoted himself for the next two years.

During his strange and secluded career of the '20's, Wittgenstein was visited on at least two occasions by Frank Ramsey, a brilliant young Cambridge mathematician who had helped in the first English translation of the *Tractatus,* who begged Wittgenstein to return to Cambridge and philosophy. Wittgenstein also had some philosophical discussions with Moritz Schlick, the founder of the famous Vienna Circle of Logical Positivists, and other members of the Circle. In March 1928, Wittgenstein heard the great Dutch mathematician Brouwer deliver a lecture on the foundations of mathematics, and it has been said that this lecture stirred him to return to the arena.[8] In any case, Wittgenstein went back to Cambridge early in 1929. He received his Ph.D. degree in June of the same year, submitting the *Tractatus* as a thesis, and the following year he was made a Fellow of Trinity College.

Wittgenstein began at once the lectures which were eventually to change the course of British philosophy. They were almost always held in his own rooms or in those of a friend in the college. Malcolm describes them as follows: [9]

> Wittgenstein sat in a plain wooden chair in the centre of the room. Here he carried on a visible struggle with his thoughts. He often felt that he was confused, and said so. Frequently he said things like 'I'm a fool!' 'You have a dreadful teacher!' 'I'm just too stupid today.' Sometimes he expressed a doubt that he would be able to continue the lecture, but only rarely did he give up before seven o'clock.
>
> It is hardly correct to speak of these meetings as 'lectures,' although this is what Wittgenstein called them. For one thing, he was carrying on original research in these meetings. He was thinking about certain problems in a way that he could have done had he been alone. For another thing, the meetings were largely conversation. Wittgenstein commonly directed questions at various people present and reacted to their replies. Often the meetings consisted mainly of dialogue. Sometimes, however, when he was trying to draw a thought out of himself, he would prohibit, with a peremptory motion of the hand, any questions or remarks. There were frequent and prolonged periods of silence, with only an occasional mutter from Wittgenstein, and the

[8] Professor Herbert Feigl has kindly informed me, in correspondence, that he and F. Waismann spent a few hours with Wittgenstein in a cafe after the lecture, and that "it was fascinating to behold the change that had come over W[ittgenstein] that evening." Whereas previously he had been reluctant to discuss philosophy, and had even had to be persuaded by Waismann and Feigl to attend the lecture at all, now "he became extremely voluble and began sketching ideas that were the beginnings of his later writings." In Feigl's opinion, "that evening marked the return of W[ittgenstein] to strong philosophical interests and activities."

[9] Malcolm, *Memoir,* p. 26.

stillest attention from the others. During these silences, Wittgenstein was extremely tense and active. His gaze was concentrated; his face was alive; his hands made arresting movements; his expression was stern. One knew that one was in the presence of extreme seriousness, absorption, and force of intellect.

During the first two or three years of his fellowship, Wittgenstein gradually fought his way out of the doctrines he had put forth in the *Tractatus,* but it seems not to have been until around 1933 that there occurred to him those basic ideas which occupied his thought to the end of his life. From the period immediately following, we have two works: the *Blue Book,* dictated to a small, carefully chosen group of his students during the year 1933-34, and the *Brown Book,* dictated to two members of the earlier group during 1934-35.[10] These were not meant for the general public, nor even for the philosophical world at large, although Wittgenstein did allow a few people to see them and to have copies. In one way or another both works found their way into the studies of philosophers in universities throughout at least the English-speaking world and doubtless far beyond that too.

When his fellowship at Trinity expired in the spring of 1936, Wittgenstein retired for nearly a year to his small secluded house on a fjord in Norway. The house was one of the few possessions he had retained from his wealthy days prior to the First World War. (He had in fact offered it as a gift to one of his wartime companions, but the latter refused it. Wittgenstein's reason for keeping the house was no doubt his deep need to have a solitary refuge where he could pursue his thoughts in as much peace as possible.) It was here, in 1936, that he began to write Part I of the *Philosophical Investigations.* (This part was completed by 1945.) He returned to Cambridge in 1937, and in 1939 he was appointed Moore's successor to his chair in philosophy. But before he could actually assume it, the Second World War broke out, and Wittgenstein once again abandoned his work to contribute to the war effort. He served as a porter in Guy's Hospital in London and later worked at Newcastle in a medical laboratory.

Returning to Cambridge after the war, Wittgenstein soon gave up his chair in order to devote himself entirely to research. His last lectures were given in the Easter term of 1947 and his resignation took effect on December 31. Once again he went into seclusion, this time on a farm in Ireland. Later he lived entirely alone in a cottage by the ocean in Galway, where his only neighbors were fishermen and some

10 These have been published.

wild sea birds which he tamed and which came to be fed every day. When this life became too strenuous for him, he moved (in the fall of 1948) to a hotel in Dublin. It was here in the following spring that he completed Part II of the *Investigations*.[11]

Wittgenstein was already a sick man. He visited Norman Malcolm from the end of July to October (1949) at Cornell, where, although ill much of the time, he was able to have some philosophical discussions with the philosophers and graduate students there. On his return to England, his illness was diagnosed as cancer. During much of the time that remained to him, he was unable to work, but at least he was up and about. He spent more than three months with his family in Vienna, from December to the end of March (1950), steadfastly refusing to divulge to them the nature of his malady; and in the fall of 1950 he even visited Norway once again with a friend. On April 29, 1951, he died in Cambridge at the house of his doctor.

Character

Some sort of curse must have been hurled by a wicked and jealous demon over the gifted children who played in the luxurious mansion of the Wittgensteins in Vienna. Ludwig's favorite sister, like their father, died slowly of cancer after several operations. Three of his four brothers committed suicide. The fourth, Paul, a brilliant concert pianist, lost his right arm in the first World War, only a few months after his highly successful debut. Ludwig himself was a strange, tormented person. He was miserably unhappy as a child and youth; when 23, he confessed to his friend David Pinsent that for nine years he had suffered from terrible loneliness and that he had continually thought of suicide. He even felt ashamed at never daring to kill himself; he had "had a hint" that he was *de trop* in the world, but had meanly disregarded it. In adult life he was haunted by fears—that he might go mad, that he would die before his work was completed, that no one properly understood his teaching. His nervous temperament cast him into frequent moods of depression and brought on outbursts of temper, which, especially when directed at his friends, were often followed by bitter self-chastisement.

Not surprisingly, his outlook on life was grim, even gloomy, and he considered himself "doomed." He looked upon the age in which he lived as a dark one. He was dismayed by the heartlessness, cruelty,

---

[11] They were not published until 1953, two years after Wittgenstein's death.

and sinfulness of much of mankind, and by the basic helplessness of the human condition. Although anything but an existentialist in his philosophical persuasion, he once told a friend that he considered Kierkegaard to be by far the greatest philosopher of the nineteenth century.[12] He understood what Kierkegaard meant by despair and agreed with his view that man by himself is in an utterly hopeless situation. Malcolm remarks:

> Of the things that came to his attention in the normal passage of events, hardly any gave him pleasure and many produced in him an emotion that was not far from grief. Often as we walked together he would stop and exclaim "Oh, my God!" looking at me almost piteously, as if imploring a divine intervention in human events.[13]

It must have distressed Wittgenstein that although wanting and needing to believe in God, he was nevertheless unable to do so.

Wittgenstein was, despite all this, full of vitality; others, by comparison, seemed only half alive. He had a most forceful and singular personality which exerted great influence over other people. No one who had any dealings with him remained indifferent; some disliked him, others were strongly attracted to him. It is difficult to see how anyone could fail to have been fascinated by him one way or another.

Perhaps his most outstanding character traits were high seriousness and integrity, which carried along with them a fierce hatred of pretense, affectation, slickness, mere cleverness, and superficiality of any sort. These traits colored all aspects of Wittgenstein's life, including his philosophical work. He occasionally chose to live quite primitively and in seclusion; but even when he was living in more civilized surroundings, his rooms were always furnished in the most austere manner imaginable. At Cambridge, for example, he had no easy chair or reading lamp, and the walls were absolutely bare. No ornaments or photographs or decorations of any kind were to be seen, save for a few flowers. It was as if Wittgenstein were unwilling to reveal his soul even to the smallest extent to people who might happen to enter his rooms. His dress, too, was unvaryingly simple: grey flannel trousers, a shirt open at the neck, a woolen lumber jacket or a leather jacket. "One could not imagine Wittgenstein in a suit, necktie, or hat," Malcolm tells us.[14] Anyone who knows the standards

---

[12] See M. O'C. Drury's contribution to "Ludwig Wittgenstein: a symposium" in *The Listener,* LXIII, No. 1609 (January 28, 1960), 164.

[13] Malcolm, *Memoir,* p. 32.

[14] *Ibid.,* p. 25.

of dress that are expected, indeed required, at Cambridge and Oxford will understand how little Wittgenstein cared for social conventions. In food, too, he preferred the simple—although the rumor that he subsisted entirely on corn flakes may have been slightly exaggerated. Malcolm reports that while Wittgenstein was staying with him, bread and cheese constituted the main portion of all his meals. "Wittgenstein declared that it did not much matter to him *what* he ate, so long as it was always the same." [15]

The one thing he could not stand in anyone was affectation or insincerity—in short, dishonesty, another aspect of Wittgenstein's outlook reminiscent of existentialism. His belief that academic life is afflicted with this sin doubtless accounts in large part for his intense dislike of it.

> He had, he said, only once been to high table at Trinity and the clever conversation of the dons had so horrified him that he had come out with both hands over his ears. The dons talked like that only to score: they did not even enjoy doing it. He said his own bedmaker's conversation, about the private lives of her previous gentlemen and about her own family, was far preferable: at least he could understand why she talked that way and could believe that she enjoyed it. [16]

One can understand why Wittgenstein might have preferred the company of his Austrian school children, Irish fishermen, and Norwegian farmers to that of his academic colleagues. One can understand too the respect he had for genuine religious conviction, even though he did not and could not share it.

But it was in his philosophical endeavors that Wittgenstein was most ruthlessly uncompromising with superficiality. Philosophy was for him profoundly serious and difficult work, and he could not abide any suggestion of slickness in carrying it out. One must do it honestly and vigorously and wholeheartedly; and one must do it for oneself—no abstract, pre-cooked theories or systems must be appealed to, as if the mere mention of their names could cause difficulties to vanish. One must look at the puzzling facts with unprejudiced eyes, and work and fight one's own way through to clarity and truth—*all* the way through. Wittgenstein demanded nothing less than complete understanding.

He naturally avoided making superficial acquaintances, but he did have the need for friends—and friends who loved him for his own sake. His reasons for giving away the fortune he had inherited

[15] *Ibid.*, p. 85.
[16] Karl Britton, "Portrait of a Philosopher," *The Listener*, LIII, No. 1372 (June 16, 1955), 1072.

were no doubt complex—a feeling of guilt at having money which he had done nothing to earn and which he thought he did not deserve, a need to prove himself by his own work and on his own merits, an overwhelming desire to avoid the innumerable complications that attend wealth, and so on. But another important reason was that he did not want to attract friends on the strength of his money. Later in life, he was plagued by the thought that some people liked him simply for the philosophic wisdom they thought they could acquire from him. Perhaps this explains the taxing tests he often put his closest friends to; he would, for example, sometimes upbraid them mercilessly for an opinion they had expressed, and then not speak to them for days. Yet, such was the magic of his personality, that they were devoted to him, even if their love was tinged with fear. It must be added that Wittgenstein was painfully aware of his own shortcomings; his criticism of others was nothing compared with his self-criticism. He once remarked, "One keeps stumbling and falling, stumbling and falling, and the only thing to do is to pick oneself up and try and go on again. At least that is what I have had to do all my life." [17]

Wittgenstein was not just a gloomy, terrifying man. He was capable of acts of great kindness and generosity, and was deeply appreciative of the kindness of others. Characteristic terms of praise in his vocabulary were 'human' and 'human being.' Being a *human* being —that is, being kind or generous or honest—was, for Wittgenstein, far more important in a person than being intelligent, clever, or refined. He had a completely original and imaginative sense of humor, as anyone who reads his later works discovers at once. In lectures and discussions, he took pleasure in inventing weird and amusing examples to illustrate his philosophical points; and, as might be expected, they were not invented merely to make people laugh—on the contrary, they served an essential purpose in his teaching. Indeed, according to Malcolm, "Wittgenstein once said that a serious and good philosophical work could be written that would consist entirely of *jokes* (without being facetious)." [18]

There is more than a merely passing similarity between the life and personality of (at least the later) Wittgenstein and those of Socrates— despite, of course, great differences.[19] Both had a close circle of disciples that they influenced enormously by the power of their intel-

---

[17] Drury, "Ludwig Wittgenstein: a symposium," p. 164.

[18] Malcolm, *Memoir,* p. 29.

[19] This comparison has been suggested by others. See, for example, Walter Kaufmann, *Critique of Religion and Philosophy* (New York: Harper & Row, Publishers, 1958), pp. 40-43.

lect and character. Neither had a uniformly salutary effect on his students; many were so impressed with their master that they tended merely to imitate him. (Wittgenstein was aware of this, and it upset him.) Both carried out their philosophical teaching by discussion, rather than by lecturing. Both thought that philosophical knowledge could not simply be transferred from the mind of the teacher to that of the student—rather, in the dialectical procedure of questions and answers, the student must come to see the truth for himself. The student was encouraged by both to think for himself: "I should not like my writing to spare other people the trouble of thinking. But, if possible, to stimulate someone to thoughts of his own." (*PI*, Preface, p. x.) The use of jargon and technical terms was shunned by both, and their examples dealt with the most ordinary and humble objects and events. Both had a loathing for artificiality and sham, and hence managed to offend and annoy a great many people. But both were loved by a small circle of friends, many of whom were also their students. Both were severe with their friends, but loved them for all that. Both were absolutely faithful to their own ideas and ideals, and gave up everything for the sake of philosophy. Both lived simply and paid little attention to their clothes, or rooms, or food, or other bodily needs—and they did so, as far as one can see, basically for the same reason: such things would have distracted them from their serious business. Both had a strong sense of duty and were willing to risk their lives in the service of the state in times of danger. I do not think it misleading to say that, although for quite different reasons, both Socrates and Wittgenstein welcomed death; in any case, it is certainly true that they each displayed the highest kind of courage in the face of death.

On Friday, April 27th, he took a walk in the afternoon. That night he fell violently ill. He remained conscious and when informed by the doctor that he could live only a few days, he exclaimed 'Good!' Before losing consciousness he said to Mrs. Bevan (who was with him throughout the night) 'Tell them I've had a wonderful life!' By 'them' he undoubtedly meant his close friends. When I think of his profound pessimism, the intensity of his mental and moral suffering, the relentless way in which he drove his intellect, his need for love together with the harshness that repelled love, I am inclined to believe that his life was fiercely unhappy. Yet at the end he himself exclaimed that it had been 'wonderful!' To me this seems a mysterious and strangely moving utterance.[20]

[20] Malcolm, *Memoir*, p. 100.

Part I

Tractatus

Logico-Philosophicus

2   The Demand for Simples

The *Tractatus* is a short, aphoristic, difficult, and haunting work. It consists of a preface plus some 80 pages of numbered propositions expressed in powerful prose. The thought is highly compressed, very often to the point of obscurity. One has the strong impression that each proposition has been carefully thought out and painstakingly worded, and that behind each lies a host of subtle, but mostly unexpressed, considerations. Hence the passages of the *Tractatus* need to be interpreted—somewhat like those in a sacred text. This comparison is not an idle one, for the book sounds very like a sacred text, as though the author were pronouncing truths which only the "elect" could possibly understand. This tone has infuriated some, but in others it has instilled an attitude which approaches religious awe. One thing, at any rate, is certain: any interpretation of the *Tractatus* is bound to be at least in part highly controversial, and an author would be extremely presumptuous in claiming that his interpretation was definitive. What is presented here is a way of looking at the main doctrines of the work that makes sense to me. My hope is that this will help the reader in his own thinking about them.

First, a word about the system of numbering in the *Tractatus*. According to Wittgenstein's own account of it (*T*, p. 7 n.), the most important propositions are those to which integers are assigned; there are seven of them, numbered 1 through 7. The decimal number indicates the "logical importance" of the proposition and the entire number (i.e., integer plus decimal) of a proposition *p* indicates on which other proposition *p* is a comment. Thus, for example, 3.3

and 3.4 are comments on 3 and less important than it; 3.31 and 3.32 are comments on 3.3 and less important than it; and so on.

Professor Erik Stenius, however, points out that Wittgenstein's actual practice accords only partially with this account.[1] Stenius argues that propositions whose first decimal is 0 (e.g., 2.01) are indeed comments on the relevant basic proposition (i.e., on 2, in the case of 2.01), but that when there is a single decimal (e.g., 2.1, 2.2) new concepts are introduced which figure essentially in the following whole-numbered proposition (i.e., 3, in the case of 2.1 and 2.2). Thus 3.1, 3.2, 3.3, and so on, are best thought of as preambles to 4 rather than comments on 3. It is true, however, that Wittgenstein's own explicit account accords fairly well with his practice in the case of propositions with two or more decimal numbers (e.g., 2.1511 and 2.1512 are comments on 2.151). At any rate, the numbering system is not nearly so rigorous and consistent as it is made to appear; it is only a rough guide to the structure of the *Tractatus*. It does, however, at least provide a convenient means of referring to the propositions.

Atomic Facts

In the *Tractatus,* Wittgenstein develops a metaphysical system from considerations of language and meaning. The metaphysical and linguistic doctrines which he held during this period are so essentially bound up with one another that neither can be understood in isolation from the other. Still, our account must begin somewhere, and perhaps the best place would be where Wittgenstein himself begins— with facts. He writes at the beginning of the *Tractatus:*

1	The world is all that is the case.
1.1	The world is the totality of facts, not of things.

.   .   .

| 1.2 | The world divides into facts.[2] |

---

[1] Erik Stenius, *Wittgenstein's Tractatus* (Oxford: Basil Blackwell, 1960). See chapter 1 for an illuminating discussion of the numbering system and general structure of the *Tractatus.*

[2] Here, and throughout this book, quotations beginning with numbers are taken from Wittgenstein's *Tractatus.* The edition cited is given in the list of abbreviations, p. xi. The numbers are all, with the one exception mentioned in footnote 13, p. 26, those assigned by Wittgenstein himself to the various propositions of the work.

Wittgenstein does not say that the world is made up of facts, or that facts are the stuff of the world. On the contrary,

2.021   Objects make up the substance of the world. . . .

Even so, these opening remarks of the *Tractatus* seem puzzling at first. One would naturally think not only that things make up the world, but also that the world is the totality of things—and that this is so just because objects do make up the world.

But there are objections, and seemingly strong ones, against this common-sense view. Whatever the world is the totality of, it might be argued, a complete list of them ought to tell us what the world is like, ought to provide a complete description of the world. But this is not the case if the world is the totality of things. From a list of all the objects that there are, one can derive only a very inadequate idea of what the world is like. If you are asked to describe a room, and in reply simply list the articles contained in it plus the walls, windows, doors, and so on, you would have performed your job very poorly. What was wanted was not just a list of objects, but also an account of what they are like and how they are arranged in the room. For example, you might have said that there is a green wicker chair by the window, that it has a red cushion with a flower pattern on it, that next to it is a stuffed moose, and so on. But what you would then be listing is not a lot of objects, but a lot of facts. The truth about the world, then, is that there are such and such facts, not that there are such and such objects.

The same point can be put in the following way. If you break the world down into objects, the result does not correspond uniquely to this actual world; any number of other possible, but nonactual, worlds, if so broken down, would yield the same result. Suppose you were asked to build a model of a certain particular room from a list of the objects it contains. There are so many possibilities of combining and arranging these objects, and so many possible qualities they might have, that your task would be a hopeless one. But you could do it if you were given a list of the facts about the room. In short, there can be any number of possible worlds composed of just the objects which compose this actual world, for those objects might be arranged in many different ways, have different histories, and so on. It is the facts that there are, not the objects that there are, that uniquely determine the world—i.e., this actual world, as distinguished from other possible worlds.

In this way, one can find Wittgenstein's view that the world is the totality of facts, not things, compelling. It is even more compelling if we think of the world not as an instantaneous, three-dimensional whole—e.g., the world as it is at the present moment—but rather as a four-dimensional space-time "worm" extending through all time. The world so conceived, one might naturally think, consists largely of innumerable facts—e.g., that Caesar crossed the Rubicon and that Socrates drank the hemlock.

If, then, it seems reasonable to view the world as a totality of facts, just what can be said about facts themselves? Wittgenstein evidently thought of a fact as being a kind of complex entity existing in the world, as being a group of things arranged or combined in a certain way—as though, for example, the fact that the cat is on the mat is the complex consisting of the cat and the mat, arranged so that the former is on the latter. That he so viewed them is shown by the kinds of statements he makes about facts and states of affairs. For example,

2.01   A state of affairs (a state of things) is a combination of objects (things).

. . .

2.03   In a state of affairs objects fit into one another like the links of a chain.

2.031   In a state of affairs objects stand in a determinate relation to one another.

It has come to be generally recognized that it is a mistake to think of facts in this way, and the later Wittgenstein [3] certainly thought his earlier view was mistaken.

Talking of the fact as a "complex of objects" springs from this confusion (cf. *Tractatus Logico-philosophicus*). [*BB*, p. 31.]

I shall not pause to give the arguments against such a view of facts; [4] the important point here is that in the *Tractatus* Wittgenstein thought of them as real complexes existing in the world. Indeed, he thought that facts have the most basic kind of reality, as is indicated by his assertion that "the world divides into facts" (*T* 1.2). To be sure,

[3] It has become customary to refer to the Wittgenstein of the *Tractatus* and "Some Remarks on Logical Form" (1929) as the early Wittgenstein, and to the Wittgenstein of *The Blue and Brown Books* and all subsequent works as the later Wittgenstein. I observe this custom here and throughout the book.

[4] For a cogent attack on it, see J. R. Lucas, "On Not Worshipping Facts," *The Philosophical Quarterly*, Vol. 8, No. 31 (April 1958), 144-56.

"Objects make up the substance of the world" (*T* 2.021), but the things that Wittgenstein meant by 'objects' are such that they cannot exist apart from facts, as we shall see (*T* 2.0121, 2.0122). So it is facts alone that can exist of themselves, independent of anything else. For Wittgenstein, then, facts are there in the world to be pictured (*T* 4.03, 4.0311, 4.032) and described (*T* 4.023) by language. And it is not at all difficult to adopt this view of facts; indeed, certain 'fact'-locutions make it seem to be the only possible view. I am thinking of expressions such as these:

It is a fact that Socrates is short.
The fact is: Socrates is short.
Certain facts about Socrates are astonishing.
He just discovered some new facts about Socrates.
If you look at the facts dispassionately, you will see that Socrates was guilty.

These expressions make the view that the word 'fact' denotes a kind of (complex) entity extremely tempting. And the early Wittgenstein—rightly or wrongly—succumbed to this temptation.

The world, then, according to Wittgenstein, divides into facts. Most facts are highly complex, and are composed of less complex facts. These, in turn, are composed of still less complex facts, and so on. Ultimately—and this is a central point of Wittgenstein's system—we get down to facts which cannot be further reduced, which do not consist of any further, less complex, facts; these can be called atomic facts. Atomic facts are not absolutely simple, because they are made up of components, but these components are not simpler facts. (What they are will be discussed presently.) Atomic facts, then, are the ultimate building blocks of the world in the sense that the world divides ultimately into them, and they are the simplest things that are self-subsistent, that can exist by themselves, in isolation.

But so far the doctrine of atomic facts has simply been stated; it has not in any way been justified. What grounds have we for supposing that complex facts break up ultimately into atomic facts? And what exactly is an atomic fact anyway? As might be expected, Wittgenstein did not arrive at atomic facts by any direct inspection of complex facts; he did not simply notice that complex facts are, as it happens, composed ultimately of atomic facts. He arrived at them, rather, from the side of language; he thought that certain considerations about language require that there be atomic facts.

In the *Tractatus,* Wittgenstein writes:

4.21   The simplest kind of proposition, an elementary proposi-
            tion, asserts the existence of a state of affairs.

To assert the existence of a state of affairs (*Sachverhalt*), as we shall
see in the next chapter, is to assert an atomic fact. What we must do
now, evidently, is examine the concept of an elementary proposition
—for it was through elementary propositions that Wittgenstein
reached states of affairs and hence atomic facts.

Russell's Theory of Descriptions

Before we attempt such an examination, however, it would be
well to look briefly at Russell's famous theory of descriptions, which
Wittgenstein considered to be his "most important production." [5] The
notion of the analysis of propositions which is embodied in the theory
is important for understanding the *Tractatus* in general, and in particular for understanding Wittgenstein's argument for the existence of
elementary propositions and hence for the existence of atomic facts.

I shall consider this theory only as it applies to phrases which
Russell called definite descriptions—such phrases as 'the author of
Waverley,' 'the present King of France,' 'the tallest building in New
York,' and so on—phrases which, as we might say, purport to name
one definite object and no other. The main point of Russell's theory is
to show that such phrases, although they appear to name one such
object, in fact never do so.

Let us begin with a general remark about meaning. It is not wholly
implausible to assume, and I think many people *may* assume, that the
meaning of any word or phrase is the object (or quality or relation, and
so on) it names. It is not unnatural to suppose, for example, that the
word 'Socrates' names a certain man, that it means that man, and
thus that he is the meaning of the word 'Socrates'; similarly, one might
easily suppose that the color red is the meaning of the word 'red.'
"As to what one means by 'meaning,' I will give a few illustrations.
For instance, the word 'Socrates,' you will say, means a certain
man; the word 'mortal' means a certain quality; . . ." [6]

[5] Malcolm, *Memoir,* p. 68.
[6] Bertrand Russell, "The Philosophy of Logical Atomism," reprinted in his
Logic and Knowledge, ed. by R. C. Marsh (New York: The Macmillan Company, 1956), p. 186. This book will hereinafter be referred to as "Marsh
volume." "The Philosophy of Logical Atomism," originally given as a series of
lectures in 1918, was first published in *The Monist,* XXVIII (1918) and
XXIX (1919).

This assumption presupposes that every word or phrase *does* name something—an object, quality, relation, or whatever. Russell realizes that this presupposition is unwarranted; for example, the word 'Cerberus,' the phrase 'the golden mountain,' and words like 'or,' 'if,' and 'all,' do not name anything. But if the assumption is restricted so as not to have this presupposition, Russell would accept it; he holds, in other words, that if a word or phrase *does* name something—if it is a true proper name, a "logically proper name"— then the meaning of that word or phrase is whatever it names.

Let us confine our discussion to nouns. According to Russell, if a noun does in fact name a certain object, then that object is its meaning, and it has that meaning in all contexts. It does not matter whether the noun stands by itself or whether it occurs in a sentence; it always has whatever meaning it has. It is just this feature which is characteristic of true proper names, according to Russell. If we consider 'Sir Walter Scott' for the moment to be a proper name,[7] it seems clear that this expression refers to a certain man whether it is written by itself on a page or occurs in a sentence. Russell maintains that definite descriptions are quite unlike proper names; contrary to appearances, they do not name any object, and thus they have no meaning in isolation. This seems at first glance like a wildly implausible view— why does not the phrase 'the tallest building in New York' name a certain building just as much as, and in the same sense that, 'Sir Walter Scott' names a certain novelist?

Russell's position here is not in the least implausible if we bear in mind his basic assumption that the meaning of a name is the object it denotes. For if we insist that all definite descriptions name objects, and we assume with Russell that the object is their meaning, what are we to say about definite descriptions like 'the round square' or 'the present King of France'? There are no actual objects that they could name, so we must either invent some nonactual objects for them to name, so that they may have a meaning, or we must say that such expressions are meaningless, since they name no objects. Neither of these alternatives is in the least tempting. We certainly do not want to introduce a new metaphysical realm into our ontology, peopled by

---

[7] Russell's final view, however, is that terms like 'Sir Walter Scott' and 'Socrates,' although counted as proper names *par excellence* in ordinary discourse, are not really proper names at all, not "logically proper names"; he held that they are really concealed descriptions—i.e., abbreviated or truncated descriptions. For his arguments in support of this conclusion, see lecture VI of his "The Philosophy of Logical Atomism."

such nonexistent objects as round squares, golden mountains, and present kings of France. Nor on the other hand do we want to say that such definite descriptions as 'the present King of France' have no meaning of any sort; for we should then have to say that the sentence 'The present King of France does not exist,' since it contains a meaningless phrase (viz., its subject), is nonsensical, whereas in fact it expresses a true proposition. Russell's theory of definite descriptions offers us a way out of this uncomfortable position.

Our error (the one which leads to the uncomfortable position), according to Russell, is in assuming that definite descriptions are proper names—for example, that 'the author of *Waverley*' is a proper name of the man also called Sir Walter Scott. Once we make this assumption, we are lost. The thing to do, we are told, is to abandon that assumption.

Before proceeding further, we might consider the following objection: "I grant that 'the round square' and 'the present King of France,' since there are no objects corresponding to them, are not true proper names; but I can see no reason why 'the present President of the United States' and 'the author of *Waverley*' should not be true proper names." One might answer this objection by arguing that the logical nature of a form of words cannot plausibly be thought to vary with empirical matters of fact. But whether Russell would agree with such an answer or not, and whether it is sound or not, it would need, in any case, an elaborate defense; Russell thought he could show that no definite descriptive phrase can be a true proper name, no matter what the world happens to contain. He presents the following argument which attempts (very badly, I'm afraid) to demonstrate this—to demonstrate that no definite descriptive phrase, not even one to which there does correspond something in existence, can be a true proper name.

> Take, for example, the following proposition: "Scott is the author of Waverley." . . . This proposition expresses an identity; thus if "the author of Waverley" could be taken as a proper name, and supposed to stand for some object *c,* the proposition would be "Scott is *c.*" But if *c* is any one except Scott, this proposition is false; while if *c is* Scott, the proposition is "Scott is Scott," which is trivial, and plainly different from "Scott is the author of Waverley." [8]

[8] Russell and Whitehead, *Principia Mathematica,* I, Second edition (London: Cambridge University Press, 1925), 67. The same argument appears in Russell's "The Philosophy of Logical Atomism," Marsh volume, pp. 245-46.

(That the proposition "Scott is Scott" is different from the proposition "Scott is the author of *Waverley*" is evident, says Russell, from the fact that George IV wished to know whether Scott was the author of *Waverley,* whereas it would be absurd to suggest that he wanted to know whether Scott was Scott. "An interest in the law of identity can hardly be attributed to the first gentleman of Europe." [9]) 'The author of *Waverley*,' Russell concludes, is not a proper name: ". . . 'The author of *Waverley*' does not stand simply for Scott, nor for anything else." [10]

The assumption that definite descriptions are proper names must be abandoned; this means that definite descriptions in isolation have no meaning. But then are not all sentences containing them meaningless? Russell answers "No," and here we get to the heart of his theory of definite descriptions. Although such phrases have no meaning in isolation, sentences containing them may have a perfectly good meaning. (Words and phrases of which this is true he calls 'incomplete symbols.') Russell claims that if we contemplate the proposition expressed by such a sentence—e.g., "The author of *Waverley* was Scotch"—we can see that it is a complex one. First of all, it states that someone wrote *Waverley;* if no one had written *Waverley,* the sentence would express a false proposition. Secondly, it states that only one person wrote *Waverley;* if two or more persons had written it, the sentence '*The* author of *Waverley* was Scotch' would again express a false proposition. Thirdly, it states that whoever wrote *Waverley* was Scotch. Hence, according to Russell, the proposition expressed by the sentence 'The author of *Waverley* was Scotch' has for its meaning the three propositions expressed by these three sentences:

(1) at least one person wrote *Waverley;*
(2) at most one person wrote *Waverley;*
(3) whoever wrote *Waverley* was Scotch. [11]

Notice that on this view, propositions containing definite descriptions which describe no object, e.g., "The present King of France is bald," now have a perfectly good meaning, but they are false, since part (1) of their analysis is false, thus making the whole proposition false.

[9] Russell, "On Denoting," Marsh volume, p. 48. The article first appeared in *Mind,* XIV (1905).

[10] Russell, "The Philosophy of Logical Atomism," Marsh volume, p. 253.

[11] Russell, *Introduction to Mathematical Philosophy* (London: George Allen & Unwin Ltd., 1919), p. 177.

Russell considered this a desirable feature of his theory, since he thought such propositions were both meaningful and false.

Let us call propositions (1)–(3) the *analysis* of the original proposition "The author of *Waverley* was Scotch." Russell thought that when such a correct analysis of a proposition is given, it tells you what the proposition really says, what it is really about. Notice that in the analysis, the definite descriptive phrase 'the author of *Waverley*,' which occurs in the original analyzed proposition, entirely disappears. Therefore, since the analysis specifies what the proposition really says, " 'the author of *Waverley*' is not a constituent of the proposition at all. There is no constituent really there corresponding to the descriptive phrase." [12] The original proposition *appears* to refer directly to (i.e., to name) something called 'the author of *Waverley*,' but the analysis shows, according to Russell, that this appearance is deceptive.

One general point which these considerations were thought to show is that the analysis of a proposition gives its true logical form. The grammatical form of the original sentence in our example is misleading; it makes it look as though the proposition has a subject/predicate logical form—as if the proposition names an entity (in the subject) and then says something about it (in the predicate). But the truth of the matter is that the proposition is really a conjunction of three other propositions (viz., propositions (1)–(3)) and has not a simple subject/predicate form at all. It is important, therefore, to distinguish grammatical and logical forms. Wittgenstein compliments Russell on this insight:

4.0031   . . . It was Russell who performed the service of show-
             ing that the apparent logical form of a proposition need
             not be its real one.

And he says earlier:

4.002(4) [13] Language disguises thought. So much so, that from the
             outward form of the clothing it is impossible to infer the
             form of the thought beneath it, because the outward form
             of the clothing is not designed to reveal the form of the
             body, but for entirely different purposes.

[12] Russell, "The Philosophy of Logical Atomism," Marsh volume, p. 248. See also p. 253.
[13] A number in parentheses after a *Tractatus* section number indicates the paragraph of the section.

There is much that can be said in criticism of Russell's claims in his theory of descriptions, and of the conclusions he drew from them, but it would not serve our present purposes to say it here. Instead, I shall simply mention two of the important issues which his theory raises. First, the theory claims that certain phrases—namely, definite descriptions—which at first glance seem to name an object, in fact do not do so. This leads one to enquire what sort of expressions in the language *do* name objects; what, in short, are the real names in the language? What characteristics must an expression possess in order to be counted a genuine name? Second, the theory claims that a proposition expressed by a certain sort of sentence can be analyzed into other, presumably simpler, propositions. This inevitably leads one to think that all complex propositions might be analyzable into simpler propositions, and these in turn into still simpler ones, and so on, until—what? Is this process of analysis possible? If so, how far can one carry it? And is there any order or structure in the results of such analysis? Russell's theory had analyzed one sort of proposition into three others; but it is difficult to see how that analysis could be generalized, so that a complex proposition of any form could be similarly broken up into three analogous propositions. Must propositions of different forms be analyzed in different ways? If so, how many different ways? Do these ways simply form a heterogeneous collection, or is it possible to reduce them to a system, or at least to characterize them all in some basic way? Again, given a certain proposition, are there several equally correct ways of analyzing it, or is there only one way?

Although Wittgenstein's first thoughts in philosophy were concerned with the foundations of mathematics, it was not long before he found himself embroiled in such questions as these. It is characteristic of him that he should have seen with the greatest clarity that these and other questions existed and demanded answers, that he should have honestly faced them and tried to deal with them, and that he should have persevered until he had found what he considered to be complete and ultimate answers. The greater part of the *Tractatus* consists of the results of these labors.

Elementary Propositions

We are now in a better position to examine Wittgenstein's doctrine of elementary propositions. First, something must be said about the meaning of his German term *'Elementarsatz.'* I have translated it as 'elementary proposition,' and that is how Pears and McGuinness render it in their translation of the *Tractatus*. Miss G. E. M. Anscombe, a leading expert on Wittgenstein and one of his literary executors, concurs with this translation.[14] But Stenius translates the term as 'elementary sentence.' [15] Evidently the 'elementary' is correct; but ought *Satz* to be rendered as 'sentence' or as 'proposition'?

A preliminary question might arise in some readers' minds: Does it make any difference which way it is translated? It does, for sentences and propositions are quite different. Propositions are the thoughts or ideas which sentences can be used to express. Sentences are composed of words in accordance with syntactical rules, and belong to some definite language, whereas propositions are not composed of words and do not belong to any language. The English sentence 'It is raining,' the German sentence *'Es regnet,'* and the French sentence *'Il pleut'* are three different sentences, but they can all be used to express the same proposition, which is not itself either English, German, or French. There are no English or French propositions. Furthermore, propositions are the sort of thing that can be true or false, but sentences cannot be true or false. If someone were to ask "Is the English sentence 'It is raining' true or false?" one would be at a loss for an answer. If, on a particular occasion, someone describes the weather by uttering the sentence 'It is raining,' what he asserts will be either true or false, but then it is the proposition he expresses, which includes a reference to a particular time and place (in this case, the time and place of the utterance of the sentence) that is true or false, not the sentence, which does not include any such reference.

In ordinary German usage, the term *'Satz'* can mean either 'sentence' or 'proposition' (or even 'clause'). The solution to our problem of how to render the term *'Satz'* in the *Tractatus* is that Wittgenstein uses it in both basic senses and so our translation of it must reflect this variation. An examination of the relevant passages will bear this out. For example, he often speaks of *Sätze* (*Elementarsätze*) as being true or false, as in *T* 4.06 (*T* 4.25, 4.26): in these passages, we must read 'proposition' ('elementary proposition'). In other

[14] G. E. M. Anscombe, *An Introduction to Wittgenstein's Tractatus* (Hutchinson University Library. New York: Hillary House Publishers, Ltd., 1959), p. 30.
[15] Erik Stenius, *Wittgenstein's Tractatus* p. 12.

passages, such as those in which he speaks of *Sätze* as being composed of words (e.g., *T* 3.141), we ought to read 'sentence.' But in the overwhelming majority of cases, by *'Satz'* (*'Elementarsatz'*), Wittgenstein means 'proposition' ('elementary proposition').

Does this mean that, as a result of the fact that the German term *'Satz'* conflates the different notions of a sentence and a proposition, Wittgenstein merely confuses the two notions? Moore seems to suggest something of the sort when he writes that in Wittgenstein's lectures during the period 1930-33, he sometimes explicitly distinguished sentences and propositions, and sometimes said things which imply that 'sentence' and 'proposition' mean the same.[16] But the truth of the matter is that Wittgenstein is well aware of the conceptual distinction between a sentence and a proposition. As we shall see, he rejects the view that a proposition is a special kind of entity—a thought or idea—separate from a sentence and which the sentence somehow expresses; on the contrary—and this is the crucial point—a proposition for him *is* a sentence *in a certain relationship* (which shall be explained later). Hence, although a proposition cannot be simply identified with a sentence, there is still a sense in which it *is*—is nothing more than—a sentence. (Similarly, an uncle cannot be simply identified with a man; but since an uncle is a man in a certain relationship, an uncle just is—is nothing more than—a man.) The fact that he holds this view of the intimate tie between a sentence and a proposition accounts for the disturbing fact that Wittgenstein does not always distinguish as carefully as one might desire between them.

We can complete this preliminary account of Wittgenstein's use of *'Satz'* by considering another term he employs: *'Satzzeichen,'* which is translated by Pears and McGuinness as 'propositional sign.' To see what this term means, look at what is written on the line below:

It is raining.   It is raining.

There are two senses of the term 'sentence.' According to the first, there are two sentences written on the line. The inscription on the left is a sentence, and so is the one on the right; thus, there are two complete sentences. But there is another sense of 'sentence' in accordance

16 G. E. Moore, "Wittgenstein's Lectures in 1930-33," Part I, *Mind*, LXIII, No. 249 (January 1954), 11. This, and the two succeeding parts of Moore's article, are reprinted in his *Philosophical Papers* (London: George Allen & Unwin Ltd.; New York: The Macmillan Company, 1959). In that book, the cited passage is found on pp. 262-63.

with which we would say that there is only one sentence, viz., the English sentence 'It is raining,' written twice on the line. Borrowing terms from C. S. Peirce, let us label the first sense of 'sentence' *sentence-token* and the second, *sentence-type.* Thus two sentence-tokens are written on the line but only one sentence-type is exemplified there. Sentence-tokens are the actual inscriptions (or sounds) written (or made) on a particular occasion, in a particular place; they are composed of individual ink marks on paper, chalk marks on blackboards, sound waves in air, or whatever. Sentence-types are universals of which particular sentence-tokens are the instances; they are not composed of actual ink marks or chalk marks or sound waves, but of shapes of ink or chalk marks, structures of sound waves, or whatever. When we speak of the English sentence 'It is raining,' we are speaking of that sentence-type. Notice how bizarre it would be to say that the English sentence 'It is raining' is composed of ink marks, although the particular instances of it, its sentence-tokens (such as the one in the earlier part of this very sentence), may well be.

Where ordinary language is concerned, by *'Satzzeichen,'* or propositional sign, Wittgenstein means a sentence-token; where a symbolic language or notation is concerned, as in symbolic logic, he means a sign in that language or notation analogous to a sentence-token. (See, for example, *T* 4.442.) So a propositional sign is any particular sign or group of signs—i.e., any sign-token—that might be used to express, or assert, a proposition. In those few passages in which *'Satz'* must be translated as 'sentence,' he means by *'Satz'* a sentence-type (or, for nonordinary languages or notations, something analogous to it). In the *Tractatus,* then—to confine ourselves for the moment to ordinary language—*'Satz'* may mean either proposition or sentence-type, and *'Satzzeichen'* means sentence-token. One thing is clear, however; in the *Tractatus,* Wittgenstein is much more interested in what sentences are used to assert—i.e., in propositions—than in the sentences themselves.

But what is an elementary proposition, according to Wittgenstein? It is one that cannot by analyzed into any further, more basic propositions (just as an atomic fact is one that does not consist of further, more basic facts). It has components (as the fact has) but not components that are themselves propositions. We have seen how Russell tried to show, in his theory of descriptions, how a certain type of proposition can be analyzed into other, simpler propositions; and these, in turn, could presumably be further analyzed. Wittgenstein is now saying that there is a class of absolutely basic propositions of which no such further analysis is possible—these are the elementary propositions.

An elementary proposition, Wittgenstein tells us, is one consisting entirely of names.

4.22   An elementary proposition consists of names. It is a nexus, a concatenation, of names.

But it must be realized that Wittgenstein is using the term 'name' in a technical sense, not in any ordinary sense. We can say such things as " 'Square' is the name of a plane figure with four equal sides," " 'Cow' is the name of a kind of animal," and " 'Socrates' is the name of a famous Greek philosopher"; these terms, however, would not be counted as names in Wittgenstein's sense. By a name, he means a term that is essentially to be contrasted with one that can be verbally defined; it is one that cannot be analyzed or defined.

3.26   A name cannot be dissected any further by means of a definition: it is a primitive sign.

Hence Wittgenstein would not count such terms as 'square' and 'cow' as names, for each of them has a definition. We might think that what are ordinarily called proper names, like 'Socrates,' ought to qualify as names in this special sense; after all, one does not find definitions of them in dictionaries. But Wittgenstein would claim that ordinary proper names do not qualify, for he would hold that their meaning can be analyzed by stating certain essential facts about the person or thing they name. He would, in short, agree with Russell that they are really abbreviated definite descriptions (see note 7, p. 23). In order for a term to be a name, there must be no possibility whatever of defining it or analyzing it—rather, there must be no way of defining it in any purely verbal way. If it names something which can be observed, then it could be defined in another way, namely by pointing to whatever it denotes and saying "The word '_____' means *this*." This kind of definition is called ostensive definition; the only possible way of defining a name is by ostensive definition, and that possibility exists only in case the name denotes something observable.

It follows from this that a name must denote something simple— something, that is, without parts or components of any kind. If it denoted something complex, it could be defined in terms of its constituents and their structure, and hence would not be a name. Wittgenstein takes another term of common speech and gives it a meaning it does not have there. The term is 'object,' and he uses it to mean something that is simple. A name, in Wittgenstein's special sense, can only denote an object.

3.203   A name means an object.

2.02   Objects are simple.

The meaning of T 4.22 is now a bit clearer: an elementary proposition is one that consists entirely of terms that denote simples.

But the question now faces us: Why did Wittgenstein think that there are any such propositions? The following passage gives us a hint:

4.221(1)   It is obvious that the analysis of propositions must bring us to elementary propositions which consist of names in immediate combination.

There do not just happen to be elementary propositions; Wittgenstein did not discover them by any kind of empirical investigation. He says there *must* be such propositions; their existence is demanded by certain considerations. It is not even necessary to produce examples of elementary propositions; Wittgenstein is certain that there must be such things as elementary propositions, and hence names and objects, even though he admits that he cannot think of a single example of one. (See *NB*, entries for 14.6.15, 16.6.15, 21.6.15.) It is certain a priori that they exist. Finding actual examples of them is a mere empirical detail, and in this Wittgenstein was not interested. Malcolm reports:

I asked Wittgenstein whether, when he wrote the *Tractatus*, he had ever decided upon anything as an *example* of a 'simple object.' His reply was that at that time his thought had been that he was a *logician;* and that it was not his business, as a logician, to try to decide whether this thing or that was a simple thing or a complex thing, that being a purely *empirical* matter! It was clear that he regarded his former opinion as absurd.[17]

But precisely what considerations make it certain a priori that there are elementary propositions, names, and objects? In a word: considerations about meaning. The main argument depends on two important assumptions:

[17] Malcolm, *Memoir*, p. 86.

(1) The (correct) analysis of a proposition gives its real meaning.

(2) The meaning of any term—with the single exception of the so-called "logical constants" (see below, p. 70)—is whatever it designates or denotes.

It will become apparent as the argument proceeds that in making assumption (2), Wittgenstein does not commit himself to the obviously false doctrine that every term must designate something *directly,* i.e., must be a true proper name. As we have already noted (p. 23), 'Cerberus' and 'the golden mountain' are counter-examples which refute that doctrine at once. Assumption (2) commits Wittgenstein rather to the different doctrine that, except for the logical constants, every term must directly *or indirectly* designate or denote something. What this means will be explained in what follows.

When Russell gave his analysis of a certain type of proposition in his theory of descriptions, he thought that the three propositions of the analysis were what the original, analyzed proposition really meant. In general, a correct analysis of a proposition was taken to express what the proposition really means. On this view of analysis, which Wittgenstein shared with Russell, the terms of a proposition can be said to signify something indirectly, *via* the terms of the simpler propositions into which it is analyzed. The terms of the analyzed proposition mean whatever the terms of the simpler propositions mean—no more, no less. Hence the meaning of the terms of the analyzed proposition may in this sense be said to depend on the meaning of those of the simpler propositions. Thus in an ordinary, verbal definition—which is one kind of analysis—the meaning of the defined term may be said to depend on those of the terms of the definition.

> 3.261(1)   Every sign that has a definition signifies *via* the signs that serve to define it; and the definitions point the way.

But if the terms of the simpler propositions of the analysis are themselves definable in other, still more basic, terms, the same thing must be true of them: their meaning will be dependent on the meaning of those other terms. This order of dependence continues as long as the terms at each level of the analysis are still definable. But the series cannot be infinitely long; it cannot be the case that proposition *A* is analyzable into a group of propositions *B,* that these are in turn analyzable into a larger group of propositions *C,* and so on ad infinitum. It cannot, for then no ordinary term would denote anything, and hence, if the meaning of a term is what it denotes, as

Wittgenstein assumed, no ordinary term would have a meaning—which is absurd. The terms of proposition *A* do not denote anything directly; they denote only *via* the terms of propositions *B*. The terms of propositions *B*, in turn, denote something only *via* the terms of propositions *C*, and so on. But unless in this progression one eventually reaches propositions whose terms denote something directly—i.e., *name* something—and do not merely lead on to further propositions, none of the terms in propositions *A, B, C, . . .* will denote anything, none of them will mean anything. These ultimate propositions must consist of nothing but names, for only such propositions are unanalyzable; any other type of proposition will only lead, by analysis, to further propositions.

Think of it in this way. There must be a completed route from words to something outside words which they denote, for that, ultimately, is their meaning. But if one word only leads to others, and they in turn only to still others, and so on forever, then words are eternally trapped in their own realm. At some point, there must be a breakthrough, for words *do* have meaning. It can only be made, according to Wittgenstein, with elementary propositions consisting of nothing but names.

In his early reflections on this subject, Wittgenstein wrote:

> But it is clear that components of our proposition can be analysed by means of a definition, and must be, if we want to approximate to the real structure of the proposition. *At any rate, then, there is a process of analysis.* And can it not now be asked whether this process comes to an end? And if so: What will the end be?
> If it is true that every defined sign signifies *via* its definitions then presumably the chain of definitions must some time have an end. [*NB*, entry for 9.5.15.]

As we have seen from *T* 3.261(1), quoted above, Wittgenstein came to think that every defined word does signify *via* the words in its definition, and hence that the process of analysis must come to an end. What it must always come to end in, of course, are elementary propositions—i.e., propositions consisting entirely of names, that is to say, of terms that cannot be further defined by other terms.

There is another, related, argument—or the suggestion of one, at any rate—to be found in the *Tractatus* for the existence of indefinable signs. This one turns upon what Wittgenstein calls the determinateness of sense of propositions. There is a necessary connection, we are told, between the alleged existence of (proper) names (i.e., simple signs—see *T* 3.202) and the determinateness of a proposition's sense:

3.23   The requirement that simple signs be possible is the requirement that sense be determinate.

If we are to read this sentence as indicating an argument for indefinable signs, we must see why this connection is a necessary one. The clue to the connection seems to be in Wittgenstein's contention that the indeterminateness of a proposition is a result of the fact that one of its terms denotes a complex.

3.24(3)   When a propositional element signifies a complex, this can be seen from an indeterminateness in the propositions in which it occurs. In such cases we *know* that the proposition leaves something undetermined. (In fact the generality-sign *contains* a prototype.)

The last sentence of this passage suggests that it is the *generality* involved in a proposition dealing with a complex that introduces indeterminateness into such a proposition's sense. This point is stated explicitly in the *Notebooks*.

It can be seen that a name stands for a complex object from an indefiniteness in the propositions in which it occurs. This comes of the generality of such propositions. [*NB*, entry for 21.6.15.]

To see how generality introduces indeterminateness, we must consider this passage:

3.24(2)   A complex can be given only by its description, which will be right or wrong.

A term which designates something complex (such as a person or a table) does so only by being a description of it; that is, the term for a complex is never a logically proper name, but is always really an implicit description of that complex. The description will become explicit in the analysis of the proposition in which the term occurs. (Since 'description of a complex' is consequently equivalent to 'definition of the term for a complex,' the point at issue here is the same as that discussed in the previous argument.)

It is this alleged fact—that a term which designates a complex is not its (proper) name but always really a description of it—that explains what Wittgenstein means by the *indeterminateness* of a proposition's sense. In the first place, there is indefiniteness concerning *which* description, of all the possible ones, is the right one. If I say "The watch is lying on the table," the expression "the watch" (to consider just the subject expression) designates something complex. It must, then, according to Wittgenstein, be an implicit description of the watch. But *what* description? At this point one kind of generality and hence one kind of indeterminateness enter in. There are all kinds of timepieces that fall under the general heading of 'watch': pocket watches of all sorts, wrist watches of all sorts, watches embedded in rings, and so on. Which of all the possible descriptions of all these different kinds of watches is involved in my proposition "The watch is lying on the table"? The proposition *as so expressed* does not say, and it is therefore to that extent indeterminate; it leaves undetermined what specific description is to be used in analyzing the general term 'watch.'

But even if this first kind of generality (and indeterminateness) could be removed, there would still remain a second kind. Given *any* description of an individual, no matter how detailed, there will always be an indefinite number of different individuals, actual or possible, that it will also fit. (See *T* 5.5302.) To say this, however, is to say that any such description is inherently and unavoidably general. A proposition containing such a description is therefore indeterminate in the further sense that it does not, as so expressed, specify which, of all the possible individuals answering to the description, is actually meant. That is left undetermined by the proposition.

If we were confined, then, to terms designating complexes—if such terms were the only kind that there are—then all propositions would necessarily be indeterminate in sense in one or both of the ways just described. It is only if there are terms designating simples—terms, that is, which are not descriptions of what they designate, but which directly and uniquely name them—that such indeterminateness of sense can be avoided. This, I take it, is the meaning of *T* 3.23 quoted above.

Wittgenstein thinks, moreover, that the simple signs (names) must not only be possible, but actual, since he holds that the sense of every proposition *is,* in fact, determinate.

> 3.251   What a proposition expresses it expresses in a determinate manner, which can be set out clearly: a proposition is articulated.

(See *PI,* sects. 98 and 99.) This determinateness is normally not apparent in the sentence which expresses a proposition; nevertheless, what the person means by that sentence—the thought or proposition which he means to express by it—is always perfectly determinate. The sentence may be vague, and, in fact, almost always is (*NB,* entry for 21.6.15), but the thought behind it, on each occasion of its use, is not. (See *T* 3.262.) Thus, for example, if I am looking at a watch lying on a table and say "The watch is lying on the table," then I do not just mean that *some* kind of watch stands in *some* sort of relation that might be called 'lying on' to *some* sort of table; I mean that *this* particular watch stands in *that* determinate relation to *that* particular table. (See *NB,* entries for 20.6.15 through 22.6.15.)

Therefore, although a proposition *as expressed in terms* T_1, T_2, . . . , *which signify complexes,* is in *that* regard doubly indeterminate in sense, nevertheless its sense is *in fact* perfectly determinate, since on each occasion of the use of the terms T_1, T_2, . . . , the speaker (or thinker) means by them something determinate. So when the proposition is analyzed and its real sense spelled out, all indeterminateness vanishes. But if so, then the analysis must end in elementary propositions which consist of nothing but simple, i.e., indefinable, terms (or names), because anything short of that will, for the reasons given, still contain some indeterminateness.

Wittgenstein concludes, what is more, that there must be simple things—i.e., objects—which the names denote. He shared with Russell the assumption that the meaning of a name is the object it denotes.

3.203   A name means an object. The object is its meaning.

Hence, if there were no such objects, the elementary propositions would consist of terms that had no meaning and would thus be meaningless. But since the meaning of all propositions depends ultimately on that of the elementary propositions (see *T* 4.411), no proposition would have any meaning, which is also absurd. Any meaningful language, then, must be founded on names, on indefinable terms that directly denote objects (i.e., simples) and which form elementary propositions.

The following passage in the *Tractatus* seems at first glance incompatible with the foregoing account:

4.2211   Even if the world is infinitely complex, so that every fact consists of infinitely many states of affairs and every state of affairs is composed of infinitely many objects, there would still have to be objects and states of affairs.

In this passage, it might appear that Wittgenstein allows the possibility of an infinite regress in the process of analyzing propositions. However, the passage can be naturally construed in a way that is perfectly consistent with his claim that the regress must come to an end with elementary propositions. It can be read, namely, as allowing the possibility not that the regress of analyses may be infinite, but rather the different possibility that when the final stage of the analysis is reached, infinitely many objects may be referred to. So there is no incompatibility between our account and T 4.2211.

Wittgenstein has what he considers to be further grounds in support of his assertion that there are simple things—i.e., objects. He states these grounds without actually producing an argument in the following passage:

> 2.0211   If the world had no substance, then whether a proposition had sense would depend on whether another proposition was true.

Since the preceding section (T 2.021) tells us that "objects make up the substance of the world," the present section clearly deals with the existence of objects. Wittgenstein thought it plainly false to say that the question of whether or not a proposition has sense (meaning) depends on whether or not some other proposition is true. (One allegedly absurd consequence of such a statement is given in the succeeding section, T 2.0212.) Therefore, if it can be shown that this unacceptable statement follows from the hypothesis that there are no simple objects, this will prove that there must be such objects.

But how can that be shown? Although Wittgenstein does not explicitly tell us, the following argument can be constructed from some of the things he does say.[18] First of all, we already know that for Wittgenstein, in order that any term (apart from the logical constants) have meaning, it must refer to something—i.e., something existent—either directly or indirectly; it must, ultimately, designate some thing or things that actually exist (in the past, present, or future). This follows at once from the assumption (2) (p. 33) that the meaning of a term is whatever it denotes. In order for a proposition to be meaningful—or, as Wittgenstein puts it, to have a sense— it must of course be composed of terms that have meaning. Hence if

---

[18] For one important part of this argument, I am indebted to James Griffin's *Wittgenstein's Logical Atomism* (London: Oxford University Press, forthcoming).

a proposition is to have sense, its terms must, in the end, designate something existent.[19]

Suppose now that I express the following proposition:

(A) The broom is in the corner.

What kind of analysis of my proposition would Wittgenstein offer? The kind of analysis he would give, at this point anyway, is indicated in the section immediately preceding T 2.021:

> 2.0201   Every statement about complexes can be resolved into a statement about their constituents and into the propositions that describe the complexes completely.

In section 60 of the *Investigations,* where Wittgenstein is discussing the doctrines of the *Tractatus,* he describes the following analysis of proposition (A), thus illustrating the kind of analysis he meant in T 2.0201:

(1) The stick is in the corner,

(2) The brush is in the corner,

(3) The stick is attached to the brush in such and such a way.

If we grant to Wittgenstein—and it is admittedly to grant a great deal—that if proposition (A) is to have sense, the terms in it must ultimately refer to something existent, then we must allow that the question of (A)'s having sense depends at least in part on whether or not the subject term, 'the broom,' ultimately refers to something existent. But notice that what I mean by 'the broom' is specified by proposition (3) of the analysis. Hence, it might seem as though the question of whether 'the broom' refers to something depends on the

---

[19] This raises grave problems for Wittgenstein. Almost everyone would admit that propositions about mythical and fictitious persons and things, and such propositions as "The present King of France is bald," make perfectly good sense. Wittgenstein himself insists that they do.

3.24(2)   . . . A proposition that mentions a complex will not be nonsensical, if the complex does not exist, but simply false.

(The claim that all such propositions are false is very dubious. "Horatio is Hamlet's best friend" looks like a true proposition; and it has been very persuasively argued by P. F. Strawson that propositions such as "The present King of France is bald" and "All John's children are asleep," where John has no children, are neither true nor false.) But if such propositions have a sense, then they must, in the end, be about certain (simple) existing objects; and it is difficult to see how this could be true. What objects, for example, are ultimately referred to by "Horatio is Hamlet's best friend"? Objects which constitute the words of Shakespeare's manuscript for *Hamlet* or of the various copies of the play? Not a very plausible answer, but none any more satisfactory seems to be available to Wittgenstein.

truth or falsity of proposition (3); in other words, it seems that we can assert that if 'the broom' does refer to something, proposition (3) is true, whereas if it does not refer to anything, proposition (3) must be false. But this assertion would be justified only if propositions (1)–(3) constituted the final or ultimate analysis of proposition (A), which they do not. As it is, the attribution of truth can be postponed; it is enough, in order for proposition (A) to have sense, that proposition (3)—and of course the others as well—merely have sense.

Proposition (3) can be further analyzed, and the propositions which occur in its analysis can in their turn be further analyzed, and so on. But suppose now that there are no absolutely simple objects. In that case, this regress of analyses will be endless; there will always be constituents of constituents of constituents . . . and so on ad infinitum; and hence, in view of the type of analysis envisioned in T 2.0201, there will always be analyses of analyses of analyses . . . and so on ad infinitum. But then how is the required reference to existents ever to be secured? Only by the *truth* of some group or other of the propositions which occur in the endless regress of analyses. This shows, then, that if there are no absolutely simple objects, then the question of whether 'the broom' of proposition (A) has an ultimate reference to existents, and hence whether proposition (A) has sense, will depend on whether certain other propositions are true. And this, according to Wittgenstein, is an intolerable situation.

But now it might occur to us that this result is unavoidable in *any* case; after all, if reference to existents is required for the sense of a proposition, then isn't the truth of some other proposition—namely, that there *is* such an existent—also always required? Wittgenstein evidently thinks not; he thinks that the situation is quite different if there are simple objects. In that case, the regress of analyses will come to an end in elementary propositions consisting of names. That these names refer to existents and, hence, that the terms of proposition (A) also do is guaranteed by the very fact that they *are* names; for since the meanings of indefinable signs are the objects they name (T 3.203), if they named no object, they would be mere meaningless marks, and not names at all. This reference to existents on the part of the elementary propositions into which proposition (A) can be analyzed is enough to guarantee that (A) has sense. It is not necessary that the elementary propositions be true, although they must, of course, have sense. The objects are the meanings of the names, and, if the names are combined in permissible ways—that is, if the elementary propositions assert that the objects are configured in ways in which they *can* (might possibly) be configured, whether or not they actually are so configured—this will be enough to ensure that the elementary propositions, and hence proposition (*A*), have sense.

There is, however, the following obvious objection to this argument. "The argument has illicitly smuggled in truths about existents, without appearing to do so, by simply *assuming* that certain indefinable signs are names. In order for an indefinable sign '*a*,' which purports to be a name, really to *be* one and not a mere meaningless mark, it is necessary that there exist an object *a* which it names. Hence, whether any elementary proposition containing '*a*' has sense or not depends on the truth of another proposition—namely, the proposition, "*a* exists." The same will be true, of course, of all elementary propositions. So as long as reference to existents is made a requirement for the sense of a proposition, the sense of a proposition must always depend on the truth of other propositions, *whether or not* there are simple objects." Wittgenstein's answer to this objection would be that "*a* exists," where '*a*' is an indefinable sign, is nonsense, and therefore not a proposition at all. His argument for this claim is given below, pp. 60-62. Hence the sense of an elementary proposition cannot depend on the truth of any such proposition as "*a* exists," for this is *not* a possible proposition.

So, according to Wittgenstein, if there are simple objects, whether 'the broom' has some ultimate reference to existents and hence whether proposition (*A*) has a sense will depend only on whether the elementary propositions of its final analysis have a sense; whereas if there are no simple objects, as we have seen, the dependence will be rather on whether some propositions somewhere in the analysis of (*A*) are true. The kind of dependence in the former case is perfectly legitimate and unexceptionable; indeed, the sense of a proposition *must* depend on the sense of the propositions which constitute its analysis. But as we have remarked, Wittgenstein regarded the kind of dependence involved in the latter case to be illegitimate. In order to avoid it, then, we must assume that simple objects exist.

*   *   *

The overall picture of language and of its connection with the world which emerges from the foregoing considerations is basically a surprisingly simple one. Imagine an ordinary complex proposition as a flat structure located at some height from the earth. It is supported from below by several simpler structures—the propositions which constitute its analysis. These are each in turn supported by further, less complex structures. Finally, just above the earth are the least complex structures possible—elementary propositions. These consist of elements—names—which are directly supported by simple things on the earth—Wittgenstein's objects. It is just here and only here, with names and objects, that the connection between language and reality is made, that language "hooks on" to reality. We may not be able to see the simple objects, nor the complexes of them (i.e., states of affairs), but they must be there to provide the ultimate foundation for the edifice of language.

We find Wittgenstein carrying on a classic—perhaps the classic—philosophical enterprise, namely that of reducing the complex to the simple. The first known Western philosopher, Thales, attempted it when he argued that all things are really just water, and most of the philosophers who followed him have tried to do the same thing, in one form or another (although there is another traditional strand in Western philosophy—the idealist one—which repudiates this entire program). The particular versions of this enterprise in comparatively modern times that resemble Wittgenstein's most closely are those of Descartes, Leibniz, Locke, and Hume. Descartes, for example, writes,

> Method consists entirely in the order and disposition of the objects towards which our mental vision must be directed if we would find out any truth. We shall comply with it exactly if we reduce involved and obscure propositions step by step to those that are simpler, and then starting with the intuitive apprehension of all those that are absolutely simple, attempt to ascend to the knowledge of all others by precisely similar steps.[20]

Leibniz talked of primitive concepts which are "not resolvable into others" and from which all other concepts are derived by "combination." Locke thought that all ideas which are not simple could, in one way or another, be reduced to simple ideas, the names of which are "not capable of any definitions"; and Hume wrote: "When we

[20] Descartes, *Rules for the Direction of the Mind,* Rule V. The quotation is taken from *The Philosophical Works of Descartes,* trans. by E. S. Haldane and G. R. T. Ross (London: Cambridge University Press, 1911-12), Vol. 1, p. 14.

analyze our thoughts or ideas, however compounded or sublime, we always find that they resolve themselves into such simple ideas as were copied from a precedent feeling or sentiment." (*An Inquiry Concerning Human Understanding,* section II.) But for a view of language which is essentially identical with Wittgenstein's, we must go back to Plato's *Theaetetus.* Wittgenstein writes in *Philosophical Investigations:*

> What lies behind the idea that names really signify simples?— Socrates says in the Theaetetus: "If I make no mistake, I have heard some people say this: there is no definition of the primary elements— so to speak—out of which we and everything else are composed; for everything that exists in its own right can only be *named,* no other determination is possible, neither that it *is* nor that it *is not.* . . . But what exists in its own right has to be . . . named without any other determination. In consequence it is impossible to give an account of any primary element; for it, nothing is possible but the bare name; its name is all it has. But just as what consists of these primary elements is itself complex, so the names of the elements become descriptive language by being compounded together. For the essence of speech is the composition of names."
>
> Both Russell's 'individuals' and my 'objects' (*Tractatus Logico-Philosophicus*) were such primary elements. [*PI,* sect. 46.] [21]

Thus, unlikely as it may seem, we find in the *Tractatus* yet another extended "footnote to Plato." [22]

[21] The passage from Plato is taken from *Theaetetus* 201D-202B. The translator notes that she translated the German translation of *Theaetetus* which Wittgenstein used, rather than the original.

[22] "The safest general characterization of the European philosophical tradition is that it consists of a series of footnotes to Plato. I do not mean the systematic scheme of thought which scholars have doubtfully extracted from his writings. I allude to the wealth of general ideas scattered through them." Alfred North Whitehead, *Process and Reality* (London: Cambridge University Press, 1929), p. 53.

3 Propositions

The Sense of a Proposition

It is an obvious, but nevertheless important, fact that we can understand a proposition that is false, or a proposition about whose truth or falsity we are in doubt. The intelligibility of a proposition, and hence also its having a meaning, are independent of its truth or falsity. Wittgenstein was well aware of this fact.

> 4.024 To understand a proposition means to know what is the case if it is true.
>
> (One can understand it, therefore, without knowing whether it is true.)

(See also *T* 4.061.) This indicates an important difference between the meaning of a name and the meaning of a proposition. Although a proposition may have a meaning even though there is no fact corresponding to it (i.e., it is false), a name cannot have a meaning if there is no object corresponding to it, because the meaning of a name *is* the object it names. (*T* 3.203.) We cannot construe propositions, then, as being names which denote facts which are their meaning. Frege had construed declarative sentences as proper names, but as a result he could not hold that they name facts. He had to find something else for sentences to denote. He actually "found" two such somethings: the True for true sentences and the False for false sentences.[1] But this was not a satisfactory solution to the problem.

---

[1] Frege, "On Sense and Reference," reprinted in Geach and Black, eds., *Philosophical Writings of Gottlob Frege* (Oxford: Basil Blackwell, 1952), p. 63. Frege explains that he means his doctrine to apply only to those uses of a declarative sentence in which the questions of the actual reference of its components and hence its truth value are at issue, and not to declarative sentences used, for example, in a play or a story.

For an explanation and partial defense of Frege's doctrine, see M. Dummett, "Truth," *Proceedings of the Aristotelian Society*, LIX (1958-59), 141 ff.

Wittgenstein marks the difference between the meaning of a name and that of a proposition by saying that a name has *Bedeutung* and a proposition has *Sinn*. Pears and McGuinness translate the first as 'meaning' and the second as 'sense': names have *meaning,* propositions have *sense*. The two terms *'Sinn'* and *'Bedeutung'* were used by Frege, but whereas he held that both names and sentences could have *Sinn* as well as *Bedeutung,* Wittgenstein holds that names have only *Bedeutung* and no *Sinn,* and that propositions have only *Sinn* and no *Bedeutung*.[2]

> 3.3   Only propositions have sense; only in the nexus of a proposition does a name have meaning.

A proposition thus does not name a situation; on the contrary, it describes it. (*T* 3.144[1] and 4.023[3].)

Frege held that the sense of a declarative sentence is the thought which it "contains," and that the thought is "not the subjective performance of thinking but its objective content, which is capable of being the common property of several thinkers." [3] The sense of a sentence is thus a rather strange kind of objective entity which is apprehensible by minds. Wittgenstein naturally wanted to avoid populating reality with such things, if he possibly could. In any case, he maintained that the sense of a proposition is the situation it describes.

> 4.031(2)   Instead of, 'This proposition has such and such a sense,' we can simply say, 'This proposition represents such and such a situation.'

A proposition, as we shall see, is a "logical picture" and

> 2.221   What a picture represents is its sense.

So the sense of a proposition is the situation it "depicts" or represents. But this way of speaking seems at first to have the effect of canceling, for the most part, the distinction between names and propositions. At least, the old problem arises: What are we to do with false propositions? If the sense of a proposition is the situation it describes or represents, then either all false propositions have no sense, since they describe no existent situation, or there must be nonexistent situations which they describe or represent. The first alternative is un-

---

[2] In an earlier work, "Notes on Logic" (reprinted in *NB*), Wittgenstein had assigned both *Sinn* and *Bedeutung* to propositions. See *NB*, p. 94.

[3] Frege, *op. cit.,* p. 62*n*.

acceptable, in view of the fact that we can understand false propositions. Hence the second alternative is forced upon us.

Wittgenstein accepts it and uses the terms 'situation' ('*Sachlage*') and 'state of affairs' ('*Sachverhalt*') in such a way that situations and states of affairs may be either actual (existent) or merely possible and nonactual (nonexistent). He speaks of "possible situations" (*T* 2.202, 3.11, 4.125, and elsewhere), and of the existence and nonexistence of states of affairs.

> 2.06   The existence and non-existence of states of affairs is reality.
>   (We also call the existence of states of affairs a positive fact, and their non-existence a negative fact.)

(See also *T* 4.25.)

States of affairs are elementary or atomic. They are what correspond to elementary propositions.

> 4.21   The simplest kind of proposition, an elementary proposition, asserts the existence of a state of affairs.

(See also *T* 4.25.) Just as an elementary proposition cannot be analyzed further into more basic propositions, so states of affairs do not consist of any more basic states of affairs. And as an elementary proposition consists only of names in combination, so a state of affairs consists only of objects in combination.

> 2.01   A state of affairs (a state of things) is a combination of objects (things).

As Wittgenstein uses the terms, 'situation' is a genus term and 'state of affairs' designates one species of situation. A state of affairs is an atomic situation; there are also nonatomic, or molecular, situations.[4]

Limiting ourselves to states of affairs, let us ask how these are related to facts (*Tatsachen*) and reality, as Wittgenstein uses these terms (e.g., in *T* 2.06). A state of affairs, we are told in *T* 2.01, is "a combination of objects (things)." Some combinations of objects exist and some combinations of objects do not exist. In some way, the former are associated with positive facts, and the latter with negative facts (*T* 2.06[2]). Let us consider positive facts first. What

---

[4] Wittgenstein thus uses the terms 'situation' and 'state of affairs' in technical senses. The reader is hereby warned that, in this book, these terms will be used as Wittgenstein uses them, not as they are ordinarily used.

exactly is a positive fact? *How* is it associated with states of affairs that exist?

The clearest answer is provided in the following pair of passages:

1.1   The world is the totality of facts, not of things.

.   .   .

2.04   The totality of existing states of affairs is the world.

These passages yield the identity of facts and existing states of affairs. From them alone, one would think that the identity is complete, that all facts are existing states of affairs. But from T 2.06(2), it seems fairly clear that existing states of affairs are to be identified not with all facts, but only with positive facts. And further, since states of affairs are atomic, we must say that only a positive *atomic* fact is an existing state of affairs. It is these positive atomic facts that ultimately comprise the world, that the world finally divides into.

Reality, we learn from T 2.06, includes more than this; it includes not only positive but also negative facts. It is understandable that some term of this sort (viz., 'reality') covering both positive and negative facts should be introduced; for the full general truth about things includes not only that, say, S is P and that R is Q (positive facts), but also that, say, R is not P and that S is not Q (negative facts). But what is a negative fact? A possible answer—but not Wittgenstein's—would be this: a negative fact is an existing combination of objects, just as a positive fact is, but the combination includes the object *not*. We shall see later on in this chapter why Wittgenstein rejects this answer. What he must hold, it would then seem, is that a negative fact, or at least the most basic kind of negative fact (i.e., one stated by the [true] negation of an elementary proposition), is a state of affairs that does not exist, a state of affairs in the condition of not-existing. Where *"S is P"* and *"R is P"* are elementary propositions, *"S is P"* asserts the existence of the state of affairs that S is P, and *"R is not P"* asserts the nonexistence of the state of affairs that R is P. The former, if true, states a positive fact and the latter, if true, a negative fact.

The world, then, includes all the positive atomic facts, all the existing states of affairs in their state of existing; reality is wider, and includes all the positive *and* negative facts, all the existing *and* nonexisting states of affairs in their respective states of existing and nonexisting. If this interpretation is correct, then Wittgenstein has apparently given to nonactual states of affairs a shadowy kind of being;

full existence is not attributed to them, of course, but rather some kind of subsistence in a strange realm of nonexistence, of mere possibility. To sum up, Wittgenstein's remarks imply, it would seem, that states of affairs—which, for reasons to be given below, are all positive—can reside in either of two realms: either in the realm of existence, in which case they are positive atomic facts and parts of the world, or in the realm of nonexistence, in which case they are parts not of the world, but merely of reality in general.

This account of the relation between the world and reality, and between facts and states of affairs seems to me to be the one that makes best sense of the passages I have cited and that fits in best with the later doctrines of the *Tractatus*. I wish it were entirely free of difficulties, but it is not. For one thing, it does not agree with what Wittgenstein says in a letter to Russell written in 1919:

> "What is the difference between *Tatsache* and *Sachverhalt?*" *Sachverhalt* is what corresponds to an *Elementarsatz* if it is true. *Tatsache* is what corresponds to the logical product of elementary props when this product is true. [*NB,* p. 129.]

But there is a more fundamental difficulty. In *T* 2.04, Wittgenstein says that the world is the totality of existing states of affairs, and my account interprets this to mean that the world is the totality of positive atomic facts. According to my account, furthermore, *T* 2.06 says that reality consists of both positive and negative facts. And yet we read almost at once:

2.063   The sum-total of reality is the world.

which implies that the world, too, consists of positive and negative facts. Something is wrong somewhere. I can think of no wholly convincing explanation for this apparent inconsistency. James Griffin suggests the following possibility.[5] Wittgenstein says:

2.05   The totality of existing states of affairs also determines which states of affairs do not exist.

(See also *T* 1.12.) So, if all the positive facts are given, all the negative facts are thereby also given, which means that there is a sense in which positive and negative facts are inseparable. Griffin suggests that when Wittgenstein speaks of the world as including both positive and negative facts, he might mean merely that positive and negative facts are inseparable in this sense, although only positive

[5] In his *Wittgenstein's Logical Atomism,* forthcoming.

atomic facts, strictly speaking, actually comprise, are actually *parts* of, the world. (Negative facts, after all, do not even exist: a negative fact is merely the nonexistence of a possible state of affairs, according to T 2.06[2].)

A state of affairs, we know, is composed entirely of objects (T 2.01 and 2.0272). Notice, now, that nonexistent, as well as existent, states of affairs must be combinations, arrangements, or configurations of *existent* objects: an existent state of affairs is an actual arrangement of existent objects, a nonexistent state of affairs is a nonactual arrangement of existent objects. A nonexistent state of affairs is neither an actual nor a nonactual arrangement of *nonexistent* objects. It is obvious that there cannot be an actual arrangement of nonexistent objects, but it might be thought that, once nonexistent states of affairs are allowed, it is possible that some of them might be nonactual arrangements of nonexistent objects. But that this cannot be the case follows at once from the doctrine that the meaning of a name is the object it denotes (T 3.203). On this doctrine, no mention can possibly be made of nonexistent objects, for any proposition which tried to do so would be nonsensical. For example, if a and b were, *per impossibile,* nonexistent objects, the names 'a' and 'b' would be devoid of meaning, meaningless (and hence not names) —for the meaning of a name is the object it denotes, and in these cases there *is* no such object. Therefore propositions purporting to say anything about a and b will all be nonsensical, since they will contain the meaningless "names" 'a' and 'b.' But if no mention can be made of nonexistent objects, if any proposition which attempts to do so is nonsensical, then the very concepts of a nonexistent object and hence of an arrangement of them (actual *or* nonactual) are unintelligible. All talk of nonexistent objects, then, including the suggestion that nonexistent states of affairs might be nonactual arrangements of them, is necessarily nonsensical. So all states of affairs, both existent and nonexistent, are arrangements of existent objects only.

It follows from this, and from the fact that objects are eternal (this point is discussed later, in chapter 5), that all possible or conceivable worlds must consist of precisely the same objects that this actual world of ours consists of. Hence the only difference there can be amongst possible worlds is in the way the objects are configured. A possible or imagined, but nonactual, world must be composed of states of affairs, and all possible states of affairs, as we have just seen, are arrangements of nothing but existent objects—i.e., the objects that compose this world of ours, the real world.

2.022   It is obvious that an imagined world, however different it may be from the real one, must have something—a form—in common with it.

2.023   Objects are just what constitute this unalterable form.

The sense of a proposition, we said, is the situation which it describes and asserts to exist. If we keep this use of the term 'sense' in mind, several passages in the *Tractatus*, which seem at first glance to be obscure or absurd, are seen to be perfectly intelligible.

4.1211   Thus one proposition 'fa' shows that the object a occurs in its sense. . . .[6]

It sounds paradoxical to speak of an object's actually occurring in the sense of a proposition; we normally do not think of actual physical water drops occurring in the sense of the proposition "It is raining." The reason we do not is that we normally distinguish between the sense of a proposition (what we, but not Wittgenstein, ordinarily call its meaning) and the fact, if any, that it describes, much as Frege did. But Wittgenstein identifies the two things, and when this is done, it is not odd to speak of objects occurring in the sense of a proposition, since they occur in the situation which the proposition describes.

Another otherwise puzzling passage is the following:

3.13(3)   A proposition does not actually contain its sense, but does contain the possibility of expressing it.

One would not ordinarily understand what it means to deny that a proposition contains its sense, but on Wittgenstein's use of the term, what it means is quite clear—the proposition does not include the situation which it describes. There are many other odd things which Wittgenstein's use of the term 'sense' sanctions—so many that one wonders whether he should not have picked another term. But at least if we bear in mind what Wittgenstein meant, we can understand what he says.

This use of the term 'sense,' whereby the sense of a proposition is the situation it describes or represents, can easily lead even the wary into puzzles and difficulties; it certainly led Wittgenstein into them

[6] The expressions 'fa' or 'Fa' are to be read: "object a has the property f (F)," "object a is an f (F)," or simply "a is f (F)."

once or twice. The main one can be explained as follows. Consider
a proposition about some complex thing—let us say, about one's
wrist watch. Suppose I assert that my watch is lying on the table. I
have then said something not about just a certain feature of the
watch, but about the whole watch. The sense of a proposition, we
are agreed, is the situation it describes, and it seems that the situation
which this proposition describes includes in it the watch—the whole
watch. But now let us recall, from the last chapter, the sort of thing
Wittgenstein sometimes meant when he spoke of the analysis of a
proposition. Here is *T* 2.0201 again:

> 2.0201   Every statement about complexes can be resolved into a
> statement about their constituents and into the proposi-
> tions that describe the complexes completely.

So, the analysis of a proposition includes propositions about the
constituent parts of whatever the proposition is about. We saw, for
example, how the analysis of proposition (*A*) about the broom included propositions about its brush and its handle (p. 39). But these
propositions of the analysis are themselves further analyzable, and
their analysis must contain propositions about the constituent parts
of whatever they are about—for example, about the constituent parts
of the brush and the handle, and so on. In this way, one can be led to
think that in analyzing the proposition about my watch, one must
eventually reach propositions which mention all the minutest parts
of the watch—since the proposition is, after all, about the whole
watch. Hence the sense of the original proposition, which is of course
expressed by these ultimate propositions into which it is analyzable,
must contain every single part of the watch, no matter how small.
Wittgenstein sometimes drew this conclusion; thus we find him
saying in the *Notebooks 1914-1916* such things as:

> When I say this watch is shiny, and what I mean by "this watch"
> alters its composition in the smallest particular, then this means not
> merely that the sense of the sentence alters in its content, but also
> *what I am saying about this watch* straightway alters its sense. The
> whole form of the proposition alters. [*NB*, entry for 16.6.15.]

But this apparent conclusion from the view that the sense of a
proposition is the situation it describes cannot under any circumstances be accepted, because it is absurd. It is absurd to maintain
that in saying something about an object one is always saying something about all its parts; if I say that my watch is shiny, it is no part

of my meaning that there is a jewel inside the watch. Evidence about there being such a jewel is completely irrelevant to the truth or falsity of the proposition I assert, and the proposition has exactly the same sense whether or not there is any such jewel. Wittgenstein was far too shrewd to be duped for very long; two days after making the above-quoted entry in his *Notebooks,* he made another, far more sensible one, which completely cancels it.

> . . . If . . . I say that this watch is not in the drawer, there is absolutely no need for it to FOLLOW LOGICALLY that a wheel which is in the watch is not in the drawer, for perhaps *I had not the least knowledge* that the wheel was in the watch, and hence could not have meant by "this watch" the complex in which the wheel occurs. [*NB,* entry for 18.6.15.]

Wittgenstein had seen that the absurd thesis which seemed to follow from the view that the sense of a proposition is the situation it describes, really does not follow from it at all. When I assert that my watch is lying on the table, the complex situation which I describe does not include situations in which all the parts of the watch occur. It includes only those situations which are essential to that thing's being a watch, and of course to its lying on the table.[7] The absurd conclusion is thus avoided; but it is easy to be led into thinking that

[7] It should be noted, however, that when situations are construed in this way, new difficulties present themselves. It is natural to think of the situation of my watch's lying on the table as being a full-bodied, three- (or perhaps even four-) dimensional complex consisting of my watch (the whole of it) and the table (the whole of it), arranged so that the first is lying on the second. When one has this picture of a situation, it seems easy enough to conceive how it can "divide into" simpler situations, and ultimately into states of affairs that are combinations of simple objects. It is easy to see, in short, how (simple) objects might be the substance of situations. When situations are thinned out in the manner indicated, however, our earlier straightforward picture of them is *ipso facto* destroyed. But then, as long as they are still thought of as being some sort of complex existing in the world—and this basic idea the early Wittgenstein could not, of course, give up—it becomes exceedingly difficult to imagine what sort of complex they could possibly be. Situations seem now to be mere abstracted aspects of the full-bodied slices of the world which we had previously thought them to be; and in fact it is not at all clear that—or how—such aspects *could* be things actually existing in the world, as the system of the *Tractatus* requires. How could (simple) objects, or anything else, be the *substance* of any such complex? They seem to be altogether too thin for substance—too insubstantial. And *which* simple objects, of all those present in the original full-bodied slice of the world, are to be the required substance of our situations as now conceived? It seems impossible to say. Difficulties such as these make our new "thin" conception of situations highly unattractive.

one must accept it, and so one must be wary. Wittgenstein was usually, but not always, wary.

We ought not, however, to be too harsh here with the view that the sense of a proposition is the situation it describes, for it is not so much that view which tempts one to the absurd conclusion just discussed as it is Wittgenstein's conception of what a proper analysis of a proposition is—namely, that the analysis of a proposition about a complex consists of propositions about its constituent parts and of propositions which describe it completely. This conception of analysis is the major villain of the piece. Wittgenstein may have been seduced into adopting it by supposing that there is a closer analogy between analyzing a chemical compound and analyzing a proposition than there is (see *PI*, sect. 90). Be that as it may, *T* 2.0201 shows that Wittgenstein had not abandoned it by the time he wrote the *Tractatus*. Indeed, we have seen in the last chapter what a crucial part this conception of analysis played in Wittgenstein's arguments for the existence of simple objects; it is, in fact, difficult to see how their existence could plausibly be argued for without it. It is thus one of the most important, and at the same time one of the weakest, props supporting the system of the *Tractatus*.

Wittgenstein uses the expression 'sense of a proposition' in another way in the *Tractatus,* and this second way must now be explained. Consider the elementary proposition *"aRb"* and its negation *"~(aRb)."* Wittgenstein tells us, employing 'sense' now in a new way, that these two propositions have opposite sense (*T* 4.0621 [3]). on Logic" (1913)—a work which is reprinted in *Notebooks 1914-* What this means is hinted at in the following passages from "Notes *1916.*

> Every proposition is essentially true-false. Thus a proposition has two poles (corresponding to case of its truth and case of its falsity). We call this the *sense* of a proposition. [*NB*, p. 94.]

· · ·

> A proposition is a standard with reference to which facts behave, but with names it is otherwise. Just as one arrow behaves to another arrow by being in the same sense or the opposite, so a fact behaves to a proposition; it is thus bi-polarity and sense come in. [*NB*, p. 97.]

(Wittgenstein is here being influenced by the fact that the German word *'Sinn'* can mean 'direction.') The proposition *"aRb"* asserts that *a* bears *R* to *b;* it thus agrees with, runs along with, the state of affairs that aRb—the proposition and the state of affairs run, as it were, in the same direction. But the proposition "$\sim(aRb)$" asserts that a does not bear R to b, and hence does not agree with the state of affairs that aRb—it runs counter to, runs against, that state of affairs. If the state of affairs that aRb exists—if a does bear R to b—then "aRb" is true and "$\sim(aRb)$" is false. Implicit in this second use of 'sense' is the notion of running along with or running against something, and hence the notion of having a direction, as an arrow has a direction.

> 3.144(2)   (Names are like points; propositions like arrows—they have sense.)

A name, such as 'a' or 'b,' is static; it does not move. It picks out an object, and that is all. But a proposition moves; the proposition "aRb" moves from a to b—it moves in that direction.

According to the first, and what I have called Wittgenstein's main, use of 'sense,' "aRb" and "$\sim(aRb)$" do not have opposite sense, but rather the same sense, for they describe the same state of affairs —namely, that aRb. "aRb" describes the state of affairs that aRb and asserts that it exists—it says that a does bear R to b. But "$\sim(aRb)$" describes the same state of affairs that aRb and asserts that it does not exist—it says that a does not bear R to b. The same reality (viz., the state of affairs that aRb) corresponds to both, they are both *about* the same state of affairs.

> 4.0621(3)   The propositions 'p' and '$\sim p$' have opposite sense, but there corresponds to them one and the same reality.

Since the same reality corresponds to both, they both have the same sense in Wittgenstein's main use of the term, although in his second use of it, they have opposite sense.[8] The two uses are related as fol-

"The *meaning* of a proposition is the fact which actually corresponds to it." (*NB*, p. 94.)

Its sense was its "direction" (see *NB*, p. 97). Referring to his own theory, Wittgenstein said:

"In this theory p has the same meaning as not-p but opposite sense." (*NB*, p. 97.)

Thus this early distinction between the meaning and sense of a proposition, found in "Notes on Logic," reappears later in the *Tractatus* as an analogous distinction between two senses of the term 'sense.'

lows: in the second use of the term 'sense,' it refers to the "direc-

---

[8] In "Notes on Logic," Wittgenstein distinguished the meaning of a proposition from its sense. Its meaning was the fact which corresponds to it.

tion" in which the objects are related *in* the situation which constitutes its reference in its first (main) use.

It is unfortunate that Wittgenstein sometimes uses important terms (e.g., *'Satz'* and *'Sinn'*) to mean different things on different occasions; this is certainly a fault in the *Tractatus.* Nevertheless, in any given passage, it is usually clear enough which way the term is being used, so that, if one keeps the different meanings in mind, he need not be misled.

Before proceeding, we might ask why Wittgenstein asserts that the same reality corresponds to a proposition and to its negation. Why should *p* and ~*p* describe the *same* situation? To consider just elementary propositions and states of affairs, why not say that the elementary proposition *"S* is *P"* describes the state of affairs of *S's* being *P* and that "~*(S* is *P)"* describes the different state of affairs of *S's* not being *P?* Why not admit, in other words, that there are both positive and negative states of affairs? Then there would be no need to have two different meanings of 'sense of a proposition': *"S* is *P"* would have one sense (in *the* meaning of 'sense'), and "~*(S* is *P)"* would have another sense (in the same meaning of 'sense').

But Wittgenstein would reject this alternative; he thought it impossible to admit the existence of negative states of affairs. To be sure, there are negative nonelementary propositions which describe negative nonatomic situations; for example, it is a (negative) fact that Nero was not Julius Caesar, that George Washington did not live in Cairo, and so on. But as we know, according to Wittgenstein, such propositions are reducible by analysis to nothing but elementary propositions. Suppose now we accepted the proposed alternative to Wittgenstein's view and admitted negative states of affairs. If we make the plausible but nevertheless debatable assumption that where *p* is an elementary proposition, there is no way of analyzing ~*p*,[9] we would have to grant that both *p* and ~*p* were elementary propositions. On the proposed alternative, then, the proposition *p* must describe the positive state of affairs that *p* and the proposition ~*p* the negative state of affairs that ~*p*. This negative state of affairs, it seems, would differ from the positive one in containing an extra

[9] It is debatable, for one could argue, for example, that even if "*x* is red" were an elementary proposition, "~(*x* is red)" can be analyzed as "*x* is green or *x* is blue or *x* is white or . . ." and so on through all possible colors. See Russell's defense of negative facts in his "The Philosophy of Logical Atomism," Marsh volume, pp. 211-16.

thing called 'not'—it would contain a negating factor. The negative state of affairs would be very like the positive one except that it would contain one more object. Similarly, the two elementary propositions p and $\sim p$ would be alike except that the negative one would contain one more name. On this view, then, the sign of negation, '$\sim$', would be a name and would denote an object.

Wittgenstein resolutely spurns this consequence; he says

4.0621(1) . . . Nothing in reality corresponds to the sign '$\sim$'.

The reason he spurns it is this: if '$\sim$' were the name of an object, then the double negation of a proposition (e.g., $\sim\sim p$) would be a wholly different proposition from the original (p), for it would describe a state of affairs with two more objects in it than the state of affairs that the original proposition describes.

5.44(4)   And if there were an object called '$\sim$', it would follow that '$\sim\sim p$' said something different from what 'p' said, just because the one proposition would then be about $\sim$ and the other would not.

Since $\sim\sim p$ says exactly what p says,[10] the suggestion that '$\sim$' is a name, and hence that there are negative states of affairs, must be abandoned. And so there can be no negative elementary propositions either: $\sim p$ is a truth-function (this notion will be discussed presently) of the elementary proposition p, and not itself an elementary proposition. (See paragraph [6] of Wittgenstein's letter to Russell, *NB*, p. 130.)

It is for these reasons that Wittgenstein says that p and $\sim p$ describe the same state of affairs, an assertion which forces him to make some such distinction as that he makes between his two meanings of 'sense of a proposition.' It seemed to him to be the only satisfactory alternative to the (impossible) admission of negative states of affairs.

Truth-functions

At the end of the last chapter, we saw that, according to Wittgenstein, in analyzing the meaning of any proposition—only now we must say, in analyzing the *sense* of any proposition—one must

---

[10] Or so Wittgenstein assumed. There are, however, some who deny the universal truth of this claim, notably logicians of the Intuitionistic School.

ultimately arrive at nothing but elementary propositions. The sense of any proposition can thus be stated completely by means of elementary propositions and propositional connectives alone; so that if one had a list of all possible elementary propositions, plus certain propositional connectives, he could say anything that is sayable by simply making selections from the list. Nonelementary propositions are just combinations of elementary propositions; they are molecular propositions which are structures, ultimately, of nothing but atomic, or elementary, propositions.

> 4.51 Suppose that I am given *all* elementary propositions: then I can simply ask what propositions I can construct out of them. And there I have all propositions, and that fixes their limits.

But the question now arises: What kind or kinds of structure do molecular propositions have? In what way or ways are elementary propositions combined in order to yield molecular ones? Wittgenstein's answer is that they are combined by truth-functional connectives alone, so that all molecular propositions are truth-functional compounds (or, for short, truth-functions) of elementary propositions. This is one of the central doctrines of the *Tractatus*.

> 5(1) A proposition is a truth-function of elementary propositions.

But what are truth-functional connectives and truth-functions? A compound proposition, compounded of the propositions p_1, p_2, . . . , p_n, is a truth-functional compound (truth-function) of p_1, . . . , p_n if and only if its truth or falsity (its truth-value) is uniquely determined by the truth-values of p_1, . . . , p_n. A connective is a truth-functional one if it compounds propositions into truth-functional compounds. On these definitions, 'and' is a truth-functional connective; for if we know the truth-values of each of the propositions "Smith is in town" and "Jones is in town," then we know the truth-value of the complex proposition "Smith is in town and Jones is in town." If either one or both of the two component propositions is false, so is the complex proposition; if both are true, so is the complex proposition. Compare this with a non-truth-functional connective, such as the causal 'because': even if we know the truth-values of the propositions "Smith failed the course" and "Smith drinks too much," we do not thereby in all cases know the truth-value of the molecular proposition "Smith failed the course because he drinks too much." Even if we know that both of the component propositions are true, we do not thereby know what the truth-value of the molecular one is—it might still be either true or false. Hence, the causal 'because' is not a truth-functional connective.

On the above definition, negation, perhaps somewhat oddly, turns out to be a truth-functional connective—oddly, because negation does not *connect* one proposition with another. Still, it is convenient to classify it as a limiting case of a truth-functional connective: the truth-value of a proposition p determines the truth-value of its negation $\sim p$. If p is true, $\sim p$ is false; if p is false, $\sim p$ is true. Thus, $\sim p$ is a truth-function of p.

All propositions, Wittgenstein says, are truth-functions of elementary propositions.[11] Given all the elementary propositions, if I knew which were true and which false, I would know everything there is to know, because the truth-value of any other proposition is entirely determined by the truth-value of its component elementary propositions. Even under these favorable circumstances, to be sure, I may not know at once the truth-value of a given molecular proposition, for I may not realize right away which elementary propositions are its components, nor precisely how they are truth-functionally connected. Nevertheless, the whole truth about the world is determined solely by the truth-values of the elementary propositions.

> 4.26   If all true elementary propositions are listed, the world is completely described. A complete description of the world is given by listing all elementary propositions, and then listing which of them are true and which false.

There is no actual proof of this central doctrine—that all propositions are truth-functions of elementary ones—offered in the *Tractatus*. The doctrine is not proved simply by showing that in the analysis of any proposition, one must ultimately reach elementary propositions. For let it be granted that, in the analysis of propositions, one must finally reach elementary ones. Still, they could not be a mere heterogeneous, unconnected heap, or mere aggregate, of such propositions. To state the sense of a complex proposition, it is not enough simply to read a long list of elementary propositions with a period after each one. The elementary propositions, as Wittgenstein

---

[11] Even an elementary proposition is trivially a truth-function of itself; for given its truth-value, its truth-value is of course thereby determined. (See *T* 5[2].)

fully realized, must be connected or combined with each other in some way. But he never explicitly tells us why all the required connectives must of necessity be truth-functional ones. Nevertheless, he did have reasons for thinking that this is the case:

1. He thought he could show that general propositions are really truth-functions of particular propositions about objects.

2. He must have thought it obvious that particular propositions about complex individuals are really truth-functions of elementary propositions.

3. In those cases where it appears that one proposition occurs in another otherwise than as an argument to a truth-function, it can be shown, Wittgenstein thought, that the appearance is deceptive.

Let us examine each of these claims individually.

1. There are two basic kinds of general propositions, universal (e.g., "Everybody in this room has a hat") and existential (e.g., "Someone is in this room and has a hat"). It might seem obvious that at least an existential proposition is a truth-function of propositions about individuals—i.e., about complexes such as persons and chairs. For example, it might at first seem obvious that "Someone is in this room and has a hat" (call it proposition A) means "Either Jones is in this room and has a hat, or Smith is in this room and has a hat, or Robinson is in this room and has a hat, or . . ." and so on until the names of all people are exhausted (call this proposition B). (We know that 'either/or' is a truth-functional connective; the compound proposition p_1 or p_2 or . . . p_n is true if at least one of $p_1, p_2, \ldots, p_n$ is true, and otherwise false.) But proposition A and proposition B do not, in fact, say the same thing at all. Admittedly, if I tell you that proposition B is true, you can then be sure that proposition A is so. But what if I tell you that proposition B is false? In that case, nothing follows about the truth or falsity of A. A could, of course, be false, but if I failed to mention even one person in the world, proposition A might be true even though B is false, since that one ignored person might be in the room and have a hat. Proposition A, then, cannot assert the same thing as proposition B, since one might be false while the other is true. Only if I add to proposition B the assertion that absolutely everyone *is* in fact mentioned in B does the falsity of B entail the falsity of A. To express proposition A, then, one cannot just express proposition B; one must

add to B the proposition that Jones, Smith, Robinson, and so on, are all the people that exist. This point could be put by saying that an existential proposition implicitly contains a universal one. Let us turn, then, to universal propositions.

By the same line of reasoning, it can be seen that universal propositions are not equivalent to a mere conjunction of propositions about complex individuals. "Everybody in this room has a hat," for example, does not mean the same thing as "Jones is in this room and has a hat, and Smith is in this room and has a hat, and Robinson is in this room and has a hat." We must add to the latter the proposition "And Jones, Smith, and Robinson are the only people in this room" (call it proposition C). Does this show, then, that universal propositions are not just truth-functions of propositions about individuals? Must we admit that any universal proposition always contains an irreducibly universal component? Wittgenstein did not think so. First, he thought that such propositions as C—i.e., universal propositions about complexes—must be reducible to a (complicated) universal proposition about objects, since he thought that objects are the sole ultimate constituents of all complexes. (See *T* 2.0201.) And second, he thought that universal propositions about objects, as opposed to those about complexes like people and chairs, must be just truth-functions of elementary propositions—i.e., of propositions about objects.

But why is there this difference between universal propositions about objects and those about complexes? Suppose the universal proposition is "All objects have property *F*." Why do we not have to add to the conjunction "Object *a* has *F* and object *b* has *F* and object *c* has *F* . . . ," the further proposition "And *a, b, c,* . . . are all the objects there are," just as we had to in the case of universal propositions about complexes? Wittgenstein's answer is that it is not possible that such an additional proposition should be required, because there *is* no such proposition; the alleged proposition would in fact be nonsense.

> 4.1272(4) Wherever [the word 'object'] is used . . . as a proper concept-word, nonsensical pseudo-propositions are the result.

The analysis of the pseudo-proposition "And *a, b, c,* . . . are all the objects there are" would have to include such propositions as "*a* is an object," and such propositions are nonsensical—or rather since there cannot be nonsensical propositions, we must say that there is no such proposition as "*a* is an object." The reason for this is as follows. Any genuine proposition must have a significant negation: if the sentence '*S* is *P*' expresses a genuine proposition, then so must '~(*S* is *P*)' and vice versa; and if '*S* is *P*' is nonsensical, so is '~(*S* is *P*)' and vice versa. For example, it makes sense to say that a book is red, and therefore it makes sense to say that a book is not red. But it does not make sense to say that truthfulness is red, and therefore it makes no sense to say that truthfulness is not red. The sentence 'Truthfulness is red' expresses no proposition, and neither does 'Truthfulness is not red.' Wittgenstein puts this point in the following way:

> 5.5151(3) The positive *proposition* necessarily presupposes the existence of the negative *proposition* and *vice versa*.

In the *Notebooks 1914-1916,* he put the same point in this way:

> In order for a proposition to be capable of being true it must also be capable of being false. [*NB*, entry for 5.6.15.]

This principle—which may be called the principle of significant negation—certainly seems to be a sound one. It does not seem possible that a given sentence should express a genuine proposition, but that its negation should be nonsensical.

If we now apply this principle to the alleged proposition that "*a* is an object," we see that it is really not a proposition at all, because its negation is not a proposition. (I assume throughout that '*a*' is a simple sign.) If we try to say "~(*a* is an object)," we produce patent nonsense. This can be seen as follows. Assume that "~(*a* is an object)" is a genuine proposition. If so, it must either be true or false. If it is true (i.e., if *a* is not an object), then the sign '*a*' denotes no object, and hence has no meaning, since the meaning of a name is the object it denotes; but this would make the sentence '~(*a* is an object)' nonsensical, since it would contain a sign with no meaning. Our assumption thus leads to absurdity; it implies that if a certain sentence (viz., '~(*a* is an object)') expresses a true proposition, then that same sentence is nonsensical (i.e., does not express any proposition). The assumption must be abandoned then. We must say that the sentence '~(*a* is an object)' does not express a genuine proposition. But then according to the principle of significant negation, the sentence 'a is an object' also fails to express a genuine proposition.[12] And since the alleged proposition "And a, b, c, . . . are all the objects there are" would have to include in the expression of its sense such sentences as 'a is an object' and 'b is an object,' that alleged proposition must itself not be a genuine proposition after all.

Therefore, according to Wittgenstein, the universal proposition "All objects have property F" is really a conjunction (and hence a truth-function) of propositions about the individual objects "a has F and b has F and c has F . . . ," and the fact that a, b, c, . . . are all the objects that there are is shown by the fact that in our grammar there are only the names 'a,' 'b,' 'c,' . . .

> . . . What you want to *say* by the apparent proposition "There are 2 things" is *shown* by there being two names which have different meanings (or by there being one name which may have two meanings).[13]

(See also T 5.535[3].) The class of objects, unlike the class of men or books, is "determined by our dictionary" or is "defined by grammar," as he put it some years later. This, at any rate, was Wittgenstein's view in the *Tractatus;* later he realized that he had been mistaken.[14]

---

[12] A similar argument would show that "a exists" is not a proposition. This shows that in such passages as that on p. 49, where I spoke of the existence and nonexistence of objects, I said something which is illegitimate; it is impossible to attribute existence or nonexistence to objects.

> 4.1272(5) So one cannot say, for example, 'There are objects', as one might say, 'There are books'. . . .

(Wittgenstein discusses this topic in *PI*, sect. 50.)

[13] Wittgenstein letter to Russell dated 19.8.19, reprinted in *NB*, p. 129ff.

[14] From a "finitist" point of view at least, the *Tractatus* view is indeed mistaken: If there are infinitely many objects, then the universal proposition "All objects have property F" cannot be the mere logical product of Fa, Fb, Fc, and so on. There is ambiguity in connection with the expression 'and so on.' Any actual logical product (such as $Fa \cdot Fb \cdot Fc$) must be a finite one, just as any actual series of numbers must be a finite one. In finite cases, the 'and so on' is harmless, for it is then merely a sign of laziness, as when one says "The alphabet consists of the letters A, B, C, and so on." But in infinite cases, the 'and so on' is clearly not a sign of mere laziness. So whereas the proposition "The alphabet consists of the letters A, B, C, and so on" can be replaced by an expression which enumerates all the letters of the alphabet, since there are only a finite number of them, the proposition "All objects have property F" cannot be replaced by a logical product of elementary propositions (such as Fa, Fb), if there are infinitely many objects, for then no such product can possibly be written out. And since Wittgenstein did not want to commit himself to there being only a finite number of objects (see T 4.2211), he should not

To summarize: a universal proposition about complexes is not analyzable as a truth-function of particular propositions about individual complexes, for the analysis must contain another universal proposition about complexes. (In our example, this was proposition C.) But, since propositions such as C *are* analyzable as truth-functions of particular propositions about *objects,* universal propositions about complexes are seen to be truth-functions of particular propositions about objects—i.e., of elementary propositions.

Note.[15] The foregoing account gives, I believe, the heart of Wittgenstein's view; but for the sake of clarity and simplicity of exposition, I deviated from the letter of his doctrine on two inessential points. In this note, in order to set the record straight, I shall say what these two points are.

First, he does not use disjunction ('either/or') and conjunction ('and') in analyzing existential and universal general propositions, but rather a single truth-functional connective in terms of which 'either/or' and 'and' (and in fact any truth-functional connective) can be defined. This single connective is H. M. Sheffer's 'neither/nor,' symbolized by a stroke, '|'; the expression '$p|q$' is to be read 'neither p nor q' or 'not-p and not-q.' (See line 12 of the chart in T 5.101.[16]) Both 'p and q' and 'p or q' can be defined in terms of Sheffer's stroke function. So Wittgenstein's analyses of existential and universal general propositions—although not actually expressed in terms of 'or' and 'and' as my account had it, but rather in terms of 'neither/nor'—do not differ in *content* from those given in my account. By using the above-mentioned definitions, his analyses and the ones I

---

have said that a universal proposition about objects is a truth-function—specifically, a logical product—of elementary propositions. He later admitted his error. (See G. E. Moore, "Wittgenstein's Lectures in 1930-33," Part III, *Mind,* LXIV, No. 253 [January 1955], 2-4 [*Philosophical Papers,* 297-99].)

[15] This note can be omitted by those readers with no elementary knowledge of logic.

[16] Sheffer's work appeared in his "A Set of Five Independent Postulates for Boolean Algebras," *Transactions of the American Mathematical Society,* Vol. 14 (1913). In point of historical fact, Sheffer symbolized 'neither p nor q' as '$p \downarrow q$': '$\downarrow$' is sometimes referred to as the dagger function. Sheffer also employed the symbol '|'—the stroke function—but he used it to signify not joint denial but rather alternative denial, so that for him '$p \mid q$' denies one or both of p and q. (See line 2 of the chart in T 5.101.) In the *Tractatus,* however, Wittgenstein chooses to symbolize joint denial by '|' rather than by '$\downarrow$', and I shall follow him in this. Accordingly, what I shall call Sheffer's stroke function is that of joint denial, even though this is not historically accurate.

gave can be translated into one another, and are thus equivalent.

Second, Wittgenstein's analyses involve two stages where I had just one; that is, when he analyzes a universal proposition about objects, he does not immediately set it down as a truth-function of elementary propositions, as I did in my account. Instead, he first expresses that proposition in symbolic notation, making use of an extension of Sheffer's stroke function. This function, as originally conceived, required that the propositions to which it is applied be actually given or at least explicitly represented; it occurred, in other words, only in such contexts as '$p|q$,' in which the individual propositions are explicitly represented (in this case by the letters 'p' and 'q'). Wittgenstein extends Sheffer's operation of simultaneous denial so that it can apply not only to propositions which are given in this way by enumeration, but also to a whole range of propositions which are not explicitly listed, but are described as being the values of a function. This he does by introducing expressions of the form '$N(\overline{fx})$.' $N(\overline{Fx})$ is the simultaneous negation of all the values of the propositional function Fx for all values of x. Suppose that the variable x has only the three values, a, b, and c, so that the only values of Fx are the propositions Fa, Fb, and Fc. Then $N(\overline{Fx})$ is the simultaneous negation of these three propositions; that is, it is $\sim Fa \cdot \sim Fb \cdot \sim Fc$. (See T 5.502 and 5.51.)

For Wittgenstein, use of this extension of Sheffer's notation of simultaneous negation constitutes the *first* stage in the analysis of any general proposition. Consider, for example, a universal negative proposition such as "Nothing is an F." This proposition can be expressed as $N(\overline{Fx})$ where Fx has as its values all the propositions obtained for all values of x. Then, in the *second* stage, it is pointed out that $N(\overline{Fx})$, being the simultaneous negation of all these values of Fx, says that $\sim Fa \cdot \sim Fb \cdot \sim Fc$ . . . and so on for all values of x. Since x ranges over everything, it thus denies that anything is an F, or in other words it asserts that nothing is an F. (See T 5.52.)

In short, Wittgenstein first finds an expression for generality, in the notation $N(\overline{Fx})$, and gets to truth-functions only by analyzing that expression. My account, on the other hand, tried to express the universal proposition as a truth-function of particular propositions about objects (i.e., elementary propositions) immediately—that is, *without* making use of any intermediate expression. (In T 5.521, he takes Russell and Frege to task for following the latter course.) But although in my account the move was made in one step, whereas in

Wittgenstein's actual account it is made in two, the end result is the same in either case—namely, truth-functions of elementary propositions. And that is the feature of Wittgenstein's account that I was mainly concerned to stress. *End of note.*

2. There is no discussion in the *Tractatus* attempting to show that run-of-the-mill propositions about complex individuals (such as chairs and people) are really truth-functions of elementary propositions; thus, Wittgenstein must have thought it obvious that this is so. But of course it is not at all obvious. Think, for example, of such a proposition as "Jones signed a check to pay his debt to Smith"; there are involved in the sense of this proposition, in one way or another, the concepts of a person, of banking and finance, of moral practices, and doubtless many others as well. It is highly implausible to maintain that this could all be expressed as a truth-function of elementary propositions. At the very least, a great deal of argument would be needed to show how this might be done, and none is provided in the *Tractatus*.

3. Wittgenstein examines, although briefly and cryptically, one kind of proposition in which his thesis seems to be false—i.e., in which one proposition appears to occur in another in a non-truth-functional way.

5.541   At first sight it looks as if it were also possible for one proposition to occur in another in a different way.

          Particularly with certain forms of proposition in psychology, such as '*A* believes that *p* is the case' and '*A* has the thought *p*,' etc.

This class of propositions would include such members as "*A* expects that *p*," "*A* wishes that *p*," "*A* is afraid that *p*," and many others. What is typical of them is that the truth-value of the whole proposition is not uniquely determined by the truth-value of *p*. For example, a person *A* can believe that it is going to rain, whether or not what he believes is true. Hence it appears that a proposition (*p*) can occur in another ("*A* believes that *p*") in a non-truth-functional way, contrary to Wittgenstein's thesis. Wittgenstein attempts to show, in an extremely short and difficult passage (*T* 5.542) that this is a mere superficial appearance, and that when such propositions are properly analyzed, they are revealed to be truth-functions of elementary propositions like all the rest. A discussion of this passage must wait until later, for, if I interpret it properly, it requires an understanding of some points which have not been made so far in our account.

*   *   *

Wittgenstein's view, then, is that all propositions are truth-functions of elementary propositions. Given all possible elementary propositions, one could construct any proposition whatever from them by using nothing but truth-functional operators. And, since H. M. Sheffer proved that all the truth-functional connectives can be defined in terms of one primitive truth-functional connective, this means that, on Wittgenstein's view, any proposition whatever can be constructed from elementary propositions by the use of the one primitive truth-functional connective.

> 5.3   All propositions are results of truth-operations on elementary propositions.
>
> A truth-operation is the way in which a truth-function is produced out of elementary propositions.
>
> It is of the essence of truth-operations that, just as elementary propositions yield a truth-function of themselves, so too in the same way truth-functions yield a further truth-function. When a truth-operation is applied to truth-functions of elementary propositions, it always generates another truth-function of elementary propositions, another proposition. When a truth-operation is applied to the results of truth-operations on elementary propositions, there is always a *single* operation on elementary propositions that has the same result.
>
> Every proposition is the result of truth-operations on elementary propositions.

(See also *T* 6 and 6.001.)

This is an extraordinary, one almost wants to say, an incredible, thesis. In the discussion above, I mentioned only three kinds of proposition, but there are many others, some of which seem *obviously* to contradict Wittgenstein's thesis. Consider, for example, this list which Miss Anscombe provides:

> Laws of inference, and, generally, logical truths.
> Statements that one proposition implies another.
> Generality—i.e., propositions containing 'all' and 'some.'
> Propositions giving logical classifications of terms and expressions—e.g., ' "to the right of" is a relation,' ' "a is to the right of b" is a proposition.'

Propositions that are important in the foundation of mathematics such as 'a is the successor of b.'

Statements about the possibility, impossibility, necessity, and certainty of particular states of affairs.

Statements of identity.

Propositions apparently expressing functions of propositions, such as 'it is good that p,' or 'p is possible,' 'p is necessary' or again 'A believes p' or 'A conceives p'; and perhaps even statements about, e.g., the beauty of pictures.

Propositions stating probabilities.

Propositions of mathematics.

Propositions stating laws of nature.

Propositions about space and time.

Egocentric propositions.

Propositions about the world as a whole, about God and the meaning of life.[17]

I think it is absurd to suggest, as my discussion in the last two or three pages has perhaps suggested, that Wittgenstein first examined with an open mind all the different types of proposition that he could think of, that it somehow occurred to him that they are all truth-functions of elementary propositions, and that he then tried to defend the thesis as best he could. No one could have arrived at any such view in that manner; no such view would ever have suggested itself to an uncommitted mind. I suggest, then, that the truth of the matter is rather this: Wittgenstein first arrived at a theory—call it for the moment theory X—which he thought was necessarily true. Theory X entailed the view that propositions are *truth-functions* of elementary propositions; it demanded that this theory of truth-functions be true. Then, finally, Wittgenstein considered all the types of proposition that he could think of, and tried to account for them all, in one way or another, on his theory of truth-functions.[18] As we shall see, some of them he ruled out as not being genuine propositions at all (as meaningless, or sheer nonsense); some he claimed are not sheer nonsense, but are nevertheless illegitimate since they try to say something which cannot be said; still others, although propositions, were said to be degenerate ones which say nothing; and the others he tried to show really are truth-functions of elementary propositions, appearances to the contrary notwithstanding.

[17] G. E. M. Anscombe, *An Introduction to Wittgenstein's Tractatus*, pp. 79-80.

[18] I am not suggesting, needless to say, that this sequence is an actual historical one; it is a sequence in the order of justification, not necessarily in the temporal order.

This mode of procedure is almost standard method with philosophers. Ever so many philosophical arguments follow this general schema:

> One would ordinarily think that all these *S*'s are of radically different kinds—that some are *P*'s, some are *Q*'s, some are *R*'s, and so on. But my theory demands that all *S*'s are essentially *M*'s. Now, these particular things (*n, m, o* . . .) which appear to be *S*'s are not really *M*'s, so they cannot really be *S*'s. And these *S*'s, which at first appear not to be *M*'s, when properly understood, are seen to be really *M*'s after all.

The procedure embodied in this schema is perfectly valid, as long as the theory in question is unassailable. (As we shall see, one of the targets of the later Wittgenstein's most withering criticism is the idea that, given any group of things called by the same name, there must be an essence which they all share.)

Theory X, which demands that all genuine propositions be truth-functions of other propositions, is Wittgenstein's famous picture theory of propositions. Miss Anscombe writes:

> . . . The picture theory does not permit any functions of propositions other than truth-functions. Indeed, we should not regard Wittgenstein's theory of the proposition as a *synthesis* of a picture theory and the theory of truth-functions; his picture theory and theory of truth-functions are one and the same.[19]

Our next big task, clearly, is to investigate this picture theory of propositions. Before turning to that task, however, let us first notice one or two consequences of Wittgenstein's theory of truth-functions.

Logical Atomism

One consequence of the theory of truth-functions is that the world divides into nothing but atomic facts; there are, for example, no irreducibly general facts. Russell had argued, on grounds indicated above (p. 59f.), that universal propositions are not just truth-functions of propositions about individuals, and that one must therefore admit some universal propositions to be basic and irreducible to any other kind of proposition. And therefore, he had urged, there must be irreducibly general facts which are not molecular constructions out

[19] Anscombe, *op. cit.*, p. 81.

of atomic facts, in order for the universal propositions to have something to correspond to.

> It is clear, I think, that you must admit general facts as distinct from and over and above particular facts.[20]

Since Wittgenstein thought, on the contrary, that universal propositions are all ultimately analyzable into elementary propositions, he did not have to postulate irreducibly general situations or general facts; and thus his world-view is to that extent, at least, tidier than Russell's. Russell had also argued for the existence of negative facts as a type of fact irreducible to atomic facts (in chapter 3 of "The Philosophy of Logical Atomism"); and Wittgenstein rejected this suggestion too. For him, all propositions are truth-functional molecules or structures of nothing but elementary propositions, and all nonatomic situations and facts are molecules or structures of nothing but states of affairs and atomic facts.

(*Note.* I am afraid that it may be somewhat misleading to speak of nonatomic situations and facts being molecules or structures of states of affairs [atomic situations] and atomic facts. This way of putting it is apt to suggest that they are molecules or structures in the same way that physical molecules or structures are composed of physical atoms and parts—in the way that a house, for example, is a structure of beams, floors, roof, and so on. But besides all the other differences in the two kinds of cases, there is this crucial difference: in the case of physical molecules or structures, all the components must at least exist, whereas in the case of situations or facts, some of the components may be components precisely by *not* existing. To take a simple example, one possible situation can be described by a proposition of the form "$p \cdot q \cdot \sim r$," where p, q, and r are elementary propositions. The states of affairs described by p, q, and r are all components of the complex situation; but if the situation exists, the states of affairs described by p and q exist [i.e., are atomic facts], while that described by r does not exist. So although to speak of nonelementary propositions being molecules or structures of elementary propositions is not, I think, apt to mislead, the analogous talk of nonelementary situations and facts being molecules or structures of states of affairs and atomic facts is slightly misleading. Still, no harm need be done if only the picture is not taken too seriously.)

20 Russell, "The Philosophy of Logical Atomism," Marsh volume, p. 236.

One might object here that complex situations cannot consist of just states of affairs, that they must include something else besides —viz., whatever it is that binds the states of affairs together into a complex whole. But Wittgenstein denies that there is anything binding them together. A complex situation is described by a truth-function of elementary propositions; the elementary propositions describe the states of affairs which make up the complex situation, so the only terms that could denote whatever it is that is supposed to bind the states of affairs together are the truth-functional operators, the so-called logical constants. It is these that might seem to denote some sort of 'logical cement.' But Wittgenstein denies that logical constants stand for or denote anything.

> 4.0312(2) My fundamental idea is that the 'logical constants' are not representatives. . . .

This can be seen as follows. The logical constants can all be reduced by definitions to Sheffer's stroke function. But $p|q$ says $\sim p \cdot \sim q$ (i.e., not-p and not-q). Wittgenstein has already shown that 'not' or '$\sim$' does not denote or designate anything, and it is obvious that the same is true of 'and' or '·'. Hence, Sheffer's stroke does not denote anything, and, since all the logical constants can be reduced to it, none of them does. (See T 5.42.) Logical constants are needed in the language to construct nonelementary propositions; they are thus indispensable syntactical devices, but they are not names, they do not represent logical cement.

Wittgenstein's philosophical view has been very appropriately entitled *logical atomism*. The term was coined by Russell [21] as a name for his own views at the time (around 1918), but Wittgenstein's system may be said to constitute a much purer version of logical atomism than even Russell's. Wittgenstein's logical atomism is at once a theory of propositions and a metaphysical theory. All genuine propositions are molecules constructed of logical atoms called elementary propositions; all situations are molecules constructed of logical atoms called states of affairs. Elementary propositions (or states of affairs) are atomic, since they cannot be further reduced to any more basic propositions (or states of affairs). [22]

---

[21] *Ibid.*, p. 178.

[22] I would be adhering more faithfully to Russell's way of speaking about logical atomism if I were to refer only to Wittgenstein's *objects* as (logical) atoms, rather than to states of affairs and elementary propositions.

I remarked that, for Wittgenstein, there is nothing which binds states of affairs together to form complex situations. The independence of states of affairs is actually more radical than that statement would indicate. They are absolutely independent of one another. A state of affairs (and hence an atomic fact) has no relations or connections of any kind with any other.

2.061　　　States of affairs are independent of one another.

2.062　　　From the existence or non-existence of one state of affairs it is impossible to infer the existence or non-existence of another.

(See also T 1.21.) It amounts to the same thing to say that elementary propositions are absolutely independent of one another:

5.134　　　One elementary proposition cannot be deduced from another.

4.211　　　It is a sign of a proposition's being elementary that there can be no elementary proposition contradicting it.

Wittgenstein could have put it more strongly: not only cannot two elementary propositions be contradictories (i.e., such that if one is true the other must be false, and if one is false, the other must be true), they cannot even be contraries (i.e., such that if one is true, the other must be false, but they may both be false). (See T 2.061, 2.062.) Two elementary propositions cannot have any such relationship to one another.

The doctrine that two elementary propositions cannot be contraries is not a very plausible one on the face of it. For example, suppose we have the two propositions (1) "a has P in degree 1 at time t_1" and (2) "a has P in degree 2 at time t_1," where 'a' designates an object and 'P' a property. Although (1) and (2) are not contradictories, they are evidently contraries. On Wittgenstein's view, then, (1) and (2) cannot be elementary propositions; for if they were, they would describe two states of affairs which are *not* independent of one another, contrary to T 2.061. Hence, (1) and (2) must be further analyzable in such a way that no pair of the resulting elementary propositions can be contraries of one another. And this seems like an impossible demand; for it seems that if, as is the case, a state of affairs S consists in a's having some property or in a's being related in some way to b (or to $c, d, e, . . .$), one can always specify at least one other state of affairs involving a (and perhaps also $b, c, d, e, . . .$) which the existence of S would exclude from existence, contrary to T 2.062.[23] It appears, therefore, as though Wittgenstein must revise his doctrine and admit that *some* states of affairs are not entirely independent of one another. Wittgenstein in fact later abandoned the doctrine that no elementary propositions can be contraries,[24] although he still maintained that they cannot ever be contradictories. This revision leaves untouched much of what Wittgenstein says in the *Tractatus* about the independence of states of affairs, for the revision applies only to those states of affairs satisfying *all* of the following conditions: (i) the same object or objects occur in them, (ii) the object has the same property, or the objects are related by the same relation, and (iii) the same moment of time is involved in all of them. States of affairs to which these three conditions do not apply can still be wholly independent of one another, and so can the elementary propositions which describe them.

But in the *Tractatus,* at any rate, if Fa and Ga are two different elementary propositions, I cannot deduce one from the other. That is, I cannot deduce one from the other directly, unaided by any other premises. If I have the additional premise "If Fa then Ga" (symbolized as $Fa \supset Ga$)—or the universal premise "All F's are G's" (symbolized as $(x)(Fx \supset Gx)$) which includes $Fa \supset Ga$ as one of its values— then from it and $Fa,$ I can of course deduce $Ga.$ But from Fa alone, Ga cannot be deduced. It might be thought that the premise $Fa \supset Ga$ must assert the existence of some sort of tie between the states of affairs that Fa and that $Ga,$ but it does not. It merely denies that a certain situation happens to obtain—namely, that where Fa is true, Ga is false. And for this there is and can be, according to Wittgenstein, no explanation, for different states of affairs are entirely independent of one another.

What is true of elementary propositions and states of affairs is also true of compound propositions and compound situations. To be sure, if a compound proposition p contains another proposition q as one of its components, it may be possible to deduce q from $p.$ To take an extremely simple example, if p is the proposition $q \cdot r,$ then I can deduce q from $p.$ Similarly, if a complex situation S_1 contains situation S_2 as one of its components, then from the existence of S_1 I may be able to infer the existence of $S_2.$ But if S_1 and S_2 have nothing in

23 For a detailed and illuminating discussion of this matter, see E. Stenius, *Wittgenstein's Tractatus,* ch. IV, and also J. Jarvis, "Professor Stenius on the Tractatus," *Journal of Philosophy,* LVIII, No. 20 (Sept. 26, 1961), 584-85.

24 In his article "Some Remarks on Logical Form," *Proceedings of the Aristotelian Society,* IX (1929).

common, then I cannot infer the existence of one from the existence of the other.

5.135   There is no possible way of making an inference from the existence of one situation to the existence of another, entirely different situation.

5.136   There is no causal nexus to justify such an inference.

The point can be put more graphically as follows: Wittgenstein's theory of truth-functions has the consequence that the only metaphysical cement there could possibly be to connect states of affairs would be logical cement—i.e., something designated by the truth-functional connectives (logical constants). But when he denies the existence of logical cement, he denies the existence of all cement. Reality, for Wittgenstein, is wholly granular; the grains (the states of affairs) are entirely independent of one another, and so are the complexes with no grains in common.

6.37   There is no compulsion making one thing happen because another has happened. The only necessity that exists is *logical* necessity.

6.371   The whole modern conception of the world is founded on the illusion that the so-called laws of nature are the explanations of natural phenomena.

Induction—whereby we predict what hitherto unobserved facts will be on the basis of what we have already observed—on this view immediately loses its validity.

5.1361   We *cannot* infer the events of the future from those of the present.
              Belief in the causal nexus is *superstition*.

There can be no valid inference from one state of affairs (or complex of them) to a different state of affairs (or a different complex of them) because each is totally unrelated to the other.

6.363   The procedure of induction consists in accepting as true the *simplest* law that can be reconciled with our experiences.

6.3631   This procedure, however, has no logical justification but only a psychological one.
              It is clear that there are no grounds for believing that the simplest eventuality will in fact be realized.

6.36311   It is an hypothesis that the sun will rise tomorrow: and this means that we do not *know* whether it will rise.

At the turn of the century, the Absolute Idealism of F. H. Bradley (1846-1924) reigned supreme in British philosophy. Bradley taught that both reality and knowledge are unified systems: every fact is connected with every other, and none can exist in isolation from all the rest. Since reality is essentially one, no truth can be completely understood in isolation from the one System of Truth; in order to know one thing, a person must know everything. Before Bradley was even in his grave, Wittgenstein had turned his august monistic philosophy exactly on its head.

4 The Picture Theory

Wittgenstein says that an elementary proposition consists of names only. But if that is the case, a difficulty immediately arises. How can an elementary proposition say or state anything? How can it tell us anything? A mere list of names cannot state a fact, and therefore cannot be true or false, as propositions are. What, for example, could the list "Socrates, Aristotle, Athens, living" possibly assert?

There is another puzzling feature of language connected with propositions. A person can understand what a proposition means even if he has never run across it before, even if it has never been explained to him what its sense is. For example, it is unlikely that anyone has previously heard this proposition: "There are now fourteen young apes playing with an African anteater on my living-room floor." And yet everyone who understands English knows what the proposition means, provided the meanings of the constituent words are known to him. The old familiar words can convey a new sense to us. This may seem like a trivial fact, but it decidedly is not; it is only something that we are used to because we meet examples of it every day. It is an extraordinary fact which demands some explanation. Out of the blue, an entirely new proposition is presented, a new combination of words is uttered, and I know at once what is meant. No one need have told me: I just "see" what it means in some way or other that needs accounting for. (Notice, by the way, that this fact provides another reason for denying that propositions are names of the facts they describe; for I cannot know the meaning of a name without having been told, or in some other way having previously learnt it.)

This puzzling feature of language is of the highest importance for its usefulness and flexibility. Think how limited language would be, and indeed how limited we would be, if each sentence had its own special meaning which was no function of the meaning of its constituent words. There would then be a stock of things that it was possible to say in the language, just as now there is a stock of words in the language which are available for use; whenever a person wanted to say anything, he could only say one or another of the standard things. Imagine an example of such a language. Suppose that by convention certain flags mean certain things—a blue flag means "It's raining in the mountains," a red flag "It's raining on the beach," a brown flag "There is snow in the mountains," and so on. No one could understand what these flags mean simply by looking at the flags themselves; the meaning of each flag would have to be explained to a person before he could know what it was, or he would have to gather what it means from the behavior of the language users. There would be no such thing as coming across a flag with a new color and knowing at once by inspection what it meant. Whenever anyone wished to say something, all he could do would be to display one of the flags, thus expressing one of the predetermined propositions. New flags could be introduced, thus enlarging the stock of sayable things, but it would be at best a tedious process with highly limited possibilities of expression. The human mind might be able to make some progress under these conditions, but a ceiling would soon be reached; it would be excessively difficult after a certain point to remember what any more sentences meant and virtually impossible to invent sentences with complex or subtle meanings. In such a language, the invention of a new sentence would be an infrequent and notable event; in our language, it is a commonplace occurrence—and not a matter of *invention* at all.

Wittgenstein places great importance on this feature of our language. In fact, he sometimes actually goes too far in this, as in the following passage:

> 4.027   It belongs to the essence of a proposition that it should be able to communicate a *new* sense to us.

Here, as elsewhere, Wittgenstein confuses proposition with propositional sign. It is not a proposition, but a propositional sign—a sentence —which communicates a sense to the hearer (reader), for that is all that the hearer hears (reader sees). Propositions may *have* new senses, but they cannot be said to communicate them. I say Wittgenstein goes too far here because I think it is perfectly possible to have a language in which propositional signs cannot immediately communicate new senses—e.g., the flag language just discussed. On the other hand, it could plausibly be argued, in favor of Wittgenstein, that unless a system of signs had elements that were combinable in different ways—i.e., unless it had a syntax—it would not constitute a *language*. (Can the birds, for example, be said to have and to use a language?) If this claim be correct, then what I have called a "flag language" would not be a language at all and *T* 4.027 would not go too far, for what it says *is* true of language with a syntax—i.e. (if the claim is valid), all languages.

Be that as it may, in our language we can express new propositions by using the old words, and our hearers can usually understand the new sense at once, without any previous acquaintance with it, without any explanation. Wittgenstein thought that there is only one possible way of explaining this vital and puzzling feature of language: the proposition must be a picture of the situation it describes and asserts to exist (or not to exist). Understanding the sense of a proposition is knowing what situation it describes. Just by looking at a proposition, I can tell what situation it describes. I can "read it off" from the proposition itself, even if the proposition is quite new to me and no one has explained its sense to me. But how could I thus "read off" the situation from the proposition itself, unless the proposition were some sort of representation, or picture, of the situation?

> 4.021   A proposition is a picture of reality: for if I understand a proposition, I know the situation that it represents. And I understand the proposition without having had its sense explained to me.

This is an extremely plausible solution to the problem. A picture has just the features which we noted a proposition has. It represents some situation beyond itself, and I can tell which situation it is merely by looking at the picture. No one need explain to me what situation it depicts; I can "read it off" from the picture itself. A picture *shows* us what it represents; similarly,

> 4.022(1)   A proposition *shows* its sense.

It is true that a proposition does not at once appear to be a picture of a situation. Ordinary pictures look like what they represent, and a proposition certainly does not look like a situation. But Wittgenstein is not asserting that a proposition is an ordinary—that is, spatial— picture of the situation it describes; it is rather a "logical picture" of it (*T* 4.03[3]). In order for one thing, A, to be a logical picture of another, B, three conditions must be met: (1) there must be a one-to-one correspondence between the components of A and those of B; (2) to every feature of the structure or form of A there must correspond a feature of the structure or form of B; and (3) there must be rules of projection connecting the components of A and those of B. Rules of projection are rules whereby given A (or B), B (or A) can be reconstructed from it. A good example is the rules connecting a musical score and an actual performance of it; given either the score or the performance, the other can be reconstructed from it. Wittgenstein uses this example.

> 4.0141   There is a general rule by means of which the musician can obtain the symphony from the score, and which makes it possible to derive the symphony from the groove on the gramophone record, and, using the first rule, to derive the score again. That is what constitutes the inner similarity between these things which seem to be constructed in such entirely different ways. And that rule is the law of projection which projects the symphony into the language of musical notation. It is the rule for translating this language into the language of gramophone records.

Remembering Wittgenstein's lifelong interest in music, one might guess that this example is what suggested to him the idea that a proposition is a picture of the fact it describes. But that is not the case.

> Wittgenstein told me how the idea of language as a *picture* of reality occurred to him. He was in a trench on the East Front, reading a magazine in which there was a schematic picture depicting the possible sequence of events in an automobile accident. The picture there served as a proposition; that is, as a description of a possible state of affairs. It had this function owing to a correspondence between the parts of the picture and things in reality. It now occurred to Wittgenstein that one might reverse the analogy and say that a *proposition* serves as a *picture*, by virtue of a similar correspondence between *its* parts and the world. The way in which the parts of the proposition

are combined—the *structure* of the proposition—depicts a possible combination of elements in reality, a possible state of affairs.[1]

The first vague suggestion of this idea may well have been planted in Wittgenstein's mind by certain doctrines of Hertz's *Principles of Mechanics;* in discussing the picture theory, Wittgenstein explicitly refers to them.

4.04   In a proposition there must be exactly as many distinguishable parts as in the situation that it represents.

        The two must possess the same logical (mathematical) multiplicity. (Compare Hertz's *Mechanics* on dynamical models.)

Here is one of the passages from Hertz that Wittgenstein was referring to:

The relation of a dynamical model to the system of which it is regarded as the model, is precisely the same as the relation of the images which our mind forms of things to the things themselves. For if we regard the condition of the model as the representation of the condition of the system, then the consequents of this representation, which according to the laws of this representation must appear, are also the representation of the consequents which must proceed from the original object according to the laws of this original object. The agreement between mind and nature may therefore be likened to the agreement between two systems which are models of one another, and we can even account for this agreement by assuming that the mind is capable of making actual dynamical models of things, and of working with them.[2]

It is, indeed, more appropriate to say that Wittgenstein's view of the proposition is that it is a model of the situation it represents, than to say that it is a picture of it. Wittgenstein occasionally uses the term 'model' in this connection.

4.01(2)   A proposition is a model of reality as we imagine it.

[1] G. H. von Wright, "Biographical Sketch," reprinted in Malcolm, *Memoir,* pp. 7-8. The following entry occurs in the *Notebooks 1914-1916:* "In the proposition a world is as it were put together experimentally. (As when in the lawcourt in Paris a motor-car accident is represented by means of dolls, etc.)" (*NB,* entry for 29.9.14). The editors of the *Notebooks* suggest that the date of this entry indicates that the incident referred to by von Wright could not very well have taken place in a trench on the East Front. (*NB,* p. 7n.)

[2] Heinrich Hertz, *The Principles of Mechanics,* trans. D. E. Jones and J. T. Walley, sect. 428. The term in the original German text which the translators have rendered as 'images' is '*Bilder*'—i.e., pictures.

The wording of *T* 4.031(1) also suggests the analogy of a model.

> 4.031(1)   In a proposition a situation is, as it were, constructed by way of experiment.

But perhaps the best way to state Wittgenstein's position is to say that the proposition is a projection (as the term is used, for example, in projective geometry) of the situation it describes. Wittgenstein uses that term as well, but it is usually the propositional sign that he speaks of as being a projection of the situation.

> 3.11(1)   We use the perceptible sign of a proposition (spoken or written, etc.) as a projection of a possible situation.

In any case, the example of a musical score is particularly instructive; most people are familiar with at least the general principle involved, and the analogy it provides is an especially close one. The individual note marks mean certain sounds, just as individual words mean certain objects. As the piece may never be performed, so the proposition may be false; and as one knows from looking at the score what the piece would sound like if it were performed, so one knows what would be the case if the proposition were true. (*T* 4.022[2], 4.024[1].) And just as one can read a new score without a special explanation, since he knows the general rules of projection of music, so one can understand a new proposition without its sense being explained, since he knows the general rules of projection of language.

One important feature of Wittgenstein's picture theory of propositions should be borne in mind, if we are to realize that certain apparent objections to it are not really damaging. It might be objected, for example, that the theory is incompatible with other things Wittgenstein has said. If a proposition is a picture of a fact, then every word or phrase in it must directly stand for something, as every note in the musical score directly stands for a particular sound; and so in the proposition "The author of *Waverley* is Scotch," the phrase 'the author of *Waverley*' must directly represent some object. But according to the theory of definite descriptions, accepted by Wittgenstein, this is not the case. Furthermore, it is absurd to suggest that in the proposition "The average American male likes baseball," the subject phrase directly names an object, as the picture theory would require it to. These and other objections to the picture theory are at once swept away by Wittgenstein's insistence that propositions *as ordinarily expressed* are not, in that form, pictures of the situations

they describe.[3] In the strictest sense, it is only elementary propositions, those consisting entirely of names, that are pictures of situations. But when any other kind of proposition is completely analyzed
into elementary propositions—i.e., when its true nature as a truth-
function of elementary propositions is fully exhibited—then it, too,
is a picture of the situation it describes. And even then, the nonelementary proposition depicts something only in virtue of the fact
that its component elementary propositions do so.

> First and foremost the elementary propositional form must portray;
> all portrayal takes place through it. [*NB*, entry for 31.10.14.]

As condition (1) (p. 78) demands, there must be a one-to-one correspondence between the components of a picture and those of the
thing pictured; hence there must be exactly as many components of
the picture as there are of the thing pictured. Since a proposition is
a picture of the situation it describes, this must hold of it too
(*T* 4.04[1]). But this requirement is met only by elementary propositions; they alone consist entirely of names, each of which directly
denotes an object.

> 4.0311   One name stands for one thing, another for another thing,
>   and they are combined with one another. In this way the
>   whole group—like a *tableau vivant*—presents a state of
>   affairs.

But there is a problem which still faces us, namely the one mentioned in the opening paragraph of this chapter. An elementary
proposition is a series of names, and how can a series of names state
a fact, how can it say anything true or false? To find an answer to
this question, let us try to answer first the preliminary question: How
can a series of names represent (picture) a state of affairs? It is
difficult to see how a list of names can be a picture. Let us ask what
the essence of an ordinary picture is. What is it about a picture that
makes it a representation of a situation? Wittgenstein answers this
question by saying:

> 2.14   What constitutes a picture is that its elements are related
>   to one another in a determinate way.
> 2.141   A picture is a fact.

There seems to be a conflict here between Wittgenstein and common

---

[3] Although Wittgenstein sometimes talks as if they were—for example, in
T 4.011.

sense, connected with the earlier one over whether the world divides into facts or into objects (see pp. 18-19). Common sense would say that the things in a picture which do the representing are the blotches of paint or ink or whatever, and that what they represent are the several objects of the scene depicted. Wittgenstein, however, disagrees with this way of describing the matter; what represents the scene, he maintains, is certain facts. Suppose the scene depicted is a room with furniture. It is not simply the individual patches of paint in themselves that represent the arrangement of the furniture in the room; for if those same patches of paint were placed differently on the canvas, they would not represent the actual arrangement of furniture at all. No, what it is about the picture that represents the arrangement of furniture is the *fact* that the several patches of paint are placed in a certain way on the canvas. For example, the fact that the blue patch is next to the red one represents the fact that the blue chair is next to the red table in the room itself.

> 2.15(1) The fact that the elements of a picture are related to one another in a determinate way represents that things are related to one another in the same way.

A picture, then, is a fact; and it represents certain features of the reality depicted only because it is a fact. If, at the risk of a slight (and, I hope, harmless) inaccuracy, we assume that the picture is analogous to an elementary proposition in the sense of being composed of simple elements, then we see that it is only the structural features of reality (e.g., the arrangement of the furniture in the room) that the picture *qua* fact represents. The nonstructural features (e.g., the items of furniture) are represented by the patches of paint.

> 2.13   In a picture objects have the elements of the picture corresponding to them.
>
> 2.131   In a picture the elements of the picture are the representatives of objects.

We may say then that, for Wittgenstein, a picture is a fact composed of elements (patches of paint). The elements represent the objects, and the fact that the elements are arranged in the way they are represents the fact that the objects are so arranged in reality.

We are now in a better position to understand how an elementary proposition can represent or picture a state of affairs. I spoke of elementary propositions as mere series, or lists, of names. I did so because that is what, at first glance, they might seem to be. But in fact Wittgenstein never speaks of an elementary proposition as being a mere series of names; on the contrary, he says it is a "nexus, a concatenation, of names" (*T* 4.22). He makes his meaning quite clear in the following passage.

3.141(1)   A proposition is not a medley of words.—(Just as a theme in music is not a medley of notes.)

(He might have added: just as the picture is not a mere medley of patches of paint.) This way of putting the matter is meant to stress the fact that there is a definite relationship among the component names, that they are arranged in a certain way that is significant—just as the patches of paint in a picture are arranged in a certain way that is significant. Consider the proposition that *aRb*—that "object *a* has or bears a relation *R* to object *b*" or, more simply, "*a* bears *R* to *b*." This proposition is expressed by the propositional sign '*aRb*.' The propositional sign, unlike the proposition, is composed of actual ink marks and is thus much more like an ordinary picture than is the proposition itself. Let us, then, concentrate on the propositional sign for the moment. (The question of the relationship between the proposition and the propositional sign, and of the relationship between both of them and a picture, will be discussed later.) A propositional sign, like a picture, is a fact.

3.14   What constitutes a propositional sign is that in it its elements (the words) stand in a determinate relation to one another.
A propositional sign is a fact.

It is only because it is a fact that a propositional sign can represent something, can be used to describe a state of affairs.

3.142   Only facts can express a sense, a set of names cannot.

In this passage, Wittgenstein once again denies that a mere list of names (or set of names, as he puts it here), can possibly say anything. He states the essence of his view of the matter in the following well-known passage.

3.1432   Instead of, "The complex sign '*aRb*' says that *a* stands to *b* in the relation *R*," we ought to put, "*That* '*a*' stands to '*b*' in a certain relation says *that aRb*." [4]

[4] To make the passage conform to my own practice in this book, I have substituted single quotation marks for the translators' double ones around '*aRb*,' '*a*,' and '*b*.' Hence I also changed their single quotation marks to double ones around the two propositions cited in this passage.

Although Wittgenstein is concerned in this passage with a propositional sign's *saying* something, the passage is, nevertheless, relevant to the mere *representing* or *depicting* of something. We can therefore adapt it to our present purposes by formulating the following variation.

(V)   Instead of, "The complex sign '*aRb*' represents (pictures) the state of affairs of *a* standing to *b* in the relation *R*," we ought to put, "*That* '*a*' *stands to* '*b*' *in a certain relation represents* (pictures) the state of affairs *that aRb.*" [5]

In reading *T* 3.1432 and (V), one must be careful to bear in mind a certain important convention, namely, that to form the name of a word, one places single quotation marks around the word itself. When we want to refer to the man Socrates, we write his name, as in "Socrates is ugly"; this is a statement about the man Socrates. On the other hand, when we want to refer to his name, we write his name inside single quotation marks, as in " 'Socrates' contains eight letters"; this is a statement not about the man Socrates, but about his name. It would make no sense whatever to say "Socrates contains eight letters"; for Socrates is a man and a man cannot be said to contain any number of letters. It would make no sense either to say " 'Socrates' was a Greek philosopher," for 'Socrates' is a word and there are no words that can sensibly be said to be philosophers. A natural extension of this convention is that to form the name of a sentence, one writes the sentence inside single quotation marks. Thus, one can say "The sentence 'Socrates is ugly' contains three words."

Keeping these conventions in mind, we see that (V) can be paraphrased as follows: we ought not to assert that the sentence '*aRb*' represents the state of affairs that object *a* stands in relation *R* to object *b* (i.e., the state of affairs that *aRb*); rather, we should assert that the fact that the sign '*a*' stands in a certain relation to the sign '*b*' represents the state of affairs that *aRb*. Suppose that *R* is the relation of *being to the right of*. Then (V) says: do not assert that the sentence '*a* is to the right of *b*' represents the state of affairs that *a* stands in that relation to *b* (i.e., that *a* is to the right of *b*); rather,

---

[5] In point of fact, Wittgenstein's real view is that it is not the propositional *sign* in itself that says something and is a picture of, or represents, something; the proposition is what says something and is a picture. But for the moment the inaccuracy involved in both *T* 3.1432 and our variation (V) on it can be ignored; it will be corrected later, p. 86ff.

assert that the fact that the sign 'a' stands in a certain relation to the sign 'b' represents that a is to the right of b. It would not be positively wrong to assert that the sentence 'a is to the right of b' represents that a is to the right of b, but it would be misleading. It would be misleading because it would make it look as though the sentence *qua* string of words represents the situation, whereas Wittgenstein's point is that it is only the sentence *qua* fact that does so. The sentence, in so far as it can be used to represent a situation, *is* a fact (*T* 3.14[2]); the second way of putting the matter makes this point explicit, whereas the first way obscures it. That is one reason why the second way is superior to the first.

Wittgenstein's claim, in short, is this: it is not the sentence (propositional sign) *qua* mere string of words that represents a situation, any more than it is the patches of paint in an ordinary spatial picture, *qua* a mere set of patches, that represents the situation depicted; rather, just as it is the fact that the patches are arranged in the way they are that represents the situation, so it is the fact that the words of the propositional sign are related in the way they are that represents the situation described. According to our present conventions, in order to represent the state of affairs that aRb, the three signs must be arranged in the following special way: first, the 'a' is written; then immediately following it on the same line comes the 'R'; and immediately following it on the same line comes the 'b.' To the left of the 'a' and to the right of the 'b' there are spaces. It is the fact that the three signs are written in this particular way that represents the state of affairs that aRb; not the mere set of signs itself.

There are several possible ways of characterizing the fact that the three signs are written in the way they are; Wittgenstein chooses to say that it is the fact that 'a' stands in a certain relation to 'b.' [6] The relation he means is that of being written just before an 'R' which is followed immediately by the 'b,' all three being written on the same line and with spaces at either end. It is the fact that the two signs 'a' and 'b' are thus related that represents the state of affairs that aRb. There is nothing which absolutely requires that the relation be that particular one; it is a matter of convention. The convention

[6] He might have said instead that it is the fact that 'a' and 'b' stand in a certain relation to 'R,' or the fact that 'a' stands in a certain relation to 'R' and 'b,' for example. I will discuss in the next chapter his reason for spurning these other possible ways of characterizing the relevant fact and for choosing the one he does.

might have arisen that if you want to represent that *aRb,* you write
the separate signs one over the other, like this: $\begin{array}{c}a\\R\\b\end{array}$. Or, it might all
have been done by colors: e.g., if you wanted to represent that *aRb,*
you would write '*a*' in black, followed by '*b*' in red, whereas if you
wanted to represent that *aSb,* you would write '*a*' in black followed
by '*b*' in green. So the actual relation which relates the signs '*a*'
and '*b*' is purely conventional; nevertheless, it is still the fact that '*a*'
stands in a certain relation—conventional though it may be—to '*b*'
that represents the state of affairs that *aRb.*

What does a propositional sign (*qua* fact) depict according to this
view? As in the case of the picture, the fact that the elements of a
propositional sign are related in the way they are represents only
the structural feature of the situation represented.

> 3.21   The configuration of objects in a situation corresponds to
> the configuration of simple signs in the propositional sign.

Of course a state of affairs really is itself just a structure; but it is a
structure of elements (viz., objects). The elements of an elementary
propositional sign stand for the elements of a state of affairs, and the
fact that the sign elements stand in a certain relation to one another
represents the fact that the objects stand in a certain relation to one
another in the state of affairs (*T* 4.0311).

We have been speaking so far of propositional signs. We must now
bring what we have said to bear on propositions themselves. Wittgenstein says that it is propositions—and primarily elementary propositions—that are pictures of reality. (See, e.g., *T* 4.01[1], 4.021,
4.03[3] and [4], 5.156[4].) He never speaks of propositional signs
as being pictures. (But see *T* 4.012.) This seems at first glance to be
incorrect. We normally think of a picture as consisting of marks or
patches of paint arranged in some way on paper or canvas or whatever, and since a propositional sign also consists of marks arranged
in a certain way on paper (or sound waves in air, or whatever), it
would seem to be the propositional sign rather than the proposition
which ought to be called a picture. This point can be made more
specific. Consider the following possible objection to Wittgenstein's
view.

"A proposition cannot be a picture, because it includes a reference
to a perfectly definite situation (viz., the situation it describes),

whereas a picture does not. This can be shown by considering this picture.[7]

Picture A

Let us assume that this is a picture of Socrates (on the left) fencing with Plato (on the right). A picture does not, in itself, refer to the specific situation it depicts; it does not, because it does not in itself make any connection between its components and the things or persons that they are meant to represent. In Picture A, for example, the left-hand figure is supposed to represent Socrates, but the figure itself does not tell us so. The figure does not make any connection between itself and Socrates. On the contrary, it could represent any number of people other than Socrates; and even if it were an exact likeness of Socrates, the connection between it and Socrates would still not be made, because any number of other people, actual or nonactual, might look just like Socrates, and the figure might represent one of them. Something in addition to the figure itself is required, then, before it can represent Socrates and no one else. The same can be said of the right-hand figure, and of the picture as a whole. So Picture A, by itself, does not depict the situation of Socrates, and no one else, fencing with Plato, and no one else; and in this a picture is unlike a proposition, which describes a situation involving perfectly specific objects. Therefore it must be the propositional sign, if anything, that is a picture, and not the proposition that is so."

Wittgenstein would agree with one main point of this objection, but he would deny one of its assumptions and hence also the conclusion of the argument. He would agree that a group of marks on paper, such as those labeled 'Picture A' above, do not in themselves depict a specific situation; they do so only if the marks are correlated with certain things or persons. When the left-hand figure is correlated with Socrates, and the right-hand figure with Plato, then, and only then, may the marks become a picture of Socrates fencing with Plato, rather than of someone other than Socrates fencing with someone other than Plato. The complex mark is not a picture

---

[7] This picture is borrowed from Wittgenstein (see *NB,* p. 7).

of a certain part of reality until the components making it up are correlated or coordinated with certain definite elements of reality— until they are "linked" with or "touch" reality.

2.1511   *That* is how a picture is attached to reality; it reaches right out to it.

.   .   .

2.1514   The pictorial relationship consists of the correlations of the picture's elements with things.

2.1515   These correlations are, as it were, the feelers of the picture's elements, with which the picture touches reality.

But how are the metaphorical notions of "reaching right out" and of "feelers" to be interpreted literally? That is, what is it for the picture's elements to be *correlated* with things? Wittgenstein says nothing explicit on this matter. At one point in the *Notebooks 1914-1916,* he speaks of the correlation as something that *I*—presumably the drawer of the picture—*do*.

> *By* my correlating the components of the picture with objects, it comes to represent a situation and to be right or wrong. [*NB,* entry for 26.11.14.]

And elsewhere in the *Notebooks,* he speaks of my—presumably the speaker, writer, or thinker of a proposition—correlating names with things (entries for 30.5.15 and 15.6.15, for example). The correlation is something that I do, then. But *how* do I do it? From what Wittgenstein says in *T* 3.11 (discussed below, p. 93ff.), I suspect he thought that correlating elements of a picture (or proposition) with elements of reality is a mental act—the mental act, namely, of meaning or intending the former to stand for the latter. For example, in Picture A, I mean (or intend) the left-hand figure to represent Socrates and the right-hand one to represent Plato, and this is how I correlate the elements of the picture with those of reality. (This mental act of meaning or intending apparently did not strike the early Wittgenstein as being in any way mysterious or puzzling, but the later Wittgenstein found it so and many pages of the *Philosophical Investigations* are devoted to a discussion of it.)

Wittgenstein thus agrees with, and even insists on, one main point of the objection. Nevertheless, the objection, he would say, is based on a false assumption which vitiates its conclusion that the propositional sign, and not the proposition, is a picture of reality. The relevant assumption is that the ink marks labeled 'Picture A' constitute in themselves a *picture*. This assumption is false, he would say; the marks themselves cannot be a picture. Suppose they appeared on a piece of paper by complete chance; for example, suppose that a pen rolled around on the paper at random, pushed by the wind, and those marks just happened thereby to be produced. Or suppose that exactly similar marks were emblazoned on a rock by a bolt of lightning. Marks thus caused, though they be exactly like the marks labeled 'Picture A,' do not in themselves constitute a picture. If we were to see the lightning produce these marks on the rock, we would not cry out "Look at this picture," much less "Look at this picture of two men fencing," much less "Look at this picture of Socrates fencing with Plato." Rather, we would say something like: "How extraordinary are these marks which the lightning has made. They look just like a picture of two men fencing." Hence it is not certain ink marks in themselves which make something a picture; the marks must be made by some conscious agent. In addition, it must not be the case that the agent makes them wholly unintentionally or accidentally. If, in walking, a man happens to kick over and spill a bottle of ink, forming picture-like marks on the floor, he has not produced a picture. *Full* intention is not, however, required; a man can absent-mindedly make some marks on paper, as in doodling, and what he draws may well be a picture.[8]

What, then, *does* constitute a picture? We must be careful in answering this question if we are to avoid confusion. There are really three points to be noted. The first point, just made, is this: a group of marks is never, in itself and no matter how produced, a picture of any sort. This being granted, it is important to distinguish further

---

[8] There is an interesting exception to what I have just said. If certain marks M are the results of a direct causal process P involving an object O, then M may be a picture of O despite the fact that they were not made by any conscious agent. For example, if a camera drops on the floor and the shutter clicks, thus producing an image of a chair on the film, the developed print is without doubt a picture of that chair. The assistance of man-made objects (e.g., film and camera) is not even necessary; thus, if for several years at a certain time each day, sunlight streams past a tree and then through a narrow cave opening, and if marks resembling the tree are thereby etched on the opposite cave wall, they will, I think, constitute a picture of the tree. So I must say that in order for marks M to constitute a picture, they must either be produced (1) by a direct causal process like P or (2) not wholly unintentionally by a conscious agent. I shall henceforth ignore pictures of type (1) and talk as though all pictures were of type (2), since the point of my discussion is to develop the analogy between pictures and propositions, and there are no propositions, I take it, that are anything like pictures of type (1).

between a picture (or mere picture) and a *representational* picture, a picture which depicts—or is "of"—something. In order for a group of marks to be a picture of any sort, they must be made not wholly unintentionally by an agent, but a person can make a picture without making a representational picture. An abstract expressionist painter puts patches of paint on the canvas, and he does so intentionally; but although what he produces is a picture, it is not necessarily a picture *of* anything (nor, of course, is it meant to be). The second point to be noted, then, is this: in order for a group of marks to be not only a picture, but a representational picture, it is necessary that the agent make the marks not wholly unintentionally and, in addition, that the marks resemble, within certain unspecifiable limits, the sort of thing depicted.

(The limits doubtless vary with at least [a] the ease or difficulty of making marks that resemble different kinds of thing, [b] the purpose of the picture, and [c] the ability of the drawer. To consider just [c]: the degree of resemblance we require in the case of a child's drawing is less than that required of an adult's. Notice, in this regard, that the kind of resemblance which any ordinary—i.e., spatial—representational picture has to what it depicts is richer and more familiar than the kind which, according to the picture theory of propositions, a proposition has to the situation it describes. To be sure, there must be a one-to-one correspondence between the elements of an elementary proposition [names] and those of the state of affairs it describes [objects], and the two must have the same "logical form"; but the proposition need not look very much like the state of affairs. And the names certainly do not look at all like the objects they mean; for example, in the elementary proposition aRb, 'a', since it is complex [i.e., made up of several lines], cannot look like the simple object a.)

There is yet a further, and for our purposes more important, distinction to be made; namely, that between a mere representational picture and a representational picture which depicts certain definite individuals. Let us call the latter type of picture a *definite* representational picture. Picture A, for example, would be a mere representational picture if it simply depicted two men fencing; it would be a definite representational picture if it depicted Socrates fencing with Plato, or Descartes fencing with Spinoza, or whatever. The third point, then, can be put as follows: in order for a group of marks to

tical in structure with a fact without picturing it. Just as we require someone to make the splotches with intent to paint the scene, so we require someone to make the marks with intent to express the fact.[12]

A note in passing: by saying that a proposition is a propositional sign in its projective relation to the world, Wittgenstein deliberately avoided the view that a proposition is a strange sort of shadowy entity. G. E. Moore, speaking of the Wittgenstein of the early 1930's, says:

> One chief view about propositions to which he was opposed was a view which he expressed as the view that a proposition is a sort of 'shadow' intermediate between the expression which we use in order to assert it and the fact (if any) which 'verifies' it.[13]

There is just the propositional sign (or sentence-token) and the situation which the proposition describes; the proposition is not a third entity over and above the propositional sign and the situation; it is just the propositional sign in a projective relationship to the situation described.

The propositional sign is given its projective relation to the world by "thinking its sense."

3.11   We use the perceptible sign of a proposition (spoken or written, etc.) as a projection of a possible situation.
            The method of projection is to think out the sense of the proposition.[14]

There are, to be sure, rules or laws of projection for language (*T* 4.0141) and it might be thought that it is these which make a propositional sign the projection of a particular possible situation. In a way, they do, but Wittgenstein would presumably claim that the statement of such a rule or law is just a shorthand way of saying that people habitually project one into the other by thinking the sense of the proposition.

In the previous chapter, it was noted that by 'the sense of a

---

12 John Wisdom, "Logical Constructions," Part I, *Mind,* XL, No. 158 (April 1931), 207.

13 Moore, "Wittgenstein's Lectures in 1930-33," Part I, *Mind,* LXIII, No. 249 (January 1954), 13 (*Philosophical Papers,* p. 265).

14 I take exception to the translators' 'think out' and translate '*das Denken des Satz-Sinnes*' as 'thinking (or to think) the sense of the proposition.' This admittedly involves me in a Germanism with no obvious meaning in English, for we, in English, never speak of "thinking the sense of a proposition." But at least I presently give this phrase a sense, and, I think, a plausible one; whereas I am not sure what could be meant by "thinking *out* the sense of a proposition."

proposition,' Wittgenstein most often meant the situation which the proposition describes. On this primary use of the phrase, the act of thinking the sense of a proposition becomes the act of meaning the propositional sign to represent a determinate situation. Suppose the proposition is an elementary one and hence that the corresponding situation is an atomic one—i.e., a state of affairs. Thinking the sense of such a proposition involves two things: (a) meaning or intending each name of the propositional sign to denote one specific object and no other (that is, correlating the name with its object), and (b) meaning that those objects are arranged in such and such a manner, that the state of affairs has such and such a structure (T 2.032).[15] So when I write down or utter an elementary propositional sign, and at the same time mean by it that certain definite objects are arranged in a certain definite way, I am thereby thinking the sense of the proposition, and using the propositional sign to express the proposition. It is only in this way that it is a picture of one specific state of affairs and no other.

Wittgenstein also uses the expressions 'sign' and 'symbol' to mark the distinction between the propositional sign and the proposition. A propositional sign is made up of signs, but a proposition is made up of symbols.

3.31(1)   I call any part of a proposition that characterizes its sense an expression (or a symbol).

3.318   Like Frege and Russell I construe a proposition as a function of the expressions contained in it.

A symbol is a sign together with its relation to the object it denotes—i.e., a sign referring to the object which it means or, again, a sign in its projective relation to an element of reality. Thus an elementary proposition, for example, is made up of elementary symbols; in this case, the constituent symbols are *names*. So an elementary proposition consists of names (T 4.22), whereas an elementary propositional sign (sentence) consists of elementary signs (words) (T 3.14). And

---

[15] Although T 2.1514 makes no mention of it, Wittgenstein would presumably want to claim that something analogous to act (b) is required in the case of ordinary pictures—such as Picture A—as well. In order for the marks comprising Picture A to represent Socrates fencing with Plato, it is not enough for the drawer to correlate the figures with Socrates and Plato (act [a]); he must also mean that they are *fencing* with one another. The same marks could, after all, be used to depict Socrates and Plato merely standing next to one another in those attitudes—or to depict any number of other situations involving Socrates and Plato. (See *PI*, p. 54, remark [b].)

just as a proposition is a propositional sign in its projective relation to a situation, so a name may be called an elementary sign in its projective relation to an object—it is an elementary-sign-meaning (or standing-for)-an-object.[16]

A sign consists of ink marks on paper, or sound waves in the air, or something of the sort, i.e., something perceptible.

3.32   A sign is what can be perceived of a symbol.

We cannot, however, actually see a symbol; for although we can see the sign, we cannot see what it is about the sign that makes it a symbol. We cannot see its relation to its object, and that is an essential part of its being a symbol. It is possible that one sign may represent two different symbols.

3.321   So one and the same sign (written or spoken, etc.) can be common to two different symbols—in which case they will signify in different ways.

Thus, for example, the sign 'bank' can mean either a sloping mound or an institution for handling money. A picture, on this view, is a symbol, and the marks or patches of paint *by themselves* merely a sign, merely "what can be perceived of [the picture]."

At this point, the following objection might be raised: "The main reason Wittgenstein had for supposing that a proposition is a picture of a situation was that a person can immediately *see* from looking at (or hearing) the proposition what situation it describes. But now he says that a proposition is a complex *symbol,* and all we can actually see (hear) of a symbol is a sign—and it certainly is true that all we can see (or hear) of a proposition is a sentence, or propositional sign. But how can I immediately 'read off' what situation a proposition describes from looking at (or hearing) it, if it is impossible to look at (hear) it at all?"

Of course, one can see (or hear) only the propositional sign, and not the proposition. (At the beginning of this chapter, it is true, I spoke as if one *could* see [hear] the proposition itself, but that was an inaccurate way of speaking which I indulged in only for the sake of simplicity of exposition, before the nature of pictures was discussed.) But the proposition *is* the propositional sign in its projective relation to the world (*T* 3.12); therefore, since I know the rules of

16 But see *T* 3.202 and 3.26 where names and simple or elementary signs seem to be identified *tout court.*

projection for language, I can immediately tell, from seeing (or hearing) the propositional sign, which proposition is being expressed and, what comes to the same thing, which situation is being described, just as a person who knows the rules of projection for music can immediately tell, from seeing the musical signs (the written notes of the score), which sequence of sounds is represented thereby.

But now we must return to the question which perplexed us at the beginning of this chapter. We began by supposing that an elementary proposition is a mere set, a series, of names; and we wondered how a series of names could possibly *state,* or *say,* anything. We soon discovered, however, that according to Wittgenstein an elementary proposition is not a series of names at all, but rather a "nexus, a concatenation, of names" (*T* 4.22), and, what is more, a picture of a state of affairs. Wittgenstein now maintains that a proposition says something just because it *is* a picture.

4.03(4)   A proposition states something only in so far as it is a picture.

But this contention merely plunges us into a new difficulty; for whereas a proposition does, indeed, say something, a picture, it would seem, does not. How, then, can a proposition say something just in virtue of *being* a picture? Let us express this latest difficulty in the form of the following objection.

"A proposition cannot be a picture, because a proposition says or asserts something, whereas a picture does not. Consider once again Picture A of Socrates fencing with Plato. The picture does not in itself *say* that Socrates is fencing with Plato. Suppose someone wanted to tell another person that Socrates is fencing with Plato; it would not be enough simply to hold up Picture A. In order to assert that Socrates is fencing with Plato, a person would have to hold up the picture and, in addition, nod or do something to indicate that this is the way things are. A person could assert that Socrates is not fencing with Plato by holding up the same picture and shaking his head or doing something to indicate that this is not the way things are. Something else, then, in addition to the picture itself, is needed before anything is actually *said.* Wittgenstein himself saw this during the period of the *Notebooks 1914-1916:*

> Can one negate a *picture?* No. And in this lies the difference between picture and proposition. The picture can serve as a proposition. But in that case something gets added to it which brings it about that

now it *says* something. In short: I can only deny that the picture is right, but the *picture* I cannot deny. [*NB*, entry for 26.11.14.]

A picture can be used to assert something, but it does not of itself assert anything; in this, it is unlike a proposition."

This objection has a point, but there is not much force to it. It would be a matter of convention if a person's holding up of an ordinary picture (like Picture A), while nodding his head, should mean that he is asserting something (in the case of Picture A, that Socrates is fencing with Plato).[17] The convention need not be even as complicated as that; the mere holding up of a picture could mean that the person asserts that this is the way things are (that *t*), and the mere holding up of a picture upside down could mean that the person asserts that this is the way things are not (that not-*t*). (So the objection is wrong in denying this possibility.) We can go still further, and make the analogy between ordinary pictures and propositions closer yet; there could easily be the convention that the very act of making a picture should mean that the artist asserts that *t*, and that the very act of making a picture with a large 'x' across it should mean that the artist asserts that not-*t*. I take it that something very like this sort of convention actually exists in the case of propositions. The very act of making the sounds '*aRb*' ('$\sim$[*aRb*]') or producing the written marks '*aRb*' ('$\sim$[*aRb*]') in a certain way does in fact mean that the person is asserting that *aRb* (that $\sim$[*aRb*]). (In fact, it is just because there *is* such a convention that Russell's and Frege's assertion sign or "judgment stroke" is quite superfluous. See *T* 4.442[2].) And on Wittgenstein's thesis that a proposition is a kind of picture, this convention reads that the very act of making the sounds or producing the written marks '*aRb*' ('$\sim$[*aRb*]') means that the person is asserting that *this,* namely the way things are pictured by the proposition, is the way things are (are not). Given this convention, it makes little difference whether we say that it is the fact that the proposition is uttered (or written) which does the asserting or whether we say that the proposition itself does it. Wittgenstein usually speaks in the latter way.

4.022(2)   A proposition *shows* how things stand *if* it is true. And it *says that* they do so stand.

17 Throughout this discussion, we must assume, of course, that the person who holds up the picture also performs acts analogous to the acts (a) and (b) discussed on p. 94. (See also note 15, p. 94.) This is tantamount to saying that we must assume the picture to be a definite representational one.

And so there is no real incompatibility between, on the one hand, the fact that according to our present conventions concerning ordinary pictures they are not in themselves deemed to say anything and, on the other hand, Wittgenstein's thesis that propositions, which do say something, are pictures.

Hence the following two doctrines of Wittgenstein are perfectly consistent:

(a) a proposition is a picture of a situation, and
(b) a proposition states, or says, something.

Wittgenstein, however, as we have seen, goes much further than merely defending the consistency of (a) and (b). He claims that (b) is true only because (a) is true.

4.03(4)   A proposition states something only in so far as it is a picture.

But in urging this, Wittgenstein seems to go too far; in our mythical flag language (p. 76), each flag says something, but none is evidently a picture of anything. In *T* 4.03(4), the emphasis ought, perhaps, to be placed on the 'something' rather than the 'states'; it might be read "A proposition states *something definite* only in so far as it is a picture." Since Wittgenstein thought that a proposition can point beyond itself and describe a certain definite situation only by being its picture, he thought a proposition has a *content,* says *something definite,* only by being a picture. That this consideration lies behind *T* 4.03(4) is shown by the two remarks which immediately precede it.

4.03(2)   A proposition communicates a situation to us, and so it must be *essentially* connected with the situation.

4.03(3)   And the connexion is precisely that it is its logical picture.

But the flags point beyond themselves and "communicate a situation to us" without being pictures; and so there is no warrant, as far as I can see, for the extreme claim of *T* 4.03(4).

*   *   *

Wittgenstein thought it absolutely certain that a proposition is a picture of reality. All that can possibly be said, therefore, is that certain picturable situations exist or do not exist. If there is no possibility of picturing a given situation, then it cannot be asserted that that situation either exists or does not exist: no conceivable proposition can say anything about it. From this, together with Wittgenstein's doctrine that all propositions are analyzable into elementary propositions, it follows—or so he apparently thought—that all propositions must be *truth-functions* of elementary propositions. Why should this be thought to follow? Well, to say that a proposition is analyzable into a group of elementary propositions is to say that whatever the proposition asserts can be asserted by that group of component elementary propositions. In fact, what the proposition asserts *is* just what they assert, since they express what it really means. The elementary propositions are (logical) pictures of states of affairs, according to the picture theory of propositions. Hence what the original proposition asserts must be assertable by a group of (logical) pictures of states of affairs. But what can a group of pictures be made to assert? Suppose I had a group of three real pictures—i.e., ordinary spatial pictures, like Picture A—call them pictures A, B, and C. Let us say that they depict states of affairs A, B, and C respectively. What complex situations could possibly be depicted and asserted to exist or not to exist using these pictures and no others? There are lots of possibilities. For example, I could put picture A on a line next to picture B, and then put picture C with a large 'x' through it next to B. This might depict the situation in which state of affairs A and state of affairs B exist, and state of affairs C does not exist. Hence, putting a picture on a line signifies asserting that the state of affairs that it depicts exists; putting one picture down next to another signifies asserting that both states of affairs depicted exist; drawing an 'x' through a picture signifies "negating" the picture. Proceeding in this way, I can depict many other situations and assert their existence, as may easily be seen. Additional procedures could be introduced to deal with still more complicated situations. For example, if I wanted to depict a situation in which it is not the case that both states of affairs A and B exist, I could put picture A next to picture B and draw one large 'x' through both of them. In this way, more and more complicated situations could be depicted—especially if one is allowed to use a given picture more than once in constructing a single compound picture. Nevertheless, there might seem to be a definite limit to the sort of situation that can thus be depicted. For example, it might be thought that I cannot depict any such alleged situation as that if state of affairs A exists, then states of affairs B and C must necessarily exist. Nothing I could do with pictures A, B, and C would evidently yield a picture of that supposed situation, or allow me to assert its existence. It would seem that all I can assert is that one or more of the basic states of affairs (A, B, and C) exist or do not exist, or that some compound situation which consists of some combination of the existence or nonexistence of these basic states of affairs exists or does not exist.

Since elementary propositions are pictures too, it would seem that the same must be said of them. Thus, if proposition M is analyzable into elementary propositions p, q, and r, then M must assert one of the following (symbolizing conjunction—i.e., 'and'—by ' · '): $p \cdot q \cdot r$; $\sim p \cdot q \cdot r$; $\sim (p \cdot q) \cdot r$; and so on through the many possibilities. In building molecular propositions out of elementary ones, negation and conjunction [18] seem to be the only operations I can use. For what else can I do with the elementary propositions—the logical pictures—but assert one (put a picture down on a line), assert the negation of one (draw an 'x' through one and put it down on a line), or assert some conjunction of these (put pictures down next to one another on a line), or assert or deny some more complicated conjunction of combinations of these? If p, q, and r, then, can be formed into molecular propositions only by using the operations of negation and conjunction (or their equivalents), then proposition M must itself really be a molecular proposition so formed. What proposition M says must be sayable by p, q, and r, because it is analyzable into them. But since negation and conjunction are truth-functional operations, proposition M is a truth-function of the elementary propositions p, q, and r. And since all nonelementary propositions are analyzable into elementary propositions, all nonelementary propositions are truth-functions of elementary propositions. Finally, since an elementary proposition is a truth-function of itself (T 5[2]), all propositions are truth-functions of elementary propositions. That this be so is demanded by the picture theory of propositions, according to Wittgenstein.

If the above reconstruction of Wittgenstein's line of thought is correct, he argued from the premises that elementary propositions are pictures of reality and that all propositions can be analyzed into elementary propositions, to the conclusion that all propositions are

---

[18] Or their equivalents. All the truth-functional operations can be defined in terms of negation and conjunction alone. And these two, in turn, can be defined in terms of Sheffer's one basic operation of simultaneous denial.

truth-functions of elementary propositions. I agree that the argument can look plausible, that those premises can make the conclusion seem inevitable; but I think the argument is not in fact valid. It may be plausible to suppose that, if you are given as materials to construct molecular propositions nothing but pictures (namely, the elementary propositions), the only operations that you could possibly perform on them would be the truth-functional ones described above. These may appear to be, if you like, the "natural" ones. But they appear to be the sole natural ones only if a certain kind of analogy guides our thinking about the matter. For example, if we conceive of the process of constructing molecular propositions on the analogy with building a jig-saw puzzle out of separate pieces, or on the analogy of constructing a comic strip out of individual pictures, then the operations of conjunction and negation may strike us as the only possible ones. But they are not. It may seem somehow natural and unavoidable that putting one picture down next to another signifies conjunction, and that putting a cross through a picture signifies "negating" the picture, but in fact it is purest convention. And there is no necessity whatever to limit ourselves to just these two conventions. For example, we could agree that rotating one picture 45 degrees clockwise and then putting another beside it signifies causal necessity; if the first state of affairs depicted exists, then it causally necessitates that the second one exists. It is no good objecting that we never observe any such connection and hence cannot know what the sign for it means, because we do not observe conjunction or negation either. In Wittgenstein's view, none of the logical constants denotes anything (*T* 4.0312[2]). Therefore, even if we grant to Wittgenstein that elementary propositions are pictures of the states of affairs they describe and that all propositions can be analyzed into elementary propositions, it by no means follows—as he evidently thought it did—that all propositions must be *truth-functions* of those elementary propositions. An extraordinary number of molecular propositions, it may be allowed, can be built up from elementary ones by using nothing but truth-functional operations. But there is no guarantee that all propositions can be so built up, because there may be other operations that are not reducible to (definable in terms of) truth-functional ones.

There is another line of thought, not involving the picture theory of propositions, which may have led Wittgenstein to the view that all propositions must be truth-functions of elementary ones. If we grant that there are elementary propositions and that they assert the existence of states of affairs, then it might seem plausible to suppose that if we had all the elementary propositions and knew which were true and which were false, we would know all that there is to know. The point can be put in the following way. Suppose there are only three possible states of affairs and that they are described by the elementary propositions p, q, and r, respectively. Then the actual world must be one of eight possible worlds—one of those described by the following propositions: $p \cdot q \cdot r$; $\sim p \cdot q \cdot r$; $p \cdot \sim q \cdot r$; $p \cdot q \cdot \sim r$; $\sim p \cdot \sim q \cdot r$; $p \cdot \sim q \cdot \sim r$; $\sim p \cdot q \cdot \sim r$; $\sim p \cdot \sim q \cdot \sim r$. If there are only three possible states of affairs, then either all three exist, or only one of the three exists, or only two of the three exist, or none of the three exists. The above eight propositions represent all those possibilities and hence one of them must be a complete description of the actual world.

4.26   If all true elementary propositions are listed, the world is completely described. A complete description of the world is given by listing all elementary propositions, and then listing which of them are true and which false.

Suppose all three states of affairs exist, so that it is the first of the eight molecular propositions above that describes our world completely. Then $p \cdot q \cdot r$ is the most that can be truly said; it expresses the sum total of all knowledge and wisdom. All that can be truly said other than the utterance of this all-encompassing description is something short of it. For example, one could assert the elementary propositions singly or doubly, or one could assert a disjunction of them, such as "either p or q." (Disjunction is another truth-functional connective, and can be defined in terms of negation and conjunction.) Thus, all that can be truly said in this admittedly meager world is some truth-function of the elementary propositions, and hence every true proposition must be such a truth-function (and so, therefore, must every false proposition, since any false proposition is the negation of a true one).

But the foregoing argument is invalid, for it rests on an assumption that begs the question. The argument asserts the following:

(A) If one knows which elementary propositions are true and which are false (i.e., which states of affairs exist and which do not), one knows all that there is to know.

Thesis (A), however, rests on the assumption

(B) There are no real connections whatever among states of affairs.

For suppose (B) were false, and that there *were* some real connections among states of affairs. Then there would be something else to be known besides which states of affairs exist and which do not— namely, what connections hold among which states of affairs and what connections do not hold among them. Thus, for example, suppose that a state of affairs k is causally related to another state of affairs l. If I knew only that k and l exist, I would not know everything there is to know. For that, I would have to know also that k and l are causally connected. The possibility of such connections cannot be ruled out a priori. So if (B) is false, (A) is also false; and (A) therefore rests on assumption (B). But since to assume (B) is tantamount to granting the conclusion that all propositions are truth-functions of elementary propositions (once it is admitted that all propositions are analyzable into elementary propositions), the argument rests on the question-begging assumption (B). At the very least, (B) stands in need of some sort of defense, some backing up, and this is not provided in the *Tractatus*. Without such independent support, there seems to be no reason for accepting it, and therefore no reason to accept any argument, like the one in the previous paragraph, which assumes it to be true.[19]

I conclude that Wittgenstein has not established that all propositions are truth-functions of elementary ones, nor do I see how that thesis could be established. He may have reasoned in one or both of the invalid ways just discussed, or he may have simply assumed the thesis uncritically; but in any case, he has not given us any good reason for thinking it true. I want to stress that my objections have no force against a view which says: let us assume that the truth-functional operations are the only ones there are and let us see how far we can get in constructing all molecular propositions out of elementary ones, using just those operations and no others. That is, my objections

[19] Wittgenstein himself remarks in "Notes on Logic" (1913):

"It may be doubted whether, if we formed all possible atomic propositions, 'the world would be completely described if we declared the truth or falsehood of each' . . ." (*NB*, p. 98). But the doubt expressed here may only have been whether some such statement as "And these are all the atomic propositions" might not also be required, in addition to the atomic propositions themselves. This is, in fact, quite likely the case, for two pages later Wittgenstein says:

"Whatever corresponds in reality to compound propositions must not be more than what corresponds to their several atomic propositions. Molecular propositions contain nothing beyond what is contained in their atoms: they add no material information above that contained in their atoms." (*NB*, p. 100.)

would not in any way impugn Wittgenstein's view of truth-functions *conceived as a program;* they have force only against that view when it is conceived as being the only possible one there could be. But that is clearly the way Wittgenstein in fact thought of it. There is not the air of a program or any envisaging of possible alternatives in the flat statement:

5(1)   A proposition is a truth-function of elementary propositions.

The consequences of Wittgenstein's doctrines that all propositions are analyzable into elementary propositions, and are in fact truth-functions of them, are of the highest importance. But before these consequences can be fully set forth, we must know more about elementary propositions. Since they consist entirely of names, and names denote objects, we must try to determine, if we can, what sorts of things Wittgenstein thought objects to be. In the next chapter, this attempt is made.

5   Objects

The main topic of this chapter will be the nature of Wittgenstein's objects. I wish to approach this topic by a consideration of his notion of a tautology, which I shall introduce by a brief discussion of some points of logic.

Logic

There are any number of different ways of classifying propositions; one of these ways results in the following classes:

(1) Those propositions which cannot under any describable circumstances be false; i.e., those of which it is inconceivable that they should be false.

(2) Those of which, although they may happen to be true (or false), it is conceivable that they should not be so; i.e., that they should be false (or true). Circumstances can be specified under which they would have to be called false (or true).

(3) Those which can never under any describable circumstances be true; i.e., those of which it is inconceivable that they should be true.

The first is the class of necessarily true propositions or, for short, of necessary propositions or necessary truths; the (true) propositions of logic and mathematics are usually placed in this group. The second is the class of empirical propositions; and the third, the class of necessarily false propositions.

105

Although logic may sometimes have been considered somewhat less impressive than mathematics, it has baffled philosophers as much as mathematics has, and for the same sort of reasons. How, for example, can a person know with absolute certainty that a given principle of logic is true, has always been true, and will always be true? Does reason have some mysterious power of apprehending relationships between timeless, changeless entities? Wittgenstein realized that his theory of truth-functions gave him a powerful new way of interpreting the truths of logic, a way that would dispel the mystery surrounding them.

Wittgenstein held, as we know, that a compound proposition is a truth-function of its constituent propositions. (It is irrelevant here that he thought the ultimate truth-functional constituents were elementary propositions.) By assigning truth-values to its constituents, the truth-value of the proposition is uniquely determined. There are usually several possible such assignments; the number will depend on the number of different constituent propositions. Consider, for example, the proposition S_1 which is the following truth-function: $\sim p \cdot (p \vee q)$. This has the form of a conjunction of two parts, $\sim p$ and $(p \vee q)$. A conjunction is true if, and only if, all its components are true. (See p. 57.) The component $(p \vee q)$ is a disjunction, and is read "either p or q." A disjunction is true if, and only if, one or more, and perhaps all, of its members are true. Thus if I say "Sam is back or Joe has gone," what I say is true if it is true that Sam is back, but false that Joe has gone; it is also true if it is true that Joe has gone, but false that Sam is back; and it is also true if it is true both that Sam is back and Joe has gone. What I say is false only if it is false that Sam is back and also false that Joe has gone.[1] As for the negation $\sim p$, it is true if p is false, and false if p is true. These three notions of negation, disjunction, and conjunction can be defined by means of truth-tables which display these characteristics (see next page). 'T' and 'F' stand for 'true' and 'false' respectively. The truth-table presents all the possible assignments of truth-values to the component propositions, and shows what the resultant truth-value of the whole proposition is in each case. Consider the disjunction $p \vee q$, for example. There are only four possibilities: both p and q are

---

[1] This is the so-called *in*clusive 'or.' There is also an *ex*clusive sense of 'or' which is such that "p or q" is false if p and q are both false and also if p and q are both true; otherwise it is true. It is the exclusive sense that is intended in such remarks as "Either he is in Finland or he is in America."

I. Negation

p	$\sim p$
T	F
F	T

II. Disjunction

p	q	$p \vee q$
T	T	T
T	F	T
F	T	T
F	F	F

III. Conjunction

p	q	$p \cdot q$
T	T	T
T	F	F
F	T	F
F	F	F

true; p is true, q is false; p is false, q is true; both p and q are false. These four assignments are represented in the four lines of the truth-table, and the table shows what the truth-value of the whole disjunction is in each case. In the third line, for example, it shows that if p is false and q is true, the whole disjunction is true, and in the fourth line it shows that if both p and q are false, the whole disjunction is false.

A larger truth-table can easily be constructed to show how proposition S_1 comes out under the various possible assignments of truth-

1	2	3	4	5
p	q	$\sim p$	$p \vee q$	$\sim p \cdot (p \vee q)$
T	T	F	T	F
T	F	F	T	F
F	T	T	T	T
F	F	T	F	F

values to its constituents p and q.[2] (Column 3 is obtained from column 1 by using truth-table I, that for negation. Column 4 is obtained from columns 1 and 2, by using truth-table II, that for disjunction. Column 5 is obtained from columns 3 and 4, by using truth-table III, that for conjunction.) It can be seen that proposition S_1 turns out to be true under only one assignment of truth-values to its ultimate constituents, p and q—namely that of falsity to p and truth to q. Under all other possible assignments, proposition S_1 is seen to be false. Since all propositions are, according to Wittgenstein, truth-functions of their constituent propositions, the truth-value of any

[2] I distinguish the *components* of proposition S_1—namely, $\sim p$ and $(p \vee q)$— from the constituents of it—namely, p and q.

proposition is theoretically determinable in a similar way; we need only know the truth-functional structure of the proposition we are interested in.

Most propositions, presumably, will be like proposition S_1; that is, they will turn out to be true under some assignments of truth-values to their constituents, and false under others. But Wittgenstein saw that there is an interesting possible special case—namely, that of a proposition which turns out to be true under all assignments of truth-values to its constituents, that is, in which the right-hand column of its truth-table contains nothing but 'T' 's. Such propositions Wittgenstein calls *tautologies*. It can be seen that the notion of a tautology gives a clear meaning to the characterization of necessary propositions —that is, class (1), mentioned at the beginning of this chapter. The characterization given there expresses a very obscure idea: what, for example, does it mean to say that a proposition "cannot, under any describable circumstances, be false"? What kind of 'cannot' or 'impossible' is that? What is the source of this impossibility? And what precisely can be meant by 'conceivable'? Might not other people, who are more talented than ourselves, be able to conceive it? These, and other questions, are at once given clear and definite answers by Wittgenstein's theory of tautology. Necessary truths are all tautologies; and this simply means that no matter what assignment of truth-values is made to its constituent propositions, it always receives, as a result, the assignment "true." This gives at last a clear and unequivocal meaning to phrases like 'cannot under any circumstances be false' and 'inconceivable that they should be false,' which have traditionally been used in characterizing necessary truths. And it also gives, of course, a clear meaning to 'necessary.'

The truths of logic, like all necessary truths, are tautologies.

6.1   The propositions of logic are tautologies.

Consider, for example, the law of excluded middle, of which the following schema is an instance: $p \vee \sim p$. The truth-table for this schema shows that it is a tautology.

p	$\sim p$	$p \vee \sim p$
T	F	T
F	T	T

Similarly, all logical propositions, according to Wittgenstein, can be shown to be tautologies. This view, if correct, would clear away some of the mystery which has traditionally surrounded the truths of logic. For example, we need no longer wonder at the fact that we can know the truth of logical propositions with certainty, and can be absolutely sure that they will never be refuted. These things are no longer surprising when it is seen that logical propositions are tautologies. Given the definitions of the logical constants (i.e., the truth-functional connectives) in their respective truth-tables, the truth of a logical proposition follows at once —automatically, as it were. It does not matter what the truth-values of the constituent propositions are; a mechanical application of the definitions of the logical constants, as given in their truth-tables, always yields a truth-value of true for logical propositions. They are true, we might say, solely in virtue of the definitions of the basic logical constants, as given in their truth-tables. And, since we ourselves set up those truth-tables in the first place, it is not surprising that we can know ahead of time that logical propositions must always be true. There is no need whatever to postulate a special realm of timeless logical objects which reason can somehow miraculously perceive; what we need is much less exalted than that—namely, the truth-table definitions of the logical constants.

Wittgenstein's view of logical propositions as tautologies thus explains, in a clearly intelligible way, the kind of knowledge we have of them; but it secures this advantage at a price—though a price that most empiricists would be only too happy to pay. The price is this: since they are tautologies, the truths of logic are completely empty, for tautologies "say nothing."

6.1   The propositions of logic are tautologies.

6.11   Therefore the propositions of logic say nothing. . . .

(See also *T* 4.461[1], 5.142, and 5.43[2].) Logical propositions are not substantial truths about special Platonic entities, nor about any other kind of entity; they are not substantial truths at all. Our knowledge of them is secured precisely by demoting them to emptiness. A tautology is empty and says nothing, simply because it is true under all conditions, no matter what reality is like. When we utter a non-empty or substantial proposition—such as "It is raining"—we make a certain claim about reality, and thus stick our neck out to some extent. A proposition of that sort claims that the facts are such-

and-such; the facts might not be so, and hence the proposition might be false. But a tautology makes no such claim. It is true no matter what the facts are, and hence it says nothing.[3]

4.461(5) (For example, I know nothing about the weather when I know that it is either raining or not raining.)

Unlike a non-empty proposition—such as "It is raining," which describes a certain situation, which picks out a certain possible aspect of reality and asserts that it exists—a tautology describes no situation at all. It does not describe a certain possible situation and assert that it exists, for if it did, it might turn out to be false; and then it could not be a tautology. Since the situation which a proposition describes is its sense, and a tautology describes no situation, we may say that it lacks sense (*T* 4.461[3]). This is not to say, however, that a tautology is nonsensical, as whatever the sentence 'Raining not raining is is' expresses is nonsensical.

4.4611 Tautologies . . . are not, however, nonsensical. They are part of the symbolism, just as 'O' is part of the symbolism of arithmetic.

Wittgenstein has a great many interesting and important things to say in the *Tractatus* about logical inference, mathematical truths, and indeed about all aspects of logic. But as they are of interest primarily to the specialist in logic, I shall not discuss them further. The main reason I had for discussing the topic at all was to introduce Wittgenstein's notion of a tautology.

Particulars

In the range of types of proposition, tautology is at one extreme; it corresponds to class (1) of the three listed at the beginning of this chapter. A tautology is always true; it leaves the entire field of facts completely open, since it is true no matter what the facts are. The opposite extreme in the range of propositions is that corresponding to class (3), which Wittgenstein calls contradiction. A contradiction,

---

[3] Wittgenstein held that although tautologies *say* nothing, they nevertheless *show* certain very general features of the world, namely its "logical properties," the "scaffolding of the world." This doctrine, which I find exceedingly obscure, is discussed in *T* 6.12-6.13.

like any proposition, is a truth-function of its constituent propositions; but instead of coming out true under all possible assignments of truth-values to its constituents, as does a tautology, it comes out false under all such assignments. An example of a contradiction is the proposition: $(p \lor q) \cdot \sim p \cdot \sim q$. That it is a contradiction can be seen from the following truth-table.

p	q	$(p \lor q)$	$\sim p$	$\sim q$	$(p \lor q) \cdot \sim p \cdot \sim q$
T	T	T	F	F	F
T	F	T	F	T	F
F	T	T	T	F	F
F	F	F	T	T	F

A contradiction completely closes down the entire field of facts; it leaves no possibilities open. "It is raining" closes the possibility that it is not raining. Similarly, "It is not raining" closes the possibility that it is raining. Hence "It is raining and it is not raining," a contradiction, closes both possibilities and hence leaves none open. It is thus at the opposite extreme from a tautology, which leaves all possibilities open. A contradiction, then, like a tautology, describes no fact and hence also lacks sense (T 4.461[3]), although it is not nonsensical either (T 4.4611). Wittgenstein says that neither a contradiction nor a tautology is a picture of reality.

> 4.462(1)   Tautologies and contradictions are not pictures of reality. They do not represent any possible situations. For the former admit *all* possible situations, and the latter *none*.

If we compare an ordinary empirical proposition to a picture painted on a canvas, then a tautology is like a bare, untouched canvas and a contradiction is like a canvas that has been completely blacked out. (See Anscombe, *An Introduction to Wittgenstein's Tractatus*, pp. 75-77, for an interesting discussion of this point.)

Tautology and contradiction, then, are the two extreme cases of propositions (T 4.46, 4.466[4]). We can know a priori that the one is true and that the other is false. But most ordinary propositions are in class (2) of our classification. They describe some definite situation and assert that it does or does not exist; hence we cannot tell a priori whether they are true or false, but must investigate or experiment or do something else to find out which is the case. It will prove convenient to have a title for these propositions, which, although significant, are neither tautologies nor contradictions. Let us call them *descriptive* propositions, since they, unlike tautologies and contradictions, describe some definite situation. But now an important question faces us. What kind or kinds of situation do descriptive propositions describe? In one sense, the answer has already been given; ultimately, they all describe states of affairs. But this answer does not take us very far. For states of affairs are composed entirely of objects, and we do not yet know, apart from their being simple, what sort of things objects are. We must now investigate this matter.

The first thing to be determined is whether, according to Wittgenstein, the class of objects includes only particulars or whether it also includes universals. This is a basic issue, for though it is difficult to characterize the differences precisely, particulars and universals are radically different sorts of things. Although they are complex and hence do not qualify as objects in Wittgenstein's technical sense, such things as Socrates, my easy chair, and the Empire State Building are particulars. They are unique individuals whose existence is limited to a certain portion of space and time. Not all particulars are both spatial and temporal, however; mental particulars, such as the mental images which someone entertains, exist through a certain stretch of time and are therefore temporal, but there is no place at which they exist ("*Where* is your image?" is a question with no answer) and so they are not spatial in any straightforward way. (It does not seem possible for there to be a particular which is spatial but not temporal.) Of particulars, it makes no sense to say that they can be attributed to—in the sense of being predicated of—anything, nor to say that there are numerous instances of them scattered throughout the world. But these things can be said of universals. In the statements "The jars are red" and "John is to the left of Joseph," a property and a relation—i.e., two universals—are attributed to (predicated of) particulars. And universals are just the sort of thing that may have many instances dispersed throughout time, or throughout space and time. They are repeatables, and they include mainly properties (redness, squareness) and relations (being next to, talking to). There are, for example, many different instances of redness—namely, all the red particulars that there are, such as tomatoes and fire engines. Particulars can be reproduced or copied, but not instanced.[4]

There is a difference of opinion among the commentators of the *Tractatus*. Copi [5] and Anscombe hold that, for Wittgenstein, objects include particulars only, while Stenius [6] maintains that they include particulars, simple properties, and relations. Russell, in his "The Philosophy of Logical Atomism" (1918), claims to be expounding Wittgenstein's ideas, and he says that "logical atoms" include both particulars and universals.[7] But as Russell readily admits, he had not discussed these ideas with Wittgenstein since 1914, nor had he any way of knowing what Wittgenstein's views were after that date. Since Wittgenstein's views might well have changed between 1914 and the writing of the *Tractatus,* we must look to this work itself for an answer to our question.

There is no doubt that Wittgenstein thought that some objects are particulars; the question is only whether or not he thought that certain simple properties and unanalyzable relations are objects also. The question arises in the context of elementary propositions and states of affairs: In the propositions Fa (e.g., a is red) and aRb (e.g., a is next to b)—assuming for the moment that they are elementary propositions—do the signs 'F' and 'R,' like the signs 'a' and 'b,' designate objects? Are the property of redness and the relation of being-next-to, objects? Are simple particulars in some way related to simple universals to form states of affairs, or are states of affairs formed by the configuration of simple particulars only?

My opinion is that, in the *Tractatus,* Wittgenstein holds that only simple particulars are objects, that all states of affairs are produced by the combination of simple particulars only. There is, admittedly, one passage in the *Tractatus* in which Wittgenstein refers to a prop-

[4] There are, or may be, things which prove embarrassing for this formulation of the distinction between particulars and universals—as I suppose there are for any such formulation. The number five, it might be argued, is a particular (although most philosophers would disagree); and yet it is not in space or time, it can be predicated of a group of particulars ("The Nobel prize winners on campus are five—i.e., five in number"), and it can be instanced. Again, God is surely a particular despite the fact that in many religions He is held to exist outside space and time. And what is one to do with space and time themselves?

[5] Irving M. Copi, "Objects, Properties, and Relations in the *Tractatus,*" *Mind,* LXVII, No. 266 (April 1958), 145-65; and his review of E. Stenius' *Wittgenstein's Tractatus, The Philosophical Review,* LXXII, No. 3 (July 1963), 382-90.

[6] Erik Stenius, *Wittgenstein's Tractatus,* pp. 61-63.

[7] Russell, "The Philosophy of Logical Atomism," Marsh volume, p. 179.

erty (viz., a shade of blue) as an object; it is T 4.123(2). But in the very next paragraph, he seems to warn us that he is here speaking loosely, that this use of the term 'object' is an odd, atypical one. Everything else he says in the *Tractatus* seems to me to require that objects be particulars, that they not include universals.

First, consider the sort of thing Wittgenstein says about objects and states of affairs.

2.01   A state of affairs (a state of things) is a combination of objects (things).

2.0272   The configuration of objects produces states of affairs.

2.03   In a state of affairs objects fit into one another like the links of a chain.

2.032   The determinate way in which objects are connected in a state of affairs is the structure of the state of affairs.

These ways of talking are appropriate only to particulars, and not to particulars and universals together. It is perfectly natural to speak of two particulars being combined or configured or connected, and so on; but it is linguistically odd to speak of an individual *a* being combined or connected with the universal "redness," or of an individual *b* and the universal "roughness" fitting into one another like the links of a chain. It is difficult to know what could possibly be meant by such expressions.

Second, Wittgenstein says:

4.24(1)   Names are the simple symbols: I indicate them by single letters ('*x*,' '*y*,' '*z*').

But '*x*,' '*y*,' and '*z*' are individual variables, not relation or property ones; their values are '*a*,' '*b*,' '*c*,' and so on—i.e., the names of particulars, not of universals.

Third, if simple universals were objects, they would presumably be named by signs of such forms as '*f*' and 'ϕ' in fx and $\phi(x,y)$, and each proposition of these forms would then be, like any elementary proposition, "a nexus, a concatenation, of names" (T 4.22). But Wittgenstein denies that propositions of the forms fx and $\phi(x,y)$ are concatenations of names; he asserts that they are rather *functions* of names (T 4.24[2]). What this means will be discussed shortly; it is enough for now simply to note that a function of names is different from "a nexus, a concatenation, of names."

Of the several arguments Copi presents in his *Mind* article (cited above in note 5) to show that Wittgenstein considered objects to include only particulars and not universals, I find the following to be the most convincing. It is based on a passage in which Wittgenstein states that

> 2.0231   . . . It is only by means of propositions that material properties are represented—only by the configuration of objects that they are produced.

The term 'material properties' is clearly meant as a contrast to 'formal properties.' Copi proceeds to show that objects can be neither formal nor material properties, and hence cannot be properties at all. In the *Tractatus,* formal properties are identified with logical properties, as in the following passage:

> 6.12(1)   The fact that the propositions of logic are tautologies *shows* the formal—logical—properties of language and the world.

Formal properties are not objects, because whereas objects can be represented (*T* 3.22, 3.221, 4.0312[1]), logical properties cannot.

> 4.12(2)   In order to be able to represent logical form, we should have to be able to station ourselves with propositions somewhere outside logic, that is to say outside the world.

> 4.121(1)   Propositions cannot represent logical form: it is mirrored in them.

(Why this is so will be explained later, but the cogency of the argument can be seen independently of any such explanation.) Material properties, however, cannot be objects either; for they are produced only by the configuration of the objects (*T* 2.0231), and an object, being simple, cannot be formed by the configuration of other objects.[8] Since neither formal nor material properties are objects, no properties are objects.

There are still other considerations which support the view that only particulars are objects. For example, consider a passage with which we are already familiar:

> 3.1432   Instead of, "The complex sign '*aRb*' says that *a* stands to *b* in the relation *R*," we ought to put, "That '*a*' stands to '*b*' in a certain relation says *that aRb*." [9]

Surely one reason that Wittgenstein puts the matter in just this way is that he wishes to distinguish sharply the signs '*a*' and '*b*,' which are the

---

[8] This sentence deviates from Copi's account. For his way of defending the point, see *Mind* (April 1958), 162.

[9] See note 4, p. 83.

names of objects, from the sign '*R*.' He thus wishes to deny that '*R*' is the name of an object. He made this quite explicit in "Notes on Logic":

> Symbols are not what they seem to be. In "aRb" "R" looks like a substantive but it is not one. What symbolizes in "aRb" is that "R" occurs between "a" and "b." Hence "R" is *not* the indefinable in "aRb." [*NB*, p. 99.]

Presumably, then, no relations among objects are themselves objects. Indeed, it can be shown that the view that objects include relations runs into a hopeless difficulty. In a state of affairs, Wittgenstein tells us, objects are configured.

2.0272   The configuration of objects produces states of affairs.

If relations were objects, then when two or more particulars were configured so as to form a state of affairs, the configuration—i.e., the relation amongst the particulars—would be another object, over and above the particulars. But then we would be lost in an infinite regress, for if the configuration of two or more particulars were an object, then presumably the configuration of the particulars and the first configuration would also be an object, and the configuration of the particulars and the first and second configurations would also be an object, and so on ad infinitum. The regress could be stopped by denying that relations can be configured with particulars, but this seems to be entirely *ad hoc* once relations are made objects. The easier and more natural thing to do is simply to deny that relations are objects in the first place, and this is undoubtedly what Wittgenstein did.[10]

There was a time when Wittgenstein thought that objects included universals; for he wrote in the *Notebooks 1914-1916,*

> Relations and properties, etc. are *objects* too. [*NB*, entry for 16.6.15.]

This sentence might be thought to show that he believed the same thing when he wrote the *Tractatus,* but I would judge that it counts rather in favor of the opposite view. Particulars and universals are radically different kinds of things; therefore, if a philosopher uses a single term (viz., 'object') to apply to both, he would certainly

---

[10] After having written this passage, I was happy to find my reasoning supported by Copi's review of Stenius' book, in which he presents a very similar argument. See *The Philosophical Review* (July 1963), 385-87.

inform us of the fact. In the *Notebooks 1914-1916*, when he did think that both universals and particulars were objects, he said so explicitly. The very fact that he makes no such statement in the *Tractatus* is a good sign that he no longer holds his earlier opinion.

In light of the foregoing considerations, there can be little doubt that Wittgenstein, in the *Tractatus*, thought that all objects are simple particulars. Only one argument of Professor Stenius' in support of the contrary view seems to have any force at all (see his *Wittgenstein's Tractatus*, p. 62). It is based on what appears to be a mistake—namely, on the idea that an object's (i.e., a simple particular's) having a property (e.g., an object a's being red) is a matter of its being configured with a universal (e.g., of a's being configured with the universal "redness"). He argues that since a state of affairs is a combination of objects, in the state of affairs of object a's being red, redness must be counted as an object—for there is no other object for a to be combined with. And since redness is a universal, some objects must be universals.

Stenius makes an unwarranted assumption in his argument; namely, that an object's having a property must be a matter of its being configured with a *universal* (viz., the property in question). But there is no need to make this assumption. Wittgenstein could perfectly well have held that an object's having a property is not a matter of its being configured with a universal, but rather of its being configured with other simple particulars. He could have maintained, for instance, that to say that a is red is not to say that a is configured with the universal "redness," but rather to say that a is configured with b, c, and d—all simple particulars—in a certain way. And since there is a lot of additional independent evidence that Wittgenstein thought that objects include only particulars, one is justified in supposing that he actually viewed the matter in this way.

Our interpretation, moreover, fits in perfectly with other things Wittgenstein says. Let us examine one important doctrine that illustrates this fact, Wittgenstein's account of properties. In order to understand what Wittgenstein says about properties, we must first see what he means by the "form" of an object.

Objects are configured or combined to form states of affairs, and I take it that this means that they are related in some way, that a relation holds among them. Wittgenstein says further that, for any given object, the types of configurations that it can enter into—the types of states of affair it can occur in—are definitely limited. Certain objects can be combined in just so many ways, other objects can be combined in another group of ways. The different ways that objects can be configured are the *forms* of the objects. Two objects that can occur in the same kind of configuration are said to be of the same form. For example, suppose that object *a* can be configured with other objects in a way that results in its being colored, then it doubtless cannot also occur in a different kind of configuration whereby it has a certain pitch and timbre. The sort of object that can have a color (perhaps a speck in a person's visual field) is not the same sort of object that can have a pitch (perhaps a note that a person hears). A speck in one's visual field cannot have a pitch, and a note cannot have a color. If object *b* can be configured with other objects in a way that results in its being colored, it has in that respect the same form as object *a*. And color is thus one form of objects; it is one basic mode of configuration of an object with others that yields its coloredness.

> 2.0251   Space, time, and colour (being coloured) are forms of objects.

At this point, my exposition seems to encounter one or two difficulties. First, I have just spoken of an object's having a color; but Wittgenstein says:

> 2.0232   In a manner of speaking, objects are colourless.

Second, we know that according to Wittgenstein objects are simple (*T* 2.02), but how can an object be simple if it has properties? In light of their simplicity, must we not say that objects have no properties whatever, that they are bare, unqualitied particulars? No. Wittgenstein speaks over and over again about the properties of objects —e.g., in *T* 2.01231, 2.0233, 4.023, 4.123—and so he certainly thought that they have properties. But then (a) how can they be simple? And (b) what sense can be made of Wittgenstein's remark that objects are colorless?

I think that on our interpretation of Wittgenstein satisfactory answers can be given to these questions. Let us consider question (a) first. If we try to think what is involved in a thing's having a quality or property—e.g., in its being red—we would, I suppose, come naturally to the view that there must be some complexity in the thing. For we can distinguish, on the one hand, the property of redness and, on the other, the thing itself minus that property (the thing itself with its other properties). This natural way of thinking —viewing each property of an object as an inherent ingredient in it—is what tempts one to assume that, if Wittgenstein speaks of objects' having properties, he cannot at the same time consistently claim that they are simple. But on our interpretation of Wittgenstein, he rejects this natural way of looking at the matter. According to that interpretation, an object's having a property P does not mean that it has an inherent ingredient P, but rather that it is configured with other objects ($a, b, c,$ etc.) in a certain way. An object's having a property just *is* its being so configured with other objects; and for this, there is no evident need for it to be complex. So on our interpretation, the simplicity of objects is perfectly consistent with their having properties.

Our interpretation also gives an immediate answer to question (b); it gives at once a plausible meaning to Wittgenstein's remark that objects are colorless. What he meant was that an object *in itself* has no color. An object of the appropriate sort has a color only when configured with other objects; but in itself, that is to say in isolation from other objects, it has no color, is colorless. Wittgenstein prefaces his remark about the colorlessness of objects with the words "in a manner of speaking" (T 2.0232); he does this because we ordinarily apply the term 'colorless' to something that might have a color, but just happens to be colorless—for example, to clear water, gin, or alcohol. But when Wittgenstein says that objects (i.e., simple particulars) are colorless, he is not using that term in this ordinary sense; for objects, in themselves, do not just happen to lack a color, as water or gin does—rather, it is unthinkable that, apart from a configuration with other objects, an object have a color.

Philosophers have sometimes construed relations as being properties of individuals; they have thought, for example, that in the propositions "Socrates is taller than Plato" and "Socrates is the teacher of Plato," properties (that of being taller than Plato and that of being the teacher of Plato) are attributed to the subject, Socrates. We see that Wittgenstein, however, takes the opposite line and reduces properties to relations: an object's having a property (e.g., being red or being C-sharp) is a matter of its being related (i.e., configured) with other objects in a certain way.

The properties of an object can be divided into two kinds: its essential properties and its accidental properties—that is, those which it must have in order to be the kind of object it is and those which it just happens to have. Wittgenstein calls the former its internal properties and the latter its external properties (*T* 2.01231, 4.123[1]). Suppose a speck in one's visual field is an object. Its being colored, its having some color or other, is one of its internal properties (*T* 2.0131[2]), while its annoying (or delighting) the person who sees it would doubtless be one of its external properties.

As we have seen, Wittgenstein also speaks of the forms (or logical forms) of objects: objects are said to have, or to be of, certain (logical) forms, and this is contrasted with the material properties that objects may have. (*T* 2.0231.) The forms [11] of an object determine what its internal (essential) properties are. For example, if an object is of the form *color,* this means that among its internal properties will be that of having some color or other, that of having some degree of saturation or other, and so on. Suppose that a speck in one's visual field is an object of this form; its having some color or other will then be one of its internal properties. But its having the determinate color it has—e.g., red—will be one of its material properties. A speck in a visual field has a certain form—it has some color or other —but a sound in an "aural field" has another, different form—it has some pitch or other. The forms of an object thus determine its internal (i.e., essential) properties, while its material properties must be counted among its external properties; for a speck in a visual field must have some color or other, but it need not be red—it could just as well have been blue or orange.

> 2.0131(2)   A speck in the visual field, though it need not be red, must have some colour: it is, so to speak, surrounded by colour-space. Tones must have *some* pitch, objects of the sense of touch *some* degree of hardness, and so on.

If we combine these distinctions with the doctrine that an object has (actual or material) properties only by being actually configured with other objects, several consequences follow. First,

> 2.0141   The possibility of its occurring in states of affairs is the form of an object.

If object *a* (like a speck in someone's visual field) is of such a form that it must have some color or other, then there is a limited range of states of affairs in which it can occur. Certain states of affairs in this range correspond to *a*'s being red; that is, if any of those states

---

[11] I am assuming that an object may be of more than one form—for example, both colored and spatial.

of affairs existed, *a* would be red. Other states of affairs in this range correspond to *a's* being blue, green, yellow, and so on. The possibility of its occurring in just this range of states of affairs is *a's* form (or one of its forms). When one of these possible states of affairs exists— when, that is, *a* becomes *actually* configured with certain other objects—then it thereby acquires a determinate material property.

> 2.0231   The substance of the world *can* only determine a form, and not any material properties. For it is only by means of propositions that material properties are represented— only by the configuration of objects that they are produced.

If one tries to strip away in thought all the properties of an ordinary complex thing such as a desk or an apple, in an effort to conceive of the essential thing in itself, he is doomed to frustration, for nothing remains. To have any sort of idea of a desk or an apple, one must think of it as having certain properties. The same is true of Wittgenstein's objects. But since an object's having properties is a matter of its being either configurable or actually configured with other objects to form states of affairs, one can only think of an object as a constituent of states of affairs. An object's having *internal* properties is the possibility of its being configured with other objects, that is, the possibility of its occurring in states of affairs; and its having *material* properties is its actually being so configured, its actually occurring in existent states of affairs (atomic facts). Therefore, an object cannot be thought of in isolation, apart from any consideration of the states of affairs in which it can or does occur.

> 2.0121(4)   Just as we are quite unable to imagine spatial objects outside space or temporal objects outside time, so too there is *no* object that we can imagine excluded from the possibility of combining with others.
>
> 2.0121(5)   If I can imagine objects combined in states of affairs, I cannot imagine them excluded from the *possibility* of such combinations.

So, to know an object is just to know what sorts of configuration it can enter into.

> 2.0123   If I know an object I also know all its possible occurrences in states of affairs.
> (Every one of these possibilities must be part of the nature of the object.)
> A new possibility cannot be discovered later.

(Notice that this way of putting it suggests that to know an object, one need only know its internal properties. Wittgenstein makes this perfectly explicit in the next section.

> 2.01231   If I am to know an object, though I need not know its external properties, I must know all its internal properties.

This strikes one as odd; one would naturally suppose that although to know what *sort* of object a given object is requires only a knowledge of its internal properties, nevertheless this would not be sufficient to know the object itself as an individual.)

At this point, the following question arises: Can an object exist with only internal (essential) properties and no material ones? In other words, can there exist an object that occurs in no *existent* state of affairs? Wittgenstein's view seems to be that every object must occur in some existent states of affairs. The latter claim is implicit in this passage.

> 2.0131(1)   A spatial object must be situated in infinite space. . . .

(See also *T* 2.0131[2].) This claim seems plausible, for we think it perfectly natural to suppose that if an object exists, it must have some *actual* properties. And yet the apparent possibility that it might have none can haunt us. Why could it not be the case that although a certain object, *a, could* be configured with other objects, it nevertheless happens not to be configured with any? Wittgenstein offers no answer to this question. Perhaps the answer lies in the fact that if there *were* such an object, *a,* there would evidently be no way of specifying *which* object it was. The simplest facts about it would be negative facts, such as $\sim(aRb)$, $\sim(aSc)$, and so on. But if there are infinitely many objects (a possibility which must be left open), then no object can be identified in this purely negative way. There are an indefinite number of objects of which it is true that they do not bear R to b, S to c, and so on. So if there were such an object *a,* nothing could *in fact* be said about it; for there would be no way of saying *which* object one was talking about. One could not even state the hypothesis itself—the hypothesis, namely, that there exists an object which occurs in no existent state of affairs. For the question "Of *which* object is this true?" is in principle unanswerable. But an hypothesis which cannot even be stated is no hypothesis at all. (It is no good replying: "But one is not forced to specify a particular object as the one of which this is true. He need only claim that there is *some* object or other of which it is true." This reply will not do, for the analysis of the hypothesis "There is some object which occurs in no existent state of affairs" must mention individual objects, in some such manner as this: "*a* occurs in no existent state of affairs, or *b* occurs in no existent state of affairs, or. . . ." And then my objection, since it applies in full force to each of these disjuncts and since the disjunction gives the real meaning of the analyzed hypothesis, counts also against that hypothesis itself.)

It is the nature of an object, one might say, to occur in certain states of affairs. It is the nature of all objects of one given form to be able to occur in the same range of possible states of affairs, and of all objects of another given form to be able to occur in another range of possible states of affairs, and so on. Hence, two objects of the same form (two specks in a visual field, for example), apart from their external properties (the redness of one and the blueness of the other) are indistinguishable from one another. Being simple, they can have no intrinsic or internal complexity by which they might differ; and since they have exactly the same nature, there can be nothing to distinguish one from the other, apart from their external properties.

> 2.0233   If two objects have the same logical form, the only distinction between them, apart from their external properties, is that they are different.

All objects, as we have just seen, are simple particulars of various forms, which are configured in different ways to produce states of affairs. It follows from this that objects are everlasting. As the configurations change, some states of affairs go out of existence, and new ones come into existence. But it is only the configurations that change, and that come into and go out of existence; the objects, being simple, are changeless, and hence indestructible, and do not either come into existence or go out of existence.

> 2.0271   Objects are what is unalterable and subsistent; their configuration is what is changing and unstable.

Objects, then, must be immortal. In the first place, they are simple, and therefore could not come into being by any sort of coming together of their components, nor be destroyed by any sort of separation of their components—because being simple they have no components. And there is, in the second place, a purely semantic reason why objects must be absolutely permanent. It must always be logically possible to describe the destruction of everything destructible, i.e., of the world as we know it. But this description will, of course, contain names, and what the names denote cannot be destructible—for what the names denote constitutes their meaning, and if that were destroyed, the names would have no meaning and the description, therefore, no sense. Wittgenstein presents the foregoing argument in the *Philosophical Investigations,* although he does not at that later time any longer accept it.

> "What the names in language signify must be indestructible; for it must be possible to describe the state of affairs in which everything destructible is destroyed. And this description will contain words; and what corresponds to these cannot then be destroyed, for otherwise the words would have no meaning." I must not saw off the branch on which I am sitting. [*PI,* sect. 55.]

Wittgenstein also gives a slightly different version of this argument in the *Investigations.* This one deals with the destruction of a single thing, rather than with the destruction of everything.

> It can be put like this: *a name ought really to signify a simple.* And for this one might perhaps give the following reasons: The word "Excalibur," say, is a proper name in the ordinary sense. The sword Excalibur consists of parts combined in a particular way. If they are combined differently Excalibur does not exist. But it is clear that the sentence "Excalibur has a sharp blade" makes *sense* whether Excalibur is still whole or is broken up. But if "Excalibur" is the name of an object, this object no longer exists when Excalibur is broken in pieces; and as no object would then correspond to the name it would have no meaning. But then the sentence "Excalibur has a sharp blade" would contain a word that had no meaning, and hence the sentence would be nonsense. But it does make sense; so there must always be something corresponding to the words of which it consists. So the word "Excalibur" must disappear when the sense is analysed and its place taken by words which name simples. It will be reasonable to call these words the real names. [*PI,* sect. 39.]

Elementary Propositions

A state of affairs is a combination of objects—and hence, a combination of simple, permanent particulars. An elementary proposition, then, must consist of nothing but the names of these particulars, and can be written like this: "*a-b-c-d*" or "*c-d-e.*" But how are such signs to be read? What are they supposed to say? Any such proposition can say several things; "*a-b-c-d,*" for example, might say that *a* is red, or that *a* bears a certain relation to *d,* or that a certain relation connects *a, b, c,* and *d.* But how can the same proposition assert several different things? Wittgenstein answers by saying that elementary propositions like "*a-b-c-d*" are the values of a function for certain arguments.

To see what this means, consider an analogy with mathematics. $x+3$ is a function which has the value 5 for the argument 2, and 7 for the argument 4—i.e., $x+3=5$ if $x=2$, and $x+3=7$ if $x=4$. The concept of a function need not, however, be confined to mathematics. For example, the father of *x* is a function which has the value James Mill (i.e., the father of John Stuart Mill) for the argument John Stuart Mill, and the value Philip of Macedonia for the argument Alexander the Great.

All the functions we have mentioned so far have taken individuals (like James Mill) or perhaps universals (like the number 5, assuming that numbers are universals) as values, but there are also functions which take propositions as values. Examples of such functions are "*x* is blue" (which may be written as "*Bx*"), "*x* is to the left of *y*" (which may be written as "*L(x,y)*" or "*xLy*"), and "*x* is above *y* and below *z*" (which may be written as "*A(x,y,z)*"). When the blanks are appropriately filled, the result is an expression signifying a proposition. For example, the value of the function "*x* is blue" for the argument '*a*' is the proposition "*a* is blue." Such functions are commonly called propositional functions, although Wittgenstein refers to them as propositional variables. (In one place— *T* 3.315—he calls them variable propositions.) Wittgenstein claims that elementary propositions like "*a-b-c-d*" are the values of certain propositional variables or functions. The proposition "*a-b-c-d*" might, for example, be the value for the arguments '*a*,' '*b*,' '*c*,' and '*d*' of the propositional function "*x-y-z-w*"—i.e., where '*x*' = '*a*,' '*y*' = '*b*,' '*z*' = '*c*,' and '*w*' = '*d*.' [12]

---

[12] A given sum, such as $3 + 5 + 6$ may be a value of different functions. For example, it may be the value of the function $3 + x + y$ for the arguments 5 and 6, or it may be rather the value of the function $3 + x + 6$ for the argument 5. In the same way, an elementary proposition like "*a-b-c-d*" may be a value of different propositional functions. It may, for example, be the value of the function "*x-b-c-y*" for the arguments '*a*' and '*d*,' or of the function "*a-b-x-y*" for the arguments '*c*' and '*d*,' or of the function "*x-b-y-z*" for the arguments '*a*,' '*c*,' and '*d*.' All these propositional functions include terms like '*a*,' '*b*,' and '*c*,' i.e., the names of specific objects. I ignore this complicating possibility in the text and confine myself to propositional functions which consist entirely of "variable names," such as '*x*,' '*y*,' '*z*,' and '*w*.'

We may speak of $3+x$ as being a function of x, and of $3+x+y$ as a function of x and y. In the same way, the propositional function "x-y-z-w" is a function of 'x,' 'y,' 'z,' and 'w.' I have been writing propositional functions in the following way: "x-y-z," "x-y-z-w," and so on. But one is not *forced* to use this notation. Just as the mathematical function $x^2+4x-8+xy$ may be abbreviated as $F(x,y)$, so the propositional function "x-y-z-w" can be written as "$R(x,y,z,w)$." Similarly, "x-y" can be written as "$S(x,y)$," and "x-y-z" as "$T(x,y,z)$." This is the notation that Wittgenstein chooses to use.

4.24   Names are the simple symbols: I indicate them by single letters ('x,' 'y,' 'z').
            I write elementary propositions as functions of names, so that they have the form 'fx,' '$\phi(x,y)$,' etc. . . .

There is, in fact, good reason for choosing this new way of writing elementary propositions. Consider the following propositional functions: "x-y," "x-y-z," "x-y-z-w," and so on. If we limited ourselves to just this notation, we could represent only one way in which a given number of objects are configurable; for example, the only way we could represent three objects as being configured would be by writing something of the form "x-y-z." But it is possible that three objects might be configurable in any number of different ways; three objects of one form might be configurable in one way, three objects of a different form in another, and so on. And so we must be able to represent different modes of configuration for a given number of objects. This can be done with a little imagination. For example, we could write not only (a) "x-y-z," but also (b) "$x\ ^{-y}_{-z}$," (c) "$^{"x}_{-y}_{-z}$," (d) "^x_y_z," and so on, each representing a different kind of configuration of three objects. Nevertheless, it is readily apparent that it is far more convenient to write propositional functions in the new, "straight-line" notation; thus, (a) can easily be written as "$R(x,y,z)$," (b) can more conveniently be written as "$S(x,y,z)$," (c) as "$T(x,y,z)$," and so on. As we have seen, Wittgenstein announces in T 4.24(2) that he chooses this latter, "straight-line" notation.

Answers to the questions which puzzled us at the beginning of this section can now be given. We wondered how something like "a-b-c," composed of nothing but the names of objects, could be read, what it could be taken to say. The source of our difficulty was simply that we were unfamiliar with this particular notation. The difficulty disappears when we realize that (1) "*a-b-c*" is the value of some propositional function—let us say, of the function "*x-y-z*"— and (2) that "*x-y-z*" is just an alternative way of writing, say, "*R(x,y,z)*." Since we are familiar with the notation, we understand how something of the form "*R(x,y,z)*" is to be read; it says that objects *x, y,* and *z* are related by the relation *R*. So if *R* happens to be the relation of "being located on the circumference of a circle of radius 3 inches," then "*R(x,y,z)*" says that *x, y,* and *z* are located on the circumference of such a circle. Since "*R(x,y,z)*" is just another way of writing "*x-y-z*," "*x-y-z*" says exactly the same thing. And since "*a-b-c*" is a value of this propositional function for the arguments '*a,*' '*b,*' and '*c,*' it says that *a, b,* and *c* are located on the circumference of a circle of radius 3 inches. Note, however, that since Wittgenstein chooses the "straight-line" notation, he would write not "*a-b-c*," but rather "*R(a,b,c)*."

The propositional function "*x-y-z*" is a function of '*x,*' '*y,*' and '*z,*' and so the most natural alternative way of writing it might thus seem to be "*R(x,y,z)*," as we did in the previous paragraph. But "*x-y-z*" is *also* a function of '*x*' alone, and hence the alternative way of writing it might just as well be "*Fx.*" For example, suppose that if three objects (of the appropriate form) are configured in whatever way is described by "*x-y-z*," this configuration results in *x*'s being red; in that case, we would doubtless want to write "*x-y-z*" as "*Fx,*" where '*F*' designates the property of being red. This explains how "*a-b-c*," a value of the propositional function "*x-y-z*" and hence of "*Fx,*" might say that *a* is red—and Wittgenstein would in fact write it as "*Fa.*"

What I have called the "straight-line" notation—e.g., "*R(x,y,z)*" or "*Fx*"—has obvious advantages over its rival—e.g., "*x-y-z*" or

"*x*
-*y*   But it also has one major disadvantage; it is not so "per-
-*z*."

spicuous" as its rival. For one thing, when one writes something of the form, say, "*R(x,y,z)*," the extra letter '*R*' makes it look as though four objects were configured in the state of affairs, rather than the actual three; but when one uses the former notation and writes something of the form "*x-y-z*," it is evident at once that there are only three objects configured to produce the state of affairs. Again, when we write something of the form "*Fx*," this notation makes it look as though there were only two objects configured in the state of affairs—F (say, redness) and x—whereas in fact there may be three or a hundred.[13] And this may mislead the reader—and has misled, as we have seen, some commentators of the *Tractatus*—into thinking that in addition to simple particulars, the class of objects also includes simple universals (e.g., redness).

It seems, therefore, that propositions written in the forms "$R(x,y,z)$" and "$S(x,y,z)$" are not pictures of the states of affairs they describe to the same extent as propositions written in the forms "x-y-z" and "$x \overset{-y}{} -z$." But is this in fact the case? Here we come to a point on which Wittgenstein's picture theory seems to come to grief. Why is this so? Let us examine the first, more perspicuous, kind of notation. Consider the values of the four propositional functions (a)-(d) (p. 126) for the arguments 'a,' 'b,' and 'c.' These values will be the propositions (a') "a-b-c," (b') "$a \overset{-b}{} -c$," (c') $\overset{\text{``}a}{\underset{-c,\text{''}}{-b}}$ and (d') "$\overset{a}{\underset{c}{b}}$." These are four elementary propositions and must, if Wittgenstein's picture theory of propositions is correct, be pictures of four states of affairs. The question that now arises about each of them is this: (1) Can anyone who knows what objects are denoted by 'a,' 'b,' and 'c' simply read off from the proposition what state of affairs is being described and being asserted to exist—that is, can he tell at once from the proposition itself, without having previously come across it, how, according to the proposition, the objects a, b, and c are supposed to be configured?—or (2) must he rather be told or learn in some other way, for each of these propositions, what kind of configuration of the objects a, b, and c it claims to exist? Let us consider each possibility.

If we admit that (2) is the case, the picture theory is largely vacuous. For what is the force of saying that an elementary proposition is a picture of a configuration of objects, if for each different type of elementary proposition I have to be told or learn by experience *what* sort of configuration of objects is being pictured? If I

---

[13] On the other hand, this very disadvantage is, in another sense, an additional advantage of our "straight-line" notation over its more perspicuous rival. The latter would have to use 100 names to represent a configuration of 100 objects, whereas the "straight-line" notation might need only two or three signs.

cannot read off from a new configuration of names (i.e., a new elementary proposition) what configuration of objects it is supposed to describe, in what sense is the former a picture of the latter? To be sure, once I am told or learn in some other way what sort of configuration of objects the proposition "*a-b-c*" describes, I can then understand all propositions of the same form (e.g., "*d-e-f*"), even though I may never have come across them before. But this is not enough to warrant calling such propositions *pictures* of states of affairs. In music, where everyone will presumably grant that the musical score is a kind of picture of a possible performance, there are general rules of projection which cover all cases; the pupil does not have to learn, one by one, a special way of interpreting each separate arrangement of notes. And where such general rules of projection are lacking, as they are in the present case (2), it is gratuitous to speak of pictures at all.

Wittgenstein would presumably opt for (1), the former alternative (and in *T* 3.315 he seems to be saying so).[14] After all, his main reason for thinking that propositions are pictures is that we can understand a new proposition without having its sense explained to us. But can this alternative possibly be correct? How can anyone who knows what objects are denoted by the names '*a*,' '*b*,' and '*c*' tell, just by looking at the proposition "*a-b-c*," what configuration of those objects that proposition asserts to exist? As far as I can see, there is only one assumption on which this could conceivably be done and even then there would be enormous difficulties. The assumption is that, in all possible states of affairs, objects are configured only spatially, i.e., that all possible states of affairs are *purely spatial* arrangements of objects. In that case, the spatial arrangement of the names in the proposition might conceivably be a picture of the spatial arrangement of the objects in the state of affairs. But the required assumption is a highly implausible one, and Wittgenstein in any case certainly offers no argument in support of it. It seems implausible on the face of it to suggest that in the analysis of all propositions—even those in which there is a reference to time or to mental happenings or to social institutions—one must in every case arrive ultimately at elementary propositions which deal only with spatial arrangements of objects. There does not seem to be any reason for thinking that this might be so.

[14] In "Notes on Logic" (1913), however, a clear preference for the previous alternative was expressed. (See *NB*, p. 98.)

In the end, then, Wittgenstein's picture theory of propositions appears to be indefensible. Either one can or one cannot "read off" from a new kind of elementary proposition what state of affairs it describes; in the latter case, the propositions are not pictures, and in the former case, although they are pictures, one must make an apparently unwarrantable assumption in order to maintain the position.

Observables

Objects, for Wittgenstein, are simple permanent particulars. But can we say any more about them? What is an example of such an object? We know from Malcolm's report (quoted on p. 32) that Wittgenstein considered the question of which things are objects to be an empirical one that he, as a logician, was not concerned with. Yet one can infer further things about them from certain of Wittgenstein's remarks and doctrines. In T 2.0251, he gives us three examples of forms which objects can have—"space, time, and colour (being coloured)." Presumably this means that some (and perhaps all) objects have spatial characteristics, some (and perhaps all) have temporal characteristics, and some (but presumably not all) are colored. From T 2.0131(2), one seems justified in concluding that Wittgenstein considered some objects (namely, tones) to have pitches and others to have some degree of hardness.

These examples suggest that the properties of objects are observable ones. But is this in fact Wittgenstein's view? Let us investigate the matter further. First, I want to say something, very briefly, about the notion of observability.

To begin with, anything that can be perceived with the unaided senses we do not hesitate to call observable. This immediately includes a host of things as observables—things such as tables and chairs; qualities such as redness, squareness, heaviness; relations such as x being between y and z in space, x being larger than y; and odd things such as pains, tickles, shadows, clouds, rainbows, mirror images, and many more.[15] Also naturally included in the class of observables are things and qualities perceivable by the senses with

[15] For the sake of simplicity, I here confine the notion of being observable to that of being directly or immediately observable, and do not include such things as governments and such relations as that of x being the father of y, which are not directly observable, but which may be granted to be definable in terms of things that are. Objects and their properties, if they are observable at all, would clearly have to be directly observable.

the aid of instruments such as the microscope. This group of things shades off into the group of things which cannot be directly perceived but whose various effects can be perceived—for example, particles which make visible traces in a cloud chamber. It is perhaps somewhat arbitrary whether we say that such particles are observable or not; but I think it more natural to say that they are not observable and that we can only observe their effects. If we allow such particles to be observables, we must also allow alleged psychic entities such as the Id and the Ego to be observables, since we can also observe their effects in human conduct—and I take it that no one would be tempted to count the Id and the Ego among observables. There remains, in any case, a vagueness about the limits of the concept: there are instances where we cannot be sure whether something ought to be called observable or nonobservable. At the same time, there are many things which are clearly nonobservable: God, the number 2, the Id. And there are many things which are clearly observable: tables, chairs, colors, shapes.

Are Wittgenstein's objects observables or not? Are his states of affairs observables or not? Before we try to answer these questions, it must be clearly stated that they were not ones with which Wittgenstein himself was in the least concerned. He treats his subject matter quite abstractly; certain considerations about meaning and analysis drove him to the conclusion that there are elementary propositions which describe states of affairs and names which denote simple objects—but the questions of whether these objects and states of affairs are or are not observable were of little, if any, interest to him. Nevertheless, the questions are important, and as Wittgenstein's expressed doctrines immediately raise them, one is justified in discussing them.

It seems clear that Wittgenstein's picture theory of propositions commits him to the view that at least states of affairs are observable. What would a picture of an unobservable state of affairs be like? And what would be the force of saying that an elementary proposition is a picture of a state of affairs, if the latter could not be observed by anyone under any conditions? The whole point of Wittgenstein's picture theory is that it allegedly allows a person to understand a new elementary proposition—to "read off" the state of affairs which it describes and asserts to exist. But if states of affairs are not observable, it is difficult to know what it could possibly be to *understand* an elementary proposition, since the sense of a proposition is the situation it describes—or what it could possibly be to "read off" the state of affairs from the proposition. Wittgenstein must hold, then, that states of affairs are observable. And he evidently did, in fact, hold this. He writes, for example,

> 2.223   In order to tell whether a picture is true or false we must compare it with reality.

An elementary proposition is a picture of a state of affairs; and in order to be able to compare a picture with what it purports to represent, the latter must be observable.

But this does not tell us whether objects themselves are observable. From the fact that states of affairs, which are configurations of objects, are observable, one cannot infer that the objects which are configured are observable. It might be only the configurations that are so. A configuration of atoms, for example, is often observable, but atoms themselves are certainly not directly observable (that is, with the naked eye) and it is conceivable that they should not be observable at all. Let us consider in turn two possibilities: (a) that objects are observables, and (b) that they are not observables.

(a) This is the alternative that has occasionally and quietly been assumed in the present chapter. For example, on p. 120, some objects were said to have colors and pitches, and presumably if something is colored or "sounding," it is *ipso facto* observable. And it does seem as though some of Wittgenstein's central doctrines commit him to this view. "Thinking the sense of a proposition," for example, involves correlating names and objects, and the possibility of such a correlation might naturally seem to rest on the observability of objects. For how could a person who expresses an elementary proposition mean the name '*a*' to designate *that* object, unless the object can be observed? In fact, Wittgenstein's fundamental doctrine that the meaning of a name is the object it denotes (*T* 3.203) appears to commit him at once to the observability of objects. On that doctrine, in order to know the meaning of a name, one has to know the object named, and it is difficult to see how this could be done unless the object were observable.

There is, moreover, some evidence—admittedly not very conclusive—in the *Tractatus* that Wittgenstein did think objects are observable. Consider, for example, this section:

> 5.5561(1)   Empirical reality is limited by the totality of objects. The limit also makes itself manifest in the totality of elementary propositions.

The meaning of 'empirical reality' is not perfectly clear, but one plausible way to construe it is as meaning observable reality; if this is correct, the passage seems to imply that objects are observable.

In spite of these arguments in favor of thesis (a), in the end it seems to me to encounter difficulties that render it untenable. First, how can a simple particular, such as an object is supposed to be, be observable? It is easy enough to understand how certain qualities which one may reasonably grant to be simple, such as redness or roughness, can be observed; but objects are not qualities, or universals of any sort, but rather particulars. Certainly all the observable individuals that one can think of—even the smallest spatial points [16]—are in some sense complex.[17] This problem could be solved if Wittgenstein would allow that by 'simple' he can only mean 'relatively simple' or 'simplest nameable in our language'. But the wording of the Tractatus suggests no such qualification—Wittgenstein evidently meant by 'simple,' 'absolutely simple.' And so the observability of objects involves the sacrifice of their simplicity, and along with it, of their immortality.

Second, it is difficult to understand, on thesis (a), how an object's having a property can be a matter of its being configured with other objects (see p. 117 of the present chapter). If, for example, a speck in one's visual field were an object, what sense could be given to the suggestion that the speck's being configured with other objects yields its having a red color? [18] Apparently, then, thesis (a) must be abandoned, and thesis (b)—that objects are not observables—must, if possible, be embraced.

(b) On this alternative thesis, objects are not observable, although configurations of them, i.e., states of affairs, are. And then no object can have an observable property either—no object can have a color, for example. For if an object were, say, red, it would be an observable, contrary to the hypothesis. (Hence T 2.0232 receives a straightforward interpretation on thesis [b].) So all observable properties are attributable only to complexes; when certain objects are configured in certain ways, this means that the resulting complexes have observable properties. Tables, books, and chairs can be colored and

---

[16] See NB, entry for 25.5.15.

[17] Wittgenstein admits in the Notebooks 1914-1916 that "we have no acquaintance with simple objects" (NB, entry for 24.5.15).

[18] And in T 6.3751(3) Wittgenstein explicitly denies that a proposition which attributes a color to a point in one's visual field can be an elementary proposition.

shaped, on this view, but not Wittgenstein's simple objects.

This second alternative strikes one immediately as being by far the more plausible of the two for Wittgenstein to hold. It does seem to be the case—indeed it seems to be necessarily the case—that only complexes can have observable properties. And much of what Wittgenstein says in the *Tractatus* can easily be accommodated to this view. For example, objects, although simple, can still be said to have properties (nonobservable ones), and the distinction between their internal and material properties can still be maintained: an object's being configur*able* with certain other objects is one of its internal properties, and its being actually configur*ed* with certain others is one of its material properties.

Even *T* 2.0251 can be plausibly interpreted on thesis (b). It says:

2.0251   Space, time, and colour (being coloured) are forms of objects.

This need not be given the interpretation I gave it on p. 118 where, for the sake of clarity of exposition, I was speaking as if thesis (a) were true. It might well mean that if an object were configurable with others so as to yield the coloredness *of a complex,* coloredness would be one of that object's forms—and similarly with the other forms of objects. This interpretation of *T* 2.0251 is perfectly consistent with thesis (b), i.e., with the nonobservability of objects.

T 5.5561(1) (quoted on p. 132), again, does not entail that objects are observable. States of affairs are observable, and hence empirical reality can be said to be limited by them. But

2.0124   If all objects are given, then at the same time all *possible* states of affairs are also given.

Therefore, empirical reality is also limited by the totality of objects; and this is so whether or not the objects are observable.

The biggest obstacle in the way of accepting thesis (b) is undoubtedly Wittgenstein's central doctrine that the meaning of a name is the object it denotes. These two positions do not seem to be compatible. For example, if object *a* is the meaning of the name '*a,*' then in order to know the meaning of the name, a person must know object *a,* and this possibility seems to be clearly ruled out by thesis (b). This does pose a difficulty for the thesis, but I think one can go some way toward resolving it. The difficulty hinges on this claim: in order to know the meaning of a name, one must know the object it denotes, for the object is its meaning, according to Wittgenstein. But must one have observed the object in order to "know" it? Well, if a name denoted a simple quality or relation, then the answer would doubtless be "Yes." For example, suppose that the color orange were alleged to be the meaning of the adjective 'orange.' If so, a man blind from birth could not know the meaning of that word, for he has not experienced, and cannot experience, the color orange. It is no good saying that it is enough if he knows that orange is the color which occurs between red and yellow in the normal spectrum or that orange is the color produced by energy of such and such a frequency. If the actual color orange is the meaning of the adjective 'orange,' then the blind man cannot know the meaning of the word, since he has never experienced, and cannot experience (observe), the color. So, at least, it could reasonably be argued.

Wittgenstein's names, however, do not denote qualities or relations, which are universals, but rather simple particulars. Must one have observed a particular in order to "know" it? If we assume that the question has a clear sense, then the answer to it is "No" if the particular is complex; one can know a complex—such as Socrates or the Taj Mahal—without having observed it, simply by learning some definitive facts about it. Then one knows it in the sense of knowing what kind of object it is and which object of that kind it is. One knows that Socrates, for example, is the philosopher who drank the hemlock. Propositions containing the words 'Socrates' or 'the Taj Mahal' are thus intelligible to lots of people who have never observed the bearers of those names.

But this is still not relevant to our present concern, for Wittgenstein's objects are *simple* particulars. One cannot know them by sensory observation, as he can know a simple (or complex) universal; nor can one know them as he can know a complex particular, by knowing what observable properties—or properties that can presumably be defined in terms of observable ones—it has, for the properties of an object, on the present hypothesis, are not observable. How, then, can one know objects at all? Wittgenstein answers:

2.0123   If I know an object I also know all its possible occurrences in states of affairs.
          (Every one of these possibilities must be part of the nature of the object.)
          A new possibility cannot be discovered later.

To know an object just *is* to know what sorts of states of affairs it can enter into, and that is to know what Wittgenstein calls its internal properties. (The states of affairs, I have argued, are observable.) To know objects in this way, it must be confessed, is not to know them very well. I cannot, for example, know them as individuals. For if we assume that a state of affairs is a configuration of objects that are all of the same form, then I cannot, in any state of affairs, distinguish one of the objects from any of the others, since none has observable properties by which it can be individually identified. I can know an object only as that kind of object which, when configured with others of the same form, yields a certain kind of (observable) state of affairs. This "remoteness" of our knowledge of objects leaves us somewhat dissatisfied; we might wish to know them better. And there are other related difficulties. It is difficult to see, for example, how a name can be correlated with an object, how I can mean the name '*a*' to designate *that* object, when I cannot pick it out from others with which it is configured in a state of affairs.

Hence, although Wittgenstein has gone part of the way towards reconciling (1) the unobservability of his objects and their properties with (2) his doctrine that the meaning of a name is the object it denotes, the reconciliation is at best only an uneasy one.

Since thesis (a)—that objects are observables—flatly contradicts other central doctrines of the *Tractatus,* and thesis (b)—that objects are not observables—is consistent with most, if not all, of the main doctrines of the *Tractatus,* we must reject the former and accept the latter. But it must be stressed once again that Wittgenstein himself, thinking it no business of his as a logician to investigate the matter, did not bother to think it through, did not even try to reconcile his main doctrines with anything like thesis (b). He came to realize later that he certainly should have—this is evident from the conversation with Malcolm in which he made it clear that "he regarded his former opinion as absurd" (quoted on p. 32). But since he did not attempt such a reconciliation, we must shift for ourselves. As it turns out, I think the thesis of the nonobservability of objects fits remarkably well into Wittgenstein's system, despite the fact that he himself made no effort to include that thesis in it.

What has been said so far may be considered to have been confined to propositions about the physical world and hence to objects that make up physical states of affairs. (By 'physical,' here, I mean anything nonmental.) It was that kind of object that was said to be unobservable in keeping with Wittgenstein's views. But are there only physical states of affairs? Are there not also mental ones? And what about the objects which are configured to produce *them?* Surely they must be observable by the person in whose mind they occur.

Let us, then, pose the following question. Must Wittgenstein not admit that there are two radically different kinds of objects: (1) those which make up physical states of affairs and are unobservable, and (2) those which make up mental states of affairs and are observable by the person experiencing them? The answer to this question seems to be that Wittgenstein cannot admit the existence of the second type of object, cannot admit mental objects. He cannot, for such objects would be (a) observable, and hence complex, and (b) not immortal, for presumably no one would want to grant that mental objects go on existing when the person in whose mind they occur ceases to be aware of them. Lacking simplicity and immortality, they cannot be admitted as objects.

But this then commits Wittgenstein to a very radical thesis indeed. If all objects and hence all states of affairs are physical, then since all propositions are analyzable into elementary propositions which describe such states of affairs, it follows that all propositions describing one's inner experiences, thoughts, feelings, actions, and the rest, must ultimately be analyzable into elementary propositions which describe only physical states of affairs—brain states, perhaps. This may be a possible thesis to hold, but it stands in need of a great deal of defense. For it seems bizarre to suggest that whenever a person describes his inner experiences, what he really says, in the end, is that certain physical states of affairs (or combinations of them) do or do not exist. In any case, if the foregoing considerations are valid, Wittgenstein seems committed to the view that all propositions about mental states and activities are really propositions about physical states of affairs, and this of course entails that mental states and certain bodily states (presumably in the brain) are identical.

Wittgenstein, however, would not be in the least moved by what has just been said; he would vigorously reject the entire discussion as invalid. He would insist that he really is not committed to any view whatever about the metaphysical status of his objects—for example, that they are all physical and make up only physical states of affairs. He would argue that on his own theory of language and propositions, there cannot *be* any such proposition as "All objects are physical; there are no mental objects." To say such a thing would be to attempt to use the word 'object' as a proper concept-word, and only "non-sensical pseudo-propositions are the result" of such attempts (*T* 4.1272[4]). Since there cannot *be* any such proposition, he can hardly be committed to it. The matter cannot even be discussed. According to his doctrines, anything that can be said—i.e., any proposition—is analyzable into elementary propositions which describe states of affairs. A state of affairs is a combination of objects; hence, all that can be said, ultimately, is that certain objects are, or are not, combined or configured in certain ways. All that can be said, then, is *how* the objects are, i.e., which ones are combined with which others and how; nothing can be said about *what* they are, and this includes what their "metaphysical status" is.

> 3.221   Objects can only be *named*. Signs are their representatives. I can only speak *about* them: I cannot *put them into words*. Propositions can only say *how* things are, not *what* they are.

Therefore, Wittgenstein would claim that if we thought we could draw an embarrassing physicalistic view from his doctrines, this simply shows that we had not mastered those doctrines. On the other hand, we shall discover in the next chapter that, according to Wittgenstein, there are some true doctrines which cannot be expressed. My own feeling is that the physicalistic thesis described earlier must be acknowledged by Wittgenstein to be one of them.

6 Facing the Consequences

The Limits

Wittgenstein's theory of propositions in the *Tractatus* has far-reaching and important consequences. All propositions, according to that view, are truth-functions of elementary propositions. It follows that there are only three kinds of propositions: (1) tautologies, those whose truth-tables assign them truth-values of truth only, (2) descriptive propositions, those whose truth-tables assign them truth-values of both truth and falsity, and (3) contradictions, those whose truth-tables assign them truth-values of falsity only. Since tautologies and contradictions "say nothing," the only kind of proposition that says anything is a descriptive proposition. And all that a descriptive proposition can say, in the end, is that certain states of affairs exist or do not exist, or that certain "truth-functional" combinations of them exist or do not exist. This, then, is all that can be said. All intelligible discourse is thus limited to assertions about states of affairs (if we leave aside the empty discourse of tautologies and contradictions). And all thought is limited in the same way, for

4   A thought is a proposition with a sense.

The limits of language and thought are thus one and the same. This does not mean that thinking must necessarily be nothing but internal speech and must therefore be done only in words. But thinking is operating with signs of some sort, and the conditions required for these mental signs to be intelligible and significant are the same as the conditions required for the verbal signs (the words) to be so. Wittgenstein's theory of the propositional sign was a perfectly general one; there was nothing in it which required that the sign be written or verbal or of any particular sort. Hence everything it entails is applicable to mental signs as well as to linguistic signs (words). In a letter to Russell in 1919, Wittgenstein wrote:

> I don't know *what* the constituents of a thought are but I know *that* it must have such constituents which correspond to the words of Language. . . . "Does a Gedanke consist of words"? No! But of psychical constituents that have the same sort of relation to reality as words. What those constituents are I don't know. [*NB*, pp. 129-30.]

It follows from this that any thought can be put into words; a thought which cannot possibly be put into words is no thought at all. A person may claim that he has some sort of inexpressible feeling, but he cannot justifiably claim to have a thought which is inexpressible. One may, of course, have a thought which *he* cannot put into words; he may, for example, have forgotten the appropriate word or words. But one cannot have a thought which it is impossible in principle to put into words.

One might think that these limitations which Wittgenstein's theory of propositions places on significant language and thought are not seriously restrictive, and that they allow us ample freedom to say and think whatever we want—whatever, in fact, we had said and thought before. But this would be a great mistake. Wittgenstein's doctrines limit significant nonempty discourse to statements of natural science. Descriptive propositions assert the existence and nonexistence of states of affairs, or some truth-functional combination of them, and this is just what the propositions of natural science do, according to Wittgenstein.

4.1   Propositions represent the existence and nonexistence of states of affairs.

4.11   The totality of true propositions is the whole of natural science (or the whole corpus of the natural sciences).

Since descriptive propositions assert all that can be said (for tautologies and contradictions say nothing), the propositions of the natural sciences assert all that can be said.

6.53   The correct method in philosophy would really be the following: to say nothing except what can be said, i.e. propositions of natural science—i.e. something that has nothing to do with philosophy— . . .

It must be remarked at once that, in these passages, Wittgenstein uses the expression 'propositions of natural science' much too broadly. One would not ordinarily count such propositions as "The sofa in my room is green" and "Suzy is older than Mary" as propositions of natural science, and yet it is clear that Wittgenstein would want to include them among descriptive propositions. What he means, then, can be put as follows: descriptive propositions include the propositions of the natural sciences and ordinary propositions of everyday life that are reducible to (analyzable into) elementary propositions.[1]

This view of descriptive propositions sets very stringent limitations on what can be said. It rules out as unsayable many things that philosophers and ordinary people have thought they could say. Categorically ruled out is all talk of things—such as certain kinds of metaphysical entities—which are neither themselves objects, in Wittgenstein's sense of the term, nor complexes of them (or, if we prefer, complexes of states of affairs). This rejection follows at once from the doctrine that any descriptive proposition must be either an elementary proposition or a truth-function of elementary propositions.

According to the *Tractatus*, then, we are severely restricted, by whatever language we speak, as to the kind of situation, the kind of reality, we can talk or think about. The limits of language, we may say, impose corresponding limits on the reality that can be described, discussed, or in any way talked or thought about (for short, the reality that can be described or thought). Wittgenstein now goes on to make an even stronger point. In the phrase 'reality that can be described or thought,' the qualifying clause 'that can be described or thought' may be dropped. One can say simply that the limits of language impose corresponding limits on reality—or, more briefly, the limits of language are the limits of reality, of the world. Indeed, the qualifying clause *ought* to be thus dropped; for one cannot say "(1) The limits of language are the limits of the only reality that

---

[1] In interpreting this statement, we must not confine the propositions of natural science to just the *true* ones, for the truth of a proposition ought not to be a condition of its having a sense, as Wittgenstein himself was anxious to insist. In *T* 4.11, however, Wittgenstein does assert that the propositions of natural science include only true ones; but if we maintain, as we must, that the sense of a proposition is independent of its truth or falsity, *T* 4.11 is inconsistent with *T* 6.53, where it is maintained that the propositions of natural science say all that can be said. If the notion of its being true is included in the concept of a proposition of the natural sciences, then our statement must be amended to read: "descriptive propositions include the propositions of the natural sciences *and their negations*, and. . . ."

can be described or thought, but of course (2) there may be some other reality beyond this limited reality." This cannot be said, because proposition (2), if it is a genuine proposition, must be a truth-function of elementary propositions, and yet by the very nature of the case, it cannot be such a truth-function. The same point can be put in this way: proposition (2) is self-refuting, for it talks about a reality which it claims cannot be talked about. But once proposition (2) is ruled out, there is no significant contrast for the phrase 'reality that can be described or thought,' and so the qualifying expression 'that can be described or thought' becomes at least redundant and should be dropped.

Indeed, not only *should* it be dropped—it *must* be dropped. For by appeal to Wittgenstein's principle of significant negation (p. 61), it can be shown that the phrase 'reality that can be described or thought' is nonsensical. It cannot be significantly applied to anything. Suppose, for example, we try to apply the phrase to a state of affairs *aRb,* by saying:

(S) "*aRb* belongs to the reality that can be described or thought."

The negation of (S) turns out to be nonsensical. For assume the opposite, i.e., assume that the negation of (S) is not nonsensical, and hence may be either true or false. Now if it were true, *aRb* would then not be a possible state of affairs; for any possible state of affairs *can* be described or thought. But if *aRb* is not a possible state of affairs, this must be due to the fact that either (i) '*a*' or '*b*' (or both) is not the name of any object, or (ii) *a* and *b,* although objects, cannot possibly be related by the relation *R;* in either case, the expression '*aRb*' would be nonsensical, and so, therefore, would the negation of (S). So if the negation of (S) is true, it is nonsensical—which is absurd. Our assumption—namely, that the negation of (S) is not nonsensical—has thus led to absurdity, and hence must be rejected. The negation of (S), therefore, must be nonsensical, and, by the principle of significant negation, so must (S) itself—and with it, the phrase 'reality that can be described or thought.' Instead of saying, then, that the limits of language are the limits of the reality that can be described or thought, we must say instead simply: the limits of language are the limits of reality, of the world.

Wittgenstein puts what I have been trying to say in the following words:

5.61   Logic pervades the world: the limits of the world are also its limits.

So we cannot say in logic, 'The world has this in it, and this, but not that.'

For that would appear to presuppose that we were excluding certain possibilities, and this cannot be the case, since it would require that logic should go beyond the limits of the world; for only in that way could it view those limits from the other side as well.

We cannot think what we cannot think; so what we cannot think we cannot *say* either.

The limits of language, then, are the limits of the world. And language is just the totality of all propositions that can be expressed in it:

4.001   The totality of propositions is language.

It is highly doubtful that any actual person could possibly know the whole of language. It would take something very close to omniscience to know all the propositions that there are; in fact, if someone knew this and, in addition, the truth and falsity of each proposition, he would of necessity *be* omniscient. In all probability, moreover, one would need an enormous amount of knowledge—more than any single person is likely to be able to acquire—even to *understand* all the terms and propositions in the (whole of) language. In the first place, it requires vast knowledge to know the exact definitions of many terms, hence to know how propositions containing them are to be analyzed, in order to know what they say. And second, in order to be able to understand all the different possible kinds of elementary proposition, one must know—presumably by observation—all the different kinds of states of affairs that they describe, and this, in all likelihood, is more than any one person can manage. *The* language is thus an ideal of which no one, probably, possesses complete knowledge; each of us has knowledge of only a limited portion of the ideal whole. That part of it which I know can be called my language. I know the meanings of only a certain number of terms. I know—have observed—only a limited number of different kinds of states of affairs, and hence know the sense of only a limited number of elementary propositions, and can therefore understand just so many propositions. *My* language is thus only a limited part of *the* language, for I do not understand every possible proposition.

Solipsism

The same sort of limits that occur in connection with *the* language, occur in connection with *my* language, and for the same reasons. Thus, just as the limits of (the) language are the limits of thought, so the limits of my language are the limits of my thought. And just as the limits of (the) language are the limits of the world, so the limits of my language are the limits of my world.

5.6   *The limits of my language* mean the limits of my world.

This leads Wittgenstein into a brief discussion of solipsism (*T* 5.62-5.64). Solipsism may be defined as the view that only one's own self and what one experiences exist; what is not experienced by oneself, including other selves, does not exist. There is a sense in which Wittgenstein agrees with solipsism. One natural way of expressing the view of solipsism is to say "The world is *my* world," and this statement, according to Wittgenstein, is quite true. But isn't this an audacious, an outrageous, thing for anyone to say? Perhaps; but actually it merely results from a special application of the argument used above in connection with the term 'reality.' We saw that the qualifying phrase 'that can be described or thought' in the expression 'reality that can be described or thought' must be dropped; 'reality that can be described or thought' reduces simply to 'reality.' In precisely the same way, 'my world' reduces to 'the world', for 'my world' means 'the world which I can describe (talk about) or think about.' Hence, my world is simply the world, just as the reality which can be described or thought is simply the reality. Solipsism is therefore a correct view.

The only trouble, says Wittgenstein, is that the thesis of solipsism cannot be expressed: what it wants or means to say cannot be said. Leaving the self aside for the moment, solipsism wants to say "(1) only what I experience exists; (2) what I do not experience does not exist." But neither (1) nor (2) is a possible proposition. Every proposition, when analyzed, is seen to be a truth-function of elementary propositions. But in the analysis of (1), we would reach utterances such as "State of affairs *aRb* exists" and hence "Object *a* exists"; and in that of (2), presumably, such utterances as "Object *c* does not exist." For reasons already discussed (pp. 60-62), such utterances are not genuine propositions, and hence what solipsism wants to say cannot be said. This is a pity, because, as we saw, what it wants to say is correct.

All is not lost, however, because although what solipsism wants to say cannot be said, it can be indicated—it can be, and is, shown. It shows itself. It shows itself in the fact that there is a one-to-one correspondence between my language and my world. I cannot *say* that my world is all there is; but that it is so can readily be seen. (Consider an analogy with seeing. I see at the present moment, let us suppose, just three things—call them *A, B,* and *C.* How do I know that these are the only things in my visual field? Not by first looking into my visual field and then looking outside it, and noticing that everything I see lies within my visual field and that nothing I see lies outside it. I do not know it by seeing both sides of the limit of my visual field. I know it from the fact that *A, B,* and *C* are the only objects that I see: their being the only things I see shows the truth of the proposition. Their being limited in the way they are shows its truth, just as my language's being limited in the way it is shows the truth of solipsism.) What I have been saying is my interpretation of the following cryptic passage:

5.62(2)   For what the solipsist *means* is quite correct; only it cannot be *said,* but makes itself manifest.

5.62(3)   The world is *my* world: this is manifest in the fact that the limits of *language* (of that language which alone I understand) means the limits of *my* world.[2]

I said that solipsism might be defined as the doctrine that only one's own self and what one experiences exist. The most natural interpretation of this view would perhaps be that there are two radically different kinds of thing in existence: (1) the thinking, knowing, experiencing self; the thing which has experiences of various kinds; the subject of experiences; and (2) that which the self experiences, the objects of its experience. But Wittgenstein thinks that solipsism should not be interpreted in this dualistic way: solipsism, properly understood, is the view that only what oneself experiences exists. The other side of the dualistic interpretation, namely, that there is also

---

2 Some commentators would translate the passage in parentheses as 'the language which I alone understand,' but native speakers of German inform me that this would be an unnatural reading of it. It means rather "the only language which I understand." See D. Keyt, "Wittgenstein's Notion of an Object," *The Philosophical Quarterly,* Vol. 13, No. 50 (Jan. 1963), 23-24, n.6.

a thinking, knowing, metaphysical self, must be rejected. There is no such entity.

> 5.631(1)   There is no such thing as the subject that thinks or entertains ideas.

Wittgenstein, in saying this, is doubtless trying to say something which cannot, on his own view of language, be said. What he means is that the word 'I' in 'I see _____,' 'I think that _____,' 'I feel _____,' and so on, is not the name of an object.

> The I is not an object. [*NB*, entry for 7.8.16.]

It is only the accidental grammatical form—as, e.g., in 'I think that _____,' —that misleads us into supposing that there is an "I," for we are naturally disposed to think that every word in a sentence designates an object. Therefore it would be better, really, to abandon this particular grammatical construction. Moore reports of the Wittgenstein of 1930-33:

> he quoted, with apparent approval, Lichtenberg's saying 'Instead of "I think" we ought to say "It thinks" ' ('it' being used, as he said, as 'Es' is used in 'Es blitzet'). . . .[3]

The "I" is not, in any case, an observable. It is never perceived by any of the senses, and it never could be, no matter how many powerful instruments we called to our aid. I see colors and shapes, but never the "I"; I hear sounds, but never the "I"; and so on. The "I," or the self, is not an observable object, any more than the eye is a visual object.

> 5.633   Where *in* the world is a metaphysical subject to be found?
> You will say that this is exactly like the case of the eye and the visual field. But really you do *not* see the eye.
> And nothing *in the visual field* allows you to infer that it is seen by an eye.
>
> 5.6331   For the form of the visual field is surely not like this

---

[3] Moore, "Wittgenstein's Lectures in 1930-33," *Mind,* LXIV, No. 253 (Jan. 1955), 13-14 (*Philosophical Papers,* p. 309). Georg Christoph Lichtenberg (1742-1799) was a German scientist, essayist, and philosopher. Some of his ideas were taken over by Wittgenstein; his influence on Wittgenstein is a subject that deserves more thorough study than it has so far received.

(This idea had been expressed much earlier in the history of philosophy by Hume and Kant, but Wittgenstein doubtless got it from his reading of Schopenhauer. See his *The World as Will and Idea,* Book I, sect. 2.) Just as in the field of vision there are various colors, shapes, physical objects, or whatever, but no seeing eye, no visual subject,[4] so in the "field of reality" there are various experienced situations, but no experiencing subject or self.

Of course, it is not the unobservability of the self which counts against its existence, for all of Wittgenstein's objects are likewise unobservable. It is, one wants to say, the peculiar *kind* of unobservability of the self which is crucial. Wittgenstein would argue as follows. If the self existed, it would have to be configurable with other objects to form states of affairs. (It could not be composite, and hence the self would have to be a simple object if it existed at all. See *T* 5.5421[2].) But if it were so configured, the resulting states of affairs, according to the (true) solipsistic view, would have to be observable by the very same self which is alleged to be one of their constituents. If we assume, as Wittgenstein must have done, that this is an absurd result—that is, if we assume that an object in a state of affairs cannot observe that very state of affairs—then we must reject the hypothesis which led to it, namely, that the self might exist. The self, then, can never be part of reality; it is "the limit of the world—not a part of it" (*T* 5.641[3]). It is that which observes reality and not a part of reality.

But once we eliminate item (1), the thinking self, from the false dualistic interpretation of solipsism, we are left only with item (2), that which one experiences—the objects of experience. Solipsism properly interpreted, then, is the view that these are all that exist. And as we saw, this view is true. But as we also saw, a solipsist cannot express his view; he cannot say "Only the things *I* experience exist." He can say only that things like tables and chairs exist, as well as things like pains, itches, and tickles. A common-sense realist, however, would say precisely the same thing in expressing *his* view. Solipsism is thus indistinguishable from realism, despite the fact that the two views are usually thought to be antithetical.

---

4 One's own eye can be made a visual object for oneself by looking at it in a mirror; but it is even so still being seen by the seeing eye, the visual subject, which is not, as such, being seen in the mirror. The visual subject (the seeing eye) forever escapes the possibility of being seen, of becoming a visual object; it is, in a manner of speaking, invisible.

5.64   Here it can be seen that solipsism, when its implications
are followed out strictly, coincides with pure realism. The
self of solipsism shrinks to a point without extension, and
there remains the reality co-ordinated with it.

In case there should be any misunderstanding on the point, it is
perhaps worth noting that Wittgenstein, in denying the existence of
the metaphysical self, is not denying to psychology its subject matter.
He distinguishes the metaphysical self (the knowing subject) from the
soul. The soul certainly exists, and there can be a natural science of
it—psychology.

5.641(3)   The philosophical self is not the human being, not the
human body, or the human soul, with which psychology
deals, but rather the metaphysical subject, the limit of the
world—not a part of it.

(See also T 6.423[2].) In addition to things like atoms and molecules, and things composed of them, which are the concern of physics,
chemistry, biology, and so on, there are also such things as pains,
itches, desires, thoughts, dreams, and images, and these are the concern of psychology. The psychological self (as opposed to the metaphysical self, which does not exist) is nothing more than the series
of thoughts, pains, desires, and so on, that occur in its history. Or
rather, since "The world divides into facts" (T 1.2), the psychological
self is just the facts which have as constituents the thoughts, pains,
desires, and so on, that occur in its history. (Note, however, that if
Wittgenstein is committed to the [inexpressible] view that mental
states are identical with physical states, as I argued on p. 137, then
he must hold that psychology is ultimately based on, and reducible
to, physiology or some other physical, or nonpsychological, science.)
    We are now in a better position to understand Wittgenstein's treat-
ment of such propositions as "A has the thought p" (let us call it
proposition Q), which seem at first glance to be counter-examples
to his central thesis that all propositions are truth-functions of elementary propositions. (See p. 65f.) His claim is that, contrary to appearances, such propositions are really truth-functions of elementary
propositions just as every other genuine proposition is. He compresses
his suggestion on this matter into the following cryptic passage:

5.542   It is clear, however, that "A believes that p," "A has the
thought p," and "A says p" are of the form "'p' says p":

and this does not involve a correlation of a fact with an object, but rather the correlation of facts by means of the correlation of their objects.[5]

Wittgenstein thinks that if you hold that the thinking, knowing subject exists as a metaphysical entity, then such propositions as Q really would contradict his central thesis of the truth-functional nature of propositions. His reason for thinking so is as follows. If there were such an entity, then the sign 'A' in proposition Q would be the name of it, and so the proposition would assert a relationship between the entity A and the thought p, which is a fact. But we know that this relationship is independent of the truth or falsity of p, for a person can have the thought p (i.e., entertain the proposition p) whether p is true or false. Hence, the truth-value of the more complex proposition Q would be independent of the truth-value of the proposition p; and so one proposition (viz., p) would occur in another (viz., Q) in a non-truth-functional way, contrary to Wittgenstein's thesis.

But Wittgenstein thinks he has shown that there is no knowing, thinking subject, and therefore that his thesis cannot be upset in the manner just described. Still, he owes us an analysis of such propositions as Q—one which will show in a positive way that they are indeed truth-functions of elementary propositions. Such an analysis is suggested in T 5.542. He says there that such propositions "are of the form " 'p' says p'." Wittgenstein cannot seriously mean that this gives the entire sense of Q, for it makes no mention of person A. The proposition that " 'p' says p" would be true whether or not A even existed, and hence it cannot be a complete analysis of proposition Q, which contains an explicit reference to person A. I suggest, therefore, that Wittgenstein here simply made an easily remedied slip, and that his analysis of Q would contain the following two propositions: (1) A has a thought expressible by the propositional sign 'p,' and (2) the sign 'p' says that p. What needs to be shown now is that propositions (1) and (2) are both truth-functions of elementary propositions. I shall now try to say, very briefly, how this might be done.

Consider first proposition (2). How can " 'p' says p" be construed as a truth-function of elementary propositions? Since we obviously cannot carry the process of analysis all the way through to the elementary propositions, let us assume it will be enough to show that

---

[5] I have altered Pears' and McGuinness' translation by interchanging single and double quotation marks throughout.

proposition (2) is a descriptive proposition—i.e., that it asserts certain contingent facts about things in the world. We will grant to Wittgenstein, for the sake of argument, that such a proposition is a truth-function of elementary ones. The procedure is justified because the main difficulty about proposition (2) is that it does not at first appear to state contingent facts about things in the world, as propositions like "The book is red" and "Americans like baseball" do. It strikes one as a strange sort of proposition, as though, on the one hand, it were a necessary truth, and yet, on the other, as though it were not a tautology. Hence, if it can be shown that these puzzling appearances are deceptive, and that proposition (2) really states contingent facts about the world, the main source of one's uneasiness about it will be removed.

But our discussion of T 3.1432 (pp. 83-86) has already shown, I think, that proposition (2) does state contingent facts about the world. That the sign 'aRb' says that a stands in relation R to b—in short, that it says that aRb—is a purely contingent matter; if there were some other conventions, an altogether different sign might be the one that said that aRb—e.g., '$\overset{a}{\underset{b}{R}}$' might have said that aRb. And the sign 'aRb,' under different conventions, might have said something other than that aRb, or it might have said nothing. Or again, the signs 'a' and 'b' might have been the names of objects other than a and b; for example, the objects now called 'c' and 'd' might have been assigned the names 'a' and 'b,' respectively. Therefore, that 'aRb' says that aRb is a matter of the purest convention; it is merely a contingent fact about the way people happen to write and interpret their signs. Hence, proposition (2) is a descriptive proposition which states this fact and may be assumed to be, like any descriptive proposition, a truth-function of elementary propositions.[6]

[6] In T 5.542, Wittgenstein speaks of the sign 'p' as though *it* said that p; and proposition (2) reflects his way of speaking in that passage. But this seems flatly to contradict T 3.1432, where we are told that we must not say "The complex sign 'aRb' says that a stands to b in the relation R." This is only an apparent contradiction, however. That it is so can be shown as follows.

3.14(1)   What constitutes a propositional sign is that in it its elements (the words) stand in a determinate relation to one another.

Therefore, the propositional sign 'aRb' is a fact—i.e., it is the fact that 'a' stands in a certain relation to 'b.' Hence, the proposition "The sign 'aRb' says that aRb" (proposition [2]) means the same as "The fact that 'a' stands in a certain relation to 'b' says that aRb" (see T 3.1432), and there is thus no contra-

Little or nothing need be said about proposition (1)—namely, that *A* has a thought expressible by the propositional sign '*p*'—as far as its being a truth-function of elementary propositions is concerned. It obviously asserts the existence of a definite situation, and is therefore a descriptive proposition which may, like all others of that sort, be granted to be a truth-function of elementary propositions. There is a question, however, about what situation it describes. What exactly *are* we asserting when we say that *A* has a thought? Wittgenstein claimed not to know what the constituents of a thought are, but he claimed to know that whatever they are, they bear the same relation to reality that words do. A thought is thus, at least in part, analogous to a propositional sign; we may say that it is, in part, a mental propositional sign. And this part of the thought is, like any propositional sign, a fact (see note 6 above). But a thought is not merely a kind of propositional sign, it is a proposition:

4 A thought is a proposition with a sense.

But since "a proposition is a propositional sign in its projective relation to the world" (*T* 3.12), a thought includes, in addition to the mental propositional sign, an act of intention which correlates the elements of the propositional sign with elements of reality. This explains why here we have "the correlation of facts by means of the correlation of their objects" (*T* 5.542). The facts that Wittgenstein refers to are (a) the fact which the mental propositional sign is, and (b) the fact in the world which the thought is of.[7] We do not have "a correlation of a fact with an object" (*T* 5.542); that is, when we say that "*A* has a thought expressible by the propositional sign '*p*' " (this is proposition [1]), we are not asserting that a fact—namely, the propositional sign '*p*'—is correlated with an object—namely, *A*. As we have seen, there is no such object. What we *are* asserting, to summarize, is (a) that a mental propositional sign '*p*' (which is a fact) occurs in *A*'s mind, and (b) that there also occurs in *A*'s mind an act of intention whereby the objects constituting the mental prop-

---

diction between proposition (2) and *T* 3.1432. When *T* 3.1432 warns us not to say that the sign '*aRb*' says that *aRb*, it means the sign *only when it is construed incorrectly as an entity or thing;* when it is clearly understood that the propositional sign is not a thing but a fact, then one can safely speak of the sign's saying something, as in *T*. 5.542.

[7] In referring to this second fact, Wittgenstein is assuming that the thought is true. But the question of the truth or falsity of the thought must be left open. Hence (b) *should* read: (b) the *situation* which the thought is of.

ositional sign are correlated with the objects constituting the fact in the world (or better, the situation) which A's thought is of.

We have just seen how Wittgenstein discusses one kind of proposition (viz., those like proposition Q) which at first seems clearly to contradict his thesis that all propositions are truth-functions of elementary ones. In this case, he tried to show that such propositions really are truth-functions of elementary ones, despite the contrary appearance. In the *Tractatus,* Wittgenstein confronts all the types of proposition that might possibly wreck his thesis and gives some account of them compatible with that thesis. Thus he has things to say about all those kinds of proposition listed on p. 66f., and about other kinds as well. As I suggested on p. 67, he does not in every case try to prove that propositions of that type are truth-functions of elementary ones, but in one way or another the thesis is defended against all comers. I shall not attempt to interpret what Wittgenstein says about many of these matters—about identity, probability, the will, death, God, and so on. His remarks are in many cases cryptic, but always stimulating and thought-provoking, and they are among the most eloquent in the *Tractatus.*

Philosophy

We cannot leave the *Tractatus* without some consideration of Wittgenstein's views on the nature and function of philosophy. All propositions, we know, are either tautologies, or contradictions, or descriptive propositions. The first two "say nothing," so that it is only descriptive propositions which are substantial, which say anything. Hence these propositions, which Wittgenstein calls the propositions of the natural sciences, assert all that can possibly be said. But

4.111   Philosophy is not one of the natural sciences.
(The word 'philosophy' must mean something whose place is above or below the natural sciences, not beside them.)

What, then, becomes of the things which philosophers try to assert? Are they mere empty tautologies—or, what is even worse, contradictions? Or are they not even propositions; are they altogether nonsensical? What about the various things set down in the *Tractatus* itself?

One of the major theses of the *Tractatus* (call it thesis E) is that the structure or form of an elementary proposition is identical with the structure or form of its state of affairs. (*T* 2.15, 2.161, 2.17, 2.18.) But this statement does not seem to be a truth-function of elementary propositions; it does not simply say that such and such states of affairs exist, and such and such other states of affairs do not exist. It asserts, rather, a relationship between all states of affairs and something other than a state of affairs. (So, at least, it could be argued; and Wittgenstein himself would so argue.) This means that thesis *E* cannot be a descriptive proposition, for all descriptive propositions are truth-functions of elementary propositions. Since it cannot be a tautology either, it cannot be any kind of proposition at all. Thesis *E*, in short, cannot be anything sayable.

The same point can be made as follows. An elementary proposition, we know, is a picture of reality—specifically, of a state of affairs. In a picture, a certain situation is depicted. The picture has the same structure as the situation. But I cannot make a picture which depicts the fact that a picture has the same structure as its situation. I can make a picture of a picture, and a picture of its situation, but I cannot, so at least it might seem, make a picture of a picture's having the same structure as its situation; that appears not to be a possible picture. If so, no such thing as thesis *E* can be said. In 1914, Wittgenstein said:

> In order that you should have a language which can express or *say* everything that *can* be said, this language must have certain properties; and when this is the case, *that* it has them can no longer be said in that language or *any* language.[8]

Like solipsism, what thesis *E* means to say is entirely true, but also like solipsism, what it means to say cannot be said. The truth of solipsism is *shown* by something—namely, by the fact that the limits of my language mean the limits of my world (*T* 5.62). The truth of thesis *E* is also *shown* by something: it is shown by the structure of elementary propositions and by that of states of affairs. If we compare these two structures, we can see that they are identical.[9] That they are identical is thus shown, but it cannot be said. Similarly, an ele-

8 "Notes Dictated to G. E. Moore in Norway" (1914), reprinted in *NB*, p. 107.
9 This, at any rate, is what Wittgenstein would apparently have to say. But again the unobservability of his simple objects raises its ugly head and creates difficulties. For if the objects in a state of affairs are unobservable, how can we note the manner of their configuration in the state of affairs?

mentary proposition shows what the structure of its state of affairs is; but it cannot *say* what it is.

> 4.121   Propositions cannot represent logical form: it is mirrored in them.
>
> What finds its reflection in language, language cannot represent.
>
> What expresses *itself* in language, *we* cannot express by means of language.
>
> Propositions *show* the logical form of reality.
>
> They display it.
>
> .   .   .
>
> 4.1212   What *can* be shown, *cannot* be said.

But now we are faced with a paradoxical situation. In the *Tractatus,* Wittgenstein states thesis *E,* and he also states that thesis *E* cannot be stated. He claims that what he says cannot be said. And thesis *E* is not an isolated case: the *Tractatus* is filled with statements that could not possibly be construed as truth-functions of elementary propositions, that are not descriptive propositions about states of affairs, that are not propositions of the natural sciences. Indeed, it is filled with nothing else; Wittgenstein would insist that no descriptive proposition—i.e., no proposition which simply states an empirical fact—has any place in a book of philosophy (*T* 4.111, 6.53). Wittgenstein is well aware of this paradox, and boldly asserts it.

> 6.54   My propositions serve as elucidations in the following way: anyone who understands me eventually recognizes them as nonsensical, when he has used them—as steps—to climb up beyond them. (He must, so to speak, throw away the ladder after he has climbed up it.)
>
> He must transcend these propositions, and then he will see the world aright.[10]

Wittgenstein does not mean that his assertions are sheer nonsense, as if he had said "Gloom black pan fowdy." Nor does he mean that

---

[10] Prof. Roderick Chisholm, in his article "Sextus Empiricus and Modern Empiricism" (*Philosophy of Science,* Vol. 8, No. 3 [July 1941]), has pointed out that the ladder analogy was anticipated by Sextus Empiricus:

". . . Just as it is not impossible for the man who has ascended to a high place by a ladder to overturn the ladder with his foot after his ascent, so also it is not unlikely that the Sceptic after he has arrived at the demonstration of his thesis by means of the argument proving the non-existence of proof, as it were by a step-ladder, should then abolish this very argument." (Sextus Empiricus, *Against the Logicians,* trans. by R. G. Bury, Book II, sect. 481 [Cambridge, Mass.: Harvard University Press, 1935], p. 489.)

they are obfuscating nonsense, like the pseudo-propositions of some metaphysicians (e.g., "The Absolute is becoming"). Wittgenstein considers his philosophical assertions to be illuminating nonsense. What he had intended to say is quite true—only, as it turns out, it cannot be said. So we must grasp what it is that he intended to say, learn the lesson—climb up the ladder. But precisely in virtue of having done so, we will no longer continue trying to say such things, for we will realize that they cannot be said. We will throw away the ladder by means of which we came to have this insight. We will see that certain important things are the case—things which are shown, but which cannot be said. But from then on we will say only what can be said, namely, the propositions of the natural sciences.

One immediately feels a sense of uneasiness with Wittgenstein's position here, and I think it is in fact untenable. In the course of the *Tractatus,* he has said certain things about the relationship between propositions and situations: that one is a logical picture of the other, that they have the same structure, and so on. We understand these doctrines, we weigh their merits and demerits, and no doubt take a stand on them, either accepting or rejecting them. But then at the end we are told that they are all nonsense, and that such doctrines cannot be stated, that they merely try to say something that can only be shown and that cannot be said. This evaluation cannot be accepted; Wittgenstein has said these things and therefore they can be said. What *is* nonsensical is to deny that what has been said can be said. (Frank Ramsey said, "What we can't say we can't say, and we can't whistle it either." [11]) What has to be abandoned, it would seem, is not only the idea that those things cannot be said, but also —and more basically—the theory (of what can be said) that implies that they cannot be said. But Wittgenstein is quite unwilling to take that course, and the reason is not far to seek. The theory of what can and cannot be said is so basic to the entire system of the *Tractatus,* that Wittgenstein could not possibly abandon it without abandoning the entire *Tractatus.* For a man with a system, this is an eminently good reason; but the fact that in order to preserve the system he had to adopt the paradoxical position of denying that what he had clearly said could be said, causes one to doubt whether the system is really sound and therefore worth preserving.

This aspect of Wittgenstein's *Tractatus* has not gone uncriticized,

[11] "General Propositions and Causality," *The Foundations of Mathematics* (London: Routledge & Kegan Paul Ltd., 1931), p. 238.

even by those who were most influenced by the book. Carnap, for example, wrote in 1935:

> I, as well as my friends in the Vienna Circle, owe much to Wittgenstein, especially as to the analysis of metaphysics. But on the point just mentioned I cannot agree with him. In the first place he seems to me to be inconsistent in what he does. He tells us that one cannot state philosophical propositions and that whereof one cannot speak, thereof one must be silent; and then instead of keeping silent, he writes a whole philosophical book. Secondly, I do not agree with his statement that all his propositions are quite as much without sense as metaphysical propositions are. My opinion is that a great number of his propositions (unfortunately not all of them) have in fact sense; and that the same is true for all propositions of logical analysis.[12]

But let us return from this brief critical excursion outside the system into its protective confines once again. All that can be said are the propositions of the natural sciences, according to Wittgenstein. Philosophy is not one of those sciences, and therefore its propositions are nonsensical, like those of the *Tractatus* itself. And this is really to say that there are no philosophical propositions (*T* 4.112[4]). But what, then, becomes of philosophy on this view? Should philosophers close up shop and become natural scientists or logicians or lens grinders, or what? Wittgenstein's answer is that there are still two useful jobs that a philosopher can do: one negative or destructive, and one positive or constructive. The negative one is this: he can point out to metaphysicians and ethicists, and others who try to say something that cannot be said, the error of their ways. He can thus curb their pretensions.

> 6.53   The correct method in philosophy would really be the following: to say nothing except what can be said, i.e. propositions of natural science—i.e. something that has nothing to do with philosophy—and then, whenever someone else wanted to say something metaphysical, to demonstrate to him that he had failed to give a meaning to certain signs in his propositions. Although it would not be satisfying to the other person—he would not have the feeling that we were teaching him philosophy—*this* method would be the only strictly correct one.

This may seem like a humble function to perform, but if effectively done, it would save hours, days, and years of the useless squabbles

---

[12] Rudolf Carnap, *Philosophy and Logical Syntax* (London: Routledge & Kegan Paul Ltd., 1935), p. 37ff.

that have traditionally occupied some philosophers. Once they saw that both their own theory and those of their opponents contain meaningless signs and are therefore pseudo-propositions, they would lose interest in the struggle and devote their energies to useful labors. They would realize that their former views were nonsensical and that the problems that had distressed them do not exist.

4.003   Most of the propositions and questions to be found in philosophical works are not false but nonsensical. Consequently we cannot give any answer to questions of this kind, but can only establish that they are nonsensical. Most of the propositions and questions of philosophers arise from our failure to understand the logic of our language.

(They belong to the same class as the question whether the good is more or less identical than the beautiful.)

And it is not surprising that the deepest problems are in fact *not* problems at all.

Good philosophy thus removes the puzzlement engendered by bad philosophy, and this is no mean achievement. The problems that had exercised philosophers in the past seemed real enough to them, and bothered them as much as if they had been real; the new, good philosophy, in showing them that their problems were nonsensical and hence did not really exist (were *"not* problems"), would thereby remove puzzlement and anxiety which definitely did exist. We shall see that, in later years, Wittgenstein still thought that good philosophy has this useful therapeutic job to do, although his view of how it ought to be accomplished changed radically.

There is another, more constructive, job for the philosopher to do, according to Wittgenstein. All propositions are truth-functions of elementary ones. But it is often the case, especially with a difficult or complicated proposition, that we do not know *which* elementary propositions it is to be analyzed into, or even what the first step towards such a complete and final analysis is. We do not, in short, know the meaning—i.e., the sense—of many propositions. We are often not clear just what it is that we are saying when we make an utterance—e.g., when we talk about democracy or art or inertia or force. A philosopher can help us in this important matter by showing us whether these utterances express genuine propositions and, if so, how they are to be properly analyzed.

4.112(1)   Philosophy aims at the logical clarification of thoughts.

.   .   .

4.112(3)   A philosophical work consists essentially of elucidations.

. . .

4.112(5)   Without philosophy thoughts are, as it were, cloudy and indistinct: its task is to make them clear and to give them sharp boundaries.

There are no philosophical propositions, as we have seen. Philosophy is thus not the endeavor to investigate realms of being and to discover new truth, new facts. Natural scientists are the only ones that are properly concerned with discovering new facts. Philosophy is therefore not a body of true propositions, as physics or biology is: it is not a theory. It consists in the activity of making theories and other propositions clear.

4.112(2)   Philosophy is not a body of doctrine, but an activity.

. . .

4.112(4)   Philosophy does not result in 'philosophical propositions,' but rather in the clarification of propositions.

Philosophy, on this view, still in a sense maintains its position as "the queen of the sciences"—a position quite compatible with its not being one of them. For philosophy tells the sciences what their propositions really mean (its positive role) and, if a scientist tries to propound a theory in such a way that one or more of the words he uses really have no meaning—for example, if he talks about "entelechies" or "vital forces"—philosophy points out to him that his theory is illegitimate, that it has no sense (its negative role). Philosophy in effect delimits the area within which scientists can intelligibly work.

4.113   Philosophy settles controversies about the limits of natural science.

Philosophy is a clarifier and arbitrator. It is like a combined lawgiver, who lays down laws of property, and a judge, who ensures that the laws of property are obeyed; but it has no property of its own. Philosophy is all form and no content.

There are many who would think that this view of philosophy demotes it from its rightfully exalted rank. One of the main traditional reasons for thinking that philosophy is a sublime discipline was the belief that, among other things, it is concerned with the basic principles of reality or being, and therefore that there are certain propositions—very important and fundamental ones at that—which belong to it exclusively. These are the principles of metaphysics. But metaphysics is ruled out by the system of the *Tractatus:* all that can be significantly said is *how* reality is (i.e., that certain states of affairs exist and that certain others do not); nothing can be said about *what* reality is—and that is what metaphysicians try to talk about (*T* 3.221). To be sure, there are many metaphysical assertions in the *Tractatus;* nothing could be more blatantly metaphysical than such statements as that objects "make up the substance of the world" (*T* 2.021), that they are simple (*T* 2.02), and indestructible (*T* 2.0271). But these are among the assertions which Wittgenstein himself declares to be nonsensical, and which must be thrown away, like the ladder (*T* 6.54). So metaphysics is to be eliminated.

Another pride and joy of philosophy—ethics—must also go. People have often looked to philosophy to tell them what things are of real value, what the good life is, and how they ought to act. If the *Tractatus* is right, they must now look elsewhere, or, rather, they must stop looking. If the terms of ethics, like 'good,' 'value,' 'ought,' and so on, have any meaning, it must be analyzable in terms of states of affairs; and if this can be done, it will be the job of the philosopher to carry out the analysis. But what the analysis will do in that case is show that ethical propositions, like any other nontrivial ones, are really descriptive propositions which therefore fall under one or another of the natural sciences—psychology, sociology, and economics being perhaps the most likely candidates in this case. And if such an analysis of ethical terms cannot be carried out, then they are meaningless expressions. In either event, there are no special objects, no special realms of being, no values which the ethical philosopher is especially qualified to examine, and no special ethical propositions in which he reports his findings. All that is true of the world is that certain objects are or are not configured in certain ways: this is all that can be said. Whether these configurations are good or bad, whether certain others would be better or worse, and whether we ought or ought not to try to change them—these are not additional facts in the world. And if they were, they could only be additional configurations of objects, and hence just what happens to be the case.

6.41　　　. . . In the world everything is as it is, and everything happens as it does happen: *in* it no value exists—and if it did, it would have no value.
　　　　　If there is any value that does have value, it must lie outside the whole sphere of what happens and is the case. For all that happens and is the case is accidental.

> What makes it non-accidental cannot lie *within* the world, since if it did it would itself be accidental.
> It must lie outside the world.

Ethical propositions, as usually understood, do not state facts, do not state what happens to be the case.[13] On the contrary, they try to say that certain situations are good or bad, ought or ought not to exist, and so on—they pass judgment on what happens to be the case. Ethical propositions thus purport to say something "higher" than ordinary descriptive propositions, which merely state facts. But if the doctrines of the *Tractatus* are correct, such things cannot be said; descriptive propositions say all that can be said. Hence ethical propositions, as usually understood, do not exist any more than metaphysical ones do.

6.42   And so it is impossible for there to be propositions of ethics.
Propositions can express nothing of what is higher.

One cannot help being struck by the basic simplicity and neatness of the system expounded in the *Tractatus*. It presents the aspect of a severe, geometrically planned, city—one which is, however, inexplicably placed in the midst of a jungle. The jungle cannot actually be seen: the city is all that is visible—there is only the suggestion, the vague feeling, that beyond the clearly illuminated straight streets lies the darkness of something unthinkable.

Inside the city, all is in order; there is an almost excessive tidiness about it. There are just three kinds of propositions: tautologies, contradictions, and descriptive propositions. Since the first two types say nothing, all that can be said is sayable by the third type. All propositions are analyzable into elementary propositions, and are in fact truth-functions of them. There are not alternative ultimate analyses of any given proposition, but only one such analysis.

3.25   A proposition has one and only one complete analysis.

---

[13] Some moral philosophers, however, would hold that they do, that propositions containing such concepts as 'good,' 'right,' 'ought,' 'duty,' and so on, are descriptive propositions which do nothing but state (or purport to state) empirical facts. In this group are some of the philosophers that G. E. Moore charged with committing the "naturalistic fallacy." (See his *Principia Ethica* [London: Cambridge University Press, 1903].) Anyone who defined 'good' in terms of pleasure alone, for example, would be holding that propositions containing that concept are purely descriptive. But in view of *T* 6.42, quoted below, Wittgenstein must reject, with Moore, any such definition of ethical terms.

Its sense is thus always perfectly determinate.

> 3.251   What a proposition expresses it expresses in a determinate
>   manner, which can be set out clearly: a proposition is
>   articulated.

Since thought bears the same relation to reality that language does,

> 4.116   Everything that can be thought at all can be thought
>   clearly. Everything that can be put into words can be put
>   clearly.

All descriptive propositions are perfectly clear, then; they describe
perfectly determinate situations. What is not always clear at once is
precisely *which* situation a given proposition describes—i.e., what
the correct analysis of it into elementary propositions actually is. It
is the job of the philosopher to tell us. The philosopher is thus the
chief electrician in our city; he provides illumination. He is also the
chief of police; he throws out those things which look alluringly like
propositions but really are not.

But there is also the jungle—or rather, the suggestion of a jungle
—and one has the feeling that Wittgenstein longs to escape into
parts of it from the city in which he has imprisoned us all.

> 6.522   There are, indeed, things that cannot be put into words.
>   They *make themselves manifest*. They are what is mystical.

According to his own theory of propositions, all that we can significantly and truly utter are tautologies (such as those of logic), the
identities of mathematics, and the descriptions of matters of empirical fact. But what about religion and ethics and art and all the rest?
What about the meaning of life? There is more, is there not, than
just the banal truths of science?

> 6.52   We feel that even when *all possible* scientific questions
>   have been answered, the problems of life remain com-
>   pletely untouched. Of course there are then no questions
>   left, and this itself is the answer.

We do have strong feelings about art, religion, the "meaning of it all";
these things engender vague, inexpressible stirrings in us—much as
half-heard jungle noises cause nameless fears in the night. The difficulty is precisely that the feelings and the stirrings are literally inexpressible. Nothing can be said about these matters—these important matters. We are condemned to perpetual silence about
them (*T* 7).

In the preface to the *Tractatus,* Wittgenstein says that the whole sense of his book can be summed up as follows:

> . . . What can be said at all can be said clearly, and what we cannot talk about we must consign to silence. [*T*, p. 3.]

He also suggests that though in the *Tractatus* the city has been cleared up once and for all, this is not, in the end, a matter of great consequence.

> . . . The *truth* of the thoughts that are here set forth seems to me unassailable and definitive. I therefore believe myself to have found, on all essential points, the final solution of the problems. And if I am not mistaken in this belief, then the second thing in which the value of this work consists is that it shows how little is achieved when these problems are solved. [*T*, p. 5.]

If any problems *are* important, then, they must be problems concerning the jungle. But the system of the *Tractatus* dismisses all that to the realm of impenetrable silence. It may be said that the later Wittgenstein came to realize that his earlier theory of language and meaning, as set forth in the *Tractatus,* had been much too restrictive, and that his new, more liberal, theory of language and meaning was designed at least in part to allow intelligible discourse about those important things which the *Tractatus* had relegated to the jungle of the inexpressible.

Influence of the Tractatus

It was inevitable that the *Tractatus,* with its neat system so powerfully expressed, should have exerted a profound influence on contemporary philosophical thought. But the *Tractatus* was primarily a Continental, one almost wants to say, a *German,* rather than an English, work. By this I do not mean just that it was written on the Continent in German, the English version appearing only three years after its completion. There may be some significance in those contingent historical facts, but what is of greater significance is the fact that its content and style are German rather than English. The *Tractatus* presents a sweeping and radical theoretical *system* of language and reality, one that is in violent opposition to ordinary common-sense ways of thinking. Such a work was bound to be more appealing to those philosophers who are given to system-building and generalization than to those who are more content to examine problems one by one, in a common-sensical way, uncommitted to any general over-arching system; and the former type of philosopher has normally been more prevalent on the Continent (especially in Germany), the latter in England. But whatever the reasons may have been, the *Tractatus* exerted its greatest influence in Austria and Germany, and far less in England.

This is not to say that it exerted no influence in England. We know already how Wittgenstein's ideas, communicated to Russell in discussion prior to 1914, influenced the latter's thought. In the preface to his "The Philosophy of Logical Atomism" (1918), Russell stated explicitly that the work was "very largely concerned with explaining certain ideas which [he] learnt from [his] friend and former pupil Ludwig Wittgenstein." [14] And when the *Tractatus* appeared in English in 1922, it was read with great interest by the younger philosophers at Cambridge—and by others in England as well—and had an immediate impact on some of them. Notable among these was Frank Ramsey, who had assisted in the first English translation of the *Tractatus,* and who wrote a splendid critical notice of it for *Mind* (1923) which must have helped stimulate interest in the work. C. D. Broad's remark, in the preface to his *The Mind and its Place in Nature* (1925), gives evidence of the fact that Wittgenstein was not without his immediate followers.

> I shall watch with a fatherly eye the philosophical gambols of my younger friends as they dance to the highly syncopated pipings of Herr Wittgenstein's flute.[15]

Nevertheless, the *Tractatus* was not widely read in England until the late 1930's, and only then, I would guess, as the result of the stunning effect produced by A. J. Ayer's *Language, Truth and Logic,* which first appeared in 1936 and set forth with brilliant clarity the tenets of Logical Positivism, a movement which owes a great deal to the *Tractatus.*

It is true that most English philosophers were practicing what the *Tractatus* preached; they were doing what it said philosophers ought to be doing—namely, analyzing propositions. But they had been doing this long before the appearance of Wittgenstein's work, under the guidance of Russell and, to an even greater extent, Moore.

---

14 Russell, "The Philosophy of Logical Atomism," Marsh volume, p. 177.
15 C. D. Broad, *The Mind and its Place in Nature* (London: Routledge & Kegan Paul Ltd., 1925), Preface, p. vii.

Moreover, the English philosophers displayed little interest in pursuing their analyses to the bitter end, i.e., all the way down to elementary propositions. They were content to analyze difficult notions in terms of concepts which were merely more familiar, more clearly understood. The philosophical temper of the day in England is well exhibited in the announced program of the journal, *Analysis,* which first appeared in 1933.

> *Analysis* will be mainly devoted to short discussions of questions of detail in philosophy, or of precisely defined aspects of philosophical questions. *Analysis* is not designed to support any particular set of conclusions. But the contributions to be published will be concerned, as a rule, with the elucidation or explanation of facts, or groups of facts, the general nature of which is, by common consent, already known; rather than with attempts to establish new kinds of fact about the world, of very wide scope, or on a very large scale.[16]

One of the major concerns of English philosophers in the '30's was the nature and value of analysis itself. As Professor Passmore puts it,

> . . . Analytical methods, it is fair to say, were more freely employed in the analysis of analysis than in the analysis of anything else.[17]

Various problems connected with analysis, and various distinctions amongst different kinds of analyses, were vigorously discussed [18]— matters of which the *Tractatus* had taken little or no cognizance.

The *Tractatus* exerted its greatest influence on the movement known as Logical Positivism, which was originated by a group of philosophers and other philosophically-minded men constituting the Vienna Circle—although the members of the Circle did not favor the name 'Logical Positivism.' The Vienna Circle was headed by Moritz Schlick, and began its life in 1922, when he was appointed professor of philosophy at Vienna University. It included, among others, the philosophers Friedrich Waismann, Rudolf Carnap, and Herbert Feigl, the sociologist Otto Neurath, the historian Victor Kraft, and the mathematicians Hans Hahn, Karl Menger, and Kurt Gödel. Wittgenstein, although living in Austria until his departure for England in 1929, never officially joined the Circle—he was, anyway, constitutionally opposed to joining groups of any kind—but

---

[16] *Analysis,* Vol. 1, No. 1 (November 1933), p. 1.

[17] John Passmore, *A Hundred Years of Philosophy* (London: Gerald Duckworth & Co. Ltd., 1957), p. 365.

[18] For a brief and clear account of some of these issues, see Passmore, *op. cit.,* pp. 364-68.

he had close personal relations with at least Schlick and Waismann, whom he continued to influence even after 1929. From 1927 to 1929, he met fairly frequently with some members of the Circle, primarily Schlick, Waismann, and Feigl. And although he was at this time extremely reluctant to discuss philosophical matters, the others did manage occasionally to persuade him to talk about philosophy, and specifically, to explicate certain doctrines of the *Tractatus*.[19]

It would certainly be false to say that the *Tractatus* was the sole inspiration of the Logical Positivist movement. The general outlook and some of the leading ideas of the *Tractatus* were already very much in the air in Vienna and elsewhere; Schlick, for example, in his *Allgemeine Erkenntnislehre* (1918) had already independently arrived at a conception of philosophy similar to Wittgenstein's. And the Positivists certainly did not accept everything they found in the *Tractatus:* the strain of mysticism, the hint of the jungle, especially, did not please the tough-minded men of the Vienna Circle. Neurath, for example, remarked about metaphysics that concerning it "one must indeed be silent, but not *about* anything." [20] Nevertheless, the book had an enormous effect on them, and on kindred groups elsewhere—for example, on the so-called Berlin School, led by such philosophers as Hans Reichenbach, Richard von Mises, Kurt Grelling, and Carl Hempel. The importance of the *Tractatus* was that it gathered together ideas and attitudes which were in the intellectual air; it organized, focused, and crystallized them, added certain brilliant and highly original ideas of its own, and presented the whole as a neat system, in a most powerful and exciting fashion. Schlick wrote in 1930:

> . . . I am convinced that we now find ourselves at an altogether decisive turning point in philosophy, and that we are objectively justified in considering that an end has come to the fruitless conflict of systems. . . . The paths have their origin in logic. Leibniz dimly saw their beginning. Bertrand Russell and Gottlob Frege have opened up important stretches in the last decades, but Ludwig Wittgenstein (in his *Tractatus Logico-Philosophicus*, 1922) is the first to have pushed forward to the decisive turning point.[21]

19 This information was very kindly provided to me by Professor Feigl.
20 Quoted by A. J. Ayer in his article "The Vienna Circle," in *The Revolution in Philosophy* (London: Macmillan & Co. Ltd., 1956), p. 75.
21 "The Turning Point in Philosophy" (trans. by David Rynin), reprinted in A. J. Ayer, ed., *Logical Positivism* (New York: Free Press of Glencoe, Inc., 1959), p. 54. The article first appeared as "Die Wende Der Philosophie" in *Erkenntnis,* Band 1, Heft 1 (1930).

I remarked earlier that the *Tractatus* is not unlike a sacred text; it did, in fact, occupy something like a position of the Bible of Logical Positivism. In its name, the Positivists waged holy war against the infidels, primarily metaphysicians and then ethicists,[22] for the greater glory of the gods—science, logic, and mathematics.

The main constructive issue that occupied the Positivists was the formulation of a theory of meaning for terms and propositions; and, as we have seen, this was one of Wittgenstein's main concerns in the *Tractatus*. But they coupled this with a concern for epistemology (theory of knowledge)—with a concern, in particular, for the foundations of empirical knowledge that was quite foreign to Wittgenstein. This dual interest of the Positivists is most clearly exhibited in their leading tenet, the so-called verifiability criterion of meaning, which they derived from the *Tractatus* in the following way. Wittgenstein had claimed that every proposition is a truth-function of elementary propositions; thus, to put it much too·simply, descriptive propositions state that certain states of affairs exist and that certain others do not. The Positivists considered Wittgenstein's states of affairs to be observable ones, so that knowledge of their existence and nonexistence is acquirable by empirical means. Suppose proposition P asserts that states of affairs s_1, s_2, and s_3 exist, and that s_4, s_5, and s_6 do not exist. If we find, upon investigation, that the former exist and that the latter do not, we have verified the proposition P; any other findings will prove it false. But these same states of affairs that are involved in the verification (or disverification) of the proposition also constitute its sense, according to Wittgenstein: on his view, what a descriptive proposition says, ultimately, is just that certain states of affairs exist and certain others do not. The Positivists concluded from all this that in order for a proposition which is nontrivial (i.e., not a tautology or a contradiction) to be significant or meaningful—that is, to have a sense—there must be some observable conditions (states of affairs) whose existence or nonexistence would verify it. These conditions constitute its sense, and if there are no such conditions, it is devoid of sense (meaningless, nonsensical). So the criterion of the meaningfulness of a nontrivial proposition be-

---

[22] Typical in this respect is Rudolf Carnap's "The Elimination of Metaphysics through Logical Analysis of Language" which appeared in the original German in *Erkenntnis,* Band 2, Heft 4 (1932). (It is reprinted, as translated by Arthur Pap, in Ayer, ed., *Logical Positivism.*) The first chapter of Ayer's *Language, Truth and Logic* is entitled "The Elimination of Metaphysics," and the sixth, "Critique of Ethics and Theology."

comes, on this view, its verifiability, the possibility of verifying it.[23] Metaphysical and ethical propositions, it was thought, obviously fail to satisfy this criterion.

This statement of the criterion, however, is a mere schema of empiricism; it needs to be developed, elucidated, and amplified. The history of Logical Positivism in the '30's is largely the story of the various attempts to do this. One main set of issues that was discussed concerned the sort of verifiability that is required for meaningfulness. Must we be able to verify the proposition with the means at our present disposal; or is it enough if we can merely describe circumstances which *would* verify it, even if we have not the technical means at present to observe any such circumstances; or is it perhaps even enough if it is in some sense "logically possible" to verify it? Is complete verifiability required, or only some degree of confirmability? The discussion of these and related issues in the journals and books of the Positivists led to more and more subtle considerations, and caused them to keep refining their criterion of empirical meaningfulness.[24] Another important issue concerned the status of the propositions that describe the basic conditions which confirm or disconfirm the descriptive proposition in question; these proposi-

---

[23] The Positivists thus construed Wittgenstein's elementary propositions to be "observation propositions"—that is, to be reports of actual or possible sensory observations. In doing so, they have been accused of putting a false interpretation on Wittgenstein, on the grounds that Wittgenstein, whose concerns were not epistemological, did not think of his elementary propositions in this way. I agree with the critics that Wittgenstein was not concerned with the epistemological question of whether or not his elementary propositions were "observation propositions," or, which amounts to the same thing, of whether or not his states of affairs were observable. Still, as I tried to show, certain basic doctrines which Wittgenstein espoused commit him to the observability of states of affairs, whether he acknowledged that they were observable or not. For this reason, I find the above criticism of the Positivists on this point unjustified; I think they were quite right to consider that the verifiability criterion of meaning has its source in the doctrines of the *Tractatus*. Wittgenstein, in one passage, even comes close to stating something very like that criterion:

4.063(2)   . . . In order to be able to say, ' "*p*" is true (or false),' I must have determined in what circumstances I call '*p*' true, and in so doing I determine the sense of the proposition.

[24] An excellent account of these changes and refinements is to be found in Carl G. Hempel's "Problems and Changes in the Empiricist Criterion of Meaning," *Revue internationale de philosophie*, Vol. 4 (1950); reprinted in Leonard Linsky, ed., *Semantics and the Philosophy of Language* (Urbana: University of Illinois Press, 1952) and Ayer, ed., *Logical Positivism*. (In the last-mentioned book, there is appended a note written by Hempel in 1958 indicating qualifications of certain points in the original article that he then wished to make.)

tions, which correspond to Wittgenstein's elementary propositions, were called 'protocol propositions' or 'protocol sentences' by the Positivists. Are they reports of the private experience of the individual observer (sense-data propositions), or do they state publicly observable facts? Are they infallibly certain or not? The Positivist literature is crowded with discussions of these questions and the points which they raise.

By 1938 the Vienna Circle had virtually broken up, and Logical Positivism, as an organized movement, did not survive the Second World War (although its spirit lives on, mainly in America, and individual Positivists still exert considerable influence). It is ironic that in the '30's, while Logical Positivism was flourishing, its life consisting largely of vigorous arguments of issues drawn in great part from his own *Tractatus,* Wittgenstein himself was busily engaged in undermining the foundations of the *Tractatus* and in constructing a new philosophy that was to be one of the chief executioners and one of the most important successors of Logical Positivism. To a consideration of his later thought, we must now turn.

Part II

Philosophical
Investigations

7 The Rejection of Logical Atomism

When he completed the *Tractatus,* Wittgenstein was convinced that its doctrines were certainly true and that the major problems of philosophy had been finally solved, at least in principle. To be sure, there were still jobs for the philosopher to do—primarily, the actual analyses of various concepts, of various types of propositions—but these were matters of detail in which Wittgenstein was not especially interested; the master plan had been fixed once and for all, and he was content to let others execute it. After the First War, then, the reasonable and honest thing for him to do was to abandon philosophy, and this he did. Strong confidence in the truth of philosophical doctrines, however, even in the case of thinkers who are deeply committed to their views, has a habit of wavering and crumbling. It happened to Wittgenstein. Whether it was the result of his talks with Ramsey,[1] his talks with the members of the Vienna Circle, or of his own independent thinking—most likely, it was the result of all three —Wittgenstein gradually lost confidence in the unassailability of the

[1] ". . . Since beginning to occupy myself with philosophy again . . . I have been forced to recognize grave mistakes in what I wrote in that first book [i.e., the *Tractatus*]. I was helped to realize these mistakes—to a degree which I myself am hardly able to estimate—by the criticism which my ideas encountered from Frank Ramsey, with whom I discussed them in innumerable conversations during the last two years of his life." (Wittgenstein, in the Preface to *PI,* p. x.)

main doctrines of the *Tractatus*. Being possessed of the highest kind of intellectual honesty, he realized, by the end of the 1920's, that there was only one possible course open to him: to return to philosophy, to reconsider his position—in short, to start over again. In 1929 he went back to Cambridge to resume his philosophical labors.

I think it is reasonably safe to say that, at the time of his return to Cambridge, Wittgenstein was not yet convinced of the falsity of the doctrines of the *Tractatus*. His extreme confidence in their truth was shaken, that is all. Otherwise he would not have submitted the *Tractatus* as his doctoral dissertation, nor written "Some Remarks on Logical Form" (1929), whose basic point of view was still that of the *Tractatus*. Nevertheless, even at this time new ideas were forming in his mind. Moore reports that Wittgenstein said to him

> something to the effect that, when he wrote it [i.e., "Some Remarks on Logical Form"], he was getting new ideas about which he was still confused, and that he did not think it deserved any attention.[2]

In the course of the next few years, he came to realize clearly that the leading ideas of the *Tractatus* were actually false.

I shall not try to trace the individual steps which his thought took during these years of transition—that is, to describe in detail how he actually worked his way out of the doctrines of the *Tractatus*. Nevertheless, it is important for us to consider those objections to his earlier views which Wittgenstein set down in the *Philosophical Investigations*. It is important that we do so, at this stage of our study, for two reasons. First, obviously, that we may see why he abandoned those views. But second—and this is far more crucial—that we may properly understand his later views. His later doctrines grow out of those objections and can be fully understood only in light of them. Wittgenstein himself makes this point in the Preface to the *Investigations*:

> Four years ago I had occasion to re-read my first book (the *Tractatus Logico-Philosophicus*) and to explain its ideas to someone. It suddenly seemed to me that I should publish those old thoughts and the new ones together: that the latter could be seen in the right light only by contrast with and against the background of my old way of thinking. [*PI*, p. x.]

2 Moore, "Wittgenstein's Lectures in 1930-33," *Mind*, LXIII, No. 249 (January 1954), 2 (*Philosophical Papers*, p. 253).

This chapter, then, will be devoted to the objections to major themes of the *Tractatus* that are formulated in the *Investigations*.

*   *   *

Two intimately related theses of the *Tractatus* had been (a) that the world divides not into things, but into facts, and ultimately into a uniquely determined set of atomic facts, and (b) that each proposition ultimately resolves itself, by analysis, into one uniquely determined truth-function of elementary propositions (which function may, to be sure, be expressed in several logically equivalent ways), i.e., that each proposition has one and only one final analysis. Behind these theses was the assumption that the constituents, and especially the ultimate constituents, of anything are fixed in the very nature of things, that for any *x,* there is only one right answer to the question "What are the (ultimate) constituents of *x?*" The later Wittgenstein came to realize that this assumption is unwarranted. How a thing divides up, or what the parts or components of a thing are, is not something uniquely determined "by reality," so that one account would be the right one and all others wrong. One account might be better for some purposes or more appropriate from some points of view, another better for other purposes or more appropriate from other points of view. For example, if one is comparing chairs of the same design but made of different materials, it might seem most appropriate to think of each chair as being composed of its design and its material; on the other hand, if one of the chairs is being considered alone, it might seem most appropriate to think of it as being composed of legs, seat, back, and so on.

> But isn't a chessboard, for instance, obviously, and absolutely, composite?—You are probably thinking of the composition out of thirty-two white and thirty-two black squares. But could we not also say, for instance, that it was composed of the colours black and white and the schema of squares? [*PI*, sect. 47.]

So the early Wittgenstein was wrong in saying that the world divides into facts and not into things. One can say, with equal propriety, that the world divides into facts *or* that it divides into objects *or* that it divides into events *or* that it divides in some other way. These are equally valid alternative ways of "dividing up" the world; one of them might be more convenient or illuminating for some purposes, others for other purposes. John Wisdom put the point in this way:

An account of the world in terms of things, an account of the world in terms of facts and an account of the world in terms of events is just an account of one world in three languages.[3]

This insight removes the plausibility of supposing that there is one and only one final analysis of anything, including propositions. For since it is possible to specify the constituents of a thing in such radically different ways, it is most unlikely that all these analyses, when pushed as far as they can go, will in every case yield the same final result.

But even more basic to the early Wittgenstein's contention that each proposition has one and only one final analysis was his assumption that every proposition has a perfectly determinate or definite sense (*T* 3.251). As we saw in chapter 2, that assumption also supported one of his arguments for the existence of simples (see *T* 3.23). In the *Investigations,* he discusses the sort of consideration that can make the assumption seem attractive.

> The sense of a sentence—one would like to say—may, of course, leave this or that open, but the sentence must nevertheless have *a* definite sense. An indefinite sense—that would really not be a sense *at all.*—This is like: "An indefinite boundary is not really a boundary at all." Here one thinks perhaps: if I say "I have locked the man up fast in the room—there is only one door left open"—then I simply haven't locked him in at all; his being locked in is a sham. One would be inclined to say here: "You haven't done anything at all." An enclosure with a hole in it is as good as *none.*—But is that true? [*PI,* sect. 99.] [4]

(See also *PI,* sect. 98.) The early Wittgenstein, in accepting the assumption, may also have had other reasons in mind. The sense of a proposition, he held, is the situation it describes; and a situation is something which either actually does, or at least might possibly, exist as part of the world. But nothing in the world can be vague or indefinite: everything is, after all, *precisely* as it is. So the sense of a proposition, being the situation it describes, must be perfectly definite. (See *NB,* entry for 17.6.15.)

In any case, if we do accept the assumption, then we may be led —as Wittgenstein was in the *Tractatus*—to the idea that every prop-

---

[3] John Wisdom, "Logical Construction," Part II, *Mind,* XL, No. 160 (October 1931), 460. Wisdom, a gifted and original disciple of Wittgenstein, has, since 1952, occupied the chair of philosophy in the University of Cambridge once held by Moore and Wittgenstein.

[4] The translator has rendered the term '*Satz*' of the original as 'sentence,' but 'proposition' would, I think, be preferable.

osition must be analyzable into elementary propositions. For it is natural to suppose that only elementary propositions are free from all ambiguities, from all possibilities of misunderstanding and misinterpretation. (See *PI*, sect. 91.) This completely analyzed, ideal form of the proposition, we then think, is its *real* logical form —as opposed to its merely *apparent* logical form, its superficial grammatical form (*T* 4.0031). This real form is hidden or buried in the proposition, and it is that hidden structure which analysis brings to light (*PI*, sect. 102-3). Such was Wittgenstein's thought in the *Tractatus*.

Wittgenstein realized that he had not simply looked at propositions objectively and found them to contain this ideal logical structure; his theories had *required* that they have it. He had had this "preconceived idea" (*PI*, sect. 108) about propositions, and had erroneously thought he could actually see in propositions what his theories required should be there.

> It is like a pair of glasses on our nose through which we see whatever we look at. It never occurs to us to take them off. [*PI*, sect. 103.]

(See also *PI*, sect. 104.) But if we take off the glasses, if we shed the preconceived idea, what do we find? We find, says Wittgenstein, that the facts do not conform to our previous requirement.

> The more narrowly we examine actual language, the sharper becomes the conflict between it and our requirement. [*PI*, sect. 107.]

We find, for instance, that it is simply not true that every proposition has a perfectly determinate sense. Many of the things we say are vague, inexact, indefinite—and this need not in any way prevent us from achieving our purposes in communication.

> If I tell someone "Stand roughly here"—may not this explanation work perfectly? And cannot every other one fail too? [*PI*, sect. 88.]

If I say something whose meaning is not perfectly definite, this may, but need not, cause a misunderstanding. If it does, the misunderstanding can generally be cleared up by an explanation which makes my meaning more definite. Of course, the words used in my explanation may in turn be misunderstood, but this trouble too can be cleared up by further explanations. Ordinarily I will be understood at once, or at least after a brief clarification; and when I am understood, the proposition that I express is as much in order as it need be. The words I use will be doing their job. It is gratuitous to insist that what I mean must be subject to a fantastically long explanation (analysis) that will remove every conceivable source of misunderstanding, every conceivable ambiguity or unclarity.

> The sign-post is in order—if, under normal circumstances, it fulfils its purpose. [*PI*, sect. 87.]

The early Wittgenstein had imposed impossible demands on a proposition. He had said, in effect, "A proposition is no good, is not really a proposition at all, unless it has a determinate sense—an absolutely determinate sense. A proposition must leave no room for ambiguity; there must be no scope for any possible doubt or uncertainty. Everything it says must be precisely specified." The fundamental error of this view lies not so much in *requiring* an absolutely determinate sense, as in thinking that the very *idea* of such a sense is even intelligible. Consider the following analogy. Suppose someone were to claim "A watch is no good unless it tells the exact time —the absolutely exact time." One ought not to fall into the trap and simply reply that even the best wrist watch in the world does not keep absolutely perfect time, but is still good enough for all practical purposes. No, the real trouble with the claim is that exactness of time cannot be thought of in that way at all—as if there were, in and of itself, some ideal of *the* absolutely exact time, divorced from all contexts and in particular from any consideration of human purposes or goals. In point of fact, what counts as exact time depends on and varies with the type of situation, including the needs and aims of the people involved. If a shopkeeper announces that his shop will be closed for exactly one month, and then keeps it shut for six weeks, his announcement is false. But he could hardly be accused of dishonesty or laxness if he opens it one minute or one hour after the month has elapsed. The standards of exactness for the timer of a 100-yard dash, on the other hand, are quite different; for if he misses the time of the winner by two seconds, his measurement is hopelessly inexact.

> "Inexact" is really a reproach, and "exact" is praise. And that is to say that what is inexact attains its goal less perfectly than what is more exact. Thus the point here is what we call "the goal." Am I inexact when I do not give our distance from the sun to the nearest foot, or tell a joiner the width of a table to the nearest thousandth of an inch?
>
> No *single* ideal of exactness has been laid down; we do not know what we should be supposed to imagine under this head—unless you yourself

lay down what is to be so called. But you will find it difficult to hit upon such a convention; at least any that satisfies you. [*PI,* sect. 88.]

If my watch measures time well enough for ordinary purposes (I am on time for appointments, do not miss trains, and so on) then it is in order as it is; and it would be silly to suggest that there is something wrong with it because by some supposed standard of "absolute exactness" it does not tell the *exact* time. What would be the force of that suggestion? Of course, I cannot use my watch to measure, say, the time it takes light to travel one mile—but no such use of my watch is ever in question. If my watch tells me when, for example, to tune in on the six o'clock news within 30 seconds or 15 seconds, then it *does* tell the exact time. For normal, everyday purposes such as this, telling time within those limits *is* telling the exact time.

Similarly, if what I say conveys my thought without causing any actual misunderstanding, then the proposition I express is in order as it is; and it is unreasonable to suggest that there is something wrong with it because by some supposed standard of "absolute determinateness" of sense it does not have absolutely determinate sense—that is, because someone, somewhere, somehow might conceivably think I meant something slightly different, or might conceivably, in his own mind, fill in the situation described with some erroneous details, details which my proposition had said nothing whatever about. Propositions need be only as detailed, as specified, as the circumstances demand. Why should they be any more so? A fisherman uses a net with a mesh just small enough to catch the fish he is after. The notion of an absolutely determinate sense of a proposition, divorced from the actual give and take of human discourse, is as mythical as that of absolute exactness (of time, length, and so on) divorced from all human activities. To the extent that the *Tractatus* had assumed the validity of such a notion, it was mistaken.

We have just seen how Wittgenstein criticized his earlier conception of the *complete and final* analysis of a proposition. But it was not only this extreme, this ideal, of analysis that was attacked—the very notion of analysis itself, so fundamental for the system of the *Tractatus,* came under fire. An important assumption of the *Tractatus* had been that a proposition can be analyzed into simpler propositions which express what the original proposition really means: the process of analysis makes the meaning (the sense) of the proposition explicit and clear.

In the *Investigations,* Wittgenstein subjects this idea of analysis to severe criticism. Consider the proposition P_1: "The broom is in the corner." This proposition may be analyzed as the following conjunction (P_2) of propositions: "The broomstick is in the corner, and the brush is in the corner, and the broomstick is attached to the brush." Does P_2 say what P_1 really means? Does P_2 express what anyone who utters P_1 means to assert? Certainly not, says Wittgenstein.

> If we were to ask anyone if he meant this he would probably say that he had not thought specially of the broomstick or especially of the brush at all. And that would be the *right* answer, for he meant to speak neither of the stick nor of the brush in particular. [*PI*, sect. 60.]

It is undoubtedly true that the broom consists of two parts and that the two parts are related to each other in the special way indicated. But from this it does not follow that any proposition about the broom must itself consist of at least three parts—two corresponding to the two parts of the broom, one corresponding to the relation between them. And does P_2 make the meaning of P_1 any clearer? Are we able to understand P_2 more easily than P_1? Again, certainly not, says Wittgenstein. He might concede that, in some unusual sense, P_1 and P_2 say the same thing (*PI*, sect. 61); but he would strongly deny that P_2 says it better or more clearly. On the contrary, P_2 is an odd, roundabout, and confusing way of saying what P_1 says clearly, simply, and straightforwardly. In ordinary circumstances, P_1, not P_2, is the more fundamental mode of expression. If one had to choose, it would be more plausible to say that P_1 expresses what P_2 really says—that it gives the meaning of P_2—than it would be to say the converse. Wittgenstein does not assert that this is always the case, that analysis never serves any useful purpose. On the contrary:

> Misunderstandings concerning the use of words, caused, among other things, by certain analogies between the forms of expression in different regions of language . . . can be removed by substituting one form of expression for another; this may be called an "analysis" of our forms of expression, for the process is sometimes like one of taking a thing apart. [*PI*, sect. 90.]

His point is simply that analysis is certainly not the only, nor even the most important, way of telling us what a given form of words really means, as he had assumed in the *Tractatus*.

Closely connected with the method of analysis is the assumption, which Wittgenstein made in the *Tractatus,* that the difference between the simple and the complex is an absolute one—that a thing is, in itself, and apart from all considerations of anything outside it, either simple or complex, and that is the end of the matter. What analysis does, it was thought, is to reduce the complex proposition, which describes a complex situation, to the (absolutely) simplest propositions—i.e., elementary propositions—which describe the (absolutely) simplest situations—i.e., states of affairs. To be sure, neither elementary propositions nor states of affairs were thought to be absolutely simple, since they both consist of parts. But they were deemed to be as simple as anything of their kind could possibly be. Moreover, it was assumed that almost any complex proposition consists of words which denote complex things, but that when it is completely analyzed, the resulting elementary propositions all consist of names which denote absolutely simple things—Wittgenstein's objects.

The correlative notions of absolute complexity and simplicity were shown by the later Wittgenstein to be groundless. Nothing, he argues, is in itself absolutely simple. Compared to the whole chess board, one of its white squares is relatively simple. But it is not absolutely simple. "But," you may object, "at least its color is absolutely simple." Wittgenstein's answer is that the color may be considered simple, but it may also be considered to be composed of pure white and pure yellow. And pure white may be considered simple, or it may be considered complex, being composed of all the colors of the rainbow (*PI,* sect. 47). The point is this: in a certain context—e.g., for some purposes, or when looked at from a certain point of view, or when compared with something else in a certain way—a thing may be called simple. In other contexts, however, that same thing may have to be called composite. Thus whether a thing is simple or composite depends on the context in which it is being considered; simplicity and complexity are not absolute qualities inhering in the thing itself. And if we insist on isolating a thing from all possible contexts, then there cannot be any question of whether it is simple or complex.

> If I tell someone without any further explanation: "What I see before me now is composite," he will have the right to ask: "What do you mean by 'composite'? For there are all sorts of things that that can mean!"—The question "Is what you see composite?" makes good sense if it is already established what kind of complexity—that is, which particular use of the word—is in question. . . . [*PI,* sect. 47.]

Consider, for example, the question: "Is a one inch line simple or complex?" Apart from any particular way of looking at it, apart from any context—i.e., in complete isolation—it is unanswerable, for it lacks sense. Wittgenstein thinks that it is a typical mistake of philosophers to try to talk of things apart from all contexts, to think of them in absolute terms.

> To the *philosophical* question: "Is the visual image of this tree composite, and what are its component parts?" the correct answer is: "That depends on what you understand by 'composite.'" (And that is of course not an answer but a rejection of the question.) [*PI*, sect. 47.]

The author of the *Tractatus*, at any rate, had made this mistake in thinking of his objects as in themselves absolutely simple. He came to realize the error of so thinking and thus freed himself of the perfectly natural temptation to seek the absolutely simple—a temptation which had led generations of philosophers seriously astray, including many of the best ones, e.g., Descartes, Leibniz, Locke, and Hume.

Another of his important earlier views which Wittgenstein extensively criticizes is his conception of meaning. In the *Tractatus*, he had thought that

(a) the meaning of any word which is a genuine proper name is the thing it denotes, and

(b) the names of his absolutely simple objects are the only genuine proper names that there are.

Hence, he said that the meaning of a name (in his technical sense) is the object (in his technical sense) it denotes (*T* 3.203). Having shown that it makes no sense to speak of absolutely simple objects, the later Wittgenstein could of course no longer accept proposition (b). But proposition (a), which was so fundamental to the system of the *Tractatus* that the system could not stand for a moment without it, remains so far intact. With the abandonment of absolutely simple objects and hence of words which do nothing but name them, it is natural to suppose that the words which are genuine proper names are such words as 'The Chrysler Building,' 'Socrates,' 'Moses,' and so on—i.e., the words that would ordinarily be called proper names. In the *Investigations*, Wittgenstein ruthlessly destroys proposition (a) as so construed—ruthlessly and surprisingly quickly. It is a misuse of the word 'meaning,' he now claims, to use it to signify the thing that corresponds to the name (*PI*, sect. 40). What corresponds to the name is its bearer, not its meaning; in the *Tractatus*, he had confused the bearer of a name with the meaning of the name. That this is a confusion can be seen at once from the following considerations. When Mr. N. N. dies, it is correct to say that the bearer of the name 'N. N.' dies, but absurd to say that the meaning of the name 'N. N.' dies. Moreover, if the name 'N. N.' really did lose its meaning when its bearer, Mr. N. N., goes out of existence (which would be the case if the meaning of the name were the object it denotes), then it would follow that it made no sense to say "Mr. N. N. no longer exists" or "Mr. N. N. is dead." But of course it makes perfectly good sense to say these things (*PI,* sect. 40). And as a plain matter of fact, moreover, a man's name does not lose its meaning when he is destroyed (*PI,* sect. 55). So the bearer of a name is one thing, and its meaning is another. The meaning of a name, says Wittgenstein, is given by the various descriptions which apply to the bearer of the name and enable one to identify it.

> We may say, following Russell: the name "Moses" can be defined by means of various descriptions. For example, as "the man who led the Israelites through the wilderness," "the man who lived at that time and place and was then called 'Moses,'" "the man who as a child was taken out of the Nile by Pharaoh's daughter" and so on. And according as we assume one definition or another the proposition "Moses did not exist" acquires a different sense, and so does every other proposition about Moses. [*PI,* sect. 79.]

I think it is unfortunate that Wittgenstein should have stressed the example of proper names in stating the objections to his earlier doctrine that the meaning of a name is the object it denotes. It is unfortunate, because it is not the case, in general, that proper names have a meaning. This point will be discussed later (pp. 252-3), so we need not pause over it here. In any case, Wittgenstein was certainly right to reject his former opinion. The meaning of a name and what it applies to (its bearers, if we like) are quite different and cannot be identified with one another without absurdity. The word 'slab' is the name of a kind of piece used in constructing buildings; if the meaning of this term were the actual slabs themselves, we ought to be able to say such things as "I broke part of the meaning of the word 'slab'" or "I laid a hundred parts of the meaning of the word 'slab' today"; [5] but such utterances are absurd.

Once the doctrine that the meaning of a name is whatever it denotes is abandoned, there is no longer any need to suppose, as Wittgenstein

---

[5] The examples are taken from Passmore, *A Hundred Years of Philosophy,* p. 429.

had done in the *Tractatus,* that there must be elements of reality which are indestructible, that if a name once denotes an object, the object must endure forever (see pp. 123-4). A name can have a meaning even though nothing exists corresponding to it. Wittgenstein admits that there may be special cases where we would have to say (A) "The word '_____' would have no meaning if a certain object *O* did not exist." But in these cases, the object *O* is not anything named by the word in question, and our statement (A) is in fact a mere truism. The special cases Wittgenstein has in mind are those in which a word is defined by reference to one particular sample.

> Let us imagine samples of colour being preserved in Paris like the standard metre. We define: "sepia" means the colour of the standard sepia which is there kept hermetically sealed. [*PI,* sect. 50.]

It is of course true that the word 'sepia' would have no meaning if that particular sample did not exist, since we have stipulated that 'sepia' means the color of this sample. Wittgenstein argues, very dubiously in my opinion, that the color of this standard sample is not one of the things denoted by the word 'sepia,' not something to which the word 'sepia' applies, i.e., we cannot say of it, "The color of this sample is sepia" (*PI,* sect. 50). The reason for this is presumably that the color of a thing is called 'sepia' when it is compared to the color of the sample and is judged to be of that same color. Hence the sample itself cannot be sepia colored, since it makes no sense to say of it that when one compares its color to itself, it is seen to be of the same color.[6] Wittgenstein says, paradoxically perhaps, that in these cases the color sample is not an object represented by the language (i.e., it is not one of the things that can be called 'sepia'), but it is rather a means of representation by the language— i.e., it plays a part in our actual use of language itself. Wittgenstein also refers to such a sample as "an instrument of our language" (*PI,* sect. 57). Hence statement (A), when applied to this case, is seen to be the barest truism; it says no more than that if the standard sample did not exist, it could not play a role in our use of language (*PI,* sect. 50). If even in this *recherché* type of case there is no warrant for saying that there must be indestructible elements which are denoted by names, it is evident that there is no warrant whatever

[6] Compare this with Wittgenstein's remark about identity in the *Tractatus:*
5.5303   Roughly speaking, to say of *two* things that they are identical is nonsense, and to say of *one* thing that it is identical with itself is to say nothing at all.

for saying so. Thus another important part of the structure of the *Tractatus* is demolished.

It is no doubt obvious that with so many of its supports—indeed, with its very foundations—swept away, the picture theory of propositions is unable to survive. It makes no sense to speak of absolutely simple, indestructible elements of reality, i.e., of what Wittgenstein had called 'objects' in the *Tractatus*. Hence one cannot speak of arrangements of such objects, i.e., of states of affairs. With no absolutely simple objects, there can be no words which do nothing but name them, and therefore no elementary propositions. Yet in the *Tractatus*, Wittgenstein had insisted that it is primarily elementary propositions that are pictures of reality, and that they are pictures of states of affairs. With the removal of both that which is supposed to be the picture and that which is supposed to be pictured, the picture theory is dissolved into nothingness. It vanishes without a trace. But quite apart from these more technical considerations, Wittgenstein came to realize that there is no reason to suppose that a proposition must be a picture of the situation it describes—that the two must have the same logical form. Malcolm relates an incident which may well have crystallized Wittgenstein's thinking on this point.

> Wittgenstein and P. Sraffa, a lecturer in economics at Cambridge, argued together a great deal over the ideas of the *Tractatus*. One day (they were riding, I think, on a train) when Wittgenstein was insisting that a proposition and that which it describes must have the same 'logical form,' the same 'logical multiplicity,' Sraffa made a gesture, familiar to Neopolitans as meaning something like disgust or contempt, of brushing the underneath of his chin with an outward sweep of the finger-tips of one hand. And he asked: 'What is the logical form of *that?*' Sraffa's example produced in Wittgenstein the feeling that there was an absurdity in the insistence that a proposition and what it describes must have the same 'form.' This broke the hold on him of the conception that a proposition must literally be a 'picture' of the reality it describes.[7]

Let us consider, finally, some of Wittgenstein's criticisms of his earlier assumptions about the mental act of meaning or intending. As we have seen, one of the problems that faced Wittgenstein in the *Tractatus* was that of explaining how a correlation is made between a word and the object it denotes, between a sentence and the situation it is used to describe—in short, how a correlation is made be-

---

[7] Malcolm, *Memoir*, p. 69.

tween language and the world. His answer was that the correlation is made by a mental act of intending or meaning: a person speaks or writes the propositional sign and, in addition, performs the mental act of intending (meaning) the different words to stand for certain specific objects, of intending (meaning) the propositional sign to describe just one specific situation, and no other. (See pp. 90-94.) This way of looking at the matter is perfectly natural. There is a great difference between, on the one hand, saying something and meaning it and, on the other hand, just saying the same words without meaning anything by them (e.g., saying them mechanically or by rote). It seems natural to say that the difference consists in the fact that in the former case, but not in the latter, something went on in the speaker's mind—he "thought the meaning of the words." Or again, suppose *P* says "Jack came today," that *Q* asks him "Do you mean Jack Smith or Jack Spratt?" and that *P* replies "I meant Jack Spratt." These utterances seem to force one to assume that when *P* said "Jack came today," he performed, at the same time, a mental act of meaning the word 'Jack' to stand for Jack Spratt, and not for Jack Smith or any other Jack. For one thing, when *P* replies "I meant Jack Spratt," his use of the past tense makes it appear as though he is talking about the previous moment, the moment at which he said "Jack came today"; he seems to be saying that at the moment he first spoke, i.e., while he was speaking, he then meant the word 'Jack' to refer to Jack Spratt and to no one else. (See *BB*, p. 39.) For another, if *P* had said "Jack came today" meaning that Jack *Smith* had come, there would have been something different in the episode from what there was when he said "Jack came today" but meant that Jack *Spratt* had come. And, since the difference would not apparently lie in anything that happened in the physical world at that time (for in both cases the very same words were uttered, and uttered in precisely the same way), it must lie in a difference in what went on in *P*'s mind when he spoke. (See *PI*, sect. 689, first paragraph.) In this way, we are led to think that intending (or meaning) something definite by the words we speak or write is a mental act— one that goes on while we are speaking or writing the words—and that it is in the performance of this mental act that the connection between our words and the world is made. This, according to my interpretation, was Wittgenstein's view in the *Tractatus*. (See above, pp. 90-94.)

He came, however, to think that his earlier view was fundamentally wrong. According to it, the act of meaning something by one's words is a different one from the act of saying them, and is a mental accompaniment of the physical act of producing the sounds. If this is so, then we ought to be able to mean something by any arbitrary series of marks or sounds. We ought, for example, to be able to say "a-b-c-d" and to accompany this by the mental act of meaning "The weather is fine" (*PI*, sect. 508). Try it; try to say "a-b-c-d" and mean by it that the weather is fine. It is very difficult. It is much too difficult. Why should it be so difficult if the mental-act view of meaning were correct? Perhaps it is only because you are not accustomed to using the letters of the alphabet as words. Then try another example.

> Make the following experiment: *say* "It's cold here" and *mean* "It's warm here." Can you do it?—And what are you doing as you do it? And is there only one way of doing it? [*PI*, sect. 510.]

Again, if the act of meaning something by certain words is a different act from speaking them, then we ought to be able to perform it without saying anything.

> Make the following experiment: say and mean a sentence, e.g.: "It will probably rain tomorrow." Now think the same thought again, mean what you just meant, but without saying anything (either aloud or to yourself). If thinking that it will rain tomorrow accompanied saying that it will rain tomorrow, then just do the first activity and leave out the second.—If thinking and speaking stood in the relation of the words and the melody of a song, we could leave out the speaking and do the thinking just as we can sing the tune without the words. [*BB*, p. 42.]

Why are these suggested experiments in some way absurd? They ought not to be absurd on the mental-act view of meaning. The patent absurdity of them is thus a sign that the view is misguided.

And there are still further difficulties with it. At what precise time, for example, is *P* supposed to perform the mental act of meaning Jack Spratt by the word 'Jack,' while he says "Jack came today"? At the exact moment that he uttered the word 'Jack'? But there hardly seems time enough to perform any kind of mental act during the very short interval of time it takes to say 'Jack.' All during the entire utterance, then? But then a speaker must often perform several such acts at the same time: for *P* meant by 'Jack,' Jack Spratt; and he may have meant by 'came,' came here to this house (rather than, say, came here to this town, or came here to this country); and by 'today,' he may have meant this morning (rather than, say, this afternoon). (See *PI,* sect. 661.) What strikes us especially about these questions is not so much their difficulty, as their extreme artificiality; and yet if the mental-act view of meaning is correct, they ought not to be in the least artificial.

On the mental-act view, the correct answer to the question "What was going on in *P*'s mind when he said 'Jack came today'?" would have to begin "He was meaning . . ." (*PI,* sect. 675). But this answer is not merely false—it is ungrammatical. "He was meaning . . ." is not a proper locution. Again, suppose that *P* had cursed Jack Spratt by saying "Damn him!" According to the mental-act view, *P* would have to perform the mental act of meaning by 'him,' Jack Spratt. But then it would be just possible that he performed the wrong act or made some mistake in his performance of the act, and that he performed the act of meaning by 'him' Jack Smith rather than Jack Spratt. And so it ought to make sense to ask *P:* "Are you sure you cursed *Jack Spratt?* Mightn't you have got it wrong, and cursed someone else by mistake?" The absurdity of these questions shows the inadequacy of the view that meaning something by one's words is a mental act accompanying the speaking of the words (*PI,* sect. 681).

Further, what kind of a mental act is the act of meaning supposed to be? Does it consist in entertaining an image of the intended thing? For example, did an image of Jack Spratt come before *P*'s mind when he said "Jack came today"? But this does not seem enough to make the required connection between the word 'Jack' and Jack Spratt. For how is the connection made between that image and Jack Spratt? Might that image not be a likeness of lots of other people who happen to look just like Spratt? You reply: "But *P* intends the image to be an image of Jack Spratt, and of no one else." But then what does *that* act of intention consist in? (See *BB,* p. 39.)

Finally, it seems absolutely certain that although sometimes something may go on in a speaker's mind when he says something, this need not be the case—even when the speaker certainly means something by his words. For example, *P* may simply have said "Jack came today," without thinking about Jack Spratt or anyone else. And yet if he were asked whether he meant Jack Spratt or not, he could truthfully reply that he did. Or, entirely absorbed in his work when his wife came in, he may have said, without shifting his attention from his work, "Jack came today," and nevertheless have meant Jack Spratt when he said it (*PI,* sects. 692, 693).

Wittgenstein thus marshals a battery of arguments against his own earlier view that words get correlated with objects and facts in the world by the performance of mental acts of intending or meaning them to refer to those things. In addition to the points just made, he also has many more things to say about meaning, some of which will be discussed later (in Chapter 11). In the end, one can only agree with his statement in the *Investigations* that

. . . Nothing is more wrong-headed than calling meaning a mental activity! [*PI*, sect. 693.]

And so yet another doctrine of the *Tractatus* is destroyed.

We are confronted here with a truly remarkable situation. The young Wittgenstein, as the result of much thought and great labor, had produced the *Tractatus,* a work which he thought settled the basic issues of philosophy once and for all. He had acquired high prestige and exerted enormous influence by means of that book: his reputation as a philosopher rested almost entirely on it. And now we are presented with the sight of Wittgenstein himself deliberately, ruthlessly, and with deadly efficiency, destroying the entire system of the *Tractatus.* Being aware of Wittgenstein's passionate intellectual honesty, we might have known he would be capable of such action; but still it is extraordinary. It brings to mind the case of Plato, who in the *Parmenides* subjected his own theory of Forms, his greatest achievement, to the most searching criticism. Plato was probably in his middle or late fifties when he composed the *Parmenides,* and he did not in later years abandon his theory of Forms, despite the fact that he apparently knew of no way to meet his own objections to it. Wittgenstein was younger than that when he began destroying his *Tractatus,* and in the years ahead of him he did not and could not keep on living in the ruins. With what must have required superhuman determination, he began the slow task of rebuilding. Over the following years there gradually appeared a new edifice; not nearly so neat as the old one, but in its own way, as impressive as anything that has ever appeared on the philosophic scene.

8 Puzzlement and Philosophy

The Trouble

While Wittgenstein was working his way out of the *Tractatus,* there doubtless came a stage in the process at which he had not yet freed himself from its dominant conceptions but at which those conceptions nevertheless struck him as unsatisfactory. At that point, he might have thought "These ideas of the *Tractatus* must be right— and yet they cannot be right." Indeed, even in 1914, before he had written the *Tractatus,* he said:

> On the one hand my theory of logical portrayal seems to be the only possible one, on the other hand there seems to be an insoluble contradiction in it! [*NB,* entry for 23.10.14.]

Wittgenstein came to think that a philosopher is bound to find himself in the unhappy state of being baffled; this malady is the philosopher's occupational disease. When a person thinks about something philosophically, he inevitably becomes puzzled. Being bewildered in this way is not, according to Wittgenstein, merely an unfortunate condition that some good philosophers happen to fall into but might have managed to avoid; it is an essential preliminary aspect, literally a pre-condition, of being a good philosopher. To know, in the fullest sense, what a philosophical problem is, entails being thus bewildered.

> A philosophical problem has the form: "I don't know my way about." [*PI,* sect. 123.]

If you are never genuinely lost, if you never suffer bewilderment, you will not feel the need for further philosophical investigations; indeed, you will not really see the point of them. At the very least, your philosophical work is likely to be trivial and barren. For this reason, Wittgenstein always tried to point out the puzzles and confusions that one naturally, or even inevitably, falls into when one probes into certain notions. If a student felt no difficulties in connection with the concepts of intention or understanding or meaning, Wittgenstein wanted to spoil his happy innocence. He wanted to make him realize that in our ordinary, apparently harmless ways of thinking about such things, a multitude of difficulties lies hidden; he would examine these ways of thinking and try to reveal the hidden confusions. He thus "hoped to show that you had confusions you never thought you could have had." [1] And John Wisdom writes:

> . . . He was always anxious to make people feel the puzzle—he was dissatisfied if he felt they had not done this.[2]

Wittgenstein made people "feel the puzzle" mainly by demonstrating that our usual and apparently coherent ways of thinking about a thing can in fact lead, by easy and natural steps, to absurdity when examined philosophically. Wittgenstein revealed the potential absurdity hidden in the most respectable thoughts.

> My aim is: to teach you to pass from a piece of disguised nonsense to something that is patent nonsense. [*PI*, sect. 464. See also *PI*, sect. 119.]

(For a good example of this, see Wittgenstein's discussion of expectation in *PI*, sect. 442.) Imagine the beginner's consternation when he finds, after philosophical reflection, that the "harmless" things he has always thought and said about something apparently commit him to some outrageous bit of nonsense.

Here we find, incidentally, yet another striking similarity between Socrates and Wittgenstein: Socrates too produced a state of helpless inarticulateness in his auditors, and he too did so deliberately, considering it an essential prelude to serious philosophical enquiry that the enquirer realize how very little he really knows, that he be thoroughly perplexed (cf. *Meno*, 84 A-D). All philosophy, he believed, begins in amazement and wonder (*Theaetetus*, 155 C-D). Therefore

---

[1] From a memoir by D. A. T. G[asking] and A. C. J[ackson], in the *Australasian Journal of Philosophy*, XXIX, No. 2 (August 1951), 77.

[2] "Ludwig Wittgenstein, 1934-1937," *Mind*, LXI, No. 242 (April 1952), 259.

he considered it necessary to start any enquiry by confusing his auditor—with the result that the latter often felt as though he had been struck by some paralyzing monster.

Meno: Socrates, even before I met you they told me that in plain truth you are a perplexed man yourself and reduce others to perplexity. At this moment I feel you are exercising magic and witchcraft upon me and positively laying me under your spell until I am just a mass of helplessness. If I may be flippant, I think that not only in outward appearance but in other respects as well you are exactly like the flat sting-ray that one meets in the sea. Whenever anyone comes into contact with it, it numbs him, and that is the sort of thing that you seem to be doing to me now. My mind and my lips are literally numb, and I have nothing to reply to you. Yet I have spoken about virtue hundreds of times, held forth often on the subject in front of large audiences, and very well too, or so I thought. Now I can't even say what it is. [*Meno,* 79 E–80 B.] [3]

Wittgenstein had said in the *Tractatus* that "*the riddle* does not exist" (*T* 6.5[2]); in the *Investigations,* his view is that philosophy starts with the riddle. (There is, however, an affinity, at a deeper level, between the two works on this point; see below, p. 327.) He thought that these philosophical puzzles had certain characteristic features. One of them is that they are very like paradoxes: that is, a set of apparently true propositions about the matter at hand leads to a conclusion about it which is wildly implausible, which contradicts what we all know to be the case, or at least which contradicts another statement for which we have grounds that are just as good. Sometimes it leads to a conclusion which seems not so much implausible as positively senseless, which can only be expressed by what strikes us as an illegitimate combination of words.

One does not have to look far for examples of these Wittgensteinian puzzles: Zeno's paradoxes of motion and multiplicity, and Kant's four antinomies are known to all students of philosophy. Book I of F. H. Bradley's *Appearance and Reality* consists almost entirely of the exposition of such puzzles. Bradley argues, for example, that space is "inconsistent," because it both is, and is not, a relation, and that causation must be continuous, and yet it cannot be continuous. In a famous chapter, he demonstrates that the notions of a quality of a thing and of a relation between two or more things are each self-contradictory and unintelligible. Presumably, this means that it makes no sense to attribute a quality to a thing—to say, for example, that a

<hr>

[3] Plato, *Meno,* trans. W. K. C. Guthrie (Baltimore, Md.: Penguin Books, Inc., 1956). Reprinted by permission.

bookcase is green—or to assert that two things are related—to say, for example, that Plato is taller than Socrates. It would be difficult to imagine conclusions more implausible than these, and yet Bradley's arguments in support of them can seem very persuasive.

The examples so far mentioned may have the air of being abstruse intellectual difficulties which could disturb only a highly sophisticated philosopher. Even if that were the case, it would of course not make them any less real. But there are equally perplexing philosophical puzzles which are closer to everyday matters, puzzles which are capable of troubling anyone. Consider the case of free will and responsibility. Nothing seems clearer than that we all have free will, that there are many actions we freely choose to do and others we freely choose not to do. We think this is what justifies us in holding people responsible for what they do and fail to do, in praising them for their good deeds and censuring or even punishing them for their bad ones. But this is only half the story. We all believe, in our everyday thinking and activity, that everything that happens has some cause. When something goes wrong with the automobile or when there is a noise in the cellar, we assume that of course something caused it. If someone were to suggest that perhaps there is no cause, we would regard his remark as extraordinary—we would not know what to make of it. The performance of an action by a human being is an event that happens, and so it too must be caused, and its causes must themselves have had previous causes, and so on. Hence the ultimate causes of a human action, it is reasonable to suppose, are factors in the remote past for which the person who acts is in no way responsible. The nature he is born with, his early training, the things that happen to him in school and at home—all these, and lots of other factors, more or less remote from the given action, determine the action. Given the person's history, everything he does could theoretically be predicted ahead of time; given all the events that have occurred in his life up to a given time, what he will do at that time must inevitably follow, for the previous causes fully determine it. In this way, we are led to conclude the opposite of what we all believe to be true: we are led to conclude that no one has free will, that no one ever really chooses to do the things he does or to refrain from doing the things he does not do. No one, in short, is responsible for any of his actions, and we ought not to praise a person for his good deeds or punish him for his bad ones. Thus we end in a quandary: people cannot ever be blamed for doing bad things—but surely lots of people, including ourselves, are very often to blame for doing bad things. Surely there is a difference between the kleptomaniac, who cannot help stealing, and the man who deliberately steals for personal gain.

There are various moves we may make here to extricate ourselves from this intolerable situation, but they do not help. We can claim, for example, that all events have causes except those human actions which are done freely, done of the person's own free will. But this move seems both entirely arbitrary and also contrary to the facts, for psychology and the social sciences seem to be moving ever closer to the ideal of being able to explain causally all human actions. But the worst of it is that even if we grant its truth, the claim is worse than useless. For if we allow that free human actions have no causes whatever, we only jump from the frying pan into the fire. We do indeed free the human action from the iron bonds of determinism; but by cutting it loose from all connections whatever, we give it too much freedom—dreadful freedom. The free human action now comes into the world out of the blue, as a kind of miracle, altogether fortuitously. Since it proceeds from *no* causes, it therefore of course proceeds from no causes in the agent himself; he, in short, is not responsible for it—nothing is—and so he cannot be blamed or praised for its occurrence.

> Actions are by their very nature temporary and perishing; and where they proceed not from some cause in the characters and disposition of the person, who perform'd them, they infix not themselves upon him, and can neither redound to his honour, if good, nor infamy, if evil. The action itself may be blameable; it may be contrary to all the rules of morality and religion: But the person is not responsible for it; and as it proceeded from nothing in him, that is durable or constant, and leaves nothing of that nature behind it, 'tis impossible he can, upon its account, become the object of punishment or vengeance.[4]

"But it is caused by his free choice, his act of will," you say? But what about *that* act, then? Does *it* not then become a mere stroke of fate, lucky or unlucky as the case may be, for which the person is again in no way responsible?

We are no better off than we were at the start. Other moves are

[4] Hume, *A Treatise of Human Nature,* Book II, Part III, sect. II (p. 411 of the Selby-Bigge edition). In this passage, Hume is not, of course, setting forth his own view; his purpose is rather to criticize the view expressed. See also F. H. Bradley's essay "The Vulgar Notion of Responsibility in Connexion with the Theories of Free-Will and Necessity" in his *Ethical Studies* (Oxford: The Clarendon Press, 1876).

still possible, but they too prove to be of no avail; we remain trapped in the puzzle. Wittgenstein once remarked to Malcolm:

> A person caught in a philosophical confusion is like a man in a room who wants to get out but doesn't know how. He tries the window but it is too high. He tries the chimney but it is too narrow.[5]

I dare say that there is no one seriously interested in philosophy who has not often found himself in this Kafka-esque situation, in which he goes around and around and from which no escape seems possible. It happens, for example, when one thinks about sense perception. Various perceptual phenomena (such as illusions and hallucinations), the fact that things present varying appearances to observers under varying conditions, and causal considerations about the physiology of sense perception—all these seem to entail that we do not directly perceive physical objects, and that all we are ever immediately aware of in sense perception are private mental appearances of objects, variously called 'ideas of sense,' 'impressions,' 'sensations,' 'sense-data,' or 'percepts.' But then we seem to be cut off from the possibility of any knowledge of the nature or qualities of physical objects, and even of their very existence. Yet this is absurd, for we obviously do know a great deal about them. And so the philosopher next tries to justify this knowledge: he claims that we can infer what physical objects are like from the qualities of our sense-data, or our reason tells us what physical objects are like, or physical objects just *are* families of sense-data. Thus the philosopher makes his intellectual moves in the effort to escape from his perplexity; but each move is stopped by insuperable difficulties, and the perplexity only deepens. The same sort of thing happens when one thinks about the relationship between mind and body, about the nature of God, about our knowledge of other minds, about the nature of truth, about identity, about the meanings of ethical terms, about universals, about a priori or necessary truth—or, in brief, about any philosophical issue. Being in this apparently hopeless state is, according to Wittgenstein, an essential aspect of the *condition philosophique,* at least in its (logically) earlier phases.

It might appear that this sort of situation can arise in any line of intellectual endeavor whatever, and not just in philosophy. Is it not possible to meet perplexing difficulties at every turn, for example, in searching for the causes of cancer, or in seeking the proper defense

[5] Malcolm, *Memoir,* p. 51.

of an accused man, or in trying to determine the nature of light or the function of a certain part of the living cell? Is there not always the possibility of falling into such an impasse whenever we use our minds, whether it be in science, law, mathematics, or even in everyday practical matters? Of course one can and often does encounter difficulties of an intellectual sort in areas other than philosophy. But they seldom have the *paradoxical* character that is typical of philosophical puzzles. To be sure, sometimes they have something like it. In a murder case, for example, one convincing set of clues may point straight at X as the culprit, and another set, equally good, at Y. But according to Wittgenstein, philosophical perplexities have another feature, not yet mentioned, which marks them off from such nonphilosophical cases and makes them disturbing in a special way. The feature is this: when in the grip of philosophical perplexity, we can expect no help from the introduction of new facts. We already know all the relevant facts about the matter at hand; there is no such thing as a new bit of information which, if we only had it, would show us the way out of our difficulties. For example, no conceivable discovery a physiologist might make would help the philosopher solve his problems about sense perception or free will. The philosopher already has all the facts he needs. Indeed, he has rather too many. His problem is not to find new facts, but to find some way of construing the facts he already has so that they do not appear to conflict with one another, so that they fit together into some kind of coherent whole. The pieces are all there—none is missing—but they refuse to fit together in any satisfactory way.

> This kind of mistake recurs again and again in philosophy; e.g. when we are puzzled about the nature of time, when time seems to us a *queer thing*. We are most strongly tempted to think that here are things hidden, something we can see from the outside but which we can't look into. And yet nothing of the sort is the case. It is not new facts about time which we want to know. All the facts that concern us lie open before us. . . . [*BB*, p. 6.][6]

(See also *PI,* sect. 89.)

It is this aspect of a philosophical puzzle that accounts for its special poignancy. In other fields, a thinker faced with seemingly insoluble difficulties can cling to the hope that in one way or another

[6] Hertz anticipates Wittgenstein's view in the introduction to his *Principles of Mechanics.* Wittgenstein acknowledges his debt to Hertz on this point in *The Blue and Brown Books,* p. 26.

he will come into possession of some new information which will lead to the solution he longs for. But a philosopher can entertain no such hope, according to Wittgenstein. His problem is radically different from that of other thinkers: he cannot be confident that what he already has is perfectly sound and that if he only knew a little more, all would be well. His trouble is that there is something profoundly wrong somewhere, something deeply unsatisfactory, something at the heart of his ways of thinking about the matter at hand. The whole issue is somehow misconceived, some fundamental mistake is being made. Only it is so deep, so basic, that he cannot get at it. The trouble, in short, lies not in the alleged "facts" to be explained, but in the philosopher's way of looking at them, in his way of thinking and talking about them. It appears to him as though there are profound difficulties about sense perception *itself,* about free will *itself,* about truth *itself,* and so on; but in fact the difficulty lies not there, but rather in the philosopher's way of viewing them. His problem, says Wittgenstein, is "not a scientific one; but a muddle felt as a problem" (*BB,* p. 6). The philosopher's unhappy state is thus not unlike that of many psychotics. A psychotic sometimes thinks that there is something quite wrong with the world, that things conspire against him, that harmless objects are fraught with danger; whereas in fact the real source of the trouble is in his reaction to these things.[7] The real source of the difficulty lies within; but, as with the philosopher, it lies so deep that he cannot find it, and he is most likely even unaware of its existence.

> The philosopher is the man who has to cure himself of many sicknesses of the understanding before he can arrive at the notions of the sound of human understanding.
> If in the midst of life we are in death, so in sanity we are surrounded by madness. [*RFM,* IV, sect. 53.]

Philosophy begins, then, in profound puzzlement. A man in the grip of a philosophical problem is a man who is intellectually sick, one who has a conceptual illness. His understanding is tied up in knots. No doubt some philosophers are never cured of their maladies and remain as deeply puzzled by sense perception, free will, and the rest, at the end of their careers as they were at the beginning. But more often, a philosopher seeks to free himself from this deplorable

---

[7] Compare this with what Wittgenstein said in the *Tractatus:*

6.43(3)   The world of the happy man is a different one from that of the unhappy man.

condition by developing a theory or system to deal with the puzzles. He may, for example, become a phenomenalist and maintain that physical objects are families of sense-data, or a determinist who claims that since all human actions are causally determined, ultimately, by conditions over which the agent has no control, no one is ever responsible for anything he does. These philosophical theories inevitably conflict with common sense, and indeed with what the philosopher himself believes in his unreflective moments.[8] Wittgenstein considers such "cures" to be worse than the original disease. But whatever the malady, it is the job of philosophy to clear up the puzzles, to cure the ills of the understanding.

> The philosopher's treatment of a question is like the treatment of an illness. [*PI*, sect. 225.]

Philosophy is thus therapeutic (*PI*, sect. 133), its aim being intellectual health. To change the analogy, if we think a man who is philosophically puzzled to be like a man trapped in a room, the aim of philosophy is escape.

> What is your aim in philosophy?—To shew the fly the way out of the fly-bottle. [*PI*, sect. 309.]

Philosophy begins in illness and seeks a cure; it begins in imprisonment and seeks freedom. But the cure and the freedom must be genuine and lasting.

> . . . The clarity that we are aiming at is indeed *complete* clarity. But this simply means that the philosophical problems should *completely* disappear. [*PI*, sect. 133.]

Such a cure requires that the real source of the difficulty be located and removed. The trouble with philosophical theories or systems (phenomenalism, for example) is that their propounders have not located the real source of their original puzzlement: they still carry it deep within their ways of thinking. And so the pain—the puzzlement—is bound to reappear. Philosophical theories, in short, break out into puzzles as disturbing and perplexing as those which they

---

[8] "The strange thing is that philosophers should have been able to hold sincerely, as part of their philosophical creed, propositions inconsistent with what they themselves *knew* to be true; and yet, so far as I can make out, this has really frequently happened."

G. E. Moore, "A Defence of Common Sense," reprinted in his *Philosophical Papers*, p. 41. This article first appeared in *Contemporary British Philosophy*, Second Series, ed. J. H. Muirhead, 1925.

were designed to resolve. They all have consequences which are paradoxical, which we know instinctively to be false. Philosophical theories are thus at best only temporary pain killers: they do not cure. They are aspirin; but what is needed is surgery.

The foregoing remarks will not be fully intelligible until we know what Wittgenstein's views are concerning (a) the sources of philosophical puzzlement, and (b) the proper methods of removing them. It is to these questions that we must now turn.

Causes of the Trouble

How does philosophical perplexity arise? How does our understanding get tied up in knots? In *The Blue and Brown Books*, Wittgenstein finds several different sources of philosophical puzzlement, the most important of them being misconceptions about language. For example, philosophers often tend to think that ordinary, everyday language is like an exact calculus, such as mathematics, and that there are definite rules which it strictly and everywhere follows. This may lead them to think that every word can be given a perfectly precise definition, one which gives *the* meaning of the word wherever it appears. But in fact most of our words do not have a perfectly precise meaning; they are often vague and indefinite, and have no sharp boundaries. And many words have several different meanings, varying with the contexts in which they occur—they are "odd-job" words. Some words doubtless have regular functions, but the words which cause philosophical troubles are not among them (*BB,* pp. 43–44). Philosophers, under the spell of the idea that ordinary language follows exact rules, look for these rules, and of course cannot find them. They then either become sceptical and think that a certain word has no meaning at all and should not be used; or else they invent a rule, perhaps thinking they have actually discerned it, and then constantly come up against examples where it produces paradoxes. (See *BB,* pp. 25–27, where these points are made, and the examples of 'time,' 'measure,' and 'knowledge' are discussed.)

What causes most trouble in philosophy is that we are tempted to describe the use of important 'odd-job' words as though they were words with regular functions. [*BB,* p. 44.]

One of the several sources of philosophical puzzlement mentioned in *The Blue and Brown Books* is developed much more fully in the

Investigations and given a central position there. Wittgenstein would never have claimed that this important source is the one and only cause of all philosophical confusion, but in the *Investigations* he seems to have considered it to be the main source of the particular difficulties with which *he* was primarily concerned. There are recurring echoes in the *Investigations* of most of the other sources of puzzlement which were discussed in *The Blue and Brown Books,* but they are mostly overpowered by the main theme. The rest of the present chapter will be devoted to an account of this primary source —which is complicated and multi-faceted—of philosophical puzzlement.

I shall begin by mentioning a basic human tendency, one which pervades a great deal of human thinking. When there are a number of things which are, for one reason or another, grouped together, we tend to ignore or at least "play down" the differences among the members of the group and to seek points of sameness among them. Furthermore, when there is a certain amount of undoubted sameness, we tend to try to make it as complete as possible—i.e., as complete as is compatible with the *obvious* differences, the differences that *cannot* be ignored. I shall dub this tendency "the craving for unity": [9] we seek unity in diversity, sameness in difference, the one in the many. For example, there is a range of individual animals grouped together in virtue of their obvious similarities, and we call this the class of horses. But we are not satisfied merely with a group of resembling particulars; we seek to find something common to all of them—the essence of horseness. The search for scientific laws of nature is also motivated by our craving for unity; we observe that several phenomena are related (and this is seldom a matter of "mere observation") and seek to find the one law which governs them all.

Philosophers from the earliest times to the present—especially rationalists—have acknowledged this craving for unity and many have considered it to be a part, or the whole, of the essence of human reason. Some have pushed the object of this craving as far as it can possibly go, and made an ultimate ideal of it. Reason, they said, can never be satisfied until it finds some first principle, some supreme truth, which explains everything—absolutely everything. Without going as far as this, however, we may still admit the existence of a

---

[9] Wittgenstein himself used the expressions 'craving for generality' and 'contemptuous attitude towards the particular case' (*BB,* pp. 17-18), but I prefer 'craving for unity.'

desire for unity and the fact that it pervades human thinking. (In the next chapter, this matter is discussed critically at some length.) There can be no doubt that our craving for unity often leads to beneficial results—in science, for example. But in his later writings, Wittgenstein is interested in the relationship, the interplay, between language and this craving as it effects philosophical problems. And his view is that in philosophy its effect is disastrous. Let us try to see why.

The desire for unity naturally governs our thinking about language, as it does our thinking everywhere. In the area of language, in fact, there is an especially strong temptation to succumb to it. All words are strings or groups of letters and therefore resemble one another to a high degree, so that one is easily seduced into thinking that they all function in the same sort of way.

> Of course, what confuses us is the uniform appearance of words when we hear them spoken or meet them in script and print. For their *application* is not presented to us so clearly. Especially not, when we are doing philosophy! [*PI*, sect. 11.]

(See also *PI*, sect. 12.) Not only individual words, but sentences also resemble one another—every sentence, after all, is a string of words. This obvious fact makes it tempting to suppose that all sentences are used in the same way.

Left unchecked, the craving for unity would seek to find a single function common to all individual words (to name something, perhaps; see *PI*, sect. 1) and a single function common to all sentences (to convey a thought, perhaps; see *PI*, sect. 304). But there are obvious differences of function that are too great to be overlooked. Consider sentences, for example. We cannot help noticing that although all sentences look or sound fairly much alike, consisting as they do of strings of words, they nevertheless are not all used for the same purpose. After all, the two sentences 'He is going to Newark.' and 'Is he going to Newark?' look very much alike, but everyone [10] realizes that the former is normally used to state that something is the case, whereas the latter is normally used to ask a question. We learn very early that differences of grammatical form generally involve differences of use or function. And so we must settle for something less than *complete* unity; we must be content to assimilate individual words and sentences to a handful of easily managed

[10] Rather, *almost* everyone; see below, p. 216.

paradigms rather than to just one. All words and sentences, we suppose, are just like one or another of these models. But our craving for unity, always operative, makes us shut our eyes to the forcing and inevitable distortion that result even from *this* degree of assimilation.

It is understandable enough that some kind of assimilation of different kinds of words and word groups should take place, given the unity-seeking character of human thinking. But now we must be more specific; we must see what particular *direction* this assimilation takes. *Which* models or paradigms, of the many we might use, do we in fact use in the area of language? In the case of individual words, the answer is: primarily, names of familiar kinds of objects, such as 'chair,' 'tree,' 'table,' and proper names, like 'John,' 'Socrates,' 'Ann'; and secondarily, names of familiar kinds of actions, such as 'running,' 'eating,' 'hitting,' and names of familiar properties, like 'red,' 'square,' 'hard' (*PI*, sect. 1). We tend to assume that all nouns function (very much) like 'chair' or 'John,' that all verbs function (very much) like 'run,' and that all adjectives function (very much) like 'red.' And we just do not think anything, or anything very definite, about conjunctions and adverbs and prepositions—we hope that they will take care of themselves somehow.

There is probably no explanation needed of why we tend to use such common kinds of words as our paradigms and to assimilate others to them—nor does Wittgenstein offer any. What more obvious choices could there be? We learn these words first, and everything about them seems clear and straightforward. We master these words almost from the very beginning and feel completely at home with them. They are easy, in fact. When it comes to more difficult words, then, like 'time,' 'mind,' 'thinking,' 'know,' 'believe,' and so on, it is quite natural that we should think of them on the model of words with which we are most familiar.

The assimilation of individual words to certain paradigmatic ones is not an isolated phenomenon; rather, it is part of, and occurs only *as* part of, a wider assimilation—namely, that of whole sentences having a given grammatical form to certain familiar kinds of sentences. In fact, to assimilate one individual word to another just *is* to assimilate sentences containing the one to sentences containing the other. What else could it be? (See below, p. 206f.) And as we shall see, we certainly do have this general tendency to assimilate grammatically similar sentences to one another, and, in particular, to take sentences dealing with familiar physical matters as our models, assimilating others to them.

You ask "Yes, but how does all this lead to philosophical puzzlement?" To answer this question, we must now consider the existence of certain kinds of mental or intellectual pictures. Wittgenstein points out that we tend to have a picture, or more than one picture, of time, space, the mind, remembering, and of the other things that have always puzzled philosophers; and we tend to think and talk of these things in accordance with those pictures. We often picture time, for example, as a vast stream which flows from the future, towards the present, and into the past, carrying events along with it. Space is pictured as a huge, perhaps infinitely huge, empty container—Plato's receptacle—throughout which physical objects are dispersed more or less densely. Wittgenstein mentions several other examples of such pictures. We speak of a machine's having certain possibilities. of movement, and we picture these possibilities as shadows of the actual movements themselves, and as being already there now in the machine (*PI*, sect. 194). We have all had the experience of trying to express an idea which is before our mind. We picture the idea as a mental entity hovering before our consciousness, and ourselves as trying to translate this thing into English (*BB*, p. 41). We picture the mind sometimes as a queer kind of entity (*PI*, sect. 196) and sometimes as a queer kind of place (*BB*, p. 40); and we picture remembering, recognizing, understanding, and so on, as mental processes akin to physical processes, only occurring in that place known as the mind (*PI*, sects. 305, 604). I think Wittgenstein would say that any philosopher in the grip of philosophical puzzlement has a certain picture of the subject of his bewilderment, and that this picture is to at least a large extent the source of his trouble.

Let us see how this may happen by considering one or two examples. One word that has traditionally caused philosophers a great deal of trouble is the word 'nothing.' One philosopher has written, for instance:

> What is to be investigated is being only and—*nothing* else; being alone and further—*nothing;* solely being, and beyond being—*nothing*. *What about this Nothing?* . . . *Does the Nothing exist only because the Not, i.e. the Negation, exists?* Or is it the other way around? *Does negation and the Not exist only because the Nothing exists?* . . . We assert: *the Nothing is prior to the Not and the Negation.* . . . Where do we seek the Nothing? How do we find the Nothing? . . . We know the Nothing . . . *Anxiety reveals the Nothing.* . . . That for which

and because of which we are anxious, was "really"—nothing. Indeed: the Nothing itself—as such—was present. . . . *What about this Nothing?—The Nothing itself nothings.*[11]

Jean-Paul Sartre, too, thinks of not-being or nothingness as a real realm lying within, or around, being.

We set out upon our pursuit of being, and it seemed to us that the series of our questions had led us to the heart of being. But behold, at the moment when we thought we were arriving at the goal, a glance cast on the question itself has revealed to us suddenly that we are encompassed with nothingness. The permanent possibility of non-being, outside us and within, conditions our questions about being. Furthermore it is non-being which is going to limit the reply. What being *will* be must of necessity arise on the basis of what *it is not*. Whatever being is, it will allow this formulation: "Being is *that* and outside of that, *nothing.*"

Thus a new component of the real has just appeared to us—non-being. Our problem is thereby complicated, for we may no longer limit our inquiry to the relations of the human being to being in-itself, but must include also the relations of being with non-being. . . .[12]

It is not difficult to imagine the problems and confusions that immediately arise from Sartre's conception of nothingness. For example:

But this intra-mundane Nothingness cannot be produced by Being-in-itself; the notion of Being as full positivity does not contain Nothingness as one of its structures. We can not even say that Being excludes it. Being lacks all relation with it. Hence the question which is put to us now with a particular urgency: if Nothingness can be conceived neither outside of Being, nor in terms of Being, and if on the other hand, since it is non-being, it can not derive from itself the necessary force to "nihilate itself," *where does Nothingness come from?* [13]

The tortured prose into which Sartre must of necessity fall in his attempt to answer this unanswerable question is truly awesome. We find such passages as the following, for example:

The Being by which Nothingness arrives in the world must nihilate Nothingness in its Being, and even so it still runs the risk of establishing

---

[11] Quotations from M. Heidegger, *Was Ist Metaphysik?* (1929), cited by Rudolf Carnap in his article "The Elimination of Metaphysics through Logical Analysis of Language" (trans. Arthur Pap); reprinted in A. J. Ayer, ed., *Logical Positivism* (New York: Free Press of Glencoe, Inc., 1959), p. 69.

[12] Jean-Paul Sartre, *Being and Nothingness,* trans. Hazel E. Barnes (New York: Philosophical Library, 1956), pp. 5-6.

[13] *Ibid.,* p. 22.

Nothingness as a transcendent in the very heart of immanence unless it nihilates Nothingness in its being *in connection with its own being.* The Being by which Nothingness arrives in the world is a being such that in its being, the Nothingness of its Being is in question. *The being by which Nothingness comes to the world must be its own Nothingness.*[14]

From these passages, it is easy to see that Heidegger and Sartre have a certain picture of nothingness; they picture it to themselves, to put it bluntly, as a kind of something, a kind of being or entity. Otherwise, Sartre would not have asked where it comes from, nor have said that we encounter it, that we are encompassed by it, and so on. These ways of talking are appropriate only to kinds of *thing* or *substance*—to be more specific, such things are said of the air or the atmosphere.

Another picture which philosophers have sometimes had and which has led to puzzlement is one that represents universals (such as redness and triangularity) to be kinds of particulars, to be individual substances. This is quite a natural picture to have. We say that red is a color. The word 'red' does not refer to any particular red thing, to any particular red patch; a given red book or red wall cannot literally *be* identical with the color red, for if any particular red thing has a valid claim to be the color red, so do all the other red things. But the word 'red' cannot designate all individual red things collectively either, because even if they should all be destroyed, there would still, one is strongly inclined to suppose, be such a thing as the color red. We could, for example, talk about it, remember it, wish there were some patches of it, regret its absence, and so on. Moreover, when I think of the color red, I am not thinking of this red book or that red wall, or of any individual object located in space and time—whatever I am thinking of is altogether different from that kind of thing. Finally, suppose two spatially separated objects are red; their colors, we say, are the same. It is not just that the color of one is similar to that of the other; they are actually identical. There is something in common between them—namely their color. But what they share cannot be anything in space; the two objects occupy different parts of space. The color red, or redness, then, must be a nonspatial object which can be manifested or exemplified in space, but which is not itself in space. Hence we can explain the sameness or identity that exists when two different objects

---

[14] *Ibid.,* p. 23.

are red: they are both instances or examples of one and the same nonspatial object, redness. They both participate or share in it.

It can also seem plausible to maintain that redness is not only nonspatial, but also nontemporal as well; for just as no spatial predicates are applicable to it (one cannot ask how big redness is, or what its shape is), so no temporal characteristics can sensibly be applied to it. One cannot say that redness at one time did not exist and then later came into being, or that redness changes, or that redness might one day cease to exist. Individual red things come into being, change, and cease to exist, but not redness itself. Redness, then, like all universals, is an eternal object, existing outside space and time.

In this way, the philosopher is led to posit a separate realm of being, populated by universals, conceived of as non-spatio-temporal objects. And as soon as he has done so, the puzzles and perplexity begin. There are few better illustrations of Wittgensteinian puzzlement than that contained in Plato's dialogue *Parmenides,* in which he subjects his own theory of Forms (i.e., universals) to searching criticism. Parmenides (whom Plato makes the critic of his theory in the dialogue) asks Socrates whether, when an individual thing participates in a Form, it receives as its share the entire Form or only a part of it. Socrates at once finds himself in a quandary, for there are insuperable objections to either alternative. Suppose we say that the Form as a whole is in each of its particular instances.

> If so, a Form which is one and the same will be at the same time, as a whole, in a number of things which are separate, and consequently will be separate from itself.[15]

And if we say, on the other hand, that only a part of the Form is in each of its instances, we are committing the absurdity of suggesting that a universal, a non-spatio-temporal entity, can be broken up into bits and scattered through space and time. (And what would happen, one wonders, when the Form was entirely used up? If redness, for example, were depleted, would it be impossible for a new red thing to appear?) There seems to be no way out of this predicament.

> Well then, Socrates, how are the other things going to partake of your Forms, if they can partake of them neither in part nor as wholes?
> Really, said Socrates, it seems no easy matter to determine in any way.[16]

15 Plato, *Parmenides,* 131 B (trans. F. M. Cornford).
16 *Ibid.,* 131 E.

As Wittgenstein puts it, describing our reaction when in the grip of a philosophical puzzle:

"But *this* isn't how it is!"—we say. "Yet *this* is how it has to *be!*" [*PI*, sect. 112.]

Plato, in the *Parmenides,* is clearly picturing the Forms as kinds of ghostly particulars, as shadowy, quasi-physical objects. Otherwise, he could not have spoken of them as he did. He would not, for example, have thought that it makes sense even to consider their being broken up into parts. And it is precisely this picture which led him into his difficulties.

So it is that the pictures he has lead the philosopher into confusion and perplexity. Examples of the sinister influence of such pictures can be multiplied indefinitely. Puzzlement abounds when the philosopher pictures:

(a) the mind as a spiritual thing which is somehow connected with certain kinds of physical organisms.

(b) the subconscious as a special region of the spiritual thing known as the mind.

(c) the memory as another, perhaps partially overlapping, region —a kind of storehouse—of the mind. (For a beautiful example of Wittgensteinian puzzlement based on this picture, see Book X of St. Augustine's *Confessions.*)

(d) a proposition as a ghostly entity apprehended by the mind and expressible by sentences.

(e) the meaning of a word as a kind of halo or atmosphere surrounding the word (*PI,* sect. 117).

(f) goodness as a nonnatural property (i.e., one not perceivable by the senses) of certain things, situations, actions, or persons.

And so on. I think it not unfair to say that many of the great traditional problems that have always bothered philosophers are based, in part or in whole, on such pictures as these.

Notice that a large part of the trouble pictures can cause is attributable to the fact that they are confining. If I think of the mind as a kind of theater, then as long as I am guided by this picture, the things I can say or think about the mind will be limited—limited, namely, to the sort of thing that can sensibly be said of theaters. There are thus two ways in which a picture can hold us captive (*PI,* sect. 115): by being so strong that no other picture of the thing in question seems conceivable to us, and by restricting the kinds of

things we think one can sensibly say about whatever it is that is pictured. Wittgenstein compared the thinker suffering from philosophical
puzzlement to a man trapped in a room and trying to escape: among
his chief jailers are his own pictures.

From what has been said so far, one might get the impression that,
according to Wittgenstein, it is only philosophers who have such pictures of things. This, however, is not his view. He claims that we all
have them, that they are entirely natural, being the product of causes
which operate on all men, not just on philosophers. These underlying
causes of the trouble-making pictures are connected with language
itself, according to Wittgenstein.

Part of the connection between this natural tendency to have
pictures and the facts of language has already been indicated: it is
the fact that our craving for unity leads us to assimilate certain "difficult" words and sentences to other "easier" or more familiar paradigms. We tend, for example, to think that all nouns are (very much)
like 'chair' and 'table,' all adjectives (very much) like 'red' and
'square,' and so on. If we assimilate *all* nouns to familiar ones like
'chair' and 'table,' then we shall naturally do so with nouns like
'time' and 'nothing' and 'redness.' We shall quietly assume that since
'chair' and 'table' name particular kinds of entities—in this case,
physical objects—then so also do these other nouns. These nouns
too must name something—not, of course, entities just like tables
and chairs, but entities at least like streams or the air. And then we
can hardly help picturing, say, time as a kind of stream; we think of
it in accordance with that picture.[17] Again, it is clear how Sartre's
picture of nothingness is the result, in great part at least, of his
assimilating the word 'nothing' to certain common nouns, and how
Plato's picture of his Forms is the result of his assimilating words
like 'redness' and 'triangularity' to proper names. Thus it is that our
craving for unity contributes to the generation of misleading pictures.

The assimilation of individual words, as remarked earlier (p. 200),
is really a matter of the assimilation of whole sentences. When Sartre
assimilates 'nothing' to the name of some physical substance, he is
assimilating certain sentences containing the former to syntactically
similar sentences containing the latter. ("There was nothing in the
room," "There was a table in the room"; "What did you see?" "I

[17] See R. Suter, "Augustine on Time with Some Criticisms from Wittgenstein," *Revue internationale de philosophie,* Fasc. 3-4, No. 61-62 (1962).

saw nothing," "I saw a table"; and so on.) And when philosophers like Plato who think that terms for universals, such as 'cowardice' and 'beauty,' are the names of special sorts of individuals, they too are assimilating grammatically similar sentences. ("Jones is reprehensible," "Cowardice is reprehensible"; "London means a great deal to him," "Beauty means a great deal to him.")

Let us consider in somewhat more detail another example illustrating how our craving for unity, when directed towards language, results in assimilations which produce misleading pictures. We say things like (a) "John cut an apple," (b) "John is digesting his supper," and (c) "John is sick." These statements say something about John: the first asserts that he performed an action, the second that a certain physiological process is going on in his body, the third that he is in a certain state or condition. These sentences are clearly intelligible, and we have no difficulty in understanding what they say. There are other sentences which bear marked grammatical similarities to them: for example, (a′) "John deduced a conclusion," (b′) "John is thinking about his holiday," and (c′) "John is upset by the news." Not only do these three sentences, in themselves, resemble the first three, but also the same grammatical moves which are permissible from the first three are permissible from the second three too. Thus adverbs like 'quickly' and 'carefully' can be inserted before the verbs in both (a) and (a′); instead of saying (a), "John cut the apple," one could just as well say "An apple was cut by John," and instead of saying (a′), "John deduced a conclusion," one could say "A conclusion was deduced by John"; and so on. What is more, the kinds of utterance that can surround each of the sentences in (a)-(c) are like those that can surround those of (a′)-(c′). Thus, questions like "Which apple did he cut?" "How long did it take him?" "When did he do it?" are appropriate to statement (a), as are the questions "Which conclusion did he deduce?" "How long did it take him?" and "When did he do it?" to statement (a′). As a result of all these, and other, grammatical similarities, we are led to think that (a) and (a′), (b) and (b′), (c) and (c′) are used in (very much) the same way. We are led to think that since (a) asserts that John performed an action, (a′) must assert that he performed an action; since (b) asserts that a process is going on in John, (b′) must assert the same; and similarly with (c) and (c′). But in the second group, the action, process, and state are evidently not physical ones. We cannot see John deducing a conclusion as we can see him cutting an apple; there are no bodily movements which are characteristic of deducing a conclusion as there are bodily movements characteristic of cutting an apple. These facts prevent us from saying that the act of deducing a conclusion is of *exactly* the same kind as that of cutting an apple, that the process of thinking is of *exactly* the same kind as that of digesting a meal, and that the state of being upset is *exactly* the same kind as that of being sick. We must say rather that they are analogous. The former are overt, publicly observable, and physical; the latter are very much like them, only they are hidden and not publicly observable. They are mental: deducing is a mental act, thinking is a mental process, and being upset is a mental state. As usual, we tend to make the analogy as close as possible (the unity as great as possible). No physical action can exist without something—a body—to do it; no physiological process, without something—a body—in which it can take place; and no physical state, without something—a body—to be in that state. Hence we assume that no mental action can exist without something—a mind—to do it; no mental process without something—a mind—in which it can take place; and no mental state, without something—a mind—to be in that state. In this way, by indulging our craving for unity, we are led by certain grammatical similarities in our language to think of the mind on the model of the body—i.e., we are led to have the picture of the mind as a ghostly kind of body. (See *BB*, p. 7.)

The kind of connection that has so far been discussed between pictures and language is an indirect one, since the link is made only through our craving for unity. But the connection goes deeper than that. The language we ordinarily speak does not merely tempt us with formal and structural analogies alone; it often incorporates in a full-blooded form the very pictures that entrap us in doing philosophy.

> A *picture* held us captive. And we could not get outside it, for it lay in our language and language seemed to repeat it to us inexorably. [*PI*, sect. 115.]
>
> . . . Such hypotheses or pictures of the working of our mind are embodied in many of the forms of expression of our everyday language. [*BB*, p. 40.]

But what does this mean? What it means will be clear, I think, if I correct a certain impression which my account may have created. By a picture, Wittgenstein did not mean a conscious and definite image. And by a person's having a picture of something, he did not mean that the person has, or tends to have, such an image whenever he thinks about that thing. It is undoubtedly true that, in some cases, having such images is an important part of having a picture of something. But in many cases, a person can have a picture of something without having, or even tending to have, any images at all in connection with it. To have a certain picture of something, as Wittgenstein uses the term, is to have a certain view of it, to think of it in a certain way, to think of it in accordance with some model or other. But what is it to do these things? Consider first a simple nonphilosophical illustration, one that Wittgenstein himself used. Suppose I think of the earth as a planet hurtling through space, and that I think, as I generally do, of my country as being near the top of the earth. I may then be led to say that I and my fellow-countrymen are standing upright and that the earth is beneath us, but that the people at the antipodes are hanging head downward and that the earth is really above them (*PI,* sect. 351).[18] In talking this way I have a certain picture of the earth. And this means that I am thinking of it in accordance with a certain model. One such model might be that of a basketball with a toy soldier glued to its surface in a standing position. If the ball is held in a certain way, the soldier is standing upright with the ball beneath him; but if the ball is held another way, the soldier is hanging head downward, with the ball above him. To have the picture of the earth that I do, is just to think of *it* as I do of the ball, to speak and think as if the earth and the people on it were related to one another just as the ball and the toy soldier are; to speak and think of the earth on the model, or on the analogy, of the ball. I may indeed in this case conjure up one or more images, and this may be a part of my having the picture. But even if I do, it is not the whole of my having the picture, and not even the most important part of it. What is important is that I talk and think of the earth in a certain way—namely, in the way I talk and think about the ball. It is this sense of 'having a picture' that Wittgenstein intends when he speaks of philosophical puzzlement. Thus, Sartre, for example, has the picture of nothingness as a kind of being; he pictures it to himself in that way, and this need not entail that he actually forms, or tends to form, a conscious image of nothingness as a kind of being. All that is required is that he speak and think of nothingness as if it were a kind of being—and this, as we saw, he does. And Plato, in the *Parmenides,* spoke of his Forms as if they

18 See also Malcolm, *Memoir,* p. 54.

were a peculiar kind of particular or individual; that is, he had that kind of picture of his Forms.

If this is what is primarily involved in having a picture, then it is easy to see how pictures can lie in our language, can be embodied in certain forms of expression—and how they are practically forced upon us. Having a picture is largely a matter of saying, or tending to say, certain things. If these things are the usual or normal things to say about the matter in question—if they are *the* typical things one says in the language—then of course one can hardly help having the relevant picture. Think, for example, of the sort of thing that one can say in English about the mind. We say such things as 'I shall keep it in mind,' 'She searched her mind for a possible explanation,' 'His mind is cluttered up with all sorts of prejudices,' and so on. These ways of speaking are just the ways we speak of a place, such as a room or a garden: 'I shall keep it in my room,' 'She searched her closet for a possible dress to wear,' 'His attic is cluttered up with all sorts of junk,' and so on. No wonder that we cannot help having a picture of the mind as a kind of mysterious place where ideas, images, memories, and so on, appear and where some of them are stored. Anyone who speaks English is almost bound to have such a picture; but whereas the ordinary man can get along quite well with such pictures, the philosopher, when he thinks philosophically about the mind, is easily led into bewilderment and confusion by them.

This picture-embodying feature of our language, of certain forms of expression, is one of the main things Wittgenstein has in mind when he speaks as if language were the main culprit responsible for philosophical puzzlement.

> Philosophy is a battle against the bewitchment of our intelligence by means of language. [*PI*, sect. 109.]
> Philosophy . . . is a fight against the fascination which forms of expression exert upon us. [*BB*, p. 27.]

Notice, by the way, that we need not have only one picture of something; on the contrary, certain forms of speech may embody one picture, while other forms embody different ones. For example, some ways of talking embody the picture of the mind as a kind of place, while others suggest as strongly that it is like an (ethereal) kind of physical object. Examples of the latter are the following: "One's mind reels at the thought of it," "He has a brilliant mind," "We need fresh, imaginative minds." These are the sorts of things we might say about certain kinds of physical objects, rather than about places; and so, along with the picture of the mind as a place, we have the picture of the mind as a (ghostly) *thing*.

> We do not realize that we *calculate*, operate, with words, and in the course of time turn them sometimes into one picture, sometimes into another. [*PI,* sect. 449.]

It is doubtless true that one kind of philosophical puzzlement results from the clash of incompatible pictures.

*   *   *

The plain man does not think about time or mind or sense perception or nothingness. He uses temporal words (e.g., 'time,' 'simultaneous,' 'before,' 'after'), mental words (e.g., 'mind,' 'think,' 'remember,' 'idea'), sense-perceptual words (e.g., 'see,' 'hear'), and the word 'nothing' with perfect ease, but does not bother himself about what time *is,* what space *is,* and so on. The philosopher, however, is just the man who has, traditionally, thought about these matters. But when he does so, according to Wittgenstein, he takes certain ordinary locutions which the plain man habitually uses and which cause him no difficulties at all, and puts peculiar interpretations on them. Wittgenstein compares a philosopher to a savage in this respect. After speaking about the notion of possibility, he writes:

> We mind about the kind of expressions we use concerning these things; we do not understand them, however, but misinterpret them. When we do philosophy we are like savages, primitive people, who hear the expressions of civilized men, put a false interpretation on them, and then draw the queerest conclusions from it. [*PI,* sect. 194.]

Philosophers make the same sort of mistake—although presumably not such crude ones—as a native I once read about in a newspaper article:

> For weeks before Independence Day, the nation was in a state of high excitement. "Does independence come wrapped in paper or do we go to the bank to get it?" a native asked an American missionary.

Lewis Carroll used to misinterpret certain forms of speech deliberately:

> "Who did you pass on the road?" the King went on, holding out his hand to the Messenger for some hay.
> "Nobody," said the Messenger.

"Quite right," said the King: "this young lady saw him too. So of course Nobody walks slower than you."

"I do my best," the Messenger said in a sullen tone. "I'm sure nobody walks much faster than I do!"

"He ca'n't do that," said the King, "or else he'd have been here first. However, now you've got your breath, you may tell us what's happened in the town." [19]

In this passage, Carroll has deliberately assimilated the word 'nobody' to the class of proper names—as if it were, for example, 'Mr. Nobody.' (See *BB*, p. 69.) Philosophers also misinterpret language, and we have seen several examples of such misinterpretation in our discussion of the causes of philosophical puzzlement.

Perhaps the main source of the philosopher's misinterpreting language is, again, his craving for unity—his tendency, when he does philosophy, to take the pictures embodied in ordinary language too seriously, to push the analogies too far. Up to a point, having pictures is harmless enough, as is shown by the fact that ordinary men have them and experience no intellectual ills thereby. But the philosopher is apt to go too far, and then he gets into trouble.

Consider, for example, the picture of the earth as being like a basketball with toy soldiers glued on it. Having this picture, I may be led to expect that if I were to dig all the way through the earth to the antipodes, the first things I would strike on emerging are the feet of the people there, the cellars of their houses, and so on. This application of the picture is perfectly all right. But other applications are not all right. Thus I would err if I were to expect that, if I flew in an airplane to the antipodes, the airplane would have to fly with the earth hovering above it, my blood would be forced to my head since my head would be hanging downwards, and so on. This would be to apply the picture wrongly, to misapply it. Again, suppose I have a picture of the mind as a kind of theater in which the self witnesses passing images, thoughts, feelings, and so on. Some applications of this picture do no harm: such would be the case if I were led to ask a person what he is witnessing now ("What is going on now in your mind?"), whether his present image is vivid or fuzzy, and so on. But if I am led to ask where precisely this theater is located, or if I feel a desire to look into another person's "theater" for myself to see what is going on (see *PI*, sect. 427), I am applying the picture wrongly. Wittgenstein gives another example in *The Blue Book*. Suppose a

[19] Lewis Carroll, *Through the Looking-Glass,* in *The Complete Works of Lewis Carroll* (New York: The Modern Library, n.d.), p. 225.

scientist tells us that matter is composed of tiny particles which are separated by spaces much larger than the particles themselves. We might then picture matter to ourselves as a thinly filled space. No harm would be done thereby; the picture is harmless enough for ordinary purposes. But harm would be done if we apply the picture wrongly: if, for example, we are led to think that even the hardest and soundest of wooden floors is not solid and that if one were to step on it, he would surely fall through. (See *BB*, p. 45.)

Pictures cause trouble, then, only when they are misapplied. Misapplying a picture is mainly a result of taking it too seriously, of pushing the model or analogy too far. Thus one gets into trouble by picturing the earth as like a basketball only when it is taken to be more like such a ball than it really is. And one gets into trouble by picturing the mind as like a theater only when it is taken to be more like a theater than it really is—for example, if one supposes it makes sense to speak of *anyone,* and not just the person whose mind it is, witnessing what goes on in it, or if one supposes it makes sense to speak of something going on in it even when there are no witnesses, not even the person himself.

It is perhaps obvious that not all the troubles caused by the misapplication of pictures will take the form of philosophical puzzlement. I see no way, for example, in which the picture of the earth as being like a basketball can lead to philosophical bewilderment. There is no philosophical puzzle known as the problem of the antipodes, nor is it readily conceivable how there might be. But by misapplying the pictures we have of universals or time or the mind or mental acts or numbers, the philosopher can be plunged into the chaos of intellectual bewilderment.

*   *   *

In this chapter, I have tried to give some idea of how, according to Wittgenstein, certain intricately connected and complex facts about language and about ourselves give rise to philosophical puzzlement. In talking about these things, I do not doubt that I have, perhaps unavoidably, given the impression that the whole thing involves conscious processes, as though, for example, the philosopher were aware of his craving for unity, of his assimilating different kinds of words and sentences to one another, or as though he knew perfectly well that he thinks of time on the model of a stream or of the mind as a kind of theater. But nothing could be further from Wittgenstein's thought. He would say that it is not even true that if these facts were pointed out to a philosopher in the grip of a philosophical problem, he would in every case agree. The sources of a philosopher's intellectual ills may be obvious to us, once they are pointed out, but they need not be obvious to the patient nor acknowledged by him in any way. If Wittgenstein is right, the patient is in fact thinking in certain ways despite the fact that he may hotly deny it. The source of his trouble may be hidden from him simply because it is so close to him (*PI*, sect. 129). Indeed, it is just when the puzzlement is most acute that he will be least likely to acknowledge the causes of his difficulty. His cure, in fact, consists at least to some extent in his coming to admit the existence of these things. This additional point of affinity between the sort of intellectual difficulties with which Wittgenstein is concerned and the sort of psychological difficulties with which Freud and modern psychoanalysts are concerned, is obvious enough.

9 The Attack on Essentialism

In the preceding chapter, it was noted that according to Wittgenstein one of the important features of human thinking—and one that plays a big part in producing philosophical puzzlement—is our craving for unity. Let us consider this craving as it affects our thinking about the uses or functions of whole sentences. Left unchecked, as we said before, our desire for unity would attempt to find one function common to all sentences, no matter what their grammatical mood. But this seems like an impossible ideal: it is just too obvious that the sentences 'Is he at home?' 'Shut the door!' 'Oh, if she were only here!' and 'The vase is red.' have radically different functions. And so we must rest content with finding one function in common to all declarative sentences, one to all interrogative sentences, one to all imperative sentences, and so on. The inevitable result, again, is assimilation; for example, we assimilate all declarative sentences to familiar ones like 'The cat is on the mat' and assume that they are all used to state some fact (describe some situation) in the same way that the simple model sentence generally is. There is no denying that this is a plausible and tempting view. The early Wittgenstein, at any rate, accepted it. All propositions, he said in the *Tractatus*—and we may reasonably assume that he thought all meaningful declarative sentences express propositions—are truth-functions of elementary propositions; hence, they all describe some more or less complicated situation. This, indeed, is their essence.

> 4.5(3)   . . . The general form of a proposition is: This is how things stand.

(See *PI*, sect. 114.)

I said that it seems like an impossible ideal to find one function common to absolutely all sentences, no matter what their grammatical mood. This is true, I think; but to keep the historical record straight, it must be remarked that the craving for unity was so strong in some philosophers that they thought the ideal was actually realized. Augustine, for example, stoutly maintained that absolutely all sentences, even those in the interrogative and imperative moods, have but a single function—to teach the hearer that something or other is the case.

> *Augustine*—What does it seem to you that we wish to accomplish when we speak?
> *Adeodatus*—As it occurs to me now, either to teach or to learn.
> *Aug.*—I see, and I agree to one of these points. For it is evident that when we speak we wish to teach. But how do we learn?
> *Ad.*—How, indeed, except by asking questions?
> *Aug.*—Even then, as I understand it, we only wish to teach. For, I ask, do you question for any other reason except that you may teach what you wish [i.e., what you want to know] to him you question?
> *Ad.*—That is true.
> *Aug.*—So now, you do see that in speaking we desire only that we may teach.[1]

(See *PI*, sects. 24 and 440.) One wants to say here that the craving for unity has got out of hand.

Our passion for unity is not, of course, confined to the field of language alone. We tend to assume that there is something in common to all horses, to all tables, to all men, to all games, to all religions, and so on. And this is a natural assumption. The class of horses, for example, cannot be a merely random one. Its members, the individual horses, no matter how different they may be in other respects, must have some characteristics in common—or so we think—for otherwise they would not be named or nameable by the single general

---

[1] *De magistro*, ch. 1, para. 1. Translation is from St. Aurelius Augustine, *Concerning the Teacher* and *On the Immortality of the Soul*, trans. by George C. Leckie, p. 3. Copyright, 1938, D. Appleton-Century Co., Inc. Reprinted by permission of Appleton-Century-Crofts.

term 'horse.' [2] These shared characteristics constitute the essence of that kind of thing, constitute "horseness." And, since everything is of some kind—it is either a man, a table, a piece of silver, or whatever —everything has an essence. There can be no gainsaying the powerful influence this idea has exerted on man's thought from the time of Plato down to the present.

One form of the craving for unity, then, is a craving for essences, and it is so strong that we tend to assume that everything actually has an essence—that it is the essence of all nouns to name some entity, or kind of entity, in the way that 'John Jones' or 'tree' do, that it is the essence of all declarative sentences to state some fact in the way that 'The cat is on the mat' does, and so on.

Wittgenstein sets out to show that the belief in essences, although widespread and entirely natural, is mistaken. Whereas philosophers have traditionally looked for sameness and unity, Wittgenstein looks for difference and multiplicity; indeed, he once remarked to a friend that he had considered using as a motto for the *Investigations* a line from *King Lear*—"I'll teach you differences." [3] According to Wittgenstein, one has only to examine, for example, the various individuals to which a given general term applies, to see that there is nothing which they all have in common. As a plain matter of fact, they do not share a common essence. Wittgenstein cites the example of games: If we look at all the things called 'games,' we will not find some characteristic(s) that they all have, in virtue of which we call them by that name. Wittgenstein's own account here is so lucid and pungent that I cannot do better than simply quote it:

> Consider for example the proceedings that we call "games." I mean board-games, card-games, ball-games, Olympic games, and so on. What is common to them all?—Don't say: "There *must* be something common, or they would not be called 'games' "—but *look and see* whether

[2] In the *Meno*, Socrates says, "We always arrive at a plurality, but that is not the kind of answer I want. Seeing that you call these many particulars by one and the same name, and say that every one of them is a shape, even though they are the contrary of each other, tell me what this is which embraces round as well as straight, and what you mean by shape when you say that straightness is a shape as much as roundness. . . . What is this thing which is called 'shape'? . . . Don't you see that I am looking for what is the same in all of them? . . . What is it that is common to roundness and straightness and the other things which you call shapes?" (Plato, *Meno*, 74 D–75 A.) The translation is from Plato, *Meno*, trans. by W. K. C. Guthrie (Baltimore, Md.: Penguin Books, 1956). Reprinted by permission.

[3] M. O'C. Drury, "Ludwig Wittgenstein: a symposium," *The Listener*, LXIII, No. 1609 (January 28, 1960), 164.

there is anything common to all.—For if you look at them you will not see something that is common to *all,* but similarities, relationships, and a whole series of them at that. To repeat: don't think, but look!— Look for example at board-games, with their multifarious relationships. Now pass to card-games; here you find many correspondences with the first group, but many common features drop out, and others appear. When we pass next to ball-games, much that is common is retained, but much is lost.—Are they all 'amusing'? Compare chess with noughts and crosses. Or is there always winning and losing, or competition between players? Think of patience. In ball games there is winning and losing; but when a child throws his ball at the wall and catches it again, this feature has disappeared. Look at the parts played by skill and luck; and at the difference between skill in chess and skill in tennis. Think now of games like ring-a-ring-a-roses; here is the element of amusement, but how many other characteristic features have disappeared! And we can go through the many, many other groups of games in the same way; can see how similarities crop up and disappear. [*PI,* sect. 66.]

These words can come as a revelation. Whereas one had always quite uncritically, and most likely also unconsciously, taken it for granted that all things called by a general term had something—an essence —in common, he sees now that it is not necessarily so. At one stroke, that assumption has been revealed and destroyed. As it falls away, one's entire view of language, and indeed of the world, is quite altered.

In all historical fairness, it must be stated that this particular insight was not original with Wittgenstein. We know that he read and admired William James' *The Varieties of Religious Experience,* first published in 1902; and in that book James makes the same point [4] about the terms 'religion' and 'government' that Wittgenstein does about 'game.' We call all sorts of things 'religions,' and it is plainly false that there are one or more characteristics to be found in each and every one of them. A philosopher can put forward a definition of the term 'religion' which he thinks captures the "essence" of religion, but he can only think he has succeeded if he concentrates on a small group of religions and ignores all others. And more likely than not, his definition will merely express his own preference for what he thinks any proper religion ought to be.

A main cause of philosophical disease—a one-sided diet: one nourishes one's thinking with only one kind of example. [*PI,* sect. 593.]

[4] See the first two pages of Lecture II.

We must not, however, rush from one extreme to the other; we must not infer from the fact that there is no essence of games or religions, that each is nothing more than a motley, disconnected group of things which are arbitrarily called by the same name. There is no warrant for thinking that the denial of essences leaves no reason whatever why a range of different things are all named by a single general term. Although they have no common essence, they have certain "family resemblances." Suppose we consider the many different activities called 'games':

> And the result of this examination is: we see a complicated network of similarities overlapping and criss-crossing: sometimes overall similarities, sometimes similarities of detail.
>
> I can think of no better expression to characterize these similarities than "family resemblances"; for the various resemblances between members of a family: build, features, colour of eyes, gait, temperament, etc., etc. overlap and criss-cross in the same way.—And I shall say: 'games' form a family.
>
> And for instance the kinds of number form a family in the same way. Why do we call something a "number"? Well, perhaps because it has a—direct—relationship with several things that have hitherto been called number; and this can be said to give it an indirect relationship to other things we call [by] the same name. And we extend our concept of number as in spinning a thread we twist fibre on fibre. And the strength of the thread does not reside in the fact that some one fibre runs through its whole length, but in the overlapping of many fibres. [*PI*, sects. 66-67.]

So there is a good reason for applying a single general term to a range of different things, only it is not what believers in essence have thought it was.

Wittgenstein's point can be generalized if we look at the matter not, as we have been doing, from the side of the things to which words apply, but rather from the side of the words. Looked at from the side of the things, his point is that there is no characteristic, or set of characteristics, which all things named by a given general term have in common—there is no essence which they all share. Looked at now from the side of the words, his point may be put as follows: no general term has a unitary meaning. As I use the term 'unitary,' a word has a unitary meaning when its meaning constitutes an indissoluble whole. That is, the statement or formulation of its meaning refers to certain definite characteristics and something must have all of them for the word to be properly applicable to it. The notion of having a unitary meaning is thus distinct from that of having a *single* meaning. If a word does not have a single meaning, it has two or more meanings; and each of these meanings may, or may not, be unitary. For some special purpose, we can, of course, *make* the meaning of a general term unitary by stipulating well-defined limits. We might lay it down, for example, that nothing shall be called a 'game' unless a score can be kept, and unless the players receive no money for their performance, and unless there is an official set of rules. The resulting concept will not, however, be *the* concept of a game, but only some part of it which we have chosen to mark off for our own special purposes. (*PI,* sects. 68-69.)

I think Wittgenstein would want to generalize this point about words. He would claim that not only such "family" words as 'game' and 'number,' but most, and perhaps all, general terms have no unitary meaning. Let us examine this claim.

Why can we say that the term 'game' has no unitary meaning? The reason is this. There is a group of characteristics C_1, C_2, C_3, . . . C_n which games typically have. Among these characteristics are the following: C_1, there are rules which govern the activity; C_2, there is the possibility of winning; C_3, it is a pleasant diversion; C_4, the players need to exercise certain skills; and so on. If *all* games had all of these characteristics, and *only* games did, then the word 'game' would have a unitary meaning; the statement of its meaning would consist of a statement of the characteristics C_1 to C_n. But in fact this condition is not met; not all games have all the characteristics. One game may have only C_1, C_2, and C_7; another may have only C_1, C_3, C_6, and C_7; another only C_2, C_5, and C_6; and so on. All that is required in order for something to be a game is that it have *some* of the cluster of game-characteristics C_1 to C_n, not that it have *all* of them. Not every combination of game-characteristics will do, of course: for example, it is not enough that something have only characteristic C_2 (the possibility of winning) in order to qualify for gamehood. In wars and duels and debates, there is the possibility of winning, but none is a game. There is no way of specifying ahead of time and in the abstract just how much *is* enough; it would be absurd to suggest, for instance, that in order for an activity to be properly counted as a game, it is a necessary and sufficient condition that the activity have some combination of four or more of the *n* game characteristics. It might well be that some activities which have only three game characteristics are without doubt games, and that others which have five are not.

The word 'game' might be called a genus term, and the concept 'game' a genus concept; there are several species of games falling under it (board games, ball games, card games, dice games, and so on); and individual games (e.g., chess, tennis, bridge), in turn, belong to one or more species. But not all general terms are genus terms or even species terms. Perhaps, then, it is only because of their special kind of generality that genus and species terms have no unitary meaning. But this is not so. Consider the term 'lemon,' for example.[5] Lemons normally have certain characteristics: a yellow color when ripe, skin of a certain thickness with a waxy texture, ovoid shape, acid taste, a size and hardness that falls within a certain range, and so on. If an object has all these properties, it is definitely a lemon; but something which lacks one or more of them may still be a lemon. It might happen that in a particular region of the world, due to atomic fallout, lemon trees started producing fruit of a pinkish color and with a sweet taste, but having all the other characteristics of ordinary lemons. These fruits would doubtless still be lemons: pink lemons, or sweet pink lemons. A thing cannot lack all, or even very many, of the typical lemon properties, and still be a lemon; but there is no one property, or group of two or three properties, which an object must have to be properly called a lemon. It must simply have some combination of the cluster of properties which lemons typically have. Thus lemons, like games, have no essence; and 'lemon,' like 'game,' has no unitary meaning.[6]

To whatever extent Wittgenstein's doctrine is true, to that extent he has dealt a powerful blow against the traditional view of essentialism. According to that view, the characteristics of any class C to whose members a common term T is applicable—the class of horses

---

[5] The example is borrowed from Michael Scriven. See his "The Logic of Criteria," *The Journal of Philosophy*, LVI (1959), 857-68.

[6] Wittgenstein's thesis, although highly plausible for terms like 'horse,' 'lemon,' and 'game,' is not at all plausible for terms like 'brother' and 'vixen'; for to be a brother, it is essential that one be male, and to be a vixen, it is essential that a fox be female. There is, then, an important distinction between those terms that do and those that do not fall under Wittgenstein's thesis. I am not sure how to characterize this distinction in any more fundamental way, but somehow or other it is one that must be made. For an interesting discussion of this perplexing subject, see Hilary Putnam's "The Analytic and the Synthetic" in *Minnesota Studies in the Philosophy of Science*, Vol. III, H. Feigl and G. Maxwell, eds. (Minneapolis: University of Minnesota Press, 1962). For an article that opposes the claim asserted in this footnote, see J. R. Bambrough's "Universals and Family Resemblances," *Proceedings of the Aristotelian Society*, LXI (1960-1), especially 212-14.

or games or trees, for example—can be divided into two distinct groups: (a) a relatively small group of essential characteristics— the qualities a thing *must* have in order to be a member of the class C, and which only members of class C have, and (b) a larger group of nonessential, or accidental, characteristics—the qualities that members of class C may or may not typically have, but in either case do not need to have in order to qualify as members of C. The essential characteristics were each supposed to be necessary, and the group of them together sufficient, for membership in the class C. Wittgenstein has attempted to break down this distinction between essential and accidental characteristics; he claims that there are not two radically distinct groups of characteristics of a class C whose members are denoted by a common term T—there is only a single cluster of characteristics, some sub-set of which, and not the *same* sub-set in every case, a thing must have in order to be a member of C, in order for the term T to be (properly) applicable to it.

Wittgenstein deals yet another hard blow to essentialism when he points out that many terms not only fail to have a unitary meaning, but also fail to have a *fixed* meaning—the cluster of characteristics associated with the term is always subject to change. For example, it is true now, as far as I know, that all fully refined sugar is white— barring the use of dyes, of course. Hence, this is one of the characteristics now belonging to the 'sugar'-cluster. But in the future, a new kind of raw material for sugar may be developed or discovered, or a new refining process for sugar may be found, and such refined sugar may turn out to be blue; in that case, the cluster of sugar-characteristics will have to be modified accordingly.[7]

If, however, we shift from everyday practical life to a discipline where a certain amount of rigor is required—to science, for example —essentialism might seem to regain its foothold. It often happens in science that certain characteristics of a substance or phenomenon are considered to be so central as to be treated as absolutely essential, as defining, characteristics of it. Wittgenstein would not want to deny this. He would not deny that for certain special purposes, such as those of a scientist, terms can and sometimes should be *given* a circumscribed, unitary meaning. But even in these cases, the unitary meaning cannot and should not be considered final and unalterable.

---

[7] In *PI*, sect. 79, Wittgenstein makes a different, but related, point—namely, that an *individual person* sometimes (perhaps always?) uses a term without a fixed meaning.

As science advances, and new theories are propounded, new facts and procedures discovered, some formerly privileged characteristics will be dropped from the inner circle and others take their place. So in science as in everyday life, terms often, and perhaps always, have no fixed meaning. (See *PI,* sect. 79.) [8]

It is difficult to determine whether or not Wittgenstein thought that all words are like 'game' and 'lemon' in having no unitary, fixed meaning; but this question need not concern us, for it is clear that he held that all words which are involved in philosophical puzzlement, all words which are philosophically interesting, have no unitary, fixed meaning. They do not, in other words, designate essences. And once we free ourselves from the belief in an essence corresponding to each word, we shall be well on the way towards freeing ourselves from at least some kinds of philosophical bewilderment.

Since it is our language which bewitches our intelligence, it is only to be expected that the belief in essences would do the greatest damage when it is applied to words. And we have seen in the preceding chapter that this is in fact the case. But a question still arises: Are we justified in rejecting essences in the field of language? It is doubtless true that there is no essence of games or lemons; but is *language* actually like that? Is it not true, for example, that all common nouns *do* name something in the way that 'tree' and 'dog' do, and that the one use of all declarative sentences, for example, is to describe how things stand, in the way that 'The cat is on the mat' does? It is not difficult to anticipate Wittgenstein's answer to these questions: Of course, he says, some nouns denote a kind of object as 'tree' does, and many declarative sentences are normally used to describe how things stand as 'The dog is on the porch' does, but these are only one kind of case among many (*PI,* sect. 3). When we suppose that all nouns name things and that all sentences are used to state facts, we are simply taking words like 'bread,' 'table,' and 'chair' (*PI,* sect. 1) and sentences like 'The dog is on the porch' and 'It is raining' as our models and thinking of all words and sentences in accordance with those models. But we should not indulge our craving for unity as quickly as that. When we took the trouble to look at the various different individual games, we found after some reflection that there is no one thing which they all have in common. If we do the same for

---

8 Wittgenstein undoubtedly owes a debt for these, and other, points to N. R. Campbell's *Physics: The Elements* (London: Cambridge University Press, 1920). On the topic discussed here, see chapter 2 of that book.

the various different words and sentences that there are, we will find, after even a superficial review of them, that there is no one thing which they all do.

> Think of the tools in a tool-box: there is a hammer, pliers, a saw, a screw-driver, a rule, a glue-pot, glue, nails and screws.—The functions of words are as diverse as the functions of these objects. (And in both cases there are similarities.) [*PI*, sect. 11.]

> Review the multiplicity of language-games in the following examples, and in others:
> Giving orders, and obeying them -
> Describing the appearance of an object, or giving its measurements -
> Constructing an object from a description (a drawing) -
> Reporting an event -
> Speculating about an event -
> Forming and testing a hypothesis -
> Presenting the results of an experiment in tables and diagrams -
> Making up a story; and reading it -
> Play-acting -
> Singing catches -
> Guessing riddles -
> Making a joke; telling it -
> Solving a problem in practical arithmetic -
> Translating from one language into another -
> Asking, thanking, cursing, greeting, praying. [*PI*, sect. 23.]

> . . . We do the most various things with our sentences. Think of exclamations alone, with their completely different functions.
> Water!
> Away!
> Ow!
> Help!
> Fine!
> No!
> Are you inclined still to call these words "names of objects"? [*PI*, sect. 27.]

This insight—that individual words and sentences function not in one way only, nor even in a small number of ways, but in a wide variety of ways—is of central importance in the later philosophy of Wittgenstein. He claims that it allows the philosopher to escape from some of his peculiar predicaments; that is, it leads the way to a resolution of much philosophical puzzlement. Once he comes to the realization that the uses of language are extremely diverse, one of the main sources of his bewilderment is immediately swept away. This knowledge will often bring with it freedom from the powerful influence of pictures; a philosopher need no longer be held captive by them. For example, after examining the various actual uses of a certain term which he had previously assumed had the sole use of naming some kind of entity, as 'tree' and 'dog' do, he may discover that it does not in fact name any entity whatever. In that case, he will naturally not be so strongly tempted to think of "it" in accordance with a particular picture or model. At least, if he is still tempted to do so, he will know that he is being tempted and that he ought not to succumb to the temptation. What is more, the grammatical similarities amongst different sentences found in ordinary language will no longer constitute such a formidable danger; the philosopher will no longer simply take it for granted that identical grammatical features entail identical kinds of meanings or uses. It was remarked earlier that Wittgenstein compared a person caught in the grip of a philosophical puzzle to a man trying to escape from a room.

> He tries the window but it is too high. He tries the chimney but it is too narrow. And if he would only *turn around*, he would see that the door has been open all the time! [9]

Part of what corresponds to turning around and seeing that the door is open, it is safe to say, is the rejection of essences, especially in the area of language; that is, the abandoning of the "one-and-only-one-use" prejudice and the realization that words have many different uses.

Before proceeding to the next chapter, in which the notion of a use of language will be examined, one point should be made. Wittgenstein said: "Philosophy is a battle against the bewitchment of our intelligence by means of language" (*PI*, sect. 109). He also spoke of language "tempting us to draw some misleading analogy" (*BB*, p. 48), of the "troublesome feature[s] in our grammar" (*BB*, p. 49), and of "grammatical illusions" (*PI*, sect. 110). In these passages, there lies the suggestion that it is the fault of our language that philosophers fall into puzzlement. But in contrast to this imputation of blame, Wittgenstein asserts:

> It is wrong to say that in philosophy we consider an ideal language as opposed to our ordinary one. For this makes it appear as though we thought we could improve on ordinary language. But ordinary language is all right. [*BB*, p. 28.]

9 Malcolm, *Memoir*, p. 51.

There is no contradiction here. Wittgenstein is saying that certain features of our language mislead us, tempt us to fall into ways of thinking that result in bewilderment; to this extent, our language is at fault. But the philosopher is also at fault. Although there are pitfalls in our language for the philosopher, he need not rush blindly into them. Language may tempt him, but he need not be tempted: or, if tempted, he need not succumb. Ordinary language was not designed with the philosopher's special interests in mind; its purpose is to allow human beings to communicate with one another so that work can be accomplished, transactions can be carried out, wishes can be expressed and satisfied, and so on. And for these purposes, ordinary language is quite adequate. We use words like 'time,' 'mind,' and 'know' with perfect ease and lucidity in our everyday conversation, and misunderstanding seldom arises. But then the philosopher comes along with his inordinate craving for unity and, gulled by certain features of the grammar of his language, is led into erroneous assumptions and fixed pictures. The result is the kind of philosophical confusion we have been considering. The philosopher, therefore, is at least as much to blame for philosophical troubles as our language is. (See *PI*, sect. 194.)

The later Wittgenstein's ambivalent attitude towards ordinary language reminds us of an analogous attitude expressed in the *Tractatus*. On the one hand:

4.002(4)   Language disguises thought. So much so, that from the outward form of the clothing it is impossible to infer the form of the thought beneath it, because the outward form of the clothing is not designed to reveal the form of the body, but for entirely different purposes.

And on the other:

5.5563(1)   In fact, all the propositions of our everyday language, just as they stand, are in perfect logical order.

A question which naturally suggests itself is this: If ordinary language is not perfect, since it tends to mislead the philosopher, why not invent a new and more nearly perfect language which will not have this unfortunate tendency? Wittgenstein admits that improvements in our terminology for some particular practical purpose or for the removal of some particular misunderstanding are perfectly possible (*PI*, sect. 132). These improvements need not be confined merely to the substitution of one isolated phrase or sentence for another, either. A whole new language can be invented to replace entire por-tions of the old. Mathematics, which has its own notation and rules, is such a language. This technical language has many important functions: it is indispensable to science and engineering, it plays a crucial role in our everyday activities, it allows us to make inferences which would be difficult or impossible without it, and so on. Hence there are eminently good reasons for expending the enormous amounts of time and energy required to develop and perfect the language of mathematics; but such effort scarcely seems warranted where the only end to be achieved is that philosophers will be less tempted, or not tempted at all, to fall into confusion. Whether such an ideal lan-guage eventually be forged or not, however, one thing is certain: what we must do, and do first, if philosophical bewilderment is to be removed, is to understand the workings of our ordinary, everyday language—for it is in *its* terms that our confusions and questions arise and are expressed.

10   Uses of Words

When we do philosophy, Wittgenstein has said, we get our understanding tied up in knots, we suffer intellectual cramps—that is, we fall into confusion. We are like flies in a fly-bottle: we buzz around and around in the same confined space, and see no way of escape. Wittgenstein has given us an account of some of the causes of our being in this unhappy state. But we want more than that—we want to be cured, we want to escape. We do, at any rate, if we are at all like Wittgenstein. Some philosophers, to be sure, officially abandon all hope of freeing themselves from philosophical bewilderment. Hume, for example, at the end of Book I of his *A Treatise of Human Nature,* finds himself in the most deplorable state of Wittgensteinian puzzlement, and the only means he can find to relieve it is to dine, play a game of backgammon, converse and be merry with his friends. But Wittgenstein would be totally unsatisfied with this kind of "solution"; he needs to clear up the puzzles and is unable to turn his back on them until he has achieved complete clarity (*PI,* sect. 133). Telling him to ignore his philosophical problems would be as effective as telling a dope addict that he ought to give up taking drugs. And so if we seek freedom as passionately as Wittgenstein does, we need to know not only why we are trapped in various different fly-bottles, but also how we are to escape from them.

> What is your aim in philosophy?—To shew the fly the way out of the fly-bottle. [*PI,* sect. 309.]

But how? How are intellectual illnesses to be cured? Wittgenstein's reply is that we must examine in detail the actual ways in which the key words involved in philosophical puzzlement are used. We run into (at least some of) these puzzles because we misinterpret our forms of speech, because we have a wrong and over-simplified view of the way language works. Such puzzles are resolved by seeing how our words actually do work, what their uses really are.

> [Philosophical problems] are, of course, not empirical problems; they are solved, rather, by looking into the workings of our language, and that in such a way as to make us recognize those workings: *in despite of* an urge to misunderstand them. [*PI*, sect. 109.]

Consider the word 'time,' for example. Let us suppose that we have given way to our craving for unity and have assumed that 'time' has the same kind of use that 'tree' or 'table' or 'river' does. Then it is likely we will be held captive by some picture or other and will suppose—wrongly—that the word 'time' is the name of a peculiar ethereal medium in which events occur, and which flows ineluctably from the future, through the present, into the past. In that case, it can be shown that we fall very quickly into philosophical puzzlement. But if we would only examine the actual situations in which the word 'time' is used and notice how it is used, we would see that it does not function as the name of any kind of ghostly medium. Once we do this, once we "command a clear view" of the uses of the word (*PI*, sect. 122), our philosophical problems are solved: there is nothing more to do, there is no further problem. There is, in particular, no additional question "But what is *time?*" still to be answered. Indeed, we will realize that the very question is illegitimate, if it presupposes, as it seems to, that time is some kind of *thing*.

Wittgenstein's claim here is not apt to be fully intelligible, much less assessable, however, until we know precisely what he means by a *use* of words. Hence, we must now turn to an examination of this notion. It is one of the most central, and at the same time one of the least clear, notions in the writings of the later Wittgenstein. From the way I have been stressing the word 'use,' one might suppose that it was the one word which Wittgenstein always employed in this connection; but not so. True, he uses the word 'use' far more often than any other, but he also speaks of the *functions* of words (e.g., *PI*, sects. 11, 17, 274, 556, 559), of the *aims* of words (e.g., *PI*, sect. 5), of their *purposes*. (e.g., *PI*, sects. 6, 8, 398), their *offices* (e.g., *PI*, sect. 402), their *roles* (e.g., *BB*, pp. 103, 108), and their *employments* (e.g., *PI*, sect. 421). There is no indication that Wittgenstein was aware of any important differences of meaning amongst these several terms, or that he would have been interested in such differences had he been aware of them. Although I think this is a mistake, and that there are important differences, I shall not try to argue the point here. Wittgenstein's central concept is clearly that of the *uses* of words, and we can, with reasonable assurance, concentrate on it. Nevertheless, we should bear in mind that characteristics associated with the concepts of function, aim, purpose, and the rest, may well have colored Wittgenstein's thinking about the use of words.

The general notion of the *use* of something is not so simple as it might appear to be. There are, for example, what might be called various different aspects of the use of a thing, and what these aspects are will vary with the kind of thing in question. In the use of a hammer, for example, there are at least the following aspects: how to use it (e.g., how to handle it), what it is used for or used to do, and, more rarely, what it can be used as (e.g., as a paperweight). In the use of olive oil, there are at least the following aspects, which form a different group from the previous one: what it is used in (e.g., in salad dressings) and what it is used for (e.g., for frying). Let us see now what different aspects there are in connection with the use of *words,* and then try to determine which of these Wittgenstein meant when he spoke of the use of words.

To begin with, there is one aspect that we can mention only to ignore hereafter. Words are used *as* the materials of most of our speaking and writing. It is words which we most often utter and write, when we utter or write something, just as it is foodstuffs that we most often use as materials when we cook. As Eliot's Sweeney so pungently put it for all of us:

I gotta use words when I talk to you.[1]

In this aspect of the use of words, all words are identical, and one word, or group of words, cannot be distinguished from another. Hence it is an uninteresting sense of 'use' for our present purposes, and I shall say no more about it.

A more significant aspect, for us, of the use of words has to do with the grammar of the word in question, with the kind of linguistic context in which the word can and cannot occur. For example, in the frame 'I slept in a _____ _____ bed last night,' the blanks can be filled with certain words without linguistic oddity, whereas if they

---

[1] T. S. Eliot, "Fragment of an Agon," in his *Collected Poems, 1909-1935* (New York: Harcourt, Brace & World, Inc., 1936).

are filled with other words, or even the same words in reverse order, the result is linguistically odd. Thus the words 'big comfortable' or 'very short' are suitable to fill the blanks, but not 'drink rum,' nor 'short very'; nor even, though to a lesser extent, 'comfortable big.' Knowing how to use a word, in this aspect of its use, includes knowing in what sort of linguistic contexts or frames the word can and cannot occur without grammatical oddity; or, to put it more actively, knowing how to construct grammatically correct word-groups (e.g., sentences) which contain that word and being able to recognize grammatically incorrect word-groups which contain it. Let us call this the *grammatical* aspect of the use of words.

Words are also used to *do* certain things, to perform certain linguistic jobs. It is this aspect which is meant when one says that the sentence 'Get out!' is normally used to issue an order, the sentence 'Is he?' is normally used to ask a question, and the sentence 'He is.' is normally used to state something. When we speak of the use of words in this way, we mean that words are used to perform certain speech acts (such as issuing orders, asking questions, and so on); hence, let us call this the *speech-act* aspect of the use of words.

It must not be supposed that the grammarians' rough classification of the grammatical moods of sentences corresponds in any easy, straightforward way to the various kinds of speech acts; that, for example, declarative sentences are always used to state something, that interrogative sentences are always used to ask questions, that imperative sentences are always used to issue orders, and so on. It would be a mistake to give in to our craving for unity in this way; for while the number of possible grammatical moods is small, the number of possible speech acts is very great indeed, and sentences of the same grammatical mood can be used to perform many different speech acts. Consider declarative sentences, for example. There is some truth in the claim that they are commonly used to "state that something is the case" or to "state something." But two points need to be borne in mind if we are to appreciate *how* much truth there is in it. (1) 'Stating something' is a highly general, abstract term with little content. It covers a multitude of more specific speech acts which are all different and which may be performed when one uses a declarative sentence—e.g., describing something, identifying something, commenting on something, reporting what one sees (hears, feels, and so on), pointing out something to someone, and so on. And (2), declarative sentences are very often used to perform speech acts which are not species of stating something at all: to issue commands (captain of a ship to one of his subordinates: "You will see that the job is finished by six o'clock tonight."), to request something ("I would like to see the manager."), to swear ("I'll be damned."), to recommend things ("I think this is the one you should buy."), to express emotion ("I wish I were dead!"), to make promises ("I promise to meet you there."), and to do any number of other things as well.

Consider, too, the variety of speech acts which can be performed with the following interrogative sentences: "Isn't it a lovely day?" "How do you do?" "Won't you help us?" "May I have the sugar, please?" "Are you out of your mind?" "How can you possibly believe that?" "Why did I do *that?*" "Isn't she pretty?" Confronted with examples like these, one sees at once the utter absurdity of assuming that whenever an interrogative sentence is uttered, the speaker is always simply asking a question.

The topic of speech acts is a highly complex and subtle one, and cannot be treated here in any detail.[2] Still, one important distinction ought to be made, even if only sketchily. It is the distinction which may *very roughly* be characterized as that between speech acts that are successfully performed in the mere act of saying certain words in the appropriate circumstances and speech acts that are not successfully performed unless the speaker's words produce some additional effect, normally an effect that concerns his hearers. Austin calls the former *illocutionary acts* (speech acts performed *in* saying something) and the latter *perlocutionary acts* (speech acts performed *by* saying something). Examples of illocutionary acts are such speech acts as describing something, issuing an order, asking a question, greeting someone, announcing an intention, making a promise, and so on. They are illocutionary acts because, in order to perform them successfully, one need only say certain words in the appropriate circumstances; there is no need that the saying of the words should produce some effect in the hearer or anywhere else.[3] Given the appropriate condi-

---

[2] The interested reader should consult J. L. Austin, *How to do things with Words* (Oxford: The Clarendon Press, 1962). Austin, White's Professor of Moral Philosophy at Oxford University from 1952 until his untimely death in 1960, was a powerful leader of English philosophy after World War II. His influence, indeed, rivaled that of Wittgenstein.

[3] This is debatable, however. Austin claims that an illocutionary act will not be "happily" or successfully performed unless a certain minimal effect is achieved on the hearer—namely, his hearing the words and understanding their

tions, to say "Get out!" *is* to issue an order, to say "It is an impressionistic painting mainly in greens and blues" *is* to describe something, to say "Where did John go?" *is* to ask a question, and so on. Examples of perlocutionary acts are such speech acts as persuading someone to do something, upsetting someone, pleasing someone, cheering someone up, confusing someone, shocking someone, amusing someone, and so on. To perform one of these speech acts, it is not enough that certain words be spoken; in addition, some effect [4] must be produced. For example, if you want to perform the speech act of pleasing your wife, you may say to her "You look lovely in that white dress." In saying this, you are complimenting her (*il*locutionary act), with the intention of pleasing her. But your intention will not be realized, and you will hence not succeed in performing the speech act of pleasing her, unless your words actually do please her—that is, unless they have that effect. Thus, pleasing someone is not an illocutionary, but a perlocutionary speech act. (Whether or not a perlocutionary act *can* only be performed by means of the performance of an illocutionary act is but one of the innumerable questions which we cannot try to answer here.)

When we speak of using words to perform speech acts—i.e., illocutionary or perlocutionary acts—we are concerned with the use of words to do, to accomplish, one thing or another. The use of words *to do* something ought to be distinguished from the use of words *in doing* something—by that I mean their use *in the course of* activities like telling a joke, relating an experience, instructing a student, presenting a report, and so on. It is normally not the case that the use of an individual sentence is by itself enough to do these things; relating an experience, for example, normally requires the utterance of several different sentences. Instead of our saying, then, that the sentence '*S* is *P*' was used to relate an experience, which would be odd, it is more natural to say that the sentence '*S* is *P*' was used *in the course of*, or *in*, relating an experience. (Analogously, instead of saying that a hammer was used to build a house, which would be odd, we ought rather to say that the hammer was used in, or in the course of, building

---

meaning and force. "I cannot," he says, "be said to have warned an audience unless it hears what I say and takes what I say in a certain sense" (Austin, *op. cit.,* p. 115). If Austin's claim be admitted, a slight reformulation of the way I have drawn the distinction between illocutionary and perlocutionary acts would be required, but this could easily be done.

[4] Or, some effect over and above the minimal one of the hearer's hearing the words and understanding their meaning and force. See the previous footnote.

the house). To mark the distinction between, on the one hand, the linguistic jobs which individual word-groups, primarily whole sentences, can be used to do (viz., perform various speech acts) and, on the other hand, such larger-scale jobs as relating experiences, presenting reports, and so on, which normally require the use of several sentences, we may call the latter *speech activities*. Let us confine the label 'speech activities' to those activities which, like relating an experience, are carried out entirely, or almost entirely, in words. This will serve to distinguish them from such other activities as harvesting a crop, building a bridge, and so on, which involve a great deal more than the use of words, although they usually do, as a matter of fact, also involve the use of words.

The distinction between speech acts and speech activities is only a very loose one. Most words or phrases that designate speech activities—e.g., 'describing something,' 'giving a report'—can also designate speech acts; descriptions can be made and reports given in a single sentence, in which case describing and giving the report are speech acts, not speech activities. If it requires 20 or 50 sentences to give a report, then there is no question but that the speaker uses each individual sentence while engaging in the (one) speech activity of giving a report, and that he does not use each one separately to give the report, i.e., to perform the speech act of giving a report. At the other extreme, if it requires but a single sentence, then the speaker no doubt uses the sentence to perform the speech act of giving a report, and does not use it "while engaging in" the speech activity of giving a report. But there will not be, in general, any definite place between these two extremes where the speech act of giving a report becomes the speech activity of giving one. Still, a distinction which is not absolutely clear-cut is nevertheless a distinction, and this one will prove to be important for our purposes.

In discussing the grammatical aspect of the use of words, I noted that individual words and phrases regularly occur in certain linguistic frames, that word-groups are normally put together in certain ways and not in others. There is another important aspect of the use of words that is concerned not with the immediate linguistic frame of individual words or phrases, but rather with the wider conditions— both linguistic and nonlinguistic—in which word-groups (including whole sentences and individual words) and even morphemes are normally used. It is what I shall call the *semantic* aspect of the use of words. (Though it is different from the grammatical aspect, the two are not, of course, unrelated.) A given word-group (e.g., a given sentence) is normally used only when certain conditions, which may be called semantic conditions, obtain—for example, when certain events have taken place, when the speaker is in a certain kind of situation, when a certain kind of object is present, and so on. To say this is to say that there are semantic regularities associated with the utterance of a given word-group. If two people, A and B, are having their dinner, with all the usual items on the table and with the salt-cellar near B, A can say "Please pass the salt" without the least oddity, without deviating from any semantic regularities, for this is the kind of situation in which those words are generally uttered. But under these same conditions A cannot say to B "Look out for that horse!" without deviating from semantic regularities, although he *can* say it without oddity—for example, if he says it playfully as part of a game they play at dinner, or if he says it in the course of telling a story to B over their dinner. So though the words "Look out for that horse!" can, in special cases, be used without oddity when there is no horse present, still *in the standard case,* when those words are uttered, there is a horse present, and the speaker is in fact warning the hearer about the horse. And so there are—indeed, must be, if there is to be a language at all—correlations, although not perfect ones, between the use of certain words and the existence of certain semantic conditions. Words normally "go with" certain semantic conditions, and do not "go with" certain others.

Semantic conditions sometimes include other utterances. For example, the words "No, he isn't here" are normally used only if a question has previously been asked (such as "Is Mr. Smith at home?"); one would be puzzled if the first thing one's wife said to him in the morning were "No, he isn't here." Words like "Fine, thank you," "I certainly will," "Did he?" and many others are also normally or regularly used only when there has occurred, immediately preceding them, another utterance of a certain type.

The foregoing brief remarks about the semantic aspect of the use of words have simplified things that are not simple, have glossed over many difficulties. But for our present purposes, which are extremely broad and general, they may, hopefully, suffice. The reader who is interested in pursuing these matters should read Paul Ziff's excellent *Semantic Analysis,*[5] from which my remarks and most of the terminology in which they are couched were drawn.

[5] Ithaca, New York: Cornell University Press, 1960.

Having made this survey of the various aspects of the use of words, let us return to the question of what Wittgenstein means by their "use." The way to escape from philosophical puzzlement, he has told us, is to abandon our a priori, over-simplified picture of the use of words, and look at the actual use of words to see what goes on.

> One cannot guess how a word functions. One has to *look at* its use and learn from that. [*PI*, sect. 340.]

(Compare his remark about games: "To repeat: don't think, but look!" [*PI*, sect. 66].) But the question now is: At *what* precisely are we being enjoined to look—at the grammatical, semantic, or speech-act aspect of the use of words? Or perhaps some other? In short, which aspect or aspects of the use of words did Wittgenstein intend? He never explicitly tells us; we must ferret it out for ourselves. I shall now try to show that Wittgenstein touches on all of the different aspects of the use of words we have distinguished: in some passages he stresses one aspect; in others, another; and sometimes he refers to all aspects collectively. But I shall also try to show that there is one aspect of the use of words he strongly emphasizes and to which he devotes his attention above all the others.

It is safe to say that Wittgenstein, in this "escape-from-puzzlement" phase of his philosophy, is almost totally unconcerned with what I have called the grammatical aspect of the use of words. To be sure, there are a few references to it, e.g., in *PI*, sects. 496, 558, and 664. But on the whole, Wittgenstein has practically no interest in purely grammatical considerations. Indeed, we know from our discussion of the sources of philosophical puzzlement that Wittgenstein considered the grammatical behavior of words and the grammatical structure of sentences to be among the main things that lead the philosopher astray. It could, I think, be argued with justice that it is mainly those with a superficial knowledge of grammar that are led into confusion by it, and that a more careful and detailed attention to grammar would help show them the error of their ways. But Wittgenstein's attitude seems rather to be: Grammar is dangerous, so avoid it!

We must not be misled by the following passage, which seems on the face of it to contradict what I have just said:

> Our investigation is therefore a grammatical one. Such an investiga-
> tion sheds light on our problem by clearing misunderstandings away.
> [*PI*, sect. 90.]

Wittgenstein is not using the term 'grammatical' here in the restricted sense it normally has; he is using it in an extremely broad sense, to mean simply *linguistic*. That is, the passage claims merely that he is investigating the use of *words;* it does not limit the investigation to what I have called the grammatical aspect of that use. In another passage, he distinguishes between surface grammar and depth grammar, and clearly implies that the former is highly misleading.

> In the use of words one might distinguish 'surface grammar' from 'depth grammar.' What immediately impresses itself upon us about the use of a word is the way it is used in the construction of the sentence, the part of its use—one might say—that can be taken in by the ear.— And now compare the depth grammar, say of the word "to mean," with what its surface grammar would lead us to suspect. No wonder we find it difficult to know our way about. [*PI*, sect. 664.]

Wittgenstein's "surface grammar" corresponds roughly to my "grammatical aspect of the use of words." In urging us to examine the use of words, he is not referring to this aspect. He is, in fact, determined to rise above it (or delve beneath it, at any rate). On the other hand, he *is* concerned with depth grammar; this, however, has to do not with the grammatical aspect of the use of words, but with one or more of the other aspects.

The semantic aspect of the use of words is one on which Wittgenstein places some importance. If we are troubled about the meaning of a word or group of words, he often urges us to look at the actual circumstances in which they are used. Here is one example:

> . . . Let us see what use we make of such an expression as "This face says something," that is, what the situations are in which we use this expression, what sentences would precede or follow it (what kind of conversation it is a part of). [*BB*, p. 179.]

Again, suppose I give someone the order "Figure out the values of *y* when *x* is given the values 1, 2, 3, . . . in the formula $y = x^2$," or the order "Add 3 to the number 1, then add 3 to the result of that addition, then add 3 to that result, and so on." These short instructions each determine, potentially, an infinite number of separate steps; the orders could never be completely carried out, yet given any step in the process of carrying them out, the orders uniquely determine what the succeeding step must be. And this may strike us as mysterious, may puzzle us. How can all those steps be already contained, in germ, in the original order? In some sense or other, it seems that I have issued an infinite order. And not only that, it seems that I have also somehow already anticipated each of the uniquely determined steps which must be taken if the order is to be obeyed. For example, in the second order, I meant my hearer to say '1003' after '1000,' '1006' after '1003,' and so on.

> Here I should first of all like to say: your idea was that that act of meaning the order had in its own way already traversed all those steps: that when you meant it your mind as it were flew ahead and completed all the steps before you physically arrived at this or that one.
>
> Thus you were inclined to use such expressions as: "The steps are *really* already taken, even before I take them in writing or orally or in thought." And it seemed as if they were in some *unique* way predetermined, anticipated—as only the act of meaning can anticipate reality. [*PI*, sect. 188.]

The pit of philosophical puzzlement yawns before us. To avoid it, Wittgenstein tells us, we ought to look at the sort of conditions which exist in the world when we say "The steps are determined by the formula _____"—i.e., look at the semantic aspect of the use of those words.

> We use the expression: "The steps are determined by the formula. . . ." *How* is it used?—We may perhaps refer to the fact that people are brought by their education (training) so to use the formula $y = x^2$, that they all work out the same value for y when they substitute the same number for x. Or we may say: "These people are so trained that they all take the same step at the same point when they receive the order 'add 3.'" We might express this by saying: for these people the order "add 3" completely determines every step from one number to the next. (In contrast with other people who do not know what they are to do on receiving this order, or who react to it with perfect certainty, but each one in a different way.) [*PI*, sect. 189.]

Wittgenstein does this sort of thing over and over again in his later writings: if we want to know what 'certainty,' 'understanding,' 'expectation,' 'thinking,' 'proof' mean, he tells us to examine the sort of situation to which these words apply. Examine the semantic conditions of their use.

Wittgenstein does not often appeal to the speech-act aspect of the use of words; this aspect plays only an insignificant—indeed, almost no—part in his philosophy. The reader of the *Investigations* may be misled on this point by the fact that in an early section of that work, Wittgenstein compares words to tools.

> Think of the tools in a tool-box: there is a hammer, pliers, a saw, a screw-driver, a rule, a glue-pot, glue, nails and screws.—The functions of words are as diverse as the functions of these objects. (And in both cases there are similarities.) [*PI*, sect. 11.]

(The term 'function' here is unfortunate; tools *per se* do not have functions. Wittgenstein is obviously using 'function' as if it meant the same as 'use.' In general, it must be acknowledged that Wittgenstein is not nearly as careful in his choice of words as one could wish.) Tools are used to do things, to perform certain acts; hammers are used to drive nails, screw-drivers to drive in screws, and so on. Hence, in comparing words and their uses to tools and their uses, Wittgenstein clearly has the speech-act aspect of the use of words in mind. But after paying lip-service to this aspect, he thereafter virtually ignores it in his actual practice. In the rare passages in which speech acts *are* mentioned, it is almost never illocutionary acts which are involved, but rather perlocutionary acts—that is, he speaks of using words to produce a certain effect in the hearer (see, e.g., *PI*, sect. 6). And even then, such acts are mostly treated slightingly, as being of little importance.

We come now to the aspect of using words that plays by far the most important part in Wittgenstein's later philosophy—namely, their use in what I have called speech activities. When Wittgenstein speaks of the use of words, it is usually this aspect of use that he has in mind. Even the important semantic aspect is largely absorbed into the general framework of speech activities, the semantic conditions being viewed as the conditions under which speech activities of various sorts can be engaged in. Accordingly, we must now examine speech activities, and Wittgenstein's conception of them, in some detail.

Wittgenstein's name for what I have called a speech activity is 'language-game,' and I shall henceforth use that expression rather than 'speech activity.' In point of fact, however, Wittgenstein uses the term 'language-game' much more broadly than I defined 'speech activity.' He includes among language-games pure speech activities —that is, activities which involve little, or nothing, except the use of words—such as telling a joke, reporting an event (*PI*, sect. 23), describing a room (*PI*, sect. 290), and giving an account of a dream (*PI*, p. 184). But he also includes such activities as constructing an object from a description, obeying orders, and play-acting (*PI*, sect. 23) which involve certain modes of nonlinguistic behavior as essential components, and not just as mere idle accompaniments in the way that gestures with the hand, say, figure in most (pure) speech activities. The following kind of activity, engaged in by a builder A and his assistant B, is a clear example of what Wittgenstein calls a language-game:

> A is building with building-stones: there are blocks, pillars, slabs and beams. B has to pass the stones, and that in the order in which A needs them. For this purpose they use a language consisting of the words "block," "pillar," "slab," "beam." A calls them out;—B brings the stone which he has learnt to bring at such-and-such a call. [*PI*, sect. 2.]

It might be thought that in such activities as these, one ought to distinguish the linguistic from the behavioral aspect, and to refer to the former alone as a language-game; but Wittgenstein states that the nonlinguistic behavior is also to be included in the language-game.

> I shall also call the whole, consisting of language and the actions into which it is woven, the "language-game." [*PI*, sect. 7.]

Let us call the former kind of language-games (i.e., those which consist entirely, or virtually entirely, in the use of words) *pure*-language-games, and the latter kind (i.e., those which include non-linguistic behavior as important, or even essential, parts) *impure*-language-games. The difference is one of degree only, and there will not, of course, be any hard and fast line separating pure- from impure-language-games. And the term 'impure' is not meant to have the slightest pejorative force. In fact, as I shall try to show, Wittgenstein considered impure-language-games to be, in an important sense, basic and held that pure-language-games are parasitic upon them in a crucial way.

Wittgenstein was impressed by the fact that to speak a language is to behave in certain highly complex ways—ways, furthermore, which require skill, and which can be rightly or wrongly, correctly or incorrectly, done. To speak a language is to exercise certain techniques, to behave in ways which exhibit various abilities. And speech behavior is not an isolated, hermetically sealed mode of behavior, entirely separate from other modes. Linguistic and nonlinguistic behavior are woven together into an intricate organic whole. Consider what is involved in a child's learning the meaning of a new word—let us say, the word 'ball.' It is not enough that the child be able simply to make the sound 'ball' or even to write the word 'ball'; a parrot or an idiot could do that, and not have the slightest notion of what the word meant. What more is required, then? Well, what has the child learned when he has learned the meaning of the word 'ball'? To begin with, he has learned to behave in certain ways; he has learned, for example, to reply "Ball" if someone, pointing to a ball, asks "What is this?" And when he himself points to a ball, he again says "Ball" or, even better, "This is a ball." It might be thought that this is enough. To see that it is not, we must consider the notion of an ostensive definition.[6]

Many, but by no means all, words—and these mostly names—can be given ostensive definitions. This kind of definition contrasts roughly with a verbal definition, such as one found in a dictionary. Consider, as an example, the names of kinds of physical objects. An ostensive definition of such a term consists in pointing to an example of the sort of thing named by the term, or perhaps a picture of one, and saying something of the form "This is a(n) _____" or "This is called 'a(n) _____.' " Thus an ostensive definition of the word 'ball' would consist in pointing at a ball and saying "This is a ball" or "This is called 'a ball' " or something of the sort. It is natural to suppose that such a definition uniquely determines the meaning of the word 'ball,' and hence that the child, in being able to repeat the maneuver, must know what that meaning is. But Wittgenstein shows that this supposition is false. In pointing to a ball, one is at the same time pointing to a round thing, to a thing of a certain color (e.g., red), to a thing of a certain size, to a thing of a certain weight, to a thing belonging to a certain person (e.g., Johnny), to *one* thing, to a thing made of a certain material (e.g., rubber), and so on. Hence, the ostensive definition, by itself, does not uniquely determine the meaning of the word 'ball,' and the child, in repeating it, does not necessarily know what that meaning is. As Wittgenstein says: "An ostensive definition can be variously interpreted in *every* case." (*PI,* sect. 28). The child, for instance, may think the word 'ball' designates the red color, the round shape, one of Johnny's toys, anything made of rubber, this particular bit of rubber, and so on. This is not to say that ostensive definitions are worthless; on the contrary, giving such definitions is one important way we have of teaching people what words mean. But they do not in themselves guarantee success; for they must in every case be properly *construed,* properly *interpreted,* properly *understood.* And the behavior of the child described at the end of the last paragraph is not nearly enough to show that he has interpreted the definition properly.

What sort of behavior on the part of the child will show that he has interpreted the definition aright, that he knows the meaning of the word 'ball'? All of the following are certainly relevant: if asked

---

[6] In what follows, I shall ignore Wittgenstein's distinction between ostensive teaching and ostensive definition (*PI,* sect. 6), because it is not relevant to our present concerns.

to fetch a ball, he brings back a ball; if asked to draw a picture of a ball, he does so; when asked which of several objects is a ball, he picks the right one; he speaks in appropriate ways—e.g., he says such things as "This ball is green and bigger than Suzy's" and does not say such things as "That is very ball—much baller than Suzy's." If he behaves in these and similar ways, we say that he has learnt the meaning of the word 'ball,' that he knows what a ball is. We may, of course, be mistaken. It may happen, for instance, that he behaves in all these right ways inside the house, but when he first sees a ball outside the house, asks "What is that?" In such a case, we might say that he had thought the word 'ball' meant a small spherical object *in a house*. This misconception can be removed by suitable instruction—i.e., training. But others may yet reveal themselves. There is no specific point after which it will be absolutely certain, without any possibility of being proven wrong in the future, that the child knows the meaning of the word 'ball.' But after observing his behavior in a variety of situations over a certain period of time, we can be reasonably certain that he does. (See *PI,* sect. 145.)

What seems to emerge from all this is that speaking a language, which of course includes understanding things said in it, is a matter of being able to *do* a variety of things, to act or behave in certain ways—and to do so under the appropriate conditions. Some of these skills are purely linguistic: a person unable to construct grammatically correct English sentences could not be said to speak English. But others are nonlinguistic—or, rather, are at once linguistic and nonlinguistic—in that they involve an interaction between using words and behaving in nonlinguistic ways. In our example, we saw that if a person is to be said to know the meaning of the word 'ball,' he must be able to do at least some of the following: to fetch balls, to draw pictures of balls, to distinguish balls from other things, and so on—and he must know when to do them, in what circumstances. If a person does not know how to act in at least some of these ways, he does not know the meaning of the word 'ball.' [7] And the same goes for

---

[7] This brief sketch is meant to apply at most only to the normal or central cases; it would have to be considerably expanded and qualified in various ways to cover all possible cases. For example, a paralyzed person might perfectly well know the meaning of the word 'ball' despite the fact that he cannot fetch balls, draw pictures of them, and so on. But even here, one could plausibly argue, there is a conceptual connection with modes of behavior; for it seems reasonable to suppose that if such a person does know the meaning of the word 'ball,' he must know what it is to do some or all of those things.

other words as well. Consider the word 'time," for example. Suppose a person claimed to know the meaning of the word 'time,' but was unable to tell time; had no idea how to measure a time interval (e.g., to determine how long the cake had been in the oven); when told always to do one thing, a, at a later time than another, b, he sometimes did a first, sometimes did b first, and sometimes did them simultaneously, despite the fact that he was trying to follow the instructions; and so on. No one would grant that the person knew the meaning of the word 'time,' for to know the meaning of that word is—apart from being able to construct grammatical sentences containing it—to be able to determine what time it is, to be able to measure time, normally (e.g., when not being perverse) to do one thing at a later time than another when told to do so, and so on.

So speaking a language—i.e., speaking and understanding it—is engaging in certain modes of behavior that exhibit a variety of abilities or skills. It is to engage in what Wittgenstein calls "forms of life" (*PI*, sects. 19, 23, p. 226). This explains Wittgenstein's provocative remark:

If a lion could talk, we could not understand him. [*PI, p. 223.*]

We could not understand a lion because even if he could utter grammatically correct sentences, his behavior would presumably be too radically different from ours. For example, suppose a lion says "It is now three o'clock," but without looking at a clock or his wristwatch—and we may imagine that it would be merely a stroke of luck if he should say this when it actually *is* three o'clock. Or suppose he says "Goodness, it is three o'clock; I must hurry to make that appointment," but that he continues to lie there, yawning, making no effort to move, as lions are wont to do. In these circumstances—assuming that the lion's general behavior is in every respect exactly like that of an ordinary lion, save for his amazing ability to utter English sentences—we could not say that he has *asserted* or *stated* that it is three o'clock, even though he has uttered suitable words. We could not tell what, if anything, he has asserted, for the modes of behavior into which his use of words is woven are too radically different from our own. We would not understand him, since he does not share the relevant forms of life with us.

It is primarily because he deems modes of behavior to be so vitally important in the use of words—and behavior, moreover, which exhibits certain skills—that Wittgenstein compares the using of words to the playing of games. (See *PI,* sect. 23.) Using language, for him, is playing language-games. Malcolm reports:

> One day when Wittgenstein was passing a field where a football game was in progress the thought first struck him that in language we play *games* with *words.* A central idea of his philosophy, the notion of a 'language-game', apparently had its genesis in this incident.[8]

It is noteworthy that in another incident, years earlier, a central idea of his early philosophy had occurred to Wittgenstein in a flash of insight. In looking at the diagram, it had struck him that a proposition is a picture of reality (see p. 78f.). And later, in watching the football game, it had struck him that using words is engaging in language-games. These flashes of insight exerted a powerful influence on Wittgenstein's thought—perhaps too powerful a one. Instead of thinking that they had provided him with useful and illuminating analogies, he seems to have thought that they had revealed to him the true nature of language. Thus in the *Tractatus,* the elementary proposition is not merely *like* a picture of the state of affairs, it *is* a kind of picture of it; and in his later philosophy, we do not merely engage in activities *like* games when we use language—we actually play kinds of games. This is remarkable, coming from a man who was well aware of the philosophical dangers of taking an analogy too seriously, and who was even concerned to warn us against doing so.[9]

For the later Wittgenstein, at any rate, words are not pictures, but pieces used in various language-games. And just as the significance of a piece in chess depends on its "role in the game" (*PI,* sect. 563) —i.e., how it can be moved, how one behaves with it—so the meaning of a word is its role in the various language-games in which it figures, the kind of behavior that surrounds its use, the kind of behavior in which its use is embedded. An expression only has meaning in— indeed only gets its meaning from—these modes of behavior. As Wittgenstein himself once put it:

> An expression has meaning only in the stream of life.[10]

Words have meaning only *as* "pieces" in the language-games which are their "original home[s]" (*PI,* sect. 116).

---

[8] Malcolm, *Memoir,* p. 65.

[9] In *The Brown Book,* Wittgenstein wrote: "[Language-games] are more or less akin to what in ordinary language we call games." (*BB,* p. 81.) But later he seems to have thought that there is a more intimate relation than mere akinship between language and games.

[10] Malcolm, *Memoir,* p. 93.

If we forget this fact, says Wittgenstein, if we forget the intimate connections between language and behavior, and try to treat words in isolation from the actual practical situations in which they are used, we end up in puzzlement.

> The confusions which occupy us arise when language is like an engine idling, not when it is doing work. [*PI*, sect. 132.]
> . . . Philosophical problems arise when language *goes on holiday*. [*PI*, sect. 38.]

Consider, for example, the notion of time. Philosophical difficulties begin when we consider temporal words in isolation from all connection with any practical situation. No puzzlement need arise if we ask what is involved in making an appointment for some future time, or if we ask how time is measured, or why time seems to go slower when we are waiting for the green light than when we are reading a good book, and so on. In these questions, the word 'time' is being considered in the context of some actual or possible situation. But we become bewildered if, severing all ties with any conceivable situation, we ask simply "What is time?" This famous example (cited in *PI*, sect. 89) is taken from St. Augustine, who writes:

> For what is time? Who can readily and briefly explain this? Who can even in thought comprehend it, so as to utter a word about it? But what in discourse do we mention more familiarly and knowingly, than time? And, we understand, when we speak of it; we understand also, when we hear it spoken of by another. What then is time? If no one asks me, I know: if I wish to explain it to one that asketh, I know not. . . .[11]

Thus philosophical perplexity arises when philosophers treat words as if they had no essential relationship to any modes of activity, to any kinds of situation in which they are normally used—when they treat them, in short, abstractly.

This tendency to treat words abstractly is actually an unhappy result of that complicated pattern of ways of thinking, discussed in chapter 8, which Wittgenstein held to be a major source of philosophical puzzlement. If the word 'time,' for example, is assimilated to the class of familiar nouns like 'river,' so that one supposes it names some quasi-physical medium, and if, more particularly, one pictures time as a kind of ethereal stream, then he will naturally think that the only philosophical problem there can be about time is that of

[11] Edward B. Pusey, trans., *The Confessions of Saint Augustine* (New York: Modern Library, Inc., 1949), p. 253.

discovering what the nature of this stream is. There will then be no need to consider the practical activities in which the *word* 'time' figures; they will take care of themselves. For example, there will be no call to take into consideration what it is to measure time or tell what time it is, or to determine that two events happened at the same time, and so on. One must simply think about time itself, and discover what its nature is, and the rest will follow easily.

Here an objection might be raised against Wittgenstein: "He makes too much of behavior. Admittedly, words are often used in the context of practical activity, in situations in which nonlinguistic behavior plays an essential part—that is, in what were called impure-language-games. Wittgenstein focuses his attention on such language-games. But words are also—and perhaps most often—used in *pure*-language-games: we commonly use words in mere conversation. What sort of nonlinguistic behavior is supposed to be relevant in these cases? There isn't any. The words that are used undoubtedly have meaning, and yet they are not woven into any pattern of nonlinguistic behavior. So it would seem that Wittgenstein's account is just inapplicable to the use of words in pure-language-games, and hence is of only limited interest."

This objection is based on far too restricted a conception of behavior; it confines behavior to nonlinguistic behavior. But Wittgenstein would certainly not do so, and there seems to be no justification for doing so.

> Commanding, questioning, recounting, chatting, are as much a part of our natural history as walking, eating, drinking, playing. [*PI,* sect. 25.]

To talk is to behave in certain ways—in linguistic ways. Often, to be sure, our use of words is embedded in nonlinguistic modes of behavior. But our very use of words is itself always a mode of behavior, even when it is not embedded, or at least not directly embedded, in other, nonlinguistic modes. Such cases can be of great importance, too. Consider the species of language-games of the genus "asking and answering questions" that we play. For example, when asked "What did you say?" we (as a rule) repeat our previous utterance or say something equivalent to it; or, if we consider it unimportant and not worth repeating, we may answer "Oh, nothing"; or, if we did not in fact say anything, we may reply "I didn't say anything." These are the sorts of move we make in *our* language-games. People in other societies might play quite different ones. If they are asked "What did you say?" they might always repeat the utterance which preceded their previous one; or they might continue just as they had intended to, only in a louder (or softer) voice; or they might answer by saying what they wish they had said, or the first thing that comes into their heads; or they might not be allowed to answer, and only a third person who is present might be allowed to do so; and so on. Each of these possibilities represents a different form of life, and each is different from our own. The differences are in some cases of great significance, and have wide repercussions in the lives of the people concerned. And it would certainly not be implausible to maintain that the meaning of the sentence 'What did you say?' is different in each case.[12]

So both (1) purely linguistic (or almost purely linguistic) behavior, and (2) behavior which is a mixture of linguistic and non-linguistic behavior, are central to Wittgenstein's conception of a language-game. Still, there is some truth in the claim that he gives a predominant position to nonlinguistic behavior. I shall now try to explain what I take this truth to be. Words can be divided into two classes: a) those which have uses in impure-language-games, and b) those which have uses only in pure-language-games. The overwhelming majority of words fall in the first class, but there are a few—mostly technical terms—which fall in the second. Let us consider each in turn, briefly.

a) Wittgenstein would of course admit that one can sit and talk, thus using words of this first sort in pure-language-games. But he would insist that their use in pure-language-games is dependent on their use in impure ones, in the sense that neither participant could understand what was being said unless he had already mastered the use of the relevant words in a range of suitable impure-language-games. Wittgenstein is not saying that such words *have* meaning only in impure-language-games; he is saying rather that the meaning of these words is *given* in such language-games, is mastered or learned in such games, and is hence essentially involved in them. Only after having once mastered these fundamental impure-language-games can one then engage in the more sophisticated pure ones. One can sit and talk about pencils, for example; describing them, discussing which

12 This example, modified for my own purposes, is borrowed from Stanley Cavell. See his "The Availability of Wittgenstein's Later Philosophy," *The Philosophical Review*, LXXI, No. 1 (January 1962), 73.

are the best kind, and so on. But he could not do this if he did not know what it is to write with a pencil, to fetch a pencil, to point to a pencil, to hand over a pencil when asked for one, to distinguish pencils from other things, and so on—that is, if he had not mastered the basic impure-language-games in which the word 'pencil' plays a part. These fundamental impure-language-games "lie in the background" when words are used in pure ones.

This is not to say that the uses of these words in pure-language-games are in any way "reducible to" their uses in the basic impure ones. Their uses in the two kinds of games are quite different. In playing pure-language-games, one behaves in very special ways: one constructs sentences, answers questions, expresses agreement or disagreement with another's remarks, and so on. These are sophisticated modes of behavior which require more skill, more intelligence, the mastery of more difficult and complex techniques, than are required for fetching or pointing to pencils. And Wittgenstein would say that the uses of a word in these pure-language-games add to its meaning, since these are different uses from the ones it has in the impure-language-games. A person who has mastered the uses of the word in both kinds of language-games has a greater and deeper understanding of the meaning of the word than a person who has mastered them only in impure-language-games. The uses of a word in impure-language-games are the *basic* ones, but by no means the *only* ones. And they are basic in the sense that if a word of this sort did not have any use in any impure-language-game, it would not have any in pure ones, and in the sense that if a person did not know how to play the impure games, he could not play the pure ones either.

b) A few words and symbols may have no uses in impure-language-games—e.g., certain special symbols in the higher reaches of logic or mathematics. They may have uses only in pure-language-games—in calculating, drawing inferences, proving theorems, and the like. (But see *RFM,* Part IV, sect. 2 (p. 133).) But there is nothing in this fact to embarrass Wittgenstein: these pure-language-games would be the "original homes" of such words, and their meaning would be given in the parts they play in those games. Wittgenstein could very well insist on this; and it is only by construing 'behavior' or 'activity' in unduly restricted ways that it could be thought that his doctrine of language-games is inapplicable to these cases.

*   *   *

In section 1 of the *Investigations,* Wittgenstein describes a picture of language (one which he considers to be inadequate and misleading) according to which each word names an object. This picture can give rise to the idea that the meaning of a word is the object for which it stands; an idea to which Wittgenstein himself had yielded in the *Tractatus,* in so far as words are restricted to what he there called names—i.e., logically proper names. We have seen to what difficulties and absurdities this idea inevitably leads. If we abandon it, but still insist on assimilating the noun 'meaning' to familiar nouns like 'tree,' then we may be tempted to think of the meaning of a word as a kind of spiritual halo or atmosphere surrounding the word, which is apprehended by the mind when it grasps or thinks about the meaning of the word. (See *PI,* sects. 117, 120.) Against both these pictures of the meaning of a word, Wittgenstein asserts the opposing claim that the meaning of a word is its use in the various language-games in which it plays a part.

> For a *large* class of cases—though not for all—in which we employ the word "meaning" it can be defined thus: the meaning of a word is its use in the language. [*PI,* sect. 43.][13]

Notice that Wittgenstein is careful to qualify his claim: "a *large* class of cases—though not for all. . . ." This is exactly what one would expect from Wittgenstein: just as there are many different kinds of games, so there are many different kinds of meanings, and not all can be identified with the use of the word which is said to have a meaning. Typically, Wittgenstein does not tell us which kinds of cases he would exclude from his general maxim, but from the very wording of sect. 43, as well as from statements elsewhere (e.g., *PI,* sects. 138, 197, 532, 561; *BB,* p. 69) which suggest an unqualified identification of meaning and use, it is clear that he regards the exceptions as trivial and unimportant. (He may have had in mind such examples as the following: the word 'Naomi' means 'my sweetness' in Hebrew, and 'George' means 'husbandman' in Greek. These meanings are not the same thing as—and indeed have little, if anything, to do with—the uses of those names in *English*-language-games.) We

---

[13] There are hints in the *Tractatus* of a connection between meaning and use, although what Wittgenstein meant in the *Tractatus* by the *use* of a sign is of course radically different from what he meant in his later works:

3.326   In order to recognize a symbol by its sign we must observe how it is used with a sense.

3.328(1)   If a sign is *useless,* it is meaningless. . . .

may safely ignore the exceptions in the discussion that follows, then, and assert that for Wittgenstein the meaning of a word is its use in the language, although bearing in mind that he considered this to be true only for the most important kind(s) of meaning(s). Wittgenstein speaks not only of the meaning of a word, but also of the sense of a sentence, as consisting in its use (see *PI,* sects. 20, 421).

What were Wittgenstein's reasons for identifying the meanings of words with their uses? Doubtless there were several reasons, but I shall mention two that I take to be as important as any. The first is this. If we are worried about the meaning of some difficult term, like 'time,' 'statement,' or 'truth,' it is foolish to consider it by itself, in complete isolation—i.e., to ask "What does 'time' ('statement,' 'truth') mean?" or "What is time (a statement, truth)?" This tendency to treat words abstractly, as we have seen, is one of the disastrous errors commonly committed by philosophers. What we must rather do is consider the word concretely, in context, in the framework of actual situations in which it occurs. And so it is with the word 'meaning.' It is fruitless to take it out of all context and ask "What does 'meaning' mean?" or "What is the meaning of a word?" These questions only reinforce the illusion that the meaning of a word is a mysterious entity of some sort. We must consider the term 'meaning' more concretely: Wittgenstein urges us to think not of what meaning is all by itself, but of what it is to explain the meaning of a word, to teach the meaning of a word to a child, to know the meaning of a word. (Similarly, not "What is time?" but "What is it to measure time?"; not "What is a statement?" but "What is involved in making a statement?")

> "The meaning of a word is what is explained by the explanation of the meaning." I.e.: if you want to understand the use of the word "meaning," look for what are called "explanations of meaning." [*PI,* sect. 560.]

And if we concentrate on these types of situations, as Wittgenstein did, there is great plausibility in the suggestion that the meaning of a word is its use. Consider what is involved in teaching a child the meaning of the word 'ball,' for example (see pp. 240-2). It is natural to think that when we teach a child the meaning of that word, what we teach him is its use—we teach him to play different language-games with it. And if teaching him the meaning is teaching him the use, then must not the meaning of the word *be* its use (or, in case it has several, its uses)? Wittgenstein evidently concluded that it is.

The second reason cuts deeper. Wittgenstein seeks to establish the general thesis that anything which conventionally points or refers beyond itself, anything which has conventional meaning, does so only by being used in certain ways. It follows that words, being of this sort, have meaning only by being used; hence it is natural to suppose that their meaning is their use. The general thesis can be explained by an example. Think of the familiar sign which consists of the initials "W.C.," with an arrow pointing to the right, thus: ⟫→. We say that this sign means that there is a water closet to the right, that the arrow points in the direction of a water closet. But *how* does the arrow point to the right? In what does its pointing in that direction consist? It cannot do so in and of itself; in itself it is simply a dead arrangement of lines. It points to the right because it is used by human beings in certain ways, because it plays certain parts in their language-games. The most important one is perhaps this: a man wants to visit a water closet, he sees the sign, walks to the right, and finds one. It is solely in virtue of this sort of game, this sort of human behavior into which it is fitted, that the arrow points to the right. If it were used in different ways, if it were embedded in different modes of behavior, the same arrow might point to the left, or straight ahead, or not point in any direction at all. (*PI,* sects. 454 and 495.) The meaning of the arrow and of the sign, Wittgenstein might say, is its use in the language.

> Every sign *by itself* seems dead. *What* gives it life?—In use it is *alive.* Is life breathed into it there?—Or is the *use* its life? [*PI,* sect. 432.]

Wittgenstein, then, identifies the meaning of a word—and the sense of a sentence—with its use(s) in the language. This identification is, I shall now argue, mistaken, although I do not think that Wittgenstein's mistake here, if it is one, has any very serious consequences for his philosophy. There are, undeniably, some more-than-accidental connections between the meaning of a word and its use. For example, if a word has a meaning, then it doubtless also has a use in the language. And there is a connection between knowing the meaning of a word and knowing how to use it: in most cases, if a person had no idea how to use a certain word, we would not allow that he knew its meaning. But these admitted connections between meaning and use are not strong enough to warrant identifying them, as Wittgenstein does.

Wittgenstein's identification is implausible on the face of it. In nonlinguistic areas, at any rate, things which have uses (e.g., tools, instruments) normally cannot sensibly be said to have meanings. Moreover, things which may sometimes have meanings—or (in case nothing nonlinguistic can be said to *have* a meaning) things which may sometimes mean something—(e.g., black clouds on the horizon, footprints in the snow, the rising pitch of someone's voice) do not, except rarely, have uses. So one would not expect the meaning of a *word* to be the same thing as its use(s) in the language, and I think it can be shown that it is not. Those connections between meaning and use which were just admitted to hold for words generally, do not hold universally, much less necessarily. Thus although in general if one knows the meaning of a word he also knows the use, and vice versa, still it is quite possible to know the meaning of a word and yet not know its use, and to know the use without knowing the meaning. An example of the former: if someone tells me (a non-Latin-speaker) that 'ultus' means revenge in Latin, I thereby know the meaning of that word, but I have no idea how or when to use it.[14] Two examples of the latter: most people know how to use the word 'amen' and the sign 'Q.E.D.,' yet far fewer know their meanings.[15] Furthermore, many words have a use in the language, but no meaning—(and this is not, of course, to say that they are meaningless, either). Most proper names, for example, have a use, but no meaning. One cannot ask "What is the meaning of 'John Paul Jones?' " but only "Who is John Paul Jones?" And in asserting that John Paul Jones was an early American sailor who was captain of the *Bon Homme Richard,* one is not defining 'John Paul Jones' nor in any way giving its meaning—for it has none—but rather identifying John Paul Jones (or describing him or doing something of the sort, depending on the circumstances). Wittgenstein's identification of meaning and use leads him to speak of the meaning of proper names and even of their definitions (*PI,* sects. 40, 79); but in so speaking, he is simply misusing the words 'meaning' and 'definition.' Those two words are not used, as a rule, in connection with proper names.[16] To be sure, some proper names have meaning—e.g., certain first names, many

---

[14] The example is borrowed from Ziff, *Semantic Analysis,* p. 189.

[15] It could plausibly be argued that 'amen' and 'Q.E.D.' have no meaning in English; but then they would count even more heavily against the identification of meaning and use, for they certainly have uses in English.

[16] This is not to deny that proper names have connotation, nor that proper names can mean something to someone—but to admit these things is not to admit that they have meaning. On these points, see Ziff, *op. cit.,* pp. 93-97.

American Indian names—but in the overwhelming majority of these cases, the meaning has nothing whatever to do with the use. I think a case could be made for saying that some words other than proper names also have uses but no meaning, but this would embroil us in a long, controversial discussion. There is no need to embark on such a project, for enough has been said already to support the claim that Wittgenstein was mistaken in identifying the meaning of a word with its use in the language.

Wittgenstein seems to have been laboring under the traditional assumption—perhaps a hold-over from the *Tractatus*—that it is the job of the philosopher to give us the real meaning of certain important words; and he is telling us that this meaning is neither the object(s), if any, denoted by the word nor any kind of spiritual atmosphere surrounding the word, but that it is rather the use(s) of the word in the language. What he might better have said, I think, is that it is not the job of the philosopher to give us the meaning of philosophically difficult words, but rather to give us their uses. As Wisdom put it, "Don't ask for the meaning, ask for the use." [17] And this is actually what Wittgenstein himself does in practice: he investigates the uses of words, and is not much concerned with their meanings. That is why I think his error in identifying meaning and use is not of much consequence: it does not seriously affect his valuable practice. It is interesting to note, in fact, that Wittgenstein himself occasionally divorces, at least by implication, the notions of meaning and use. After describing a simple language-game involving the word 'five,' he says:

> But what is the meaning of the word "five"?—No such thing was in question here, only how the word "five" is used. [*PI*, sect. 1.]

In another passage, he virtually says what I have just suggested that he should have said—namely, that the philosopher ought to abandon his preoccupation with meanings and concentrate on the uses of the terms that puzzle him:

> If we look at the example in §1, we may perhaps get an inkling how much this general notion of the meaning of a word surrounds the working of language with a haze which makes clear vision impossible. It disperses the fog to study the phenomena of language in primitive kinds of application in which one can command a clear view of the aim and functioning of the words. [*PI*, sect. 5.]

17 John Wisdom, "Ludwig Wittgenstein, 1934-1937," *Mind*, LXI, No. 242 (April 1952), 258.

It is Wittgenstein's claim that if we examine the various uses of the words which involve us in philosophical puzzlement—that is, if we examine the variety of language-games in which they play a part —we shall free ourselves at last from bewilderment. We shall no longer be tempted, as we were while under the influence of our craving for unity and of the pictures which are embedded in our language, to think that these words function in one way only—for example, as the name of some mysterious entity, act, process, or whatever. We shall no longer assimilate all words and sentences to a few fixed and familiar standards or paradigms, an assimilation which "had prevented us from seeing facts with unbiassed eyes" (*BB,* p. 43). And we shall be free of the "bias, which forces us to think that the facts *must* conform to certain pictures embedded in our language" (*ibid.*). If we look at the language-games we play with the word 'time,' for example—making appointments, telling what time it is, measuring lengths of time,[18] and so on—the temptation to think of time as an ethereal medium or stream in which events occur disappears, and so, therefore, do the puzzles about time which have plagued so many philosophers. This major claim of Wittgenstein is, of course, so far just a claim; it has not been justified. What is needed to justify it are separate detailed examinations of the language-games we play with the words which have proven to be philosophically troubling: 'time,' 'space,' 'meaning,' 'understanding,' 'intending,' 'know,' 'believe,' 'true,' 'beauty,' 'fact,' and the rest. Wittgenstein does this for many of these words in his later writings. And in his examinations of the uses of individual words Wittgenstein's genius shows clearly forth.

[18] The phrase 'measuring lengths of time' is a choice example of an expression into which a misleading picture is built. And see the bewilderment into which the picture casts St. Augustine:

That I measure time, I know; and yet I measure not time to come, for it is not yet; nor present, because it is not protracted by any space; not past, because it now is not. What then do I measure? [*Op. cit.,* p. 264.]

Wittgenstein refers to this passage in *BB,* p. 26.

11 Mind and Its Place in Language

One of the truths that were apparent to both the early and the later Wittgenstein is that words and sentences in themselves are dead —they are mere vibrations in the air or marks on paper, and as such have no meaning. In order for language to be the living thing we know it to be—the means whereby we communicate with one another, give advice, ask questions, and so on—something besides air vibrations or marks on paper is required. What seems to be required are various kinds of mental acts or processes. Consider the speaker: if he is actually to *assert* something, for example to say something definite about certain specific objects, he must not only utter the appropriate sounds—he must also mean something by them. If he utters the sentence 'The lion is in the corridor' he must mean by 'the lion' one particular beast, by 'the corridor' one particular place, and so on; otherwise, he will not have made the assertion, not have stated, that the lion is in the corridor, but only made a string of noises. If those same noises had been made by the wind or by a person talking in his sleep, they would not constitute an assertion; for *that,* we want to say, there must be some *thought* behind the words. Consider now the hearer: if the speaker's words are to mean anything to him, he cannot simply *hear* them and no more. Someone completely ignorant of the language can do that, can hear the sounds, but they say nothing

255

to him. No, the hearer must also understand the words—some process must go on in his mind.

> It seems that there are *certain definite* mental processes bound up with the working of language, processes through which alone language can function. I mean the processes of understanding and meaning. The signs of our language seem dead without these mental processes: and it might seem that the only function of the signs is to induce such processes, and that these are the things we ought really to be interested in. [*BB*, p. 3.]

(See also *PI*, sect. 358.)

Hence it may strike us that Wittgenstein's emphasis of the *use* of words—i.e., the language-games in which they figure, the modes of behavior in which they are embedded—is misguided. It seems as though the use of the words is merely an outward effect of what is essential, as though the way speakers of the language behave is a mere consequence of their mental acts of meaning and their mental processes of understanding words.

Wittgenstein is deeply concerned in his later writings with the alleged mental act of meaning and the alleged mental process of understanding. He is not, to begin with, in the least surprised that we tend to think of meaning and understanding as mental acts or processes, as events that take place in the mind and which manifest themselves in our action. What he says in the following passage about mental states applies with equal force to mental acts and processes.

> There is a kind of general disease of thinking which always looks for (and finds) what would be called a mental state from which all our acts spring as from a reservoir. [*BB*, p. 143.]

(See also *PI*, sect. 146.) The source of this "disease" is, above all, a picture—and one that is, as usual, embedded in certain forms of expression. For example, when a person is given an order, we say that he must at least understand it if he is to carry it out—in fact, that he must do so before he can carry it out. These ways of putting the matter tempt us to think that an act or process must occur in his mind prior to his overt action. Thus, these forms of expression can lead us to posit an intermediate step—something which Wittgenstein considers to be a "grammatical fiction" (*PI*, sect. 307).

> We are treating here of cases in which, as one might roughly put it, the grammar of a word seems to suggest the 'necessity' of a certain

intermediary step, although in fact the word is used in cases in which there is no such intermediary step. Thus we are inclined to say: "A man *must* understand an order before he obeys it." . . . [*BB*, p. 130.]

(See also *PI, sect.* 431.)

Again, consider the term 'thinking.' Many of the things we say about speaking are correlated with things we say about thinking in such a way that it is almost impossible to avoid the assumption that as 'speaking' designates a physical process, so 'thinking' designates a parallel mental process which accompanies it. Such a picture is embodied in those forms of expression.

> We very often find it impossible to think without speaking to ourselves half aloud,—and nobody asked to describe what happened in this case would ever say that something—the thinking—accompanied the speaking, were he not led into doing so by the pair of verbs "speaking"/"thinking," and by many of our common phrases in which their uses run parallel. Consider these examples: "Think before you speak!" "He speaks without thinking," "What I said didn't ·quite express my thought," "He says one thing and thinks just the opposite," "I didn't mean a word of what I said," "The French language uses its words in that order in which we think them." [*BB*, p. 148.]

It is one of the later Wittgenstein's major concerns to cure us of this particular "intellectual illness." He undertakes to do so by showing us that the various different "mental" or "psychological" words—e.g., 'thinking,' 'remembering,' 'feeling'—do not always and only designate inner states, acts, or processes. The terms which we are about to consider—'meaning' and 'understanding'—are cases in point.

What he tries to show is that we use the words 'meaning' and 'understanding' in a wide variety of situations, in many different circumstances; and that it is simply false to suggest that there is one and only one circumstance—namely, the occurrence of an act or process in a person's mind—which can justify us in applying those terms. What determines whether the words 'meaning' and 'understanding' can appropriately be applied to a person P in any given situation is the nature of the situation and its wider context—for example, what sort of person P is, how much P knows about the matter at hand, what it is he is alleged to mean or understand, what led up to the situation, and especially how P does, or would under suitable conditions, act after the situation. What goes on in P's mind, if anything, is rarely, if ever, *the* circumstance which warrants the correct application of the terms 'meaning' and 'understanding.'

Meaning

What tempts us to think of meaning as a mental act is not those locutions in which meaning is attributed to words or sentences, certain natural phenomena, and so on. It is rather those in which *people* are said to mean something. These, then, are the locutions we are now concerned with. Here are some sentences in which a few of them occur:

(a) When I said it, I meant it.

(b) When I said "John is coming," I meant John Smith, not John Jones.

(c) When I told you to teach the children a game, I meant a *nice* game, not Russian Roulette.

(d) What did he mean by that cryptic remark?

The first three, (a), (b), and (c), are the most relevant to our present purposes, for it is the sorts of mental acts seemingly referred to in them that appear most strongly to give life and significance to our words. Hence, I shall confine myself to them.

Let us discuss (a) first. There can be no doubt that there is a manifest difference between on the one hand saying something in jest or as a joke, saying something absentmindedly or without thinking, and so on, and on the other hand saying something and meaning it. But notice that cases of a person's saying something and meaning it are rather special. It is simply not true that whenever a person makes an utterance which cannot be characterized as 'absentminded' or as 'said without thinking,' he *means* what he says. Ordinary, everyday remarks cannot, in general, be described as cases of the speaker's saying something and meaning it—nor as cases of the speaker's saying something and *not* meaning it either. To take a humble example: If someone asks me what time it is and I, looking at my watch, reply "Eight o'clock," it hardly seems possible, in normal circumstances, even to raise the question of whether or not I meant what I said. I did not say it and mean it, nor say it and not mean it: I just said it. In special circumstances, however, that question might well be raised. For example, if one of my hearers thought it was only six o'clock and had an important appointment at seven, he might ask whether I really meant it when I said it was eight o'clock. So the alleged act of meaning what one says cannot be required for *every* utterance, for *every* use of language. Still, it can sometimes be said of people that they say something and mean what they say, and so the matter is worth discussing.

Many of the things we say about saying something and meaning it embody the picture of the latter as a conscious mental process running along concurrently with the physical process of speaking. But if asked to specify just what this alleged mental process consists in, just what is actually supposed to take place in the mind whenever we mean something which we say, we are hard pressed to give any sort of plausible account. One suggestion might conceivably be this: When someone says something and means it, what happens is that he says to himself, while or just before he speaks, the same sentence or its equivalent; whereas if someone says something and does not mean it, he says nothing to himself inwardly. On this view, presumably, if a person says something but really means something *else,* he must say to himself a different sentence which expresses this something else while, or just before, he speaks overtly. Despite the exceeding implausibility of this account, Wittgenstein admits that something like it may sometimes happen, although he insists that such cases are extremely rare (*BB,* pp. 34-35). It is much more often the case that when a person says something and means it, he experiences a characteristic feeling of meaning what he says. Compare the difference in feeling between saying to an old and good friend you have not seen in years "I shall be delighted to see you tonight," and saying this to a crashing bore who has just invited himself to your party tonight. (See *BB,* p. 146.)

But we cannot suppose, on the basis of these two possible accounts, that *whenever* anyone says something and means it, something must go on in his mind while he speaks. Nothing of the sort need happen; quite often a person means what he says when he simply speaks in a certain "sincere" tone of voice or has certain "earnest" facial expressions or makes certain characteristic bodily gestures (e.g., he pounds on the table). (See *BB,* pp. 35, 148.)

But it still might be thought that although what constitutes meaning what one says is not necessarily anything that goes on in a person's mind, nevertheless it must at least be something that happens *at the time the person speaks.* But Wittgenstein denies even this.

> There may be cases where the presence of a sensation other than those bound up with gestures, tone of voice, etc. distinguishes meaning what you say from not meaning it. But sometimes what distin-

guishes these two is nothing that happens while we speak, but a variety of actions and experiences of different kinds before and after. [*BB*, pp. 144-45.]

For example, suppose Professor Smith says that Jones is not going to receive a passing grade for the course, and that as he says it he performs no special mental act, has no special inner experience, and that he says it in no special tone of voice, and so on. He just says it—in a perfectly ordinary way, in the course of an ordinary conversation. It might nevertheless be true that he means what he says. For example, suppose one of his hearers had thought that Jones was a brilliant student; he might well ask Professor Smith "But do you really propose to flunk Jones?" If Smith honestly replies "Yes, I'm afraid so; I have no other choice," he clearly meant what he said; and if he proceeds to give Jones a failing grade, or to call Jones in and tell him he has failed the course, then in the absence of extraordinary circumstances, there can be no doubt that he meant what he said. If Professor Smith acts in these or similar ways, one can correctly assert that he meant what he said—even though nothing special, either physical or mental, occurred while he was speaking. And if we will still insist that there *must* have been some special act at the time he spoke, we are being misled by grammatical similarities. We are supposing, in short, that "He said it and meant what he said" is just like "He said it and smiled" or "He saw it and touched what he saw."

The following two points need to be made. First, as we have seen, there is no *one* thing—such as a unique inner experience or mental process—that happens in all cases of someone's meaning what he says. Second, whether or not the occurrence of something *C* justifies us in saying, in a given situation, that a person *P* means what he says, depends very much on the nature and context of the situation. For example, if we know *P* very well, and he says something in a certain tone of voice, we may be (rightly) sure that he means what he says; but in another situation, *P* or someone else may say something in that very same tone of voice and *not* mean what he says. Again, Wittgenstein points out that one can have the feeling which is characteristic of meaning what one says when one is lying (*BB*, p. 146).

In the light of these considerations, there are two extreme positions one might adopt. (a) " 'Meaning what one says' *must* mean one thing, *must* refer to just one act: therefore, all those different things—

tone of voice, inner experience of meaning what one says, and so on —which sometimes happen, on different occasions, when a person means what he says, must all be mere symptoms of something deeper; and this something deeper is the *real* act of meaning what one says."

What Wittgenstein's answer to this position is should be clear by now. The desire to find something in common to all cases of meaning what one says is just another instance of the craving for unity, and in particular, of the desire to find an essence. But if we actually examine all the different cases in which a person means what he says, we just do not find any such essence.

Faced with this reply, we might be tempted to adopt the opposite extreme position: (b) " 'Meaning what one says' is hopelessly ambiguous; it means different things in different situations. Sometimes it means 'the person speaks in a certain tone of voice,' sometimes it means 'the person has a feeling of meaning what he says,' and sometimes it means other things as well."

Wittgenstein asserts that *in certain special circumstances* the sentence '*P* meant it' and the sentence '*P* said it in a certain tone of voice' may mean the same thing—in the sense that it will not matter which one of the two you use—but *in general* they do not mean the same thing. (See *BB*, pp. 146-47; and also *PI*, sect. 183 and *BB*, p. 115, where this point is made in connection with 'Now I can go on' and 'He can continue' respectively.) This, however, provides no cause for alarm; it is just another example of Wittgenstein's by now familiar doctrine that general terms or phrases usually, and perhaps always, refer to a range of different cases which have a family resemblance.

Let us turn now to the much more important kind of meaning involved in locutions (b) and (c) (p. 258). Here we have to do not with a person's saying something and meaning what he says; but rather with his saying something and meaning something more or less definite or specific, O, by an individual word or phrase, W, that he utters. O may be a particular physical object or person (in the utterance "When I said 'John is coming,' I meant John Smith, not John Jones," W is 'John' and O is John Smith); a more or less vague range of numbers (in the utterance "When I said 'take a few,' I meant 8 or 10, not 55," W is 'a few' and O is the range of numbers in the vicinity of 8 to 10); a color (in the utterance "When I said 'That is magenta,' I meant the ashtray, not the sofa, and I meant its color, not its shape," W_1 is 'that,' O_1 is the ashtray, and W_2 is 'magenta,'

O_2 is the color of the ashtray); and so on. Part of the negative or destructive side of Wittgenstein's later views about this kind of meaning has been discussed earlier (pp. 183-87); but that account must now be supplemented.

As we have just seen, Wittgenstein admits that *sometimes,* i.e., in some circumstances, "meaning what one says" is a mental occurrence. It is far more tempting to suppose that this new kind of meaning— meaning something O by a word or phrase W—is a mental occurrence, in particular, a mental act; but at the same time it is far more difficult to defend the claim that it is, for there are compelling reasons against it. In particular, it seems difficult or impossible, as we shall see, to specify any mental act that will do the job required. And Wittgenstein does, in fact, adopt a tougher attitude toward the "mental-act" view of *this* kind of meaning than he does toward that view of the previous kind.

As usual, Wittgenstein stresses the importance of the nature and context of the situation in which and of which the locutions we are presently concerned with are used. He would admit that there are certain characteristic experiences which often, although by no means always, accompany a person's saying something when he means something O by a word or phrase W which he uses—e.g., having an image of O. But he insists that none of these experiences ever actually constitutes, in itself and in isolation, a person's act of meaning O. It is the nature and context of the situation in which he speaks that is important and that determines whether he means O or something else. Once we see the importance of the situation and its surroundings, we realize that the experiences which characteristically accompany the act of speaking are of little or no importance. They are seen to be much more like mere accidental accompaniments of the person's "meaning O," than essential parts of it.

Let us consider a concrete example to bring out these points. Suppose Jones, in giving an ostensive definition of the term 'elliptical' to someone, points to an elliptical ashtray and says "That is elliptical." Jones meant by 'that' (W_1) the ashtray (O_1), and by 'elliptical' (W_2) the shape of the ashtray (O_2), not its color, size, material, number, or anything else about it. In fact, he not only meant the shape of the ashtray as opposed to its color, size, material, and so on; he also meant the particular shape of the ashtray—viz., elliptical— as opposed not only to other particular shapes (such as square, circular, egg-shaped, and so on) but also as opposed to more generic

shapes (such as closed, curvilinear, esthetically pleasing, and so on).
I shall concentrate on W_2 and O_2, and ignore W_1 and O_1, in what
follows.

What does Jones' "meaning the particular shape" consist in? How,
precisely, does he go about meaning that shape and nothing else? He
does not do it by the mere physical act of extending his arm, with
pointed index finger, in the direction of the ashtray; for then nothing
would distinguish his meaning its shape from his meaning its color,
or its size, or any one of a number of other things (*PI*, sect. 33). This
sort of consideration, in fact, reinforces the natural temptation to
think of meaning as a mental or inner occurrence—i.e., we are inclined to suppose that since his meaning the shape is not the mere
physical act of pointing, it must therefore be some nonphysical act
of pointing performed in his mind.

Perhaps when Jones means the shape of the ashtray, what he does
is *concentrate his attention* on its shape, and not on its size or color
or anything else. This is a plausible suggestion and requires some
discussion. First of all, it must be remarked that although in *this* case
(i.e., of Jones and the ashtray) the suggestion is indeed plausible, still
it cannot reasonably be thought that it applies to *every* case, or even
to *many* cases, of a person's meaning something O by a word W.
Wittgenstein cites the following counter-example.

> Imagine someone simulating pain, and then saying "It'll get better
> soon." Can't one say he means the pain? and yet he is not concentrat-
> ing his attention on any pain.—And what about when I finally say "It's
> stopped now"? [*PI*, sect. 667.]

Again, suppose you point to a chess piece and say "This is called
the 'king.'" By 'this' (W) you mean this *chess piece* (O)—not this
particular bit of wood. Your meaning the chess piece by 'this' cannot
consist in concentrating your attention on the chess piece, for how
would that differ from concentrating your attention on this particular
bit of wood, which you do *not* mean by 'this' in this instance? How
do you concentrate your attention on this thing *as* a chess piece,
on the *chess-piece-ness* of this bit of wood? (See *PI*, sect. 35.)

Wittgenstein admits that in the present sort of case (i.e., where O
is the color or shape of an object) the person often does something—
and not always the same thing—which can, *in the special circumstances of the case*, be called "concentrating his attention" on O (*PI*,
sect. 33). Very well, let us suppose that Jones *does* concentrate his
attention on the shape of the ashtray as he says "That is elliptical."

Still, his act of meaning the particular shape of that ashtray by 'elliptical' cannot consist *just* in his concentrating his attention on the shape of the ashtray. That may be part of it, but it cannot be the whole of it, nor even a very important part of it. For if Jones thought the word 'elliptical' refers to any conic section, he might still concentrate his attention on the shape of the ashtray while he says "That is elliptical," and yet he would not mean by 'elliptical' the particular shape (i.e., elliptical) of the ashtray. What is far more important than what he concentrates his attention on while he speaks, is the way he goes on to behave (or the way he habitually behaves) with respect to the word 'elliptical'—how he *uses* it, in short (for example, what shapes he would *call* 'elliptical'). Thus, concentrating one's attention, even if it does occur when someone means something O by a word W which he uses, is little more than an idle ritual. It *does* nothing.

What other possible kind of mental act could constitute Jones' meaning by 'elliptical' the particular shape of the ashtray when he says "That is elliptical"? Could it be the occurrence in his mind of the image of an ellipse as he speaks? This might occasionally happen. But how can the fact that the image of an ellipse comes before Jones' mind as he speaks constitute, in and of itself, his meaning by 'elliptical' the particular shape of that ashtray? It is not a satisfactory reply to say: "Because the shape of the image is the same as the shape of the ashtray." For suppose Brown says "That is elliptical" and has an image exactly like Jones' as he says it. He still might very well *not* mean the particular shape of that ashtray, for he might think that 'elliptical' means any pleasing curvilinear shape and might have chosen the elliptical image as an example of such a shape merely because the ashtray happened to have that particular shape. Is the difference, then, that Jones *means* his image to represent the particular shape of the ashtray while Brown means *his* image to represent any pleasing curvilinear shape? Yes, most likely; but then we still need to know how they do *that*. Or consider the following case: Smith, too, has the wrong idea about what the word 'elliptical' means, but *he* thinks it denotes the color red. Pointing to a red elliptical ashtray, he says "That is elliptical," and a red elliptical image comes into his mind as he speaks. According to the suggested reply, Smith would have to mean by 'elliptical' the shape of the ashtray, because his image has the same shape as the shape of the ashtray. But he does not; he means the color of the ashtray. It seems as though we are forced to say that Jones must *mean* his image to represent the *shape* of the ashtray, and Smith must *mean* his image to represent the *color* of the ashtray. But then how do they do that? The appeal to images seems incapable of solving the problem of what it is for a person to mean something *O* by a word *W* which he uses; it merely introduces the need for further acts of meaning, which still have to be explained.

I shall try to put this point in a slightly different way. Our original reason for appealing to the mental act of meaning was the following. Words in themselves are lifeless; for example, words which name or refer to something do not establish the connection which exists between themselves and what they designate or refer to. The connection, we thought, must be made by a mental act of meaning: the speaker means his words to stand for something, and that is how the connection between words and the world is made. But, as we have just seen, if the alleged act of meaning consists merely in conjuring up an image, it will not do what we require it to do. In our example, no appeal to any mental image will help to explain the connection between Jones' words and the shape of the ashtray. A picture on a piece of paper would serve as well as the mental image, and there would still be a gap between any such picture and what it is supposed to represent. That is to say, one would still need to know how the connection between the picture and what it represents is to be established. (One obviously cannot answer that the mind also makes *that* connection by conjuring up another image, for then we would be embarked on an endless regress.) So the bridge from words to the world cannot be built of anything as insubstantial as mental images.

If we now pursue the matter further and ask how the connection *is* made between a person's image, or the corresponding picture he might draw, and what he means it to represent, we find that the answer lies not in any essentially mental activity but rather in the way he uses, or would use, the image or picture, the applications he makes, or would make, of it. As we have seen in discussing the picture theory of the *Tractatus,* an image or picture is not, *in itself,* a picture of this or that; the later Wittgenstein sees that what it is a picture of depends on how it is used.

> Imagine a picture representing a boxer in a particular stance. Now, this picture can be used to tell someone how he should stand, should hold himself; or how he should not hold himself; or how a particular man did stand in such-and-such a place; and so on. . . . [*PI,* p. 11.]

(See also *PI,* p. 54, paragraph [b].) Let us return to our example. Jones' elliptical image, we want to say, represents the particular shape of the ashtray—he means it to represent that. And it does represent that because Jones *uses* or *applies* it in certain ways—for example, because he applies it to this, that, and the other object which are all elliptical (he says they have the *same* shape as it), and because he refuses to apply it to this, that, and the other object which are not elliptical (he says they do not have the same shape as it). Brown's elliptical image, on the other hand, is a picture not of the particular shape of the ashtray, but rather of any curvilinear shape, and Smith's elliptical image is a picture of the color red; and this, too, is a matter of the ways they go on using or applying their pictures, or would go on using or applying them—ways which are different from each other and from the ways Jones uses *his* elliptical image.

But the ways in which Jones, Brown, and Smith use or apply their elliptical images are inseparable from, indeed are nothing more than, the ways they use the *word* 'elliptical.' We said, for example, that Jones applies his image only to elliptical objects; but this is just to say that he calls, or would call, them 'elliptical.' Jones' image may at most *guide* his use of the term 'elliptical'—but remember that the very same image can guide a person in totally different ways, as illustrated by the cases of Jones, Brown, and Smith. Nevertheless, merely *having* the image, in itself, does nothing—in particular, it cannot constitute Jones' (so-called act of) meaning by 'elliptical' the shape of the ashtray. For the image must be *meant* in a certain way, and how it is meant is a matter of how Jones uses the word 'elliptical.' (See *PI,* sects. 139-41.)

The image, then, is not any essential part of Jones' meaning by 'elliptical' the particular shape of the ashtray. It is, to borrow a phrase from Wittgenstein, like an illustration to a story (see *PI,* sect. 663), and it is so in two respects. First, just as it is the story which determines what the illustration represents, so it is Jones' use of the term 'elliptical' which determines what his image represents. And second, just as the illustration is mere "dressing," an inessential accompaniment of the story, which is a matter of what is written or spoken; so the image is a mere accidental accompaniment of Jones' meaning by 'elliptical' the shape of the ashtray, which is a matter of the situation in which he speaks and of its surroundings—in particular, of how he goes on, or would go on, to use the term 'elliptical.'

It seems to have become quite clear that as far as what Jones means by 'elliptical' is concerned, it simply does not matter, or matters exceedingly little, what goes on in his mind—for example, what images he has or what he concentrates his attention on. Nothing special may go on in his mind and his attention may be concentrated on nothing in particular, or on something irrelevant—and yet he doubtless means the shape of the ashtray by 'elliptical' when he says "That is elliptical." And what determines that he means the shape is the way he uses the word 'elliptical': the fact that he goes on (or would go on) to point to other objects of (what we too would call) the same shape and to call them elliptical too; the fact that if his hearer were to point to a square object of the same color as the original ashtray and ask "Is this elliptical too?" he would answer "No"; the fact that he might add "I am speaking of the shape, not the color" or even "I mean the shape"; and so on. So his "meaning the shape" is a matter of the situation surrounding his saying "That is elliptical," and especially of the actual or potential behavior, both linguistic and nonlinguistic, which surrounds the utterance. It is not a matter of what goes on in his mind while he speaks. Quite generally, nothing that happens at any one particular moment in a person's mind can possibly be definitive of whom or what he means by a certain word or phrase. Wittgenstein expresses this point in a pungent epigram:

> If God had looked into our minds he would not have been able to see there whom we were speaking of. [*PI*, p. 217.]

(See also *PI*, pp. 216-18.)

In the following passage, Wittgenstein refers to 'meaning' in a slightly different sense from the one we are now concerned with, but he would say the same about 'meaning' in our present sense.

> And nothing is more wrong-headed than calling meaning a mental activity! Unless, that is, one is setting out to produce confusion. (It would also be possible to speak of an activity of butter when it rises in price, and if no problems are produced by this it is harmless.) [*PI*, sect. 693.]

To speak of the rise in price of butter as an activity of the butter is misleading, because it draws attention to the wrong thing. It suggests (wrongly) that in order to understand what is going on, we ought to look to the butter itself, rather than to other things, such as the consumer, the dealers, the cost of other commodities, and so on. Similarly, to speak of a person's meaning something O by a word or phrase W as a mental activity—i.e., as an activity of his mind—is misleading, since it suggests (wrongly) that in order to understand what is going on, we ought to concentrate our attention on what happens in his mind when he speaks, rather than on other things, such as the situation in which he speaks, how he uses the word or phrase *W* before and afterwards, and so on.

The point can also be put in the following way. We picture a person's meaning something *O* by a word or phrase *W* as a mental act that occurs at the time he speaks. Part of having this picture is supposing that in order to discover the meaning of the phrase 'meaning something *O* by a word or phrase *W*,' we must focus our attention on what goes on in the person's mind while he speaks. But of course the phrase is simply not used like that; it does not refer—or, at the very least, does not refer *only*—to what goes on in the person's mind while he speaks. We have seen that it has, as it were, a wider scope—one that takes in his past and future behavior, for example. What Wittgenstein says in the following passage about 'think,' he would also say about 'meaning something *O* by a word or phrase *W*'—and indeed about 'understanding' too.

> In order to get clear about the meaning of the word "think" we watch ourselves while we think; what we observe will be what the word means!—But this concept is not used like that. (It would be as if without knowing how to play chess, I were to try and make out what the word "mate" meant by close observation of the last move of some game of chess.) [*PI*, sect. 316.]

It should be remarked in passing that Wittgenstein's point about "psychological" words like 'thinking,' 'meaning,' and 'understanding' can be generalized into an important truth about language. It is that there are many expressions which *seem* to do nothing but refer, in a direct and straightforward way, to some condition, action, quality or whatever, of a thing or person at a given indicated moment; but which in fact imply something further about the situation—all sorts of different things, depending on the expression. For example, we are tempted to think that "He is asleep" merely describes someone's present state—eyes closed, regular breathing, oblivious to most ordinary sensory stimuli, and so on. But the term 'asleep' says much more than that. It implies that the person *went* to sleep in one of the usual ways, and that he did not faint, or that he was not, say, hit over the head or hypnotized; and it implies that his present state has not been going on uninterruptedly for, say, three months; and so on. So the word 'asleep' does not simply cast a spotlight on a certain feature of the present moment; its beam is wider than that. Again, consider the expression 'is sitting down'[1] (in the "state" or "condition" sense, not in the "act" sense in which a person can be in the process of sitting down): to say of someone that he is sitting down is not simply to describe the present position of his limbs. For if he had fallen unconscious into a chair, or if he had had a convulsive fit so that his limbs had frozen in a sitting position and he was then placed in a chair—then he would not now be sitting down. To be sitting down, one must have sat down. In all these cases, what goes on (or is the case) at the time referred to is indeed important, but only in light of the wider situation.

> What is happening now has significance—in these surroundings. The surroundings give it its importance. [*PI*, sect. 583.]

This insight—that words, even quite ordinary and familiar ones, often have "packed into them" much more than meets the eye—is an extremely interesting and important one; that it is so is frequently demonstrated in Wittgenstein's later writings. We shall find the point illustrated again in the following section.

Knowing How to Go On

Ideally, after considering the speaker's meaning something, we ought to consider next the other side of the coin—namely, the hearer's understanding what he hears. This seems clearly to be essential to the working of language, and it seems also to be essentially a mental process or state—something that goes on or exists in the mind of the person who understands. Wittgenstein readily admits that this is an entirely natural way to regard understanding. We say such things as "Since he understood what I said, he did the right thing," and "Because he understood the principles involved, he was able to solve the problem." Embodied in these and other ways of talking is the picture of a person's (process of) understanding as the mental cause of his overt behavior, as a mental reservoir from which his actions flow. This picture is yet another manifestation of a "general disease of thinking" (*BB*, p. 143) from which we ought, according to Wittgenstein, to be cured.

I shall not, however, attempt a discussion of the concept of understanding, for it is too difficult and complex. Instead, I shall confine

[1] This example I owe to Bernard Williams.

myself to something which is at once more manageable and yet very closely akin to understanding: the notion of knowing how to go on, as it occurs in the following example of Wittgenstein's. Suppose a person *A* writes down a short sequence of numbers which forms the beginning of a series, and *B,* watching him, is to continue the series when "the light dawns," when he sees or knows what the series is and can continue it on his own—when, in short, he knows how to go on. Let us suppose that *A* writes down the numbers 1, 5, 11, 19, 29; and that at "29" *B* exclaims "Now I know how to go on," and proceeds to develop the series. It may strike us that his "knowing how to go on" is a mental act or process that occurred at the moment he spoke, or just before it, and from which his subsequent behavior flowed as from a source. Well, what *did* happen when *B* claimed that he knew how to go on?

> Various things may have happened; for example, while A was slowly putting one number after another, B was occupied with trying various algebraic formulae on the numbers which had been written down. After A had written the number 19 B tried the formula $a_n = n^2 + n - 1$; and the next number confirmed his hypothesis.
>
> Or again, B does not think of formulae. He watches A writing his numbers down with a certain feeling of tension, and all sorts of vague thoughts go through his head. Finally he asks himself: "What is the series of differences?" He finds the series 4, 6, 8, 10 and says: Now I can go on. [*PI,* sect. 151.]

We may think that this shows that *B*'s knowing how to go on must be something that went on in his mind, as, or just before, he spoke. But to think so would be a mistake. As Wittgenstein points out, *B* may have engaged in no mental activity and yet he may have been perfectly justified in claiming that he knew how to go on. The passage just quoted continues with these further examples of what *B* may do while *A* is writing down his numbers:

> Or he watches and says "Yes, I know *that* series"—and continues it, just as he would have done if A had written down the series 1, 3, 5, 7, 9.—Or he says nothing at all and simply continues the series. Perhaps he had what may be called the feeling "that's easy!" (The feeling of a slight quick intake of breath, as when one is mildly startled, is such a feeling.) [*PI,* sect. 151.]

Are we seriously tempted to think that any of these experiences— e.g., a "feeling of a slight quick intake of breath"—are what *B*'s alleged act or process of knowing how to go on consists in? Hardly, and yet that is all that may have happened as, or just before, *B* said—and justifiably said—"Now I know how to go on." The feeling of a slight quick intake of breath (feeling S) *by itself* is simply not enough; it is at most a mere sign that *B* knows how to go on—when considered, for example, against the background of his previous experience, in which he regularly *did* know how to go on whenever he had feeling S. So it may be *true,* and we may be justified in asserting, that *B* knows how to go on in this present instance when he has feeling S. But the feeling is not the knowing. And of course the ultimate and best justification for our assertion that *B* knows how to go on—the acid test, as it were—is his actual success, his actually going on to develop the series in the right way. (See *PI,* sects. 320, 324.)

But someone may object: "I see now that *B*'s knowing how to go on is not *in every case* a mental occurrence. But sometimes, surely, it is. For example, when *B* tries different formulas, doesn't the sudden occurrence of the right one to him constitute his knowing how to go on?"

It cannot be true that *in all circumstances* whenever the right formula occurs to *B, B* must know how to go on. There are many possible situations in which the right formula occurs to *B* and he does not know how to go on. *B* might not, for example, know what the formula means or, even though knowing what it means, he might fail to realize that it is the correct one (*PI,* sect. 152).

Still, *in some cases,* "*B* knows how to go on" might be said to mean the same as "*B* has just thought of the formula," despite the fact that in general they do not have the same sense. Under some circumstances we would be quite willing to substitute "*B* has thought of the formula" or "the formula has occurred to *B*" for "*B* knows how to go on"; for we might sometimes say "*B* knows how to go on —I mean he has just thought of the formula." We might be willing to talk in this way, for example, if *B* is a competent mathematician and we know full well that the only thing that had kept him from seeing what the series is was that he had not yet hit upon the right formula. In other circumstances—for example, if *B* is just learning for the first time what a series is—we would not be willing to substitute "*B* has just thought of the formula" for "*B* knows how to go on," although we might be willing to substitute "*B* has just learnt how to develop a series" for it. (*PI,* sect. 183.)

So "*B* knows how to go on" means different things in different situations, in different kinds of cases. Similarly, the utterance "He can walk now" means different things in different situations: "He can walk now—I mean his leg is sufficiently healed," "He can walk now—I mean he has just learned how," "He can walk now—I mean his work for the day is finished," and so on (see *BB*, pp. 114-15; *PI*, sect. 183). We may say, then, that just as there is no essence of games, and that games form a family of different cases; so neither a person's knowing how to go on (developing a series) nor a person's being able to walk has an essence, and each forms a family of different cases.

Does this mean that *B*'s knowing how to go on, although it cannot *in every case* be a mental process or state, nevertheless at least *sometimes* is? For example, in those special cases where *"B* knows how to go on" means "The formula has occurred to *B,"* is his knowing not an occurrence that takes place in his mind? Yes and no. The formula may have come to him in thought and if so this was doubtless a mental occurrence; but there is nothing *essentially* mental about it. The formula might just as well have come to him "on paper," as it were; and even if it came into his mind as a thought, the thought could be replaced without loss by written symbols—by the formula being written out on a sheet of paper, for example.

Furthermore, even in such cases, there are still essential connections with *B*'s behavior. First, we are willing to substitute "The formula has occurred to *B"* for *"B* knows how to go on" only where *B* is a competent enough mathematician, where we think *B* has mastered the techniques involved in developing series of this degree of difficulty. But this simply means that in the past *B* has been successful in actually writing out (or saying) series of this type when the formula has occurred to him. (See *PI*, sect. 179.) Second, even though we may be perfectly justified in asserting that *B* knows how to go on when the formula has occurred to him, if his subsequent behavior is deficient, in one or more of a certain variety of ways, we may have to deny that he knew how to go on. This might happen, for example, if he suddenly forgot how to work with formulas of this sort and could not develop the series any further.

So there are all kinds of experiences—feelings, mental activities of different sorts, and so on—which characteristically occur when *B* knows how to go on (although sometimes *B* knows how to go on without experiencing anything at all). In the appropriate circumstances, the occurrence of these experiences may justify us in claiming that *B* knows how to go on. But even when they do occur, none of these experiences *is* B's knowing how to go on. If it were, B's subsequent performance with respect to the series would be totally irrelevant to the issue of whether or not, when he said "Now I know how to go on," he did in fact know how to go on; but it is not irrelevant. On the contrary, the most nearly conclusive test of that is his actually going on to develop the series in the right way. (This test, however, is not perfectly conclusive; there will be special cases in which B does not succeed in developing the series correctly and yet in which we would agree that he did know how to go on when he said he did; and conversely, special cases in which B does go on correctly and in which we would not agree that he knew how to go on when he said he did. See *PI,* sects. 181, 184, 323.) His actually going on, we may say, is the most important test of his knowing how to go on.

The following objection might arise at this point: "I agree that I need tests or evidence or grounds for determining whether another person knows how to go on; I have to know, for example, something about his previous training in arithmetic and how good he is at developing series. Only if I know this, may I be sure that he knows how to go on when the right formula occurs to him. But my own case is different, surely. When the formula occurs to me, I know, without any grounds, without any consideration of my own past performances, that I know how to go on. So isn't my knowing how to go on just this mental event of my thinking of the formula?"

It is true that given the circumstances that I have learnt mathematics, used such formulas before, and so on, I am entirely justified in saying "Now I know how to go on" when the right formula occurs to me (*PI,* sect. 179). And I am justified without any grounds, without considering any evidence, without applying any criteria to myself (*PI,* sect. 324). Even so, the formula's occurring to me is not the same thing as my knowing how to go on; for in some cases—although not all—even though the right formula occurs to me and I feel certain I know how to go on, I may have to deny later that I did know how to go on when I said I did. This might happen if my subsequent performance turned out to be faulty in certain ways (*PI,* sect. 181).

The truth seems to be, then, that the various experiences which people characteristically have when they know how to go on are tokens or signs that they know how to go on; they are not (identical with) the knowing, but "characteristic accompaniments" of it (*PI,* sect. 321). So it is a mistake to think that when B says "Now I know how to go on," he is reporting the occurrence of one or more of these typical experiences. "Now I know how to go on" is not a description of a mental state; it is a "signal," and it is rightly employed if *B* does, or at least would in the appropriate circumstances, proceed in the right way (*PI,* sect. 180). It is an "exclamation," and may be compared to "an instinctive sound, a glad start" (*PI,* sect. 323), very like "Aha!" or "Yes!" And the main test of whether it is a "valid" one is how *B* does, or would, go on.

When we examine the wide variety of situations in which the words "I know how to go on" and *"B* knows how to go on" are used and how they are used, the view that knowing how to go on is a unique mental act or process becomes hopelessly implausible. What Wittgenstein says about understanding applies equally well here:

> In the sense in which there are processes (including mental processes) which are characteristic of understanding, understanding is not a mental process. [*PI,* sect. 154.]

Far more important, as far as *B*'s knowing how to go on is concerned, than what occurs in his mind, are the circumstances of the situation— such circumstances as *B*'s training in arithmetic and how he goes on to act. For even when one or another of the characteristic accompaniments of knowing how to go on occurs, it is still these circumstances that justify the use of the sentence *"B* knows how to go on."

Wittgenstein would say the same of understanding an utterance. To consider just one simple example: suppose *A* says to *B* "That is elliptical" and thereby gives him a proper ostensive definition of 'elliptical.' The crucial factors determining whether *B* understands the definition are not what takes place in his mind (what images he may have, for example), but the circumstances surrounding the situation: how much English *B* knows, and especially how he proceeds to act afterwards—for example, whether he goes on to apply the word 'elliptical' to just the right objects, i.e., the objects that we (the speakers of English) would apply it to. We use the phrases 'knowing the meaning of a word' and 'understanding an utterance' in a wide variety of circumstances. In some, but by no means all, circumstances, something that goes on in the person's mind may be involved. But (a) whatever this may be, it is not essential that it take place, and (b) the character of his behavior, both before and after the actual situation, is virtually always the controlling and overriding consideration.

It is difficult to escape the ever-present temptation to think that there *must* be something irreducibly mental about a person's understanding something—that some sort of mental act, process, or experience is at least an essential part of it. Wittgenstein certainly feels the full force of this temptation and grapples with it strenuously and at length. He deals, for example, with the following kinds of questions. When *B* is given a sequence of numbers and told to continue the series, does he not often guess or have an intuition as to how to proceed—and are not these mental acts of guessing and intuiting what is meant by his understanding? (*PI,* sects. 210-14.) Again, everyone has had the experience of suddenly understanding something, or understanding something "in a flash"; is this experience not one of understanding, and is it not a mental one? (*PI,* sects. 138, 139, 151, 155, 179, 180, 183, 184.) We cannot here follow Wittgenstein down all these fascinating and tortuous roads of his thought; but the reader who does so will agree, I think, that he shows quite convincingly that a person's understanding something is not a process that occurs in his mind.

"But isn't this all negative? Wittgenstein has told us that meaning what one says, meaning something *O* by a word or phrase *W,* and now understanding something, are none of them mental acts or processes. But what, then, *are* they?"

This is a question which Wittgenstein steadfastly refuses to answer; he would, in fact, consider it unanswerable. The question asks, in effect, for the essence of meaning and understanding, what their real nature is; and of course Wittgenstein would deny that they have an essence. And so he would think it a great mistake to attempt an answer to the question, just as he would consider it a mistake to attempt an answer to the question "What is a game?" Once we have an over-all view of the variety of situations in which the terms 'meaning' and 'understanding' are used, and of the various criteria for their use, there is nothing more to know about what meaning and understanding are. To know their use, Wittgenstein would say, is to know their meaning.

Wittgenstein admits that the words of our language, *qua* mere marks on paper or sounds in the air, are dead and meaningless. He is willing to admit that if language is to be the vital and important thing we know it to be, speakers must mean something by their words and hearers must understand what is meant. But he tries to show that these admissions do not commit one to the view that the workings of our language are shot through with irreducibly mental acts, processes, or experiences, or that such workings are unintelligible without them. He tries to show that meaning and understanding are not matters of what goes on in people's minds, but rather matters, ultimately, of how they behave, how they use words, and thus he seeks to strengthen and corroborate his central thesis that what gives life and significance to words is their use—i.e., the way they figure in various language-games, the modes of behavior in which they play a part.

Names Again

It might seem that the most felicitous way to summarize one of the points made so far in this chapter would be to say:

(A) 'meaning' and 'understanding' are not the names of, do not denote, mental states or occurrences.

I may have said as much, or strongly suggested it, myself. But this would not be an accurate statement, unless it were qualified. There are standard or paradigm examples of names—proper names ('John Jones,' 'Socrates'), names of colors ('red'), names of kinds of physical objects ('table'). If statement (A) is interpreted as saying that there are no mental states or occurrences x and y which bear the same sort of relationship R to the words 'meaning' and 'understanding,' respectively, as John Jones bears to the word 'John Jones,' or as red color patches bear to the word 'red'—if that is what statement (A) asserts, then it is true enough.

If statement (A) is read in another way, however, it is not true. There is a sense of 'name' and 'denote' in which it may be said of virtually any word that it names or denotes something; that 'five' denotes a number, that 'towards' denotes a relative direction, that 'slab' denotes a kind of building block, that 'remembering' and 'understanding' and 'meaning' denote mental processes, and so on for every, or nearly every, word. But to say this is to say very little—next to nothing. Compare Wittgenstein's remark about "signifying something":

> When we say "Every word in language signifies something" we have so far said *nothing whatever;* unless we have explained exactly *what* distinction we wish to make. [*PI*, sect. 13.]

To say in this weak sense that 'five' denotes a number is to say only that 'five' is a number-word rather than, for example, a color-word or a mental-process-word—i.e., that it has uses like those that 'one,' 'six,' and 'ten' have, and not like those that 'red,' 'blue,' and 'green,' nor like those that 'remember,' 'understand,' and 'think,' have. You say to a worker "Bring me five slabs"; he returns and says "I've found the slabs, but I can't find the five." You might—albeit somewhat pedantically—reply "No, no! 'Five' designates the *number* of slabs I wanted, not another kind of building block." This remark does not assert that there is some entity called 'the number five' (in fact, it denies it); rather, it simply rules out the worker's false assumption that 'five' and 'slab' have similar uses. (See *PI,* sect. 10.)

One *can* say, then, that meaning is a mental act and that understanding and thinking are mental processes; properly construed, these statements, though trivial, are true enough. But there is also a danger in so speaking, for given our craving for unity and our consequent tendency to assimilate words and phrases to familiar paradigms, it tempts us to suppose that meaning and understanding and thinking are not altogether different from *physical* acts and processes.

> One might say "Thinking is an incorporeal process," however, if one were using this to distinguish the grammar of the word "think" from that of, say, the word "eat." Only that makes the difference between the meanings look *too slight.* (It is like saying: numerals are actual, and numbers non-actual, objects.) An unsuitable type of expression is a sure means of remaining in a state of confusion. It as it were bars the way out. [*PI,* sect. 339.]

Perhaps the best way to express Wittgenstein's position would be as follows. In a trivial sense of 'name' and 'denote,' all, or at least most, words name or denote something. This, however, says very little. The word 'name,' like the word 'game,' covers a multitude of different cases: there is no one essential name-relation, any more than there is a single essence common to all games. There is a certain relation (or group of relations) between the name 'John Jones' and the man John Jones, and a different one (or group) between the word 'red' and red things—but if you think that for every word, and in particular for 'meaning' and 'understanding,' there exist things to which they bear just *those* kinds of relations, then you are sadly mistaken. Philosophers have taken the trivial truth that all (or most) words denote something, and, with their craving for unity, have construed it to mean that all words are correlated with something in the same ways that 'tree' is correlated with trees; and have thereby helped to project themselves into the dark night of philosophical puzzlement. They have thoughtlessly poisoned a harmless truth and made it deadly.

I shall conclude this section with a brief account of Wittgenstein's views about the sorts of relations which connect a name and what it names. The relations vary from case to case (*PI,* sect. 38); but let us concentrate our attention on some of the paradigm examples of a name's denoting something, such as 'John Jones' 's denoting a certain man, and 'tree' 's denoting a familiar kind of object. It may strike us that here we are confronted with a deeply mystifying aspect of language. On the one side, there is the name, and on the other, the thing named: here the word 'tree,' there the object with trunk, branches, roots, and leaves. The two things are completely unlike, so there is no natural relation connecting them. And yet they are intimately connected somehow, for the former denotes, is the name of, the latter. But how is this connection made? How can a word, a mere scribble on a piece of paper, reach out beyond itself and establish a tie with a kind of object totally unlike itself? The relation between the name and the thing named thus looks like a mysterious one—indeed, like an impossible one.

What, then, is this strange relation (rather, what are these strange relations) between a name and what it is the name of—or in short, between language and the world? This question is a theme running through all of Wittgenstein's writings, both early and late. It was one of *the* central issues which exercised him in the *Tractatus,* and certainly one of his major worries in the later works too. In the *Tractatus,* Wittgenstein had thought there was one essential name-relation, and to the question of its nature, he had given the answer which always comes most naturally to hand when there is something mysterious to be explained; he said (if I interpret his words correctly) that the mind makes the connection by meaning or intending the name to designate the object. But as he later realized, this is merely an apparent solution to the problem, not a real one. No appeal to any workings of the "mechanism of the mind" is going to solve the problem of how names and the things named are related; for that appeal, as we have seen, succeeds only in re-introducing the same difficulty in a new, mysterious medium.

And so we are puzzled. We stare at a word—at some ink marks on paper—and then at an object or person somewhere (the thing named by the word), and we are baffled as to how one *can* be the name of the other, how the two can possibly be connected. The connection between them seems to be wholly mysterious. The mystery, however, is not impenetrable. It is not an "ontological mystery," existing in the very nature of things. It is an artificial one, created by the abstract way we, as philosophers, have been viewing the matter.

> This is connected with the conception of naming as, so to speak, an occult process. Naming appears as a *queer* connexion of a word with an object.—And you really get such a queer connexion when the philosopher tries to bring out *the* relation between name and thing by staring at an object in front of him and repeating a name or even the word "this" innumerable times. For philosophical problems arise when language *goes on holiday*. And *here* we may indeed fancy naming to be some remarkable act of mind, as it were a baptism of an object. [*PI*, sect. 38.]

(See also *BB*, p. 172.) What we have done, and what has created the aura of mystery, is what philosophers habitually do: we have taken the name and the thing named out of the actual concrete situations in which they figure, out of the "stream of life" in which they participate, and have then—not surprisingly—found ourselves unable to understand the connection between them. The answer, of course, is to put them back into their natural home, that is, into the language-games in which alone they are connected and in which alone their connection can be understood. Once we do this, the mystery vanishes without a trace. Look at the language-games, and at the ways the name and the thing named are there related, and you will see at once what the connection between them is—or rather, what the connections between them are. Look, for example, at the language-game described in the *Investigations,* section 2 (quoted above, p. 240). *A* calls out 'slab' and *B* fetches a slab. This is the sort of thing we mean when we say that the word 'slab' is the name of a certain kind of object—namely, of a slab. And of course there are lots of others, lots of other language-games in which connections between the name and the thing named are established. (See *PI*, sect. 37; and also *BB*, p. 172 and *PI*, sect. 53, in which other examples are graphically presented.) There is thus no *one* relation between a name and the thing it names.

> . . . It is clear that there is no one relation of name to object, but as many as there are uses of sounds or scribbles which we call names. [*BB*, p. 173.]

There are as many relations between a name and the thing named as there are language-games in which they play a part. In any given language-game—such as that described in *PI, sect.* 2, for example—the connection between them is entirely straightforward and presents no problems for our understanding. But a philosopher, with his inordinate craving for unity, does not want to contemplate the untidy range of diversified language-games—and this reluctance proves to be his undoing. Abstracting them from all language-games, from all contexts of their employment, he considers the name and the thing named by themselves, and seeks to discover *the* relation uniting them. And of course he fails.

> . . . We, in a sense, simplify matters by saying that the name has a peculiar relation to its object, a relation other than that, say, of being written on the object, or of being spoken by a person pointing to an object with his finger. A primitive philosophy condenses the whole usage of the name into the idea of a relation, which thereby becomes a mysterious relation. [*BB,* p. 173.]

As Wittgenstein goes on to point out in this passage, the same thing happens when the philosopher deals with meaning and understanding and other mental activities. What meaning and understanding consist in is revealed only in the course of time and in a wide variety of the person's behavior. But the philosopher, trying to find the one thing which is their essence, oversimplifies the matter and collapses the modes of behavior into a single mental act or process. And then he is puzzled by this mental act or process, and cannot make head or tail of it! Philosophers, by considering matters abstractly, ignore the details of actual human behavior and thereby create trouble for themselves.

> In order to see more clearly, here as in countless similar cases, we must focus on the details of what goes on; must look at them *from close to.* [PI, sect. 51.]

*   *   *

In this chapter we have seen how Wittgenstein seeks to justify his view that, although several vital aspects of the workings of language seem to require mental acts or processes, this is actually not so. All that is actually required, in addition to the words themselves, is the behavior of human beings, the language-games which they play with the words. It is, in short, the use of words which gives them life. In use, they are alive.

12 Sensations and Talk of Them

At this point, one may begin to wonder what lies behind Wittgenstein's strenuous denial that words like 'meaning' and 'understanding' refer to private mental happenings. The most natural view, surely, is that they do refer to such happenings; why should it ever occur to anyone to deny it in the first place? We all constantly experience things which enter and leave and re-enter our consciousness, things which are directly accessible only to ourselves. And there are words in our language to refer to many of these things—words like 'pain,' 'itch,' 'ache,' 'image,' 'fear,' 'anger,' and many more. These are names for things which each of us experiences privately: only I feel my own toothache, for example. You cannot feel my toothache, nor I yours. But your toothache is doubtless qualitatively similar to mine, since the structures of our bodies are very similar. And so, although many words in our language denote physical things and events which are publicly observable by all, other words denote items in each of our separate consciousnesses, things directly observable only by the one person in whose consciousness they occur. All this seems undeniable. What is to be gained, then, by denying that 'meaning' and 'understanding' denote private mental occurrences? For even if they do not, there is still a host of words that do name such things. And if the realm of the mental so surely exists and can so easily be talked about, what reason could there be for wanting to deny that mental acts or processes play a vital part in the workings of language?

It is quite wrong to suggest that Wittgenstein, in his treatment of meaning and understanding, was originally motivated by any general considerations about the mental, or about the relationship between language and the mental. On the contrary, in *The Blue and Brown Books* he was quite willing to admit that expressions like 'meaning what one says' and 'understanding' do sometimes, albeit rarely, refer to private mental acts, processes, or states. (See, e.g., *BB,* pp. 146, 147.) But in the course of writing the *Investigations,* Wittgenstein became more and more reluctant to concede even this much. In the later parts of that work, he insists, for example, that 'meaning' is never the name (in any nontrivial sense) of a mental happening:

> Someone tells me: "Wait for me by the bank." Question: Did you, *as you were saying the word,* mean this bank?—This question is of the same kind as "Did you intend to say such-and-such to him on your way to meet him?" It refers to a definite time (the time of walking, as the former question refers to the time of speaking)—but not to an *experience* during that time. Meaning is as little an experience as intending. [*PI,* pp. 216-17.]

(See also *PI,* sect. 693 and p. 218.) An important part of the explanation of this change, I suggest, is that Wittgenstein had gradually worked out certain general views about language which, if true, would make it impossible that any word should have the function of naming (in any nontrivial sense) a private inward occurrence, act, process, or state. It is the purpose of this chapter to explain these views. I shall concentrate on a class of words which seem to constitute the most powerful counter-examples to Wittgenstein's thesis; namely, words like 'pain,' 'itch,' 'tingle,' and so on. These words seem *obviously* to name private sensations—and yet Wittgenstein would evidently want to deny it.

First of all, it is important to be as clear as we can at the outset about just what Wittgenstein is denying—although this will hopefully become clearer as we proceed with his account. He is not denying that there is a (trivial) sense in which 'pain,' for example, is the name of a sensation. In this sense, 'pain' denotes a sensation, as 'five' denotes a number, as 'understanding' denotes a mental process, and as virtually every word denotes something—that is, 'pain' is a sensation-word and has uses closely allied with 'twinge,' 'ache,' 'tickle' and the other sensation-words, just as 'five' is a number-word and has uses closely allied with 'one,' 'two,' 'ten,' and the other number-words. This much is obvious and no one would wish to deny it.

The point over which dispute arises is *how* the word 'pain' denotes a sensation, in what the denoting or name-relation consists in this case, what sort of connections exist between the word and the sensation. It is quite natural to suppose that the relations between 'pain' and a certain familiar kind of private sensation are very similar indeed to those between, say, 'red' and a certain familiar kind of publicly observable property. After all, we seem to refer to people and attribute the sensation to them ("He is in pain," "I am in pain") just as we refer to objects and attribute the color to them ("That is red," "His book is red"). We talk about pains, in short, very much as we talk about colors or sounds or textures, so the name-relation in the two kinds of cases, we think, must be very much the same. It is this view which I shall refer to as the view that 'pain' and the other sensation-words are the names of, or denote, private sensations. And it is just this view that Wittgenstein is most anxious to rebut.

On the face of it, one would immediately suppose that Wittgenstein could not possibly be right. Let us grant the special arguments about 'meaning' and 'understanding' and admit that they are not the names of inward occurrences; this still leaves a great many words which must, we feel, denote items occurring in a person's consciousness and which he alone experiences. Is it not simply absurd to deny that 'toothache,' for example, is the name of one such item? Wittgenstein, in his middle period, i.e., in the early 1930's, would not have thought of doubting this common-sensical attitude. Moore says this about Wittgenstein's lectures of 1932-33:

> . . . As to the . . . proposition . . . 'I have toothache,' the point on which he seemed most anxious to insist was that what we call 'having toothache' is what he called a 'primary experience' (he once used the phrase 'direct experience' as equivalent to this one); . . .[1]

Wittgenstein also implied that the word 'toothache' in the two propositions "I have toothache" and "He has toothache" has the same meaning in both cases; hence, a person who expresses the second proposi-

[1] Moore, "Wittgenstein's Lectures in 1930-33," Part III, *Mind*, LXIV, No. 253 (January 1955), 13 (*Philosophical Papers*, p. 308). In the next few references to this article, the page numbers will be those of the *Mind* volume; the corresponding page numbers of *Philosophical Papers* will also be given, preceded by the letters '*PP*.'

tion is attributing the very same kind of thing to another person that he would be attributing to himself if he were to express the first proposition (Moore, pp. 12-13; *PP,* pp. 307-08). Of course, I cannot directly experience the other fellow's toothache, but I justifiably "conclude" that he is experiencing just what I experience when I have toothache since he behaves just as I do when I have one (Moore, p. 12; *PP,* p. 308).

Yet Wittgenstein noticed that there are a number of important differences between "I have toothache" and "He has toothache." It makes perfectly good sense to wonder whether or not another person has toothache, but there can be no such thing as a person's wondering whether he himself has toothache or not. It can seem to me that he has toothache, but it cannot seem to me that I have toothache (Moore, p. 12; *PP,* p. 307). In fact, although I can collect evidence and perhaps verify that you have toothache, the whole notion of collecting evidence and verifying that I have toothache is absurd. What is more, I might make a mistake in identifying another person who has toothache ("I thought it was Jones who had toothache, but I see now that I was mistaken—it is the man groaning over there in the corner"); but it is not sensible to suggest that when I have a toothache, I need to identify the person who has the toothache (i.e., myself) and that I might make a mistake in doing so ("Let's see, is it I or someone else who has this toothache?") (*BB,* p. 67). Wittgenstein marked these differences by saying that 'I have toothache' and 'He has toothache' have different meanings (Moore, p. 11; *PP,* p. 307). Since the difference in meaning cannot be accounted for by a difference of meaning in the word 'toothache' in the two propositions, it must be due to a difference in meaning between the subject terms 'he' and 'I.' It is, of course, obviously true that 'he' and 'I' have different meanings; but Wittgenstein is thinking here not of this obvious difference that 'he' is used to refer to another person while 'I' is not. He means rather that the whole concept of a person is radically different in the two propositions "He has toothache" and "I have toothache." Wittgenstein expressed this difference by saying that the two propositions are not two values of the single propositional function 'x has toothache' (Moore, p. 12; *PP,* p. 307). Wittgenstein's discussion here is fascinating (*BB,* pp. 66-74; Moore, pp. 10-16; *PP,* pp. 306-12), but I shall not pursue it, since his thought was to take a new turn which is of greater importance for our purposes.

By 1933, as we have just seen, Wittgenstein had already partially broken away from the plausible view that propositions like (1) "He has toothache," "He is in pain," and like (2) "I have toothache," "I am in pain" are not importantly different in their logical characteristics. Nevertheless, he still at that time agreed with its underlying assumptions. These assumptions were that words like 'toothache' and 'pain' are the names (in a nontrivial sense) of sensations which people sometimes experience; that when I assert truly "I have toothache" or "I am in pain," I am describing the state of my consciousness (i.e., I am asserting that there is included in it a sensation called 'toothache' or 'pain'); and finally that when I assert of another person "He has toothache" or "He is in pain," I claim that he is experiencing the same sort of sensation that I do when I have toothache or am in pain. But these assumptions were now to fall under Wittgenstein's critical scrutiny.

The view which these assumptions express—let us call it View *V* —despite its naturalness and plausibility, has absurd consequences, according to Wittgenstein. First of all, if the proposition "He is in pain" claims that the person referred to has a certain sensation before his consciousness, then I can never know for certain whether any proposition of that sort is true—that is, I can never know whether another person is in pain or not—for I cannot feel another person's pain. The best I can do is infer from his behavior, or his reports, or from some other evidence, that he is in pain; but such inferences can always be wrong, for the other person might always be shamming or play-acting or joking. "I can only *believe* that someone else is in pain, but I *know* it if I am" (*PI,* sect. 303). Wittgenstein regards this consequence of View *V* as absurd, as plainly false.

> If we are using the word "to know" as it is normally used (and how else are we to use it?), then other people very often know when I am in pain. [*PI,* sect. 246.]
> Just try—in a real case—to doubt someone else's fear or pain. [*PI,* sect. 303.]
> I can be as *certain* of someone else's sensations as of any fact. . . . Am I less certain that this man is in pain than that twice two is four? [*PI,* p. 224.]

Whatever account we are going to give of 'pain' (and the other sensation-words), Wittgenstein is certainly right that we at least sometimes know—and with certainty—that another person is in pain, and that any view which denies this possibility is so far wrong.

"But mightn't the other person be shamming?" one objects. The answer is that in some cases it is evident that a person is shamming, in others it is probable or at least quite possible that he is, but that in still other cases we know that he is not shamming. "Surely, however, even the man who has been hit by a car might just conceivably be shamming; in fact there will always be at least a conceivable doubt that another person is in pain, and hence we can never know that he is." The answer to this is that if a merely conceivable doubt is going to prevent us from knowing that another person is in pain, then it is going to prevent us also from knowing anything—for example, that you are now reading a book or even that 2 plus 2 equals 4. A Cartesian wicked demon might always be deceiving us, so there is always at least a conceivable doubt. There comes a point in such situations when further doubt is no longer merely a sign of excessive caution, but a sign of irrationality. "Doubting," as Wittgenstein says, "has an end" (*PI*, p. 180).

> "But, if you are *certain,* isn't it that you are shutting your eyes in face of doubt?"—They are shut. [*PI*, p. 224.]

If there is no positive reason for doubt, no basis whatever for it, then it is unreasonable to doubt. In fact, it is difficult to determine what doubting, in these cases, can possibly *be*. Suppose a man claims to have at least a conceivable doubt that he has a hand: he pinches it, shakes it, rubs his face with it, picks up a pencil with it, and presumably continues to use it in the usual ways. And yet he claims that he entertains at least a conceivable doubt that the hand exists. What does his doubt consist in? Not just in his saying "I have a doubt," for that is in itself an empty ritual, as Wittgenstein might put it. Doubting cannot just be saying "I doubt." But what else is there here? After his tests, all the man's actions are those of a man who does not doubt that he has a hand. What is really doubtful, then, is that he does have a doubt—even a conceivable doubt. And the same goes for the man who says of the car victim: "I know he is bleeding and screaming, and I shall certainly rush to his aid—get doctors and all the rest. Still, there is a conceivable doubt that he is putting it all on." If all there is to his doubting is just his saying these words, then one wants to say that he has no doubt.

Wittgenstein now makes an even stronger point. If 'pain' is the name of a sensation which I experience only in the privacy of my own consciousness, then I cannot even understand what it would mean to say that another person has a pain—that another person feels just what I feel when I have a pain. That statement would then be unintelligible to me. If the word 'pain' denotes, for me, an item in my consciousness, then pain can exist only when I am aware of it. It makes no sense to say that although I no longer feel the pain, nevertheless it is going on all the same. 'Subconscious pain' is an expression without a use. Therefore one essential feature of a pain is that I feel it, and I would be guilty of contradicting myself if I said that there is a pain which I do not feel, but which another person feels.

"But wait a minute, not so fast. It is only an essential feature of *my* pains that I must feel them, not an essential feature of *all* pains. It is essential to any pain that it be felt, but not necessarily by me. To be sure, I only know what pain is from my own case, but surely I can imagine that someone else feels something exactly like what I feel when I have pain." Wittgenstein would reply, I think, that on the view he is attacking, there can be no distinction, for me, between *my* pains and *all* pains; for all the pains I ever meet with, or can conceivably ever meet with, *are* my pains. And is it so obvious that I *can* understand what it is for another person to feel exactly what I feel? How can I be sure that I understand the suggestion that he does?

"But if I suppose that someone has a pain, then I am simply supposing that he has just the same as I have so often had."—That gets us no further. It is as if I were to say: "You surely know what 'It is 5 o'clock here' means; so you also know what 'It's 5 o'clock on the sun' means. It means simply that it is just the same time there as it is here when it is 5 o'clock."—The explanation by means of *identity* does not work here. For I know well enough that one can call 5 o'clock here and 5 o'clock there "the same time," but what I do not know is in what cases one is to speak of its being the same time here and there.

In exactly the same way it is no explanation to say: the supposition that he has a pain is simply the supposition that he has the same as I. For *that* part of the grammar is quite clear to me: that is, that one will say that the stove has the same experience as I, *if* one says: it is in pain and I am in pain. [*PI*, sect. 350.]

(See also *PI*, sect. 351.) The point is this: one cannot tell just by looking at a sentence whether it makes sense or not. Consider the schema "It is 5 o'clock in the afternoon in (or on) _____." It might seem that the name of any place whatever can go in the blank, and the resulting sentence be intelligible. This is in fact so for places like Newark, New Jersey or Bangkok, Thailand—but it is not so for a place like the sun. It may seem, at first glance, that 'It is 5 o'clock in the afternoon on the sun' is a sentence which could be used to make an intelligible assertion: it is, after all, a perfectly good English sentence (see *PI,* sect. 348). But the appearance of intelligibility is deceptive, for one cannot specify any conceivable conditions which would count as its being 5 o'clock on the sun. It makes no sense to speak of determining the truth of the assertion that it is 5 o'clock on the sun, and therefore the assertion is unintelligible. The very notion of its being a certain time (of its being such-and-such o'clock) presupposes a system of time zones, and one can speak of its being a certain time only for a point or limited area within a time zone (including, of course, the entire time zone itself). So one can speak of its being 5 o'clock in San Francisco or on the West Coast, but not of its being 5 o'clock in America or 5 o'clock on earth—or on the sun. Therefore, although all sorts of images may occur to me when someone says "It is 5 o'clock on the sun," still I cannot conceive that it is so—that it is the same time on the sun that it is here.

And similarly, says Wittgenstein, on the view that 'pain' is the name of a private sensation, I cannot conceive that another person feels the same sensation that I do when I feel a pain. True, I can imagine all sorts of things in connection with those words—e.g., I can imagine that I look just like him and that I feel a pain sensation— but this is not enough for the intelligibility of the suggestion. There are in fact no specifiable conditions under which I could determine that another person feels the same sensation I do: to do that, I would have to be able to feel his pain (see *PI,* sect. 253), and that is impossible. He can, of course, describe his pain to me as 'sharp,' 'dull,' 'severe,' and so on, but this is no help whatever; for I have no way of telling what corresponds to these adjectives in this case. The adjectives are here being used analogically, and unless I have some conception of what they are being applied to—and this is precisely what I lack—I can have no idea of what they are supposed to mean. Since there is no way of specifying how the truth of the assertion "He feels the same sensation I do" could possibly be determined, the assertion is unintelligible. No state of affairs would *count* as his feeling the same sensation I do, just as no state of affairs would count as its being 5 o'clock in the afternoon on the sun. It is no good replying "Of course some state of affairs counts as his feeling the same sensation I do—namely, his feeling the same sensation I do," because the same reply could be made in support of the intelligibility of "It is

5 o'clock on the sun" or "The Absolute is green" or anything else you like.

A possible objection: "But the suggestion that another person who is in pain is feeling the same thing I do when I am in pain *must* be intelligible, because I can surely imagine that it is so." To this, Wittgenstein replies as follows:

> If one has to imagine someone else's pain on the model of one's own, this is none too easy a thing to do: for I have to imagine pain which I *do not feel* on the model of the pain which I *do feel*. That is, what I have to do is not simply to make a transition in imagination from one place of pain to another. As, from pain in the hand to pain in the arm. For I am not to imagine that I feel pain in some region of his body. (Which would also be possible.) [*PI*, sect. 302.]

If I think I can imagine that another person experiences the same private sensation of pain that I do when I am in pain, it would be well to look closely at what I claim to be able to do. What *exactly* do I do when I imagine this? Part of it, at least, must be that I imagine him feeling a private sensation. But can this be done? I surely can imagine him having a broken arm or a black eye; that is easy. But what must I imagine to imagine him feeling a private sensation? I imagine, let us say, a private sensation of pain, just like the ones I have when I am in pain. And, it must be added, I imagine that *he* is having it. But there's the rub, for how do I do *that?* When I feel a sensation of pain, there is no item in my consciousness, separate from the pain, which is *me* (my ego), which is me feeling the pain. There is simply the pain (*T* 5.631). How, then, can I imagine anything corresponding to *him* feeling the pain? Here is one possible reply: "When I feel a pain, I also generally experience other things—for example, I see parts of my body. Now, I could imagine a pain sensation accompanied by the seeing of parts of another person's body, as they would appear to him when he looks at his body. Perhaps this would be to imagine him feeling a pain sensation." This will not do; for how does it differ from imagining *myself* feeling the pain, only now having a different body? In fact, isn't this just what I would be imagining? When I imagine anything, I really imagine myself seeing it (hearing it, tasting it, and so on); thus, when I imagine a man with a black eye, I imagine myself seeing such a man. And when I imagine a pain, I cannot help imagining myself having it. The suggestion that I might imagine another person having a private sensation just like mine turns out to be nonsensical. (For a different argument purporting to prove the same point, see *BB*, p. 53.)

If the foregoing arguments are valid, then the thesis that 'pain' denotes a private sensation has the absurd consequence that the assertion that another person is in pain is an unintelligible one.

Wittgenstein presses relentlessly on, and points out additional absurd consequences of View *V*. If it were correct, and 'pain' and the other sensation-words denoted items in (or of) one's consciousness, then when a sensation appears before a person's mind, he must identify that item (as, say, a pain rather than an itch or an ache or a twinge). In that case, the possibility arises at once that he might make a mistake in his identification. He might always misidentify it, and hence it must always be possible for him to wonder whether he has done so or not. Consequently, all of the following remarks ought to make perfectly good sense: (a) "How do you know you are in pain?" (Moore, *op. cit.*, p. 307), (b) "I think I am in pain, but I may be mistaken," (c) "I don't know whether I am in pain or not" (*PI*, sects. 288, 408), (d) "I know I am in pain" (*PI*, sect. 246), (e) "I believe I am in pain," (f) "I seem to be in pain," (g) "I doubt whether I am in pain" (*PI*, sects. 246, 288), (h) "Let me find out if I'm in pain or not" (*PI*, sect. 246), (i) "I wonder whether I'm in pain or not." But all these utterances strike us at once as odd: we want to say that one *cannot* wonder whether he is in pain or not, or merely think he is, and so on. As Wittgenstein says:

> That expression of doubt has no place in the language-game. [*PI*, sect. 288.]

And yet if we deny, as View *V* does, that there are any *essential* connections between the use of the word 'pain' and the normal manifestations of pain in human behavior, and insist that 'pain' simply denotes a private sensation, then all those remarks would indeed be in order.

> . . . If we cut out human behaviour, which is the expression of sensation, it looks as if I might *legitimately* begin to doubt afresh. My temptation to say that one might take a sensation for something other than what it is arises from this: if I assume the abrogation of the normal language-game with the expression of a sensation, I need a criterion of identity for the sensation; and then the possibility of error also exists. [*PI*, sect. 288.]

Since, however, there really is no possibility of error, View *V* cannot be correct.

So far, Wittgenstein has been attacking what he takes to be several absurd consequences of View *V*. Now he turns to a more direct attack on the view itself. One thing, to begin with, seems perfectly certain: if there were no overt manifestations or expressions of pain—i.e., if people just inwardly *had* pains, but did not cry or groan or grimace or plead for help—then there is no conceivable way that anyone could learn the use of the word 'pain.' But then 'pain' could not be a word in any language. And so it must be granted by anyone that there is at least this connection between pain and pain behavior: pain behavior plays an indispensable part in the teaching and learning of the word 'pain.' For suppose that there were no such behavior and that one day I had a sensation *x;* and assume that *x* is a sensation which I *now* in fact call 'pain.' Under these conditions how could I possibly know that sensation *x* is properly called 'pain,' that is, that it is what people who speak English call 'pain'? I could not.

> If I know it only from my own case, then I know only what *I* call that, not what anyone else does. [*PI*, sect. 347.]
> "What would it be like if human beings shewed no outward signs of pain (did not groan, grimace, etc.)? Then it would be impossible to teach a child the use of the word 'tooth-ache.' " [*PI*, sect. 257.]

When a word is the name of something, I learn what it means by having other people point out examples of it to me or by observing what they apply it to, and then by going on myself to apply the word to further examples. In this latter process, what determines whether I have gotten it right or not is whether I apply the word to appropriate or to inappropriate things, and the only possible way of telling which is the case is for other people to confirm my application when it is correct and to rebut it when it is incorrect. But nothing of this sort can happen in the case of private sensations: I might continually apply the word 'pain' to the wrong sensation and no one would ever be able to tell me that I was doing so. Therefore, I could not possibly learn how to use the word 'pain.'

To this, the following objection might be made: "But of course you could teach a child how to use the word 'pain' even under these odd conditions. All you would have to do is hold a lighted match to his hand, or stick him with a pin, and tell him that that is what pain is" (*PI*, sect. 288). But in the absence of any overt behavior, of any reaction on the child's part, there would be no guarantee whatever that he felt anything. In fact, in the absence of any reaction, we would not have so much as the *idea* that he might feel anything, just as we do not have this idea in the case of stones or plants (*PI*, sect. 283). And whether or not he did feel anything when the pin is inserted into his flesh, how could we determine if he interprets our ostensive definition aright? How can we tell that by 'pain' he does not understand 'sticking a pin in one's flesh' or 'damaging one's flesh'? It is no good replying "These alternative possible interpretations of the ostensive definition can be eliminated by telling the child that 'pain' does not denote any overt action or state of affairs which everyone can observe, but that 'pain' is rather the sensation which only he can feel when the pin goes into his flesh." This reply won't do, because it is just as difficult to conceive how, on the present hypothesis, the child can learn the use of the words 'sensation' and 'feel' as to conceive how he can learn the use of the word 'pain.' (*PI*, sect. 257.) And even if the child does understand the words 'sensation' and 'feel,' the big difficulty still stares us in the face: how can we be sure that it is *pain*—i.e., a sensation like ours—which he feels when the pin goes in? He might simply have felt the pin rending his flesh and nothing more, or it might have caused him to have a ringing sound in his ears, or anything at all.

The foregoing considerations do not show that 'pain' is not the name of a private sensation. They show only that some outward manifestations of pain are required for the teaching and learning of the use of the word 'pain.' A child falls down and begins to cry, holding his knee; we tell him that it hurts, that he feels pain, and we comfort him, assuring him that it will soon be better. The child observes other people: his mother touches a hot stove, jerks her hand away, shakes it, grimaces, and claims that it hurts, is painful—and he knows from experience what he himself feels when he touches hot things and when he acts like that. In short, the child learns that certain modes of behavior are correlated with an inner sensation whose name is 'pain.' The overt behavior—the grimaces, the jerking of the hand away, and the rest—are external manifestations or expressions of the inward feeling; they let other people know that one is experiencing that private sensation. Words like 'I have a pain' and 'I am in pain' are descriptions of one's inward state; they, too, inform other people of how it is with us, inside. The outward manifestations are necessary in order for a child to learn what pain is—he learns that pain is the sensation correlated with those manifestations—but they are not the pain, nor any part of it. This, at any rate, is what View *V* asserts, and it is the most it can claim.

Wittgenstein launches a powerful attack against even this modified version of the original view, and specifically against the claim it shares with the original view that 'pain' is the name of, or denotes, a private sensation. He asks what the alleged naming or denoting relation can *be* in this case. An answer to this question is required, because

> . . . we call very different things "names"; the word "name" is used to characterize many different kinds of use of a word, related to one another in many different ways. . . . [*PI*, sect. 38.]

It is in answering this question that Wittgenstein takes violent exception to View *V*. According to that view, 'pain' denotes a sensation in a way quite analogous to the way that, say, 'red' denotes a familiar kind of observable property. In each case, there is the word on one side ('red' or 'pain') and what is named on the other (the color or the pain), and 'pain' is the name of what it denotes in much the same way that 'red' is the name of what it denotes. The only significant difference in the two cases is that whereas a color is public, observable by all, a pain is private, observable only by the person whose pain it is; but this difference has no effect on the naming or denoting relation, which is essentially the same in both instances. So says View *V*. In opposition to this, Wittgenstein will maintain that the privacy of pain makes a great deal of difference to the way in which 'pain' denotes a kind of sensation, and that it is wholly misguided to think that the relation between 'pain' and the sensation is of the same kind as the relation between 'red' and the physical property called by that name.

Wittgenstein begins by asking his usual question:

> How do words *refer* to sensations?—. . . How is the connexion between the name and the thing named set up? [*PI*, sect. 244.]

Once this question is asked, it quickly becomes apparent that the ways in which the names of public objects and qualities denote their objects cannot be even remotely like the ways in which 'pain' denotes a sensation. As we saw in the last section of the last chapter, the connection between the name of a public object, e.g., 'tree,' and its object is established by, and consists in, certain modes of human behavior—in pointing to trees, counting trees, drawing pictures of trees, planting trees, and so on. But in almost none of these general kinds of behavior does the word 'pain' play a part: I cannot point to a pain (although I can usually point to the place of a pain), nor show you a pain, nor draw a picture of a pain, nor fetch you a pain. I can do practically none of the things I can do with physical objects or colors or shapes, i.e., with publicly observable things, and so the modes of behavior in which alone the connection between the name of something public and the thing it names is made are not available in the case of 'pain.'

A defender of View *V* might offer the following rejoinder: "Your requirements are too stringent. Of course there are many language-games in which the names of public things play a part and in which the names of private sensations cannot perforce play any part. But still some of the language-games in which words like 'pain' might play a part are sufficiently similar to the sorts of language-games we play with the names of public things to warrant the thesis that 'pain' and similar words are the names of private sensations in very much the same way that 'red' and 'tree' are the names of physical things. For example, suppose a man suddenly experiences a sensation E that he has never had before. He can focus his attention on it and give it the name 'E.' This corresponds to an ostensive definition that one person might give another of the name of something publicly observable, only here the person gives it to himself, and instead of pointing physically to the thing named, as in a standard ostensive definition, he points to it mentally. Then he may even keep a diary and write down the sign 'E' whenever he experiences the same sensation again, noting the time and place of its occurrence—much as he might keep a diary record of the times he has seen a certain kind of tree or bird. Why are these activities not sufficiently similar to activities surrounding the use of names of publicly observable things to support my thesis that words like 'pain' are names of private sensations?" (See *PI,* sect. 258.)

The words of this rejoinder seem to make perfectly good sense; they correspond to a quite definite picture. But how is the picture to be applied? What precisely do the activities described *come to?* If we try to answer this question in detail, the rejoinder collapses and reveals itself to be nothing but empty words. Consider the alleged private ostensive definition. It is certainly true that a man can focus his attention on a sensation and say "Let this be called 'E.'" In itself, however, that performance is but an idle ritual: a sign is not transformed into the name of a thing merely by focusing one's attention and saying a few magical words—as it were, linking the sign and the thing by a mystical spiritual tie. The ritual must have some actual practical consequences if it is to be an act of giving a name to something.

Why can't my right hand give my left hand money?—My right hand can put it into my left hand. My right hand can write a deed of gift and my left hand a receipt.—But the further practical consequences would not be those of a gift. When the left hand has taken the money from the right, etc., we shall ask: "Well, and what of it?" And the same could be asked if a person had given himself a private definition of a word; I mean, if he has said the word to himself and at the same time has directed his attention to a sensation. [*PI*, sect. 268.]

And the very least that is required in the way of consequences is that the sign 'E' shall be used to refer only to the sensation E and to no other, that it shall be used regularly to refer to the same (kind of) sensation as the original one which figured in the private ostensive definition. Is that what happens in the private diary?

Wittgenstein argues that any such book would be a mere sham record, and not a genuine one. He does this by trying to show that the sign 'E' is not a sign at all, not the name of the sensation E or of anything else. His argument proceeds as follows. The alleged diarist —call him Paul—has no way whatever of knowing whether he always applies the sign 'E' to a sensation which is the same as the original one, or whether he applies it to a different one each time, or whether he sometimes applies it to the same sensation, sometimes to a different one. And the trouble is not simply that his powers are inadequate for the performance of a very difficult task; rather, according to Wittgenstein, the task is impossible in the very nature of the case. Paul performs his alleged private ostensive definition at time t_0, and resolves to call a certain sensation—call it E_0—by the name 'E.' The next day, at time t_1, he experiences a sensation—call it E_1—and having the impression that E_1 is the same as E_0, makes a suitable entry in his diary: "E again." But the trouble is [2] that there is no conceivable way of telling whether his impression is correct or not, whether E_1 really is or is not the same as E_0. There is certainly no external check. Paul cannot, for example, ask his friend Jones to corroborate his impression of identity! "Well, can't he just remember what E_0 was like and thereby see that E_1 is just like it?" This suggestion provides no help whatever. For what is his act of remembering supposed to consist in? Having an image of E_0? But then how can he tell that this image faithfully represents E_0? How can he tell, in fact, no matter what his act of remembering consists in, whether he is truly remembering what E_0 was like or whether he is only under

[2] Rather, *one* of the troubles. There is also a problem about the use of the word 'same' in this situation. See *PI*, sect. 378.

the impression that he is doing so? His recollection, even granting that it is something different from his impression that E_1 is just like E_0, is as much in need of authentication as the impression, and hence cannot be thought to provide that very authentication. If Paul were to appeal to his memory to back up his impression, he would be like a man who checks up on the veracity of a report in the morning newspaper by buying another copy of it. (*PI*, sect. 265.)

Wittgenstein argues next that under these conditions the question of the correctness or incorrectness (rightness or wrongness) of Paul's use of the sign 'E' cannot arise, and that hence the very concept of correctness or incorrectness fails to apply. The point is not that no one can tell whether, when Paul makes his subsequent diary entries 'E' at times $t_1, t_2, t_3 \ldots$, he is using the sign 'E' correctly or incorrectly. It is rather the stronger point that it makes no sense to wonder whether he is using it correctly or incorrectly, or in any other way to think or speak of his doing so. (Analogously, it is not merely difficult or impossible to tell whether a table is good-natured or not; it makes no sense to speak of a table's being good-natured or ill-tempered.) Wittgenstein argues, in support of this contention, that wherever there is no conceivable way of distinguishing right from wrong, correct from incorrect, the concepts of right and wrong, of correct and incorrect, cannot apply. To put it another way, whenever there is no distinction between a thing's seeming right and its actually being right, one cannot speak of right or wrong. (*PI*, sect. 258.) Consider the following games, for example: (a) The players sit in a circle. The first player says a word, and the next player is to say another word which strikes him intuitively as being the word which ought to come after the first one. The third player does the same, and so on around the circle. (b) The first player is to arrange various wooden objects on a board until they seem right to him. The second player is to rearrange them until they seem right to him, and so on. In these games, the distinction between seeming right and being right collapses, and this means that one cannot sensibly speak of right or wrong. Provided the players play the game honestly—that is, in (a) the players say the word that really does strike them as the right one, and in (b) the players arrange the objects in a way that really does strike them as right—then what would it mean to say that in (a) the second player uttered the right word, but the third player the wrong one, or that in (b) the third player's arrangement was correct, but the second player's was incorrect? Such concepts cannot get a foothold in these games. Nor, says Wittgenstein, do they apply to Paul's diary entries. Paul might always "make a mistake" in identifying his sensations, now putting an 'E' down in his book when he has sensation E, now when he has a different sensation S, now when he has a different one T, and so on; and there is no conceivable way that he could tell he was doing it, that he did not in every case have the same sensation E. But then we cannot speak of his making a mistake at all, nor therefore of his using the sign 'E' correctly or incorrectly; for, as in the games (a) and (b), the distinction between seeming to be correct and actually being so vanishes.

It follows from this that Paul's diary is not a record of the times he has had sensation E at all; he goes through the motions of keeping such a record, and it may even seem very clear to him that he is keeping such a record, but he is not. This conclusion can be put in another way which is more directly relevant to our present concern. Paul's mark 'E' is not the name of one of his private sensations— it is not a sign or a word of any sort. In order for a sound or mark to be a word, it must at least be possible to use it correctly or incorrectly: there must be some circumstances in which it would be correct to use it, and others in which it would be incorrect. Otherwise, it is, as we might say, a *mere* sound or mark. But if Wittgenstein's arguments above are sound, the concept of correctness and incorrectness does not apply to Paul's mark 'E'; therefore, that mark cannot be a word or sign of any kind, and a fortiori not the name of a sensation.

One reason we may still have for wanting to accept the view that 'pain' is the name of a private sensation is this: when a person is in pain, the really important thing for him is the sensation which he is feeling, for that is what is unpleasant or even horrible; hence it seems necessary and desirable to have a name for this sensation, so that one can tell other people that one has it. Wittgenstein sets about destroying this line of defense of View *V*.

> The very fact that we should so much like to say: *"This* is the important thing"—while we point privately to the sensation—is enough to shew how much we are inclined to say something which gives no information. [*PI,* sect. 298.]

Everyone acknowledges that sensations are private, that no one can experience another person's sensations, so that the special felt quality of each person's sensations is known to him alone and to no other. Thus, when you are in pain, I do not know, cannot know, the character of your sensation—whether, for example, it is exactly like what I might feel if my hand were wounded as yours is now, or whether it is something altogether different. (See *PI*, sect. 272.) Hence, if one supposes, as does View *V*, that 'pain' denotes a private sensation and that the sentence 'I am in pain' is used to assert that the speaker is experiencing a private sensation of pain, then one is supposing that "I am in pain" conveys no information whatever, has no real use at all. "But," someone objects, "at least it tells the hearer that the speaker feels *something*." No, it does not even tell him so much, for perhaps the speaker uses the sentence 'I am in pain' when he feels nothing. (See also *PI*, sect. 294.) So this view deprives the sentence 'I am in pain' and the word 'pain' of any use. If 'pain' denotes a private sensation, then it is not a working part of the machine of language, but a mere idle ornament with no function whatever.

> Suppose everyone had a box with something in it: we call it a "beetle." No one can look into anyone else's box, and everyone says he knows what a beetle is only by looking at *his* beetle.—Here it would be quite possible for everyone to have something different in his box. One might even imagine such a thing constantly changing.—But suppose the word "beetle" had a use in these people's language?—If so it would not be used as the name of a thing. The thing in the box has no place in the language-game at all; not even as a *something:* for the box might even be empty.—No, one can 'divide through' by the thing in the box; it cancels out, whatever it is. [*PI*, sect. 293.]

The analogy with pain is perfectly clear. If 'pain' is supposed to denote a somewhat (including a nothing) which each person can observe only in his own case, then the somewhat "cancels out"; and if the sole function of the word 'pain' is to denote it, the word is at once deprived of any use.

One possible misunderstanding must be avoided at all costs. Wittgenstein is not denying that when a person is in pain, he very often and perhaps always feels something frightful, nor even that this something is terribly important to the person himself and to others. He is only denying a particular thesis about language, namely that the word 'pain' names or designates this something that the person feels, in a way which is even remotely like the way that the words for publicly observable things name or designate them. In the language-games we play with words like 'tree' and 'red,' trees and redness (red things) play some part, and it is in these games that the connection between the name and the thing named is established. But in the numerous language-games we play with the word 'pain,' private sensations play no part, and so 'pain' cannot denote them in anything like the way that 'tree,' for example, denotes that kind of object. What does play a part in pain language-games is pain behavior (e.g., groaning, crying, clutching the affected part) and pain-comforting behavior (e.g., saying soothing words, administering sedatives, applying bandages, fixing pillows)—in short, the external circumstances in which the word 'pain' is used. The private sensations, whatever they may be, play no part at all. (See *PI*, sect. 271.) Consider the language-games which involve another person's being in pain. Suppose, for example, that we come upon a man who has just been run over by a car—he is moaning, bleeding, crying out for help, and says he is in great pain. We rush to help him, see that doctors are called, do everything we can to make him comfortable and put his mind at ease. It is such modes of behavior, both linguistic and nonlinguistic, on his part and ours, that enter into this kind of pain language-game; but his private sensations do not enter in. They are completely unknown to us; we have no idea what he might be feeling—what the beetle in his box might be like. But this is no epistemological tragedy, no metaphysical stumbling block to the playing of the language-game, for they are not in the least needed. We proceed in exactly the same way no matter what his sensations may be like.

"But surely in my own case, my sensations enter into pain language-games!" It is doubtless true that, in most cases, your sensation is what matters most to you at the time; and Wittgenstein would not want to deny this. He only wants to reject the idea that in these language-games, when you use the word 'pain,' you are referring to your sensation and telling other people that you have it—that you are talking about what is going on before your consciousness. If, after you say to someone "I am in pain," he sympathizes with you, comforts you, does what he can to help you, then the word 'pain' has done its work—and it was not used to tell him the nature of what you had before your consciousness, because that cannot be told.

Private sensations, then, do not enter into pain language-games, any more than the contents of a pictured pot "enter into" the picture.

> Of course, if water boils in a pot, steam comes out of the pot and also pictured steam comes out of the pictured pot. But what if one insisted on saying that there must also be something boiling in the pictured pot? [*PI*, sect. 297.]

It would be absurd to start talking about the liquid in the pictured pot; to wonder, for example, whether it is water or tea or soup or some strange exotic liquid. There is no answer to such questions; the liquid in the pot is no part of the picture—and language-games which involve the picture do not contain references to the contents of the pot. Similarly, pain language-games do not contain references to our private sensations, since these, like the contents of the pictured pot, cannot be talked about. The point is not that private sensations are nothing, or do not exist, or are not important, or anything of the sort; the point is rather that nothing can be said about them, and hence they play no part in our language-games. They are "as nothing" in those language-games. Wittgenstein sums up his position on the matter in the following way:

> "And yet you again and again reach the conclusion that the sensation itself is a *nothing*."—Not at all. It is not a *something,* but not a *nothing* either! The conclusion was only that a nothing would serve just as well as a something about which nothing could be said. [*PI,* sect. 304.]

*   *   *

The foregoing arguments are designed to show that sensation-words are not the names of inward experiences in any way analogous to that in which 'tree' or 'red' are the names of familiar kinds of object or property. These arguments are primarily negative. But sensation-words, since they are words in our language, must have some legitimate uses. If they do not have uses akin to words like 'tree' and 'red,' what uses do they have? Let us turn now from Wittgenstein's treatment of what these uses are not, to his account of what they are. Here again, I shall follow Wittgenstein in using 'pain' as the primary example.

First of all, a distinction must be made between first-person, present-tense uses of 'pain,' as in "I am in pain," and other uses, as in "He is (you are, they are) in pain." It is clear, upon reflection, that there are radical differences in the two kinds of cases. Thus, all the remarks (a)-(i) (p. 290), which deal with one's own pain, are odd, but they become readily intelligible when suitable changes are made so that they deal with another person's pain. For example, (a) "How do you know you are in pain?" is odd, but not (a′) "How do you know he is in pain?"; and (b) "I think I am in pain, but I may be mistaken" is odd, but not "I think he is in pain, but I may be mistaken"; and so on. Again, there is nothing strange about the remark "Judging from the way he is behaving, I would say that he is in pain," but nothing could be made of the remark "Judging from the way I am behaving, I would say that I am in pain." I shall begin with Wittgenstein's account of first-person, present-tense pain utterances, and then go on to his account of other kinds.

What do "I am in pain" and "I have a pain" mean? What are their uses? Well, we can teach a child how to use them. The child falls down or burns himself, and begins to cry or scream; we comfort him with some such words as "There, there. I know it hurts, I know you have a pain now, but it will soon be all right," and we may try to relieve the pain with medication, pills, or whatever. The child soon learns that the words "I am in pain" or "I have a pain in my knee (hand, wrist, tooth)" are appropriate in this sort of situation; and he learns that in these situations, if he wants comforting or some relief of his condition, it is not necessary to cry or groan or hold the affected part—and in fact, that in our culture the natural pain behavior (crying and so on) is approved of less and less as one grows older. The same purposes can be achieved simply by using the suitable words—"I am in pain" or "I have a pain in my toe." So, saying these words is new or learned or acquired pain behavior, as contrasted with the unlearned or natural pain behavior of crying, screaming, and the rest. (*PI*, sect. 244.) To say "I am in pain" is not to state that one's consciousness contains a frightful private sensation: it is more like groaning *because* one has such a frightful sensation. The sentence 'I am in pain' has a use similar to the words 'Ouch' and 'Ow.' No one would claim that the word 'Ouch' is the name of private sensation and that when one utters it, he is stating that he has such a sensation; the utterance "Ouch!" is a learned expression or manifestation of pain. Similarly, the utterance "I am in pain," although it is not *obviously* a sophisticated manifestation of pain because of its misleading grammatical structure, nevertheless is just that. We must not make the mistake, Wittgenstein tells us, of assuming that 'pain' must denote something, and that if it does not denote a private sensation, then it must denote some natural pain behavior which may accompany one's use of the word. The word 'pain' does not denote anything.

"So you are saying that the word 'pain' really means crying?"—On the contrary: the verbal expression of pain replaces crying and does not describe it. [*PI*, sect. 244.]

This view, if correct, explains the oddity of remarks (a)-(i) (p. 290) very neatly. For example, it shows why it makes no sense to speak of being mistaken about being in pain or of wondering whether one is in pain or not; for it makes no sense to speak of being mistaken about one's own groaning or crying, or to speak of wondering about them. These latter things make no sense because groaning and crying do not express statements, and it is only about things which can be so expressed that mistakes can be made, or that one can wonder. And on Wittgenstein's view, what goes for moaning and crying also goes for the utterance "I am in pain." It might seem to some that Wittgenstein has gained this advantage at rather too high a price—namely, that of having to admit that "I am in pain," at least when used in place of a cry, is not a statement and therefore not capable of being either true or false, nor of having a contradictory. It certainly looks like a statement, and certainly seems to be capable of truth or falsity and of being contradicted. If Wittgenstein is right, however, when used in place of a cry, it can only be truth*ful* or misleading, as "Ouch" can be. If someone says "Ouch!" when he feels nothing unpleasant, he is not lying, but he is doing something akin to it. He is misleading his audience, much as a liar does, despite the fact that he has not made a false statement. Wittgenstein can claim the same for "I am in pain," but he has to deny that it is actually a statement. And there are passages where he comes close to doing so:

> To say "I have pain" is no more a statement *about* a particular person than moaning is. [*BB*, p. 67.]

This quotation reveals another interesting aspect of Wittgenstein's position. He not only denies that 'pain' in "I am in pain" denotes a private sensation; he also denies that the 'I' in it denotes a particular person, namely oneself.

> "When I say 'I am in pain,' I do not point to a person who is in pain, since in a certain sense I have no idea *who* is." And this can be given a justification. For the main point is: I did not say that such-and-such a person was in pain, but "I am. . . ." Now in saying this I don't name any person. Just as I don't name anyone when I *groan* with pain. Though someone else sees who is in pain from the groaning. [*PI*, sect. 404.]

(See also *BB*, p. 68 and *PI*, sect. 410.) These remarks, of course, do not apply to other-person pain utterances (e.g., "He is in pain"), to first-person non-present-tense utterances (e.g., "I was in pain"), or to many other first-person, present-tense utterances (e.g., "I have a scar on my hand," "I have a cat"). But we cannot here delve into Wittgenstein's brilliant treatment of these matters.

As might be expected, Wittgenstein does not think that "I am in pain" has one and only one use, namely, as a cry of pain, as a bit of sophisticated pain behavior. In some contexts, it has that use; but in other contexts, others.

> We surely do not always say someone is *complaining*, because he says he is in pain. So the words "I am in pain" may be a cry of complaint, and may be something else. [*PI*, p. 189.]

Consider the words "I am afraid." In a frightening situation, these words can be wrenched from one involuntarily, in which case they are very like a cry of fear, a fear reaction. But they are not always like that. Depending on the circumstances, they can be a request for help or reassurance, an angry self-reprimand, a report of one's dispositions in a certain area, or even a report of one's present state of mind.

> A cry is not a description. But there are transitions. And the words "I am afraid" may approximate more, or less, to being a cry. They may come quite close to this and also be *far* removed from it. [*PI*, p. 189.]

Wittgenstein is careful to warn us that these different uses are not always, and are perhaps never, entirely distinct or separate; on a given occasion, the words "I am afraid" may have two or more of these uses, although one may be predominant.

> Are the words "I am afraid" a description of a state of mind?
> I say "I am afraid"; someone else asks me: "What was that? A cry of fear; or do you want to tell me how you feel; or is it a reflection on your present state?"—Could I always give him a clear answer? Could I never give him one? [*PI*, p. 187.]

Wittgenstein would say the same sort of thing about "I am in pain." Sometimes, those words too are wrenched from one, in which case they amount to a cry of pain. Wittgenstein was perhaps more interested in this use than in the others, and emphasized it above them; but he would never deny the existence of the other uses. The words "I am in pain" may be a request for assistance or compassion or both; or they may be used to hint that one desires the hearer to leave the room ("I am in pain; perhaps I'd better just rest quietly alone"). In other contexts, these words, but especially more specific pain reports, such as "I have a splitting headache" or "I have a pain in my lower abdomen," may be used to describe one's inner state.

If Wittgenstein would admit this last point, as I think he would, does this mean that he must abandon his previous arguments and concede that 'pain' may be the name, in a strong sense, of a private sensation? I think not. Wittgenstein points out that there are important differences among descriptions, depending on what they are descriptions *of*.

> But isn't the beginning the sensation—which I describe?—Perhaps this word "describe" tricks us here. I say "I describe my state of mind" and "I describe my room." You need to call to mind the differences between the language-games. [*PI,* sect. 290.]

(See also *PI,* sect. 24.) In describing my room, one of the main things I do is to utter the names of various things in the room or of its parts, and then ascribe to them certain of their more salient characteristics, so that my hearer will know what the room is like—in particular, what it looks like. That is usually the whole point, the whole purpose, of a description of a *room.* But we must not think, Wittgenstein tells us, that all descriptions have the same purpose—that is, we must not be misled by the grammatical similarity between "He describes his room," "He describes his state of mind," and so on, into thinking that they all refer to the same sort of activity. On the contrary:

> What we call *"descriptions"* are instruments for particular uses. Think of a machine-drawing, a cross-section, an elevation with measurements, which an engineer has before him. Thinking of a description as a word-picture of the facts has something misleading about it: one tends to think only of such pictures as hang on our walls: which seem simply to portray how a thing looks, what it is like. [*PI,* sect. 291.]

The purpose of some descriptions—for example, those analogous to machine-drawings—is not to tell the hearer what the thing looks like, but rather to instruct him accurately as to how the thing is to be built or repaired or whatever. And Wittgenstein would insist that when "I am in pain" is a description of one's inner state, it is most certainly not the purpose of this description to tell the hearer what the objects before the speaker's consciousness feel like, what the nature of his private sensations are. No words can ever do that, as Wittgenstein has tried to show. Therefore, describing one's inner state, unlike describing one's room, does not involve naming certain objects and then attributing characteristics to them. Hence Wittgenstein does not have to grant that 'pain' can be the name of a private sensation. What then *is* the purpose of descriptions containing the word 'pain'? There is no single answer to this question; one must simply look at actual cases and see what purposes they serve. Such a description might, for example, sometimes serve the purpose of indicating to the speaker's doctor what the source of the trouble is ("I have a burning pain in my throat; perhaps you'd better have a look at my tonsils"), or what remedy ought to be tried, or whether the remedy already used is being successful or not. Or it might give a person's reason for not being able to accept an invitation ("Come along to the movies tonight." "No, I can't; I have a dreadful headache, and don't feel like going out"), and so on.

Now we must turn from the uses of 'I am in pain' to those of sentences like 'He is in pain' and 'They are in pain.' One thing, at least, is certain: to say "He is in pain" is not to cry out in pain. It is to say something about someone else, something which can be true or false, about which we may be mistaken, about which we can conjecture and doubt, and so on. But what? It need hardly be stated at this late stage that, according to Wittgenstein, to say "He is in pain" is certainly not to say that a private mental object denoted by the word 'pain' is before the other fellow's consciousness. Is it, then, to describe his behavior, to assert that he is exhibiting some kind of pain behavior? The short answer to this question is "No"; but some explanatory discussion is in order.

The first point to be made is this. According to Wittgenstein, certain modes of behavior are essential to the concept of pain, in the sense that the notion of pain is applicable only to things that behave in these ways. This is connected with the fact discussed earlier (pp. 291-2) that the use of the word 'pain' is learned, and *can* only be learned, in situations characterized by pain behavior (or by some reference to pain behavior, at least).[3] It is not merely false to ascribe pain to things that cannot behave so—it is unintelligible, it makes no sense, to do so.

[3] Quite generally, there is, for Wittgenstein, a connection between the circumstances in which a word is learned and/or taught, and the meaning of that word, although the connection is not so simple (nor simpleminded) as some critics of Wittgenstein have made out. For a discussion of this point, see the section entitled *Criterion* (especially the first paragraph) of Norman Malcolm's "Wittgenstein's *Philosophical Investigations*," *The Philosophical Review*, LXIII, No. 4 (October 1954), 530-59. (Reprinted in *The Philosophy of Mind*, ed. V. C. Chappell (Englewood Cliffs, N.J.: Prentice-Hall, Inc., 1962).) My account of Wittgenstein's views in the present chapter owes a great deal to Malcolm's review.

Look at a stone and imagine it having sensations.—One says to one-self: How could one so much as get the idea of ascribing a *sensation* to a *thing*? One might as well ascribe it to a number!—And now look at a wriggling fly and at once these difficulties vanish and pain seems able to get a foothold here, where before everything was, so to speak, too smooth for it. [*PI*, sect. 284.]

Only of what behaves like a human being can one say that it *has* pains. [*PI*, sect. 283.]

(See also *PI*, sect. 281.) This view differs markedly from that ac-cording to which 'pain' is the name of a private sensation as 'tree' is the name of a publicly observable object: on that view, the only thing essential to the concept of pain is a certain sensation or feeling, and all so-called pain behavior is a mere consequence, a mere contingent accompaniment, of that sensation. If this view were right, then it ought to be easy to conceive that inanimate objects, like pots, pans, and stoves, might be in great pain, but simply happen not to express or manifest it in their behavior. But there is something absurd in this idea; we really cannot conceive of pots and pans having pains. In fairy tales, to be sure, pots and pans are said to see and hear and feel pain and be angry; but then they also talk and move in various ways. (*PI*, sect. 282.) Where there is no possibility of pain behavior, there is no possibility of pain either. Of course the words "The stove is in pain" may lead us to have one or more images, just as the words "It is 5 o'clock on the sun" may do. But in neither case can the pic-ture be applied; hence in neither case can one understand what is being said. (*PI*, sect. 351.) The picture cannot be applied, for nothing follows from it; one cannot do anything with it. One would not, for example, dream of comforting the stove. Indeed, what would it be to comfort a stove?

"But can't I imagine myself having pains and turning to stone while they continue? And wouldn't this be an example of a stone's having pains?" (*PI*, sect. 283.) Suppose we allow the intelligibility of this suggestion. Even so, it does not describe a situation in which a stone has a pain. Once the behavior is cut away, by my turning to stone, the pain, as it were, floats free of me. In place of a person in pain, there are now two things—a free, disembodied pain with no bearer and a block of stone—which have nothing to do with one an-other. What could possibly connect the pain with the block of stone, so that one could say the stone *has* the pain? As Wittgenstein says, "What has . . . pain to do with a stone?" (*PI*, sect. 283.) The con-clusion is that pain behavior is an essential part of the concept of pain. And this is surely right; for if a person does not wince or grimace or cry out, or at least have an inclination, desire, or tendency to do one or more of these things, then he is not, cannot be, in pain.

It does not follow from this, however, that we can simply equate a person's being in pain with his actually exhibiting pain behavior. A person can be in pain and suppress all pain behavior for a time— perhaps even for quite a long time. (See *PI*, sect. 281.) But notice that he does have to *suppress* it: in these cases, there must be at least a tendency, a proneness, to exhibit pain behavior, even if one manages to suppress the tendency. Conversely, a person can exhibit pain behavior without being in pain; he can be shamming, play-acting, giving a demonstration, and so on. Moreover, one can easily imagine automata behaving in all the ways humans behave when they are in pain, and yet we would not suppose that the automata were in pain. So, more is involved in another person's being in pain than his simply exhibiting pain behavior. But what more? The natural temptation is to reply: "In addition to behaving in a certain way, he must also be *feeling pain*." This is clearly the right answer: the idea of pain doubtless enters into these language-games. But the important question is: *how* does this idea enter in? "Well, I see that he is groaning and clutching his side, and I hear him say 'My side hurts.' However, if I am to look upon this as a genuine *pain* situation, rather than a bit of play-acting, for example, I must also believe that the fellow feels pain." Again, Wittgenstein would agree, but he would want to know what it is to believe that the other fellow is feeling a pain. Does it involve having the image or picture of a private sensation, just like one's own pain, hovering before the other fellow's consciousness? Wittgenstein has already argued against this suggestion. The representation of pain enters into the language-game, he will admit, only not as an image or picture. (*PI*, sect. 300. I translate *'Vorstellung'* as 'representation,' rather than 'image' as the translator has it.)

The representation of pain enters in, I suggest, not by any reference to a mental object behind the pain behavior and causing it, but rather by a reference to the *circumstances,* including the various sorts of *surroundings,* of the present pain behavior. To believe that the person who is now pain-behaving really is in pain is to view the situation as being of a certain kind, as having, for example, a certain "before" and "after," as fitting into a certain kind of wider situation. If I thought that the present pain behavior were part of one kind of situation (for example, if I thought that it resulted from a desire to fool the onlookers), I would not regard it as a manifestation of real pain; but if I thought it were part of another kind of situation (for example, if I thought it resulted from a knife wound or an internal disorder), then I *would* regard it as a manifestation of real pain. (Compare this with what was said in the previous chapter about the importance of the context when we are dealing with meaning and understanding.)

Believing that another person is in pain also has another aspect to it; this aspect is what Wittgenstein called the "attitude" of the believer. Consider the differences between a situation in which we are dealing with what we take to be an automaton exhibiting pain behavior and one in which we are dealing with a human being exhibiting the same behavior; in the latter case, but not the former, we believe that the other feels pain. Malcolm reports that in lectures, Wittgenstein discussed an imaginary tribe of people who had the idea that their slaves were all automata, soul-less machines with human bodies.[4] Some of the masters' dealings with these slaves would be the same as those between a master and a human slave; for example, the master would let a slave rest when it complained of being tired, would feed it when it was hungry, and would try to heal it if it complained of being sick—although I imagine the master would speak not of healing it, but of repairing it, and not of its being hungry, but of its needing food or being low on food. (We, at least, do not speak of our automobiles as being hungry when they need fuel; but then of course they do not have human bodies, either!) On the other hand, some of the masters' dealings with these mechanical slaves would be radically different from a master's dealings with a human slave.

> . . . They would *look* at the slaves in a peculiar way. They would observe and comment on their movements *as if* they were machines. ('Notice how smoothly his limbs move.') They would discard them when they were worn and useless, like machines. If a slave received a mortal injury and twisted and screamed in agony, no master would avert his gaze in horror or prevent his children from observing the scene, any more than he would if the ceiling fell on a printing press.[5]

We do not treat other human beings in these ways. We do not look at a person in the way we look at a machine; a machine does not

4 Malcolm, *op. cit.,* pp. 548-49.
5 *Ibid.,* pp. 548-49.

look back at us, and this makes a difference. We do not send in-curably sick people off to a place of dismemberment to be sold for chemicals, as we send cars to a junk yard to be sold for scrap. We comfort people in pain and seek to cheer them up; it is unthinkable that we should do this to a machine. And so on. All this can be sum-marily stated by saying that our *attitude* towards automata, towards machines in general, is radically different from our attitude towards people.

Here one might be inclined to retort: "Of course my attitude towards people is very special: this is because I believe they have souls, that is, that they are conscious." But do we *believe* this? It is extremely odd to speak of belief in this connection—as odd as it is to say that we believe, as we walk down the street, that the ground will not give way beneath our feet. We simply talk and act towards the other people we encounter every day as one *does* talk and act towards beings with souls (beings who are conscious), just as we walk down the street as one *does* walk on solid ground. The questions of whether other people have souls and of whether the ground is solid simply do not arise. "But then aren't you still making the assumption that they do have souls?" An assumption is something that can be doubted, and normally I do not and cannot doubt that other people have souls (are conscious).

> . . . Just try to keep hold of this idea [that the people around one are automata, lack consciousness] in the midst of your ordinary inter-course with others, in the street, say! Say to yourself, for example: "The children over there are mere automata; all their liveliness is mere automatism." And you will either find these words becoming quite meaningless; or you will produce in yourself some kind of uncanny feeling, or something of the sort. [*PI*, sect. 420.]
> Doesn't a presupposition imply a doubt? And doubt may be entirely lacking. Doubting has an end. [*PI*, p. 180.]

However, there can be unusual circumstances in which such a doubt is perfectly possible: if a person's looks and actions are sufficiently peculiar, I may begin to wonder if he is not perhaps an automaton. But suppose I resolve the doubt in favor of his being a person, so that I now believe he has a soul. What happens when I acquire this belief? I look at him and act towards him as I do toward conscious beings: I adopt that attitude—and to have the belief *is* to have the attitude. It may seem as though my attitude toward him is one thing and my belief that he has a soul another thing, a thing which accounts for the first; but this is not the case. To be sure, all sorts of pictures may be connected with the words "This man has a soul"—for example, a picture of a spiritual sphere inside his head or hovering just above it, or perhaps of an ethereal substance spread throughout his body. But if we seek to determine how this picture might be applied, in order to see what the belief that he has a soul actually amounts to, we find nothing but the way I look at him, talk to him, act toward him—in short, nothing but my attitude toward him.

My attitude towards him is an attitude towards a soul. [*PI*, p. 178.]

To believe he has a soul *is* just to look at him in the way I do, to act toward him in the way I do (for example, comforting him in sorrow, laughing with him at jokes, discussing people and events with him), to react to him in the way I do—in short, to have the attitude toward him that I do. There is nothing else for the belief to consist in, save for the idle accompanying images, if any, and they do not matter.

Let us now focus our attention on the finer distinction which is of more immediate concern to us—the distinction, namely, between believing that one person is in pain and believing that another is not in pain, where both are exhibiting the same pain behavior. If we look at what actually goes on in the two sorts of cases, we find again a difference in attitude. Here is one example. If a kindly shop foreman believes that one of his workers is in pain, he pities him, sympathizes with him, sends for the doctor, gives him medicine, and does similar things. If he believes that he is not in pain, he acts quite differently: he is cold and unresponsive, tells him to get back to work and stop malingering, and so on. Having these attitudes is one way, one form, of believing those things. Thus, although the foreman pities the worker *because* he believes the man is in pain, the pity is not something wholly different from the belief, but part of it; just as when one kicks the ball because one is trying to score a goal, the kicking is not something wholly different from the trying, but part of it.

Pity, one may say, is a form of conviction that someone else is in pain. [*PI*, sect. 287.]

"But I still can't help thinking that when I believe another person is in pain, I believe that he is experiencing something, a private sensation, very much like my own pains, and that this is why I pity him, comfort him, and so on." Wittgenstein is unimpressed by claims that one cannot help thinking or saying such-and-such.

> Being unable—when we surrender ourselves to philosophical thought —to help saying such-and-such; being irresistibly inclined to say it— does not mean being forced into an *assumption,* or having an immediate perception or knowledge of a state of affairs. [*PI,* sect. 299.]

What is important is not the mere words, but what they mean. Of course one cannot help thinking that (a) the other fellow over there, groaning and holding his side, is feeling something, feeling pain; but this does not mean that you are forced to assume that (b) he is experiencing a private sensation just like yours. Wittgenstein has argued at length that such an assumption is senseless. The picture we have may seduce us into supposing that when we think (a) we are *ipso facto* thinking (b). This picture, like so many others, lies in our language, in certain modes of expression. Well, then, imagine that we dispense with the words.

> I tell someone I am in pain. His attitude to me will then be that of belief; disbelief; suspicion; and so on.
> Let us assume he says: "It's not so bad."—Doesn't that prove that he believes in something behind the outward expression of pain?— His attitude is a proof of his attitude. Imagine not merely the words "I am in pain" but also the answer "It's not so bad" replaced by instinctive noises and gestures. [*PI,* sect. 310.]

When the words are replaced by groans and comforting gestures which do the same job as the words, we may not be so tempted to think that the original hearer was concerned about some private mental content that lies behind the other fellow's pain behavior.

"But mustn't there be some explanation of *why* we treat people, and specifically people in pain, differently from the way we treat automata and those we believe to be malingering or shamming? And what could this explanation possibly be but our beliefs that people have souls, that people in pain *feel* something frightful, while automata have no souls, and people who are shamming pain do not feel anything frightful?" But as Wittgenstein has tried to show, these alleged "explanations" are futile, for they reduce either to absurdity or to emptiness. If the belief that other people in pain "feel something frightful" is interpreted to mean that they have a frightful private sensation called 'pain' before their consciousness, the suggestion is absurd; and if it is interpreted in a legitimate manner, the explanation then reduces to the empty tautology that we treat people in a certain way because we treat them in that way. Thus Wittgenstein would say, I think, that one must not look for explanations here, but must simply note a form of life.

> What has to be accepted, the given, is—so one could say—*forms of life*. [*PI*, p. 226.]

We just do treat people differently from automata, and people we believe to be in pain differently from people we believe to be shamming. This is the way we do things, this is our form of life. It is not the only possible one: we might conceivably treat other people and animals as the masters in Wittgenstein's example treat their mechanical slaves. Some of Descartes' followers thought animals were automata and actually put them into hot ovens; they noted with interest and in the best scientific manner how those complicated mechanisms operated under those conditions—emitting ear-splitting barks and cries, clawing violently at the oven door, and so on. That is a possible form of life, but it is not one of ours. (Nor, of course, is it the sadist's; if a sadist were to put live dogs into a hot oven, his attitude toward them would be quite different from that of Descartes' dispassionate scientific followers.) Nor is it possible to appeal to private sensations to explain our forms of life, to explain the language-games we play with words like 'pain.' Private sensations play no part in these language-games and could not possibly explain them. We must, in fact, resist the temptation to *explain* our language-games at all.

> Our mistake is to look for an explanation where we ought to look at what happens as a 'proto-phenomenon.' That is, where we ought to have said: *this language-game is played*. [*PI*, sect. 654.]
> The question is not one of explaining a language-game by means of our experiences, but of noting a language-game. [*PI*, sect. 655.]

I have been concentrating on 'He is in pain' as it is used to state something about a person; but as with 'I am in pain,' Wittgenstein would assert that this sentence can have many different uses, depending on the circumstances. It can be used to request help (for example, when the wife of a victim of an automobile accident says it to a policeman), to suggest that he be given a sedative (when a nurse says it to the doctor), and so on. The notion that 'pain' is the name, in a nontrivial sense, of a private sensation proves to be a decided hindrance in our attempt to see what the numerous uses of the word 'pain' actually are. (See Wittgenstein's remarks about 'remember' in *PI*, sect. 305.) This misguided notion is part and parcel of the idea that language always functions in one way, always serves the same purpose: to convey thoughts—which may be about houses, pains, good and evil, or anything else you please. [*PI*, sect. 304.]

And it is this false and grossly over-simplified idea about language that Wittgenstein is above all anxious to destroy.

* * *

In this chapter, I have tried to present Wittgenstein's position as fairly and sympathetically as I know how. His words on these matters, more so than on most others, are often difficult to interpret, and I may very well have misunderstood him. In any case, his ideas are obviously highly controversial and there are certainly powerful objections which could be urged against some of his arguments, although I cannot deal with them here. But whether one accepts or rejects his conclusions, there is no denying the power and originality of what Wittgenstein has to say in defense of his views.

13   Philosophy

Gilbert Ryle has said that the "master-issue" with which Wittgenstein was concerned above all others was that of the nature of philosophy itself. What sort of activity is philosophizing? With what kind of problem should a philosopher deal? How should he proceed in his business? [1] Whether this was his master-issue or not, there can be no doubt whatever that these questions exercised him greatly throughout his career as a philosopher. Wittgenstein was by no means the first philosopher in history to have been, as it were, professionally self-conscious; but it is he, more than anyone else, who is responsible for the fact that philosophers in general are today more mindful of the nature of their enterprise than ever before.

We have seen how, according to Wittgenstein, a philosopher tends to fall into confusion and bewilderment, to get his understanding tied up in knots, and that his main job is to rescue himself from this unhappy condition. His mission in life is to escape from the traps, set for him by language, into which he has unfortunately wandered. Wittgenstein tells us that what we must do is examine the language-games we play with certain crucial words, in order to discover the actual uses they have there. But this makes it sound as though the philosopher's work is a haphazard, easy, and passive affair, and Wittgenstein certainly did not so conceive of it. To be sure, the philosopher must look at "the details of what goes on" (*PI*, sect. 51), but he must not do his looking in a completely random manner. He

[1] Gilbert Ryle, "Ludwig Wittgenstein," *Analysis*, Vol. 12, No. 1 (October 1951), 6.

must not simply, in a mindless way, gather specimen after specimen of the language-games we play with puzzling terms. This would result not in the cure of the original distress, but rather in further complications—he would then be in grave danger of being overwhelmed by too much data. He must select his examples carefully with a view to shedding light on a particular perplexity; for his description of the uses of words

> gets its light—i.e. its purpose—from the philosophical problems. [*PI*, sect. 109.]

There can be no question of laying down general rules to be followed in solving each and every philosophical problem, rules for arranging examples in every kind of case so that puzzlement will be dispelled. Problems in different conceptual areas present special difficulties of their own, and one must deal with each in a slightly different manner. Still, there are certain techniques or devices which are widely useful.

> There is not *a* philosophical method, though there are indeed methods, like different therapies. [*PI*, sect. 133.]

One of the "methods" that Wittgenstein recommends and uses is "finding and inventing *intermediate cases*" (*PI*, sect. 122). As we have seen, there is probably no word of any philosophical interest that has but a single use; we play several different language-games with each word or expression. But if the puzzlement surrounding a given expression is to be effectively and permanently dispelled, we must have a general, over-all idea of how that expression actually works; and for this, it is not enough to have a mere list of three or four uses of the expression with no evident connection among them. As Wittgenstein says:

> A main source of our failure to understand is that we do not *command a clear view* of the use of our words. [*PI*, sect. 122.]

To get such a view, we must see *connections* between the most obvious uses, between those that first come to mind; and these are not always obvious. Hence we need examples of intermediate uses of the term in question—links, as it were, between the central cases. When we have such examples, we can see how one use shades off gradually into another, and how, therefore, they form a kind of loose unity—the unity, in fact, of a family. This device is helpful not only for understanding a single word, e.g., 'looking,' but also for understanding a phrase containing it, e.g., 'looking in one's memory.'

What makes us use the expression "seeking in our memory," when we try to remember a word?

Let us ask the question "What is the similarity between looking for a word in your memory and looking for my friend in the park?" What would be the answer to such a question?

One kind of answer certainly would consist in describing a series of intermediate cases. One might say that the case which looking in your memory for something is most similar to is not that of looking for my friend in the park, but, say, that of looking up the spelling of a word in a dictionary. And one might go on interpolating cases. [*BB*, p. 129.]

Wittgenstein says we must not only find, but also invent, intermediate cases; that is, we must not concentrate our attention solely on the standard or familiar situations in which a term is used, but we must also think of less familiar ones, even of ones which may never have in fact occurred. For example, if we are asked to think of what it is for a person's course or path to be guided, we might think at once of a person following the green arrows in the subway or taking a guided tour through a museum. But it would be well to think also of these other cases:

You are in a playing field with your eyes bandaged, and someone leads you by the hand, sometimes left, sometimes right; you have constantly to be ready for the tug of his hand, and must also take care not to stumble when he gives you an unexpected tug.

Or again: someone leads you by the hand where you are unwilling to go, by force.

Or: you are guided by a partner in a dance; you make yourself as receptive as possible, in order to guess his intention and obey the slightest pressure.

Or: someone takes you for a walk; you are having a conversation; you go wherever he does.

Or: you walk along a field-track, simply following it. [*PI*, sect. 172.]

Wittgenstein not only described language-games we *do* or *could* play with a given term, but also those which, as things now are, we *cannot;* our understanding of something is increased not only by an account of the thing itself, but by contrasts with various things which it is not. Sometimes he imagined language-games which ought to be perfectly unexceptionable *if* a certain view about the word in question were true; but it turns out that there is something odd about the language-game, and so it is shown that the view about the word must somehow be mistaken. He uses this technique, as we have seen, against the view that 'meaning' denotes a peculiar mental act.

> Make the following experiment: *say* "It's cold here" and *mean* "It's warm here." Can you do it?—And what are you doing as you do it? And is there only one way of doing it? [*PI*, sect. 510.]

Sometimes he imagines certain very general features of the world to be different from what they are, and then describes the language-games we would play in such a possible world. This, too, often provides an illuminating contrast to our actual language-games.

> Let us imagine the following: The surfaces of the things around us (stones, plants, etc.) have patches and regions which produce pain in our skin when we touch them. (Perhaps through the chemical composition of these surfaces. But we need not know that.) In this case we should speak of pain-patches on the leaf of a particular plant just as at present we speak of red patches. I am supposing that it is useful to us to notice these patches and their shapes; that we can infer important properties of the objects from them. [*PI*, sect. 312.]

Philosophers have sometimes thought that, *as things now are,* "I have a pain" is just like "I see something red." In the passage just quoted, Wittgenstein describes a world in which they would indeed be very much alike, but the radical differences between that world and this one shows how wrong those philosophers were.

Another kind of illuminating contrast which Wittgenstein often makes is that between the term in question and other related words and expressions. He tries to show how the uses of the term are closely related to one or two other words which may not at first sight seem to have anything to do with it:

> The word "agreement" and the word "rule" are *related* to one another, they are cousins. If I teach anyone the use of the one word, he learns the use of the other with it. [*PI*, sect. 224.]
> The use of the word "rule" and the use of the word "same" are interwoven. (As are the uses of "proposition" and the use of "true.") [*PI*, sect. 225.]

(Note, too, the example of 'understand,' 'be able to,' 'can,' in *PI*, sect. 150. See also *PI,* sect. 492.) And of course it will be equally helpful to show that expressions which may seem superficially to be close conceptual neighbors are in fact miles apart. To make these contrasts is not to tell the whole story, but it marks a real advance in our understanding.

> Imagine we had to arrange the books of a library. When we begin the books lie higgledy-piggledy on the floor. Now there would be many ways of sorting them and putting them in their places. One would be

to take the books one by one and put each on the shelf in its right place. On the other hand we might take up several books from the floor and put them in a row on a shelf, merely in order to indicate that these books ought to go together in this order. In the course of arranging the library this whole row of books will have to change its place. But it would be wrong to say that therefore putting them together on a shelf was no step towards the final result. In this case, in fact, it is pretty obvious that having put together books which belong together was a definite achievement, even though the whole row of them had to be shifted. But some of the greatest achievements in philosophy could only be compared with taking up some books which seemed to belong together, and putting them on different shelves; nothing more being final about their positions than that they no longer lie side by side. The onlooker who doesn't know the difficulty of the task might well think in such a case that nothing at all had been achieved. [*BB*, pp. 44-45.]

Another device frequently employed by Wittgenstein is that of inventing primitive language-games. Our actual language-games are enormously complicated, and it is therefore often difficult to disentangle their various different parts or aspects. Hence, Wittgenstein found it helpful to invent elementary language-games in which some particular aspect of our sophisticated ones would show forth more clearly. (For examples of these simple games, see *PI*, sects. 1, 2, 48.) He did not think of these primitive games as being "ideal simples" which are somehow already present in our language-games, as if they could be reached by analyzing ours; but we can learn about our games by noting how they resemble, and how they differ from, the simple ones.

Our clear and simple language-games are not preparatory studies for a future regularization of language—as it were first approximations, ignoring friction and air-resistance. The language-games are rather set up as *objects of comparison* which are meant to throw light on the facts of our language by way not only of similarities, but also of dissimilarities. [*PI*, sect. 130.]

The foregoing devices or "methods" are aids to the philosopher, and nothing more. There can be no question of setting down a system of rules which can be followed mechanically by anyone and which will ensure that the aim of complete understanding will be secured. And it is clear that the philosopher's job of discovering the uses of words is no mere matter of passive observation: it is a creative task that requires skill, insight, and imagination.

Wittgenstein's methods are meant to help the philosopher to

describe the uses of words, but not just any description will do. As Wittgenstein says:

> What we call *"descriptions"* are instruments for particular uses. [*PI*, sect. 291.]

The special purpose of a philosopher's descriptions of the uses of words is to give a "perspicuous representation" of these uses (*PI*, sect. 122)—to give one a clear, over-all view of them, so that his previous puzzlement will be finally dispelled. As Wittgenstein remarked in a lecture, he sought to give "the morphology of the use of an expression." [2] By a clever arrangement of the various language-games one does or might play with a certain crucial expression, the philosopher is able to *see* how it works. It will seldom, or never, be possible to formulate a statement which neatly summarizes his results —a statement which, for example, gives the rules which govern the use of a term or which gives the definition of the term. The desire for such statements is misguided, and a person who has it is in the grip of those very forces which cause philosophical puzzlement.

> The man who is philosophically puzzled sees a law in the way a word is used, and, trying to apply this law consistently, comes up against cases where it leads to paradoxical results. [*BB*, p. 27.]

Most of the expressions of our ordinary language, and certainly the vast majority of the philosophically interesting ones, do not follow any strict rules, do not have any strict meaning which can be clearly stated.

> . . . Remember that in general we don't use language according to strict rules—it hasn't been taught us by means of strict rules, either. *We*, in our discussions on the other hand, constantly compare language with a calculus proceeding according to exact rules. [*BB*, p. 25.]
>
> Many words in this sense . . . don't have a strict meaning. But this is not a defect. To think it is would be like saying that the light of my reading lamp is no real light at all because it has no sharp boundary. [*BB*, p. 27.]

In any case, the philosopher's job is to give a certain sort of description of the uses of words; his task is a purely descriptive one.

> Philosophy really *is* 'purely descriptive.' [*BB*, p. 18.]

(See also *BB*, p. 125.) Above all, says Wittgenstein, the philosopher must not take it upon himself to *explain* anything.

---

2 Malcolm, *Memoir*, p. 50.

> We must do away with all *explanation,* and description alone must take its place. [*PI,* sect. 109.]

In the past, philosophers have had the tendency to try to explain our language-games, to explain the sorts of thing one says about time, sense perception, sensations, knowledge, and so on. They have given us philosophical theories. A notable example is the theory, or the theories, of sense-data. Everyone is familiar with the language-games in which words like 'illusion,' 'dream,' 'hallucination,' 'looks,' 'seems,' 'appears,' and others, play their parts. ("It looks elliptical from here, but it is really round," "I thought the stick was bent, but it was an illusion—it was really straight," "He thought there were pink rats on his bed-clothes, but it was all an hallucination.") In an effort to explain these language-games, philosophers have introduced what most of them took to be a new kind of entity—namely, a sense-datum, i.e., an object of "direct awareness" or of "immediate perception." In all kinds of sense awareness, they argued, a person is confronted with nothing but sense-data. If one or another version of a theory based on this idea is accepted, it was thought, all these language-games will become intelligible, will be understood. The history of philosophy is littered with the disastrous consequences of these alleged explanations, and Wittgenstein thinks it is a fundamental mistake to attempt them.

Wittgenstein, I believe, has one particular kind of explanation primarily in mind—namely, one like the example just cited, in which a language-game is allegedly explained by reference to some private mental entity, act, process, or whatever. (See *PI,* sects. 655, 656.) But a language-game is, of necessity, an entirely public affair—for the reasons given in the last chapter. Everything about it, all aspects of it, lie open to public view. As Wittgenstein says, "Nothing is concealed. . . . Nothing is hidden." (*PI,* sect. 435.) The private sensation of pain, for example, plays no part in pain language-games, as we have seen. And this is why explanations—at least of the kind he means—are impossible.

> Since everything lies open to view there is nothing to explain. For what is hidden, for example, is of no interest to us. [*PI,* sect. 126.]

(Whether Wittgenstein is justified in spurning *all* kinds of explanation in philosophy is a question too vast to be discussed here.)

A philosopher who tries to explain a language-game, to give it some "foundation," is actually merely introducing new language-games, usually with a new notation. We all habitually play numerous language-games with object-words ('chair,' 'table'), property words ('red,' 'square'), action-words ('run,' 'eat'), and so on; a sense-datum philosopher invents new games with words in his sense-datum terminology. There may be, and in fact almost certainly are, many interesting relations between these two sorts of games.

> It is like the relation: physical object—sense-impressions. Here we have two different language-games and a complicated relation between them.—If you try to reduce their relations to a *simple* formula you go wrong. [*PI*, p. 180.]

It is wrong to think that language-games with words like 'chair' and 'run' can be "reduced" to the philosopher's sense-datum language-games, or that the latter are in some way basic and can explain the former. They are different games with complicated relations to one another, and they involve different ways of looking at things (*PI*, sect. 401)—but that is all.

Because a philosopher's proper job is a purely descriptive one, he does not and cannot put forward any theories or any theses.

> . . . We may not advance any kind of theory. There must not be anything hypothetical in our considerations. [*PI*, sect. 109.]

There are no philosophical doctrines or theories. Wittgenstein once expressed this point, perhaps in a slightly exaggerated way, by saying "I hold no opinions in philosophy" [3]—there are no opinions, i.e., debatable doctrines, to be had in philosophy. Wittgenstein's position here is, in an important way, the same as the one he took in the *Tractatus* (although of course much of what lies behind them is different):

> 4.112(4)   Philosophy does not result in 'philosophical propositions,' but rather in the clarification of propositions.

And since the things which the philosopher describes are mainly familiar, everyday language-games, there is a sense in which he tells us nothing new, nothing we did not already know, for we know quite well how to play those games. Philosophy, says Wittgenstein, "only states what everyone admits" (*PI*, sect. 599).

> If one tried to advance *theses* in philosophy, it would never be possible to question them, because everyone would agree to them. [*PI*, sect. 128.]

[3] John Wisdom, "Ludwig Wittgenstein, 1934-1937," *Mind*, LXI, No. 242 (April 1952), 259.

(Here, by the way, is yet another affinity between Socrates and Wittgenstein.

> Wittgenstein once observed in a lecture that there is a similarity between his conception of philosophy . . . and the Socratic doctrine that knowledge is reminiscence: although he believed that there were also other things involved in the latter.[4]

The doctrine that knowledge is reminiscence is, however, perhaps more Platonic than Socratic.) So, the philosopher is neither a theoretical scientist who gives us explanatory theories, nor an empirical scientist who discovers new facts: he is not a scientist at all.

> It was true to say that our considerations could not be scientific ones. [*PI*, sect. 109.]

Compare this with the remark in the *Tractatus:*

> 4.111(1)   Philosophy is not one of the natural sciences.

The philosopher is rather an assembler and an arranger.

> The work of the philosopher consists in assembling reminders for a particular purpose. [*PI*, sect. 127.]
> The problems are solved, not by giving new information, but by arranging what we have always known. [*PI*, sect. 109.]

(See also *PI*, sects. 89, 415.) The philosopher puts before us familiar data about our language-games and arranges them in such a way that we achieve a clear over-all view of the uses of certain expressions. In this way he attempts to dispel the puzzlement which has plagued us.

"But if the philosopher simply tells us what we already know, why is he needed?" Part of the answer is that he is needed to arrange the data, discover intermediate cases, and so on. But there is another point which is perhaps even more important. The things which a philosopher tells us about our everyday language-games are such obvious things that we commonly overlook them and need to be reminded of them. They are so constantly before our eyes, so ever-present, that we tend to "look right through them"; we fail to notice them because of their very obviousness.

> The aspects of things that are most important for us are hidden because of their simplicity and familiarity. (One is unable to notice something—because it is always before one's eyes.) The real foundations of his enquiry do not strike a man at all. Unless *that* fact has at

_____

[4] Malcolm, *Memoir*, p. 51.

some time struck him.—And this means: we fail to be struck by what, once seen, is most striking and most powerful. [*PI*, sect. 129.]

It takes a man of great philosophical skill and insight to pick out the obvious and to realize its profound importance; this is one of the most difficult things in the world to do and it falls to the lot of the philosopher, before anyone else, to attempt it. (See *PI*, sect. 89.) To mention just one familiar example from the history of philosophy: There are no facts cited in Hume's famous analysis of causality that are not perfectly obvious, that we all did not already know. (He may have ignored some important facts, drawn faulty inferences from certain facts, and so on—his analysis, in short, might be faulty—but that is another matter.) But what genius Hume displayed in noticing these "trivialities," in realizing their significance, and in presenting them to us in a way which makes us see it too!

Nevertheless, when Wittgenstein says that the philosopher states only what everyone admits, what we already know, and that there are no philosophical theses or theories, he is overstating his case. When he refers to "what we already know," he means primarily— if I may put it too crudely—(a) statements about the world, about empirical matters of fact, and (b) statements about what one can and cannot sensibly say. He does not mean certain statements about language and meaning, and about the relationship between language and the world; for about these, he himself most certainly puts forward theses with which not everyone would agree, which not everyone would accept. When the philosopher points out that we can often know that other people are in pain or that it makes no sense to say "I wonder if it is *I* or someone else who is experiencing this pain," he is indeed stating something that we would all admit—trivialities, if you like. But when Wittgenstein makes such claims as that the meaning of an expression is its use in the language, that 'pain' does not denote a private sensation in the way that 'red' denotes a kind of quality, and that the connection between a name and the thing named is made in human behavior, he is undeniably offering controversial philosophical theses which are far from trivial.

* * *

What are we to say now about Wittgenstein's general view of the nature of philosophy? Is not his view of what philosophy is and what it can do more than a little disheartening? If philosophy can in the end only tell us what we already know, then all the grand and up-lifting theories which have been put forward by philosophers in the past—about the immaterial nature of the soul, about eternal realms of being in which meanings and values exist, about a Supreme Being with infinite attributes, and so on—must be abandoned. We are left with nothing but an arrangement of trivialities. Wittgenstein readily accepts this rather gloomy appraisal:

> Where does our investigation get its importance from, since it seems only to destroy everything interesting, that is, all that is great and important? (As it were all the buildings, leaving behind only bits of stone and rubble.) What we are destroying is nothing but houses of cards and we are clearing up the ground of language on which they stand. [*PI,* sect. 118.]

If he is willing to accept this destruction of the entities, realms of being, acts, and processes posited by philosophers, it is because he considers them to be the misbegotten issue of the philosophers' mis-conceptions about language. Those entities, acts, and realms of being are mere dreams—dreams of our language (see *PI,* sect. 358). And they are dangerous dreams, for they inevitably produce puzzlement, and Wittgenstein thought the primary aim of (good) philosophy is therapeutic, is to rid us of our intellectual illnesses.

It seems to me, however, that although this conception of philoso-phy as therapy is a fascinating and highly original one, and one in which there is a great deal of truth, nevertheless it is unduly re-stricted. We know that Wittgenstein actually suffered great torment in wrestling with philosophical problems, and so it is not surprising that *for him* the most important thing that philosophy can do is to release one from such agonies. We might go still further, and grant him that philosophy usually or even always begins with bewilder-ment; but there seems to be no real warrant for concluding that it is the *one* job of philosophy to set our minds at rest. Why, when we are cured, should we stop gaining knowledge of the workings of language, and of lots of other philosophically interesting things as well? Why should we not continue gaining such knowledge simply for its own sake? Happily, Wittgenstein himself did just that in prac-tice; many of his discussions are interesting and illuminating in themselves, and have no obvious connection with any particular philosophical puzzle.

We know that Wittgenstein had no great respect for most of the philosophers of the past:

During the walk Wittgenstein assured me (laughing) that no assistant lecturer in philosophy in the country had read fewer books on philosophy than he had. He said he had never read a single word of Aristotle, although he had lately read much of Plato and with much profit. As for Hume and Kant, it was all very well for me to read them because I was not yet as experienced in philosophical thinking as he was: but he could not sit down and read Hume—he knew far too much about the subject of Hume's writings to find this anything but a torture.[5]

It is perhaps no accident that Wittgenstein should have ignored Aristotle and found a kindred soul in Plato, nor even that he should have taught at Cambridge, where Plato has always been more deeply entrenched than Aristotle, rather than at Oxford, where the reverse is the case. For Plato, like Socrates, looked upon philosophy as something whose main aim is to do us some supreme good, as being the way, indeed, to spiritual salvation. He thought that only the philosopher can have complete spiritual health, and although his orientation was primarily moral, and although his conception of spiritual health and sickness differed from Wittgenstein's conception of intellectual illnesses and their cure, still the resemblance is striking. One of Plato's most famous myths, for example, contains a picture of the philosopher which is remarkably similar to metaphors used by Wittgenstein: in the myth of the cave, the philosopher is depicted as a prisoner who has escaped from a cave, just as in Wittgenstein, a successful philosopher is a fly who has escaped from a fly-bottle or a man who has escaped from a room in which he had thought he was trapped. For Aristotle, on the other hand, and for his descendants at Oxford—e.g., J. L. Austin—philosophy is not primarily therapeutic. The joy they get from philosophy is not primarily the joy of redemption, but the joy of discovery, the disinterested joy of knowledge for its own sake. There is the touch of the poet and the mystic in both Plato and Wittgenstein, but none in Aristotle or Austin. For Plato and Wittgenstein, philosophy is much more like art than it is like science; art is a matter of vision, where one *sees* things that cannot be said, and so is philosophy. (See *PI*, sect. 401.) For Aristotle and Austin, however, philosophy is much more like science than it is like art; neither would have any truck with ineffable visions. Which of these two general attitudes towards philosophy does one prefer? That, perhaps, is a matter of temperament, of spirit.

[5] Karl Britton, "Portrait of a Philosopher," *The Listener*, LIII, No. 1372 (June 16, 1955), 1072. The walk mentioned here occurred in 1946.

Wittgenstein, like Plato, had a spirit that yearned for the ideal, for something far away and pure, a spirit that despised the existing conditions of the here-and-now. He thought, for example, that the time in which he lived was a dark age. In philosophy, too, there is a sense in which he always—both in his early and his later writings— judged the actual to be in some degree unsatisfactory. In the *Tractatus,* the ideal he sought was that of a logically perfect language in which the true logical form of a proposition could be perspicuously presented. Ordinary language (i.e., language that we all use every day), though adequate for practical purposes, obscures vision and hides the skeletal form (*T* 4.002[4]). In his later period, Wittgenstein resigned himself, as it were, to the necessities of life, and his ideal was not nearly so remote as it had been in the *Tractatus.* (Compare the analogous shift in Plato from the *Republic* to the *Laws.*) We are all raised on ordinary language and can never altogether escape it, and if we use it in legitimate ways, we have little or no need to do so. But if only philosophers, including Wittgenstein himself, could stop using language in improper ways! And if only our language could be purged of the misleading pictures, embodied in it, that lead them astray! Wittgenstein always longed for the pure, the clean, the un- cluttered, the *primitive*—in his philosophy as in his life. He, like Plato, had little taste for the muddied flux of actuality. Aristotle and Austin, on the other hand, were lovers of the actual—they delighted in it. Between such men there is a fundamental difference in attitude toward the world.

* * *

Despite all the enormous differences between the *Tractatus* and the *Investigations,* there are still some points of resemblance. Perhaps the most important of these is that both books are concerned to mark out the limits of sense, to indicate the boundary between what can intelligibly be said and what cannot be said. To be sure, the boundary is drawn differently in the two books: the range of the sayable, for example, is greatly extended in the later work, and the boundary is described in a much more simple, straightforward way in the earlier one (see *PI,* sect. 499). Still, to draw some boundary is one of Wittgenstein's major aims in both. In pursuing this task, he was carrying on, in his own way, the work started in modern philosophy by Locke, Hume, and Kant.

Another striking point of agreement between the *Tractatus* and the later works of Wittgenstein is in the over-all, general conception of a philosophical problem, its source or cause, and its solution—though of course the details of the two conceptions are, on the whole, radically different. In his preface to the *Tractatus,* Wittgenstein wrote:

> The book deals with the problems of philosophy, and shows, I believe, that the reason why these problems are posed is that the logic of our language is misunderstood. [*T,* p. 3.]

(See also *T* 4.003.) These same words could occur without oddity in the *Investigations,* although they would there have to be construed differently. In the *Tractatus,* what he meant was that we sometimes think a proposition asserts the existence of one situation when actually it asserts the existence of quite a different one, or perhaps it even (purports to) assert the existence of no possible situation whatever and is therefore in fact nonsensical. In the *Investigations,* too, philosophical problems are said to arise because we misinterpret our forms of language, and part of what this means may be what the *Tractatus* doctrine meant—but, as we have seen, it is also more complicated than that. In both the *Tractatus* and the *Investigations,* problems can be removed by a careful study of language, which is therefore the proper job of philosophy.

> 4.0031 All philosophy is a 'critique of language.' . . .

In the *Tractatus,* explaining what a proposition means is a matter of analyzing it, breaking it down, showing what particular truth-function of which elementary propositions it ultimately is. This is not, of course, the kind of thing Wittgenstein had in mind in the *Investigations.* Yet in both works the problems are based on misunderstanding, and once this is removed, the problems disappear; they are revealed to have been really no problems at all. In the *Tractatus* Wittgenstein said:

> 4.003(3) And it is not surprising that the deepest problems are in fact *not* problems at all.
>
> 6.5(2) *The riddle* does not exist.

So, too, in the *Investigations:* the difficulties are unreal ones which we have created for ourselves, and when we see things aright, the problems vanish as if by magic.

The early Wittgenstein, like Plato, was a philosophical aristocrat in that he cared little for the deliverances of common sense or for the niceties of ordinary language. As a philosopher, he was thus much haughtier in his early days than he was later. There is this further sense, too, in which his early philosophy was more "arrogant" than his later. In the *Tractatus,* Wittgenstein had considered philosophy to be entirely a priori; and he thought, moreover, that the nature of language, which can be discovered by a process of a priori reasoning, determines the nature of reality. Most notably, he deduced, by a process of pure reasoning about language, that there *must* be simple objects. This is a bold, not to say pretentious, claim. No such claim is made, or even dreamt of, in the *Investigations.* On the contrary, we are told there that we must look—humbly, as it were—at how language is actually used and learn from that; and there is no suggestion that this examination will yield a direct insight into the nature of reality, although the results of such an examination doubtless have important metaphysical implications.

Wittgenstein mellowed somewhat, both as a person and as a philosopher, as he grew older. As a young man, he was, I should guess, audacious and full of confidence that when he set to work on any project, his considerable abilities would ensure ultimate success. He argued, apparently as an equal, with Frege and Russell about the most difficult and esoteric matters, ones in which they were acknowledged masters. The *Tractatus,* he thought, solved the problems of philosophy, in principle at least, once and for all. (See his preface to the *Tractatus.*) But then he fought a war, read Tolstoy, became a village schoolteacher and a gardener in a monastery, and lived among simple Irish fishermen. He grew more humane. This is shown in his actions and in his attitudes. For example, as a young man, he called people he disliked "philistines," whereas in his later years, he praised others by calling them "human beings." It is shown also in his philosophy. Before the First World War, Wittgenstein had been dogmatically anti-Christian,[6] but his reading of Tolstoy mitigated this attitude. Thereafter, he respected genuine religious faith, even that—perhaps especially that—of the most simple people.[7] In philosophy, the early Wittgenstein was not primarily concerned with the thoughts and language of ordinary folk; he was far more interested in those of scientists, mathematicians, and logicians. And there was more than

---

[6] Bertrand Russell, "Ludwig Wittgenstein," *Mind,* LX, No. 239 (July 1951), 298. See also Malcolm, *Memoir,* p. 72.

[7] See Norman Malcolm, "Ludwig Wittgenstein: a symposium," *The Listener,* LXIII, No. 1610 (February 4, 1960), 207.

just a slight suggestion that, although ordinary language was all right for the humble tasks of everyday life, it ought to be abandoned in favor of a technical, ideal language when important, theoretical issues are treated. But in the *Investigations,* he was primarily concerned with what we all say and think in the course of our normal daily activities, and his main task was to get these things straight, to understand them. He did not rule out the possibility or even the desirability of reforming ordinary language, but he had no thought of doing so himself.

> Such a reform for particular practical purposes, an improvement in our terminology designed to prevent misunderstandings in practice, is perfectly possible. But these are not the cases we have to do with. [*PI,* sect. 132.]

In his later period, he was not so confident, either as a person or as a philosopher, as he had been earlier.[8] He thought that we are all doomed, that we all need help.[9] His attitude toward life was almost despairing. In philosophy, so far was he from thinking that he had solved all philosophical problems, in principle or otherwise, that, as Malcolm reports,

> he was constantly depressed, I think, by the impossibility of arriving at understanding in philosophy.[10]

And now, instead of offering the philosopher the final solution to all his problems, as before, he offers him mainly—assistance, help, remedies for his intellectual problems, methods of cure.

> As regards his own work, he said it did not matter whether his results were true or not: what mattered was that 'a method had been found.' [11]

Wittgenstein was painfully aware of the fact that he was not himself a great teacher,[12] but he shared this characteristic with those who are: he did not so much pronounce doctrines, as teach a skill, an art. This was his final legacy to us.

[8] But of course Wittgenstein was never what one could call a happy or completely confident man. See p. 10.

[9] *Ibid.,* p. 208.

[10] Malcolm, *Memoir,* p. 32.

[11] Moore, "Wittgenstein's Lectures in 1930-33," *Mind,* LXIV, No. 253 (January 1955), 26. (*Philosophical Papers,* p. 322.)

[12] See Malcolm, *Memoir,* p. 62ff.

Selected Bibliography

ABBREVIATIONS

A	*Analysis*
AF	*Archivio di filosofia*
AJP	*Australasian Journal of Philosophy*
BJPS	*British Journal for the Philosophy of Science*
I	*Inquiry*
JP	*The Journal of Philosophy*
M	*Mind*
P	*Philosophy*
PAS	*Proceedings of the Aristotelian Society*
PBA	*Proceedings of the British Academy*
PPR	*Philosophy and Phenomenological Research*
PQ	*The Philosophical Quarterly*
PR	*The Philosophical Review*
PS	*Philosophical Studies (Irish)*
PSc	*Philosophy of Science*
R	*Ratio*
RIP	*Revue internationale de philosophie*
RM	*The Review of Metaphysics*
TLS	*The Times Literary Supplement*

General

Passmore, J., *A Hundred Years of Philosophy*. London: Gerald Duckworth & Co., Ltd., 1957.

Pears, D. F., G. A. Paul, and others, *The Revolution in Philosophy*. London: Macmillan & Co., Ltd., 1956.

Urmson, J. O., *Philosophical Analysis.* Oxford: The Clarendon Press, 1956.

Warnock, G. J., *English Philosophy Since 1900.* London: Oxford University Press, 1958.

Weinberg, J. R., *An Examination of Logical Positivism.* London: Routledge & Kegan Paul, Ltd., 1936.

Tractatus Logico-Philosophicus

BOOKS

Anscombe, G. E. M., *An Introduction to Wittgenstein's Tractatus.* New York: Hillary House Publishers, Ltd., 1959.

Black, M., *A Companion to Wittgenstein's Tractatus.* Forthcoming from the Cornell University Press.

Griffin, J., *Wittgenstein's Logical Atomism.* Forthcoming from the Oxford University Press.

Maslow, A., *A Study in Wittgenstein's Tractatus.* Berkeley: University of California Press, 1961.

Plochmann, G. K. and J. B. Lawson, *Terms in Their Propositional Contexts in Wittgenstein's Tractatus: An Index.* Carbondale: Southern Illinois University Press, 1962.

Shwayder, D. S., *Wittgenstein's Tractatus: A Historical and Critical Commentary.* Unpublished Ph.D. dissertation, Oxford University.

Stenius, E., *Wittgenstein's Tractatus.* Oxford: Basil Blackwell & Mott, Ltd., 1960.

ARTICLES

Allaire, E. B., "Tractatus 6.3751," *A,* XIX (1958-9).

———, "Types and Formation Rules: A Note on Tractatus 3.334," *A,* XXI (1960-1).

Anscombe, G. E. M., "Mr. Copi on Objects, Properties and Relations in the *Tractatus,*" *M,* LXVIII, No. 271 (1959).

Bernstein, R. J., "Wittgenstein's Three Languages," *RM,* XV, No. 2 (1961).

Black, M., "Some Problems Connected with Language," *PAS,* XXXIX (1938-9); reprinted as "Wittgenstein's *Tractatus*" in Black, *Language and Philosophy.* Ithaca: Cornell University Press, 1949.

Copi, I. M., "Tractatus 5.542," *A,* XVIII (1957-8).

———, "Objects, Properties, and Relations in the *Tractatus,*" *M,* LXVII, No. 266 (1958).

———, review of E. Stenius, *Wittgenstein's Tractatus, PR,* LXXII, No. 3 (1963).

Daitz, E., "The Picture Theory of Meaning," *M*, LXII, No. 246 (1953); reprinted in *Essays in Conceptual Analysis*, ed. A. Flew. London: Macmillan & Co., Ltd., 1956.

Dummett, M., "Nominalism," *PR*, LXV, No. 4 (1956).

Evans, E., "Tractatus 3.1432," *M*, LXIV, No. 254 (1955).

——, "About '*aRb*,'" *M*, LXVIII, No. 272 (1959).

Gasking, D. A. T., "Anderson and the *Tractatus Logico-Philosophicus*," *AJP*, XXVII, No. 1 (1949).

Geach, P. T., review of *Tractatus* as translated into Italian by G. C. M. Colombo, *PR*, LXVI, No. 4 (1957).

——, review of *Tractatus* as translated into English by D. F. Pears and B. F. McGuinness, *PR*, LXXII, No. 2 (1963).

Hintikka, J., "On Wittgenstein's 'Solipsism,'" *M*, LXVII, No. 265 (1958).

Jarvis, J., "Professor Stenius on the *Tractatus*," *JP*, LVIII, No. 20 (1961).

Keyt, D., "Wittgenstein's Notion of an Object," *PQ*, XIII, No. 50 (1963).

McGuinness, B. F., "Pictures and Form in Wittgenstein's *Tractatus*," *AF*, Nos. 2-3 (1956).

"The Passionate Philosopher," *TLS* (May 1, 1959).

Ramsey, F. P., "Critical Notice" of the *Tractatus*, *M*, XXXII, No. 128 (1923); reprinted in Ramsey, *The Foundations of Mathematics*. London: Routledge & Kegan Paul, Ltd., 1931.

Rhees, R., "Miss Anscombe on the *Tractatus*," *PQ*, X, No. 38 (1960).

——, "The *Tractatus*: Seeds of Some Misunderstandings," *PR*, LXXII, No. 2 (1963).

Schwyzer, H. R. G., "Wittgenstein's Picture-Theory of Language," *I*, V, No. 1 (1962).

Sellars, W., "Naming and Saying," *PSc*, XXIX, No. 1 (1962).

——, "Truth and 'Correspondence,'" *JP*, LIX, No. 2 (1962).

Shapere, D., "Philosophy and the Analysis of Language," *I*, III, No. 1 (1960).

Shwayder, D. S., "Critical Notice" of E. Stenius, *Wittgenstein's Tractatus*, *M*, LXXII, No. 286 (1963).

Stenius, E., "Wittgenstein's Picture-Theory: A Reply to Mr. H. R. G. Schwyzer," *I*, VI, No. 2 (1963).

The Blue and Brown Books

Bouwsma, O. K., "The Blue Book," *JP*, LVIII, No. 6 (1961).

Moore, G. E., "Wittgenstein's Lectures in 1930-33," Part I, *M*, LXIII, No. 249 (1954); Part II, *M*, LXIII, No. 251 (1954); Part III, *M*, LXIV, No. 253 (1955). All three parts reprinted in Moore, *Philosophical Papers*. London: George Allen & Unwin; New York: The Macmillan Company, 1959.

Kreisel, G., "Wittgenstein's Theory and Practice of Philosophy," *BJPS,* XI, No. 43 (1960).

Philosophical Investigations

BOOKS

Pole, D., *The Later Philosophy of Wittgenstein.* London: The Athlone Press, University of London, 1958.

ARTICLES

Albritton, R., "On Wittgenstein's Use of the Term 'Criterion,' " *JP,* LVI, No. 22 (1959).

Aldrich, V. C., "Pictorial Meaning, Picture-Thinking, and Wittgenstein's Theory of Aspects," *M,* LXVII, No. 265 (1958).

Ambrose, A., review of *PI, PPR,* XV, No. 1 (1954).

Ayer, A. J., "Can There Be a Private Language? Symposium," *PAS,* Supp. Vol. XXVIII (1954).

————, "Privacy," *PBA,* XLV (1959).

Bambrough, J. R., "Universals and Family Resemblances," *PAS,* LXI (1960-1).

Carney, J. D., "Private Language: The Logic of Wittgenstein's Argument," *M,* LXIX, No. 276 (1960).

Cavell, S., "The Availability of Wittgenstein's Later Philosophy," *PR,* LXXI, No. 1 (1962).

Daly, C. B., "New Light on Wittgenstein," Part I, *PS,* X (1960); Part II, *ibid.,* XI (1961-2).

Feyerabend, P., "Wittgenstein's *Philosophical Investigations,*" *PR,* LXIV, No. 3 (1955).

Findlay, J. N., "Wittgenstein's *Philosophical Investigations,*" *RIP,* VII, No. 25 (1953).

Garver, N., "Wittgenstein on Private Language," *PPR,* XX (1959-60).

Hervey, H., "The Problem of the Model Language Game in Wittgenstein's Later Philosophy," *P,* XXXVI, No. 138 (1961).

Horgby, I., "The Double Awareness in Heidegger and Wittgenstein," *I,* II, No. 4 (1959).

Linsky, L., "Wittgenstein on Language and Some Problems of Philosophy," *JP,* LIV, No. 10 (1957).

Malcolm, N., "Wittgenstein's *Philosophical Investigations,*" PR, LXIII, No. 4 (1954); reprinted in *The Philosophy of Mind,* ed. V. C. Chappell. Englewood Cliffs, N. J.: Prentice-Hall, Inc., 1962, and in Malcolm, *Knowledge and Certainty: Essays and Lectures.* Englewood Cliffs, N. J.: Prentice-Hall, Inc., 1963.

————, "Knowledge of Other Minds," *JP,* LV, No. 23 (Nov. 6, 1958);

reprinted in *The Philosophy of Mind,* ed. V. C. Chappell, and in Malcolm, *Knowledge and Certainty, ibid.*

Rhees, R., "Wittgenstein's Builders," *PAS,* LX (1959-60).

Rorty, R., "Pragmatism, Categories, and Language," *PR,* LXX, No. 2 (1961).

Strawson, P. F., "Critical Notice" of *PI, M,* LXIII, No. 249 (1954).

Suter, R., "Augustine on Time with Some Criticisms from Wittgenstein," *RIP,* XVI, Nos. 61-62 (1962).

Unsigned review of *PI, TLS* (Aug. 28, 1953).

Wellman, C., "Wittgenstein and the Egocentric Predicament," *M,* LXVIII, No. 270 (1959).

———, "Our Criteria for Third-Person Psychological Sentences," *JP,* LVIII, No. 11 (1961).

———, "Wittgenstein's Conception of a Criterion," *PR,* LXXI, No. 4 (1962).

Wisdom, J., "A Feature of Wittgenstein's Technique," *PAS,* Supp. Vol. XXXV (1961).

Remarks on the Foundations of Mathematics

Ambrose, A., "Wittgenstein on Some Questions in Foundations of Mathematics," *JP,* LII, No. 8 (1955).

Anderson, A. R., "Mathematics and the 'Language Game,'" *RM,* XI, No. 3 (1958).

Bernays, P., "Comments on Ludwig Wittgenstein's *Remarks on the Foundations of Mathematics,*" *R,* II, No. 1 (1959).

Chihara, C. S., "Wittgenstein and Logical Compulsion," *A,* XXI (1960-1).

Cowan, J. L., "Wittgenstein's Philosophy of Logic," *PR,* LXX, No. 3 (1961).

Dummett, M., "Wittgenstein's Philosophy of Mathematics," *PR,* LXVIII, No. 3 (1959).

Duthie, G. D., "Critical Study" of *RFM, PQ,* VII, No. 29 (1957).

Goodstein, R. L., "Critical Notice" of *RFM, M,* LXVI, No. 264 (1957).

Kreisel, G., "Wittgenstein's *Remarks on the Foundations of Mathematics,*" *BJPS,* IX, No. 3 (1958).

———, "Wittgenstein's Theory and Practice of Philosophy," *BJPS,* XI, No. 43 (1960).

Index